A Brief History of Flight

A Brief History of Flight

From Balloons to Mach 3
and Beyond

T. A. Heppenheimer

John Wiley & Sons, Inc.

New York • Chichester • Weinheim • Brisbane • Singapore • Toronto

Copyright © 2001 by T. A. Heppenheimer. All rights reserved

Published by John Wiley & Sons, Inc.
Published simultaneously in Canada

Library of Congress Cataloging-in-Publication Data:

Heppenheimer, T. A.
    A brief history of flight : from balloons to Mach 3 and beyond /
T. A. Heppenheimer.
      p. cm.
    Includes bibliographical references.
    ISBN 0-471-34637-3 (cloth : alk. paper)
    1. Aeronautics—History. I. Title.

  TL515.H455 2000
  629.13'09—dc21   00-026290

Printed in the United States of America

10 9 8 7 6 5 4 3 2 1

To Dawn and Torrey;
to Alex and Raizel.
May you live long and prosper.

Contents

Acknowledgments

THIS IS the third book on the history of aerospace that I have written for Hana Lane, my editor at John Wiley. The two earlier books are *Turbulent Skies* (1995), on commercial aviation, and *Countdown* (1997), on space flight. It is a pleasure to note the continuing support of Ms. Lane, and of this publisher.

Within this book, many of the chapters draw on published articles that I have written for magazines. I am glad to note their editors: At *Air and Space,* Linda Shiner and Patricia Trenner. At *High Technology*, Herb Brody, Peter Gwynne, and Paul Kinnucan. At *Invention and Technology,* an affiliate of *American Heritage,* Fred Allen, Fred Schwarz, and Richard Snow. These are people that I have worked with through the years.

A number of people have granted interviews that have provided me with source material. Many of their names appear at the back of this book, in the notes to chapters 19, 23, and 25. Other interviewees include:

> *Boeing:* Maynard Pennell, George Schairer, Jack Steiner, Joseph
>   Sutter, John Swihart
> *Douglas:* Elayne Bendel, Harry Gann
> *SR-71:* James Eastham, Captain Steve Grzebiniak, Ben Rich
> *Voyager:* Dick Rutan, John Roncz
> *Washington, D.C.:* Philip Klass, John Pike
> *World War II attack on Yamamoto:* Rex Barber, John Mitchell

A number of people have helped me with photos and artwork. I am glad to express appreciation to Jane Colihan, at *American Heritage.* To Dill Hunley of NASA's Dryden Flight Research Center. To Frieda Johnson of Edwards Air Force Base. To David Burgevin and

Kristine Kaske, at the National Air and Space Museum. To Tonya Rutan and Kelly Hall, at Rutan Aircraft Factory. To Alex "A. J." Lutz, at the San Diego Aerospace Museum. To Hugh Morgan, formerly of the U.S. Air Force. To Carolyn Schlegel of Learjet, Inc.

This book's dedication takes note of two recent marriages within my family. Last September my wife's daughter, Dawn Ciarrocchi, married her longtime sweetheart, Torrey Mills. In February my son Alex Heppenheimer married his own fiancée, Raizel Goldblatt. To these happy couples, I wish lives of good cheer and good fortune.

—T. A. Heppenheimer
Fountain Valley, California
April 11, 2000

PART *1*

Beginnings

Beautiful Balloons 1

MORE THAN two hundred years ago, King Louis XVI ruled at Versailles. The U.S. Constitution had not yet been written; Napoleon was merely a young lad in his teens. Yet it was in this era that aviation, complete with pilots, first began to take shape. More than a century before the Wright brothers, two Montgolfier brothers, Joseph and Étienne, invented the hot-air balloon. Their invention then took to the skies with astonishing rapidity. Men crossed the English Channel by air before they did so using steam, for steamships still lay well in the future.

Joseph and Étienne were two of sixteen children born to Anne and Pierre Montgolfier, a prosperous paper manufacturer in the French town of Annonay, near Lyon. Joseph, born in 1740, was a large man of powerful build, casual in his clothes, nondescript in his general appearance. He married a cousin, Thérèse, who was quite attractive. They had two children, and were happy together.

Joseph had a fine memory, readily learning lengthy songs and long poems by Voltaire. Yet he could forget the most basic things. Once he stayed with Thérèse at an inn, went out for a stroll the next morning, and left her in the room as he walked onward, lost in thought. His casual ways extended to his general attitudes, for he rarely became angry or lost his temper. They also encompassed his business practices, for he took little heed in his borrowing and spending, often calling on his father or other family members to rescue him from creditors.

When he was young, his father had sent him to a school run by Jesuits. He rebelled against its strictness and escaped into the country. Here he lived as a vagabond, working on farms and sleeping where he could. This did not last long, for the family soon retrieved him and sent him back to school. He put up with lessons in theology as best he could, but he also nurtured a growing interest in arithmetic, chemistry, and mechanics. A clerk in a bookstore slipped him texts, which certainly were not part of the approved curriculum, and Joseph devoured them, writing essays and drawing extensive diagrams in note-books. This self-education proved critical to his eventual success.

A cousin, Mathieu Duret, had studied science in Paris and had some familiarity with a burgeoning new field: the chemistry of gases. Joseph Black, a Scottish chemist, had discovered carbon dioxide in 1756, as the first gas distinguishable from common air. England's Henry Cavendish followed in 1766 with "inflammable air," hydrogen, while Joseph Priest-ley found oxygen in 1774. Duret told Montgolfier what he knew of these matters when they spent time together during 1777, with hydro-gen drawing particular interest. This gas took effort to prepare, but it had less than one-tenth the density of air. A lightweight bag of paper or cloth, filled with hydrogen, might rise into the sky.

During the next several years, Montgolfier continued to pursue his checkered career. He went to Avignon and enrolled in a local diploma mill, studying law, while helping himself to the new books that circu-lated freely within that town. His legal training did him little good, though, for early in 1782 he spent several days in a debtors' prison in Lyon. His family bailed him out, again, and he returned to Avignon.

One evening in November, sitting in his room, Joseph contemplated a picture that showed a recent siege of the British fortress of Gibraltar. It had withstood assault both by land and by sea, and Montgolfier asked himself: might it be taken by air? The evening was cool, with a fire close at hand. As he watched the hot smoke rise, he considered that fire-heated air might be buoyant like hydrogen, and far easier to prepare.

He built a lightweight framework of thin wood and covered it with taffeta fabric. It had a large hole in the bottom, and he inserted paper and ignited it. It worked! The device rose from its support and bumped against the ceiling. With fire now burning in his mind, he wrote a brief letter to his brother Étienne: "Get in a supply of taffeta and of cordage, quickly, and you will see one of the most astonishing sights in the world."

Whereas Joseph Montgolfier was casual and largely self-educated, Étienne was a sound business manager who had received a good techni-cal education. Born in 1745, he was the youngest, which gave him little hope within the family business. He nevertheless was marked for a pro-fessional career, and went to Paris to study architecture. This field in-cluded elements of civil and mechanical engineering, and Étienne won the attention of a well-known architect, Jacques-Germain Soufflot. Soufflot gave him commissions, and Étienne proceeded to build his reputation.

Pierre Montgolfier, the family patriarch, had placed his hopes in the oldest son, Raymond, and in 1761 had selected him to be the next head of the paper factory. But Raymond died in 1772, at age forty-two, and Pierre bypassed his intermediate sons as he turned to Étienne. Though only twenty-seven, this young man had already shown that he was solid and reliable. His career in Paris now was flourishing, but he saw that it was up to him to take charge of this factory, which was the source of the family's modest fortune. He returned to provincial Annonay and threw himself into running the plant. He improved its manufacturing methods, leading it to renewed prosperity.

After sending his letter, Joseph hastened home to repeat the experiment, this time in the open air. He built a similar fabric-covered box and sent it to a height of seventy feet, as it stayed aloft for a full minute. Just as Joseph had hoped, Étienne indeed was astonished, and they proceeded to build a much larger version, nine feet across. They tried it in mid December, working at the bottom of a ravine. Even before they had finished heating its air, it developed so much lift that it broke a restraining cord and flew freely, finally coming down after a flight of nearly a mile.

Truly, Joseph and Étienne had hold of something exciting. They talked of little else during the next several months, as they pursued a program of experiments. Drawing on experience from the impromptu flight of December, they learned to measure lifting force by having test devices break cords of known strength. Their early versions resembled box kites, with fabric-covered wooden frames, but a spherical cloth bag offered more promise. Taffeta and similar fabrics leaked heat readily; paper used as backing held the heat in, and there certainly was no shortage of paper at the home of Montgolfier.

By April 1783, they were ready with the real thing: a bag of sack-cloth lined with three thin layers of paper, weighing 500 pounds. It was 35 feet across and enclosed 28,000 cubic feet, holding more than a ton of air. A large open mouth at the bottom allowed it to inflate without catching on fire. The brothers built it in segments, fastening them together with 1,800 buttons. It was globe shaped; Joseph and Étienne called it a ball, or *ballon*.

Initial trials took place during that month, and again the *ballon* showed its power. Ropes held it in place during the initial experiment, which showed that it could be safely inflated. Four strong laborers held it during the second test, three weeks later. Its lift increased so rapidly that two of these men let go of their tethers, whereupon the balloon raised the other two off their feet. They saved themselves by releasing their own lines, and the big gas bag again flew free before landing on a nearby farm.

The brothers now arranged for a public demonstration, to be held in the marketplace of Annonay on June 5. A regional assembly of deputies was meeting in that town during this week, representing nobles and the Third Estate, and could send a report to Paris. The day was rainy, but the Montgolfiers nevertheless went ahead. They piled dry straw and wool within a brazier, added alcohol, and set it alight. As its hot air swelled the balloon, the brothers suspended this heater below its gaping mouth to counteract cooling from the rain.

Four husky peasants held it down, pulling on ropes. Étienne told them to let go, and the balloon rose suddenly, quickly reaching three thousand feet. Winds aloft carried it for a mile and a half before it landed in a vineyard. The brazier tipped over and ignited the cloth, and in a foretaste of many such aeronautical disasters to come, the flight of this balloon ended in a fire that consumed it.

Nevertheless, the thing had been done; the onlookers indeed had seen the achievement of flight. The minutes of the assembly duly included a discussion of this curious event, and by late June this report was in Paris and in the hands of the controller general of finance, Lefèvre d'Ormesson. He saw that the matter was worth pursuing and sent a letter to the marquis de Condorcet, head of the Academy of Science. Condorcet set up an investigative panel that included Antoine Lavoisier, a founder of the science of chemistry. Another member, Nicolas Desmarest, had known Étienne for some time through a mutual interest in papermaking, and had letters from him describing the Montgolfiers' work on balloons in Annonay.

Newspapers in Paris also picked up the story. The *Feuille Hebdomadaire* ran a letter from a landowner near Annonay on July 10; the *Journal de Paris* published a more informative article on July 27, apparently drawing on Condorcet's committee as a source. Jacques Charles, a well-born gentleman with a strong interest in science, also heard of the new invention. He was widely known in Paris for his public lectures and demonstrations. He resolved to build his own balloon and to fly it as a public spectacle, with one of his friends arranging to sell tickets and to charge admission to the show. Further, Charles would use hydrogen.

England's Henry Cavendish had first produced this gas in 1766, by treating shavings of iron, zinc, and tin with sulfuric acid. Lavoisier was quite familiar with this gas, and had coined its name. Charles knew it as well, for he had often prepared it in demonstrations, arranging for it to flow through a glass tube and blow soap bubbles. These rose toward the ceiling, and he would touch them with a candle flame to make them pop. Hydrogen was difficult to prepare in quantity, and Charles had not stretched his imagination beyond bubbles. But when he learned of the events in Annonay, he quickly made the mental leap.

Paris had resources far surpassing those of any provincial town; if Charles was to produce hydrogen in substantial volumes, this certainly was the place to try. Moreover, a local artisan had developed a suitable material for Charles's balloon: a lightweight taffeta made gas-tight with a solution of rubber in turpentine. People called this hydrogen balloon a *charlière;* Charles and his promoters set August 27 as the date of its ascent. The location, the Champ de Mars, was a military parade field that in time became the site of the Eiffel Tower.

The new *charlière* was thirteen feet across, considerably smaller than the hot-air *montgolfière* of Annonay. This reflected the fact that hydrogen had far greater lifting power. Charles expected to produce his hydrogen by using iron filings and dilute sulfuric acid, with the iron in a barrel and the acid added through a bunghole. Problems arose during the inflation, and Charles improvised solutions on the spot.

The chemical reaction produced heat and evaporated some of the acid, which condensed within the balloon, threatening to eat through its lining. Workers responded by interrupting the inflation repeatedly to remove this vitriol. They also wrapped wet cloth around a copper tube that channeled hydrogen into the balloon, for this tube was becoming excessively hot. The balloon's undersurface also became quite warm, and had to be cooled with sprays of water from a pump.

"Let the modern reader imagine what was going on here," the historian Charles Gillispie has written. "In a small, enclosed courtyard in a densely populated section of the city, a handful of largely inexperienced people were collecting an unprecedented quantity of the most inflammable gas known through a tube too hot to touch into the confinement of a rubberized bag that was close to catching fire if it was not first chewed through by sulfuric acid."

It took a thousand pounds of iron and five hundred pounds of acid to produce enough hydrogen to fill the balloon to capacity. Charles had allowed several days for such preparations, and had it one-third full by the end of the first evening. On the next day, his men had to do it all over again, for one of them had mistakenly opened the valve. This time the effort went more smoothly. Charles had kept these preliminaries from public view by working within a secluded courtyard, and now told his ground crew to move the balloon to the Champ de Mars. The men did this in the dead of night, to avoid causing a public commotion.

Ticket holders began to enter the grounds in midafternoon, as the balloon received its final addition of hydrogen. This took time; rain clouds gathered, and the mood of the crowd became stormy as well. Then, at 5:00 P.M. a cannon fired, and the fully inflated balloon was released. It soared upward swiftly, remaining in sight for only two minutes before vanishing into the clouds at fifteen hundred feet. It continued onward, rising higher and higher until it burst, due to the reduced air pressure at altitude.

The collapsing gas bag, still with plenty of hydrogen, fell to the ground near the present-day location of Le Bourget Airport, after a flight of some fifteen miles. Curious peasants watched it bound on landing, as if it were alive. As its hydrogen continued to escape, it gave off a foul odor. This resulted from impurities within the gas, probably including hydrogen sulfide, which produces the stench of rotten eggs. These people now set upon it with pitchforks, then tied the remains to the tail of a horse.

Meanwhile, Étienne had arrived in Paris during July. He began meeting with members of Condorcet's commission early in August, and secured a promise of funding. Then, when his costs became too large for the Academy, the Ministry of Finance stepped in with further help. The controller general, d'Ormesson, knew his way around the king's court, and helped Étienne make arrangements for a new flight that would take place at Versailles, in front of the royal family. This was indeed astonishing; it was as if the Wright brothers had gone directly from Kitty Hawk to the White House. But King Louis XVI was easily bemused by novelties. The date was set for September 19.

An old friend of Étienne's, Jean-Baptiste Reveillon, had been a client during his days as an architect. Reveillon owned a wallpaper factory, with plenty of room on the grounds, and allowed Étienne to use it freely. The new balloon placed paper both outside and inside the taffeta envelope, and Reveillon was quick to contribute his artistic talents. For King Louis and Queen Marie Antoinette, the design had to be elegant indeed. Reveillon colored it azure blue, with the king's initial stylized in gold, along with painted bands and draperies that might have been velvet and that certainly were fustian.

A preliminary test, on September 11, went superbly. It took only nine minutes to fill the balloon with heat from a brazier, and this balloon lifted eight men who had tried to hold it down with ropes. Others took hold of the restraining lines and brought the balloon under control. Étienne had previously arranged to demonstrate his balloon for Condorcet's commission, and he sent word requesting the presence of its members for the following morning.

Daylight brought rain, but no commissioners. Nevertheless, other dignitaries showed up, leaving Étienne with no choice except to proceed. He inflated the balloon—and the rain turned into a downpour. Soon the decorated blue paper covering was a soggy mess, with no hope of salvaging it for use at Versailles. To meet the king's schedule, he and his colleagues worked frantically through the next four days and nights, crafting an entirely new balloon. It was fifty-seven feet tall and forty-one feet in diameter, making it somewhat shorter than the balloon of September 12, and it used varnished taffeta, avoiding the need for paper. Reveillon nevertheless took care to paint it a royal blue, with large stylized letter Ls set between circling bands of gold.

The hydrogen-filled *charlière* had already demonstrated free flight, and Étienne knew he had to do more. He thought of having the balloon carry a sheep. His brother Joseph, with whom he was exchanging letters, urged him to "take a cow. That will create an extraordinary effect, far more so than a panicky sheep that no one will be able to see." But cows were heavy, so Étienne stuck to his guns—and his sheep. He added a duck and a rooster, with the three passengers riding within a cage, through which their heads and tails protruded.

Across two centuries, Étienne himself describes the flight at Versailles, for he wrote of it in a lengthy letter to his wife:

> At one o'clock, we set off a round of ammunition and lighted the fire. Two or three puffs of wind raised doubts about the feasibility of the experiment. . . . The machine filled in seven minutes. It was held in place only by ropes and the combined efforts of fifteen or sixteen men. A second round went off. We redoubled the gas, and at the third round, . . . everyone let go at once. The machine rose majestically, drawing after it a cage containing a *sheep*, a *rooster*, and a *duck*. A few moments after takeoff a sudden gust of wind tilted it over on its side. Since there was insufficient ballast to keep it vertical, the top afforded the wind a much larger surface than the part where the animals were. At that instant I was afraid it was done for. It got away with losing about a fifth of its gas, however, and continued on its way as majestically as ever for a distance of 1,800 fathoms where the wind tipped it over again so that it settled gently down to earth.[1]

Paris in 1783 was the Paris of Dickens's *A Tale of Two Cities*, with most of its people being poor, preoccupied with the daily matters of working and eking out a living. But its more privileged residents had time for other things, and they went wild over the new invention. A baron wrote that among the people he knew, "all one hears is talk of experiments, atmospheric air, inflammable gas, flying cars, journeys in the sky." The excitement even reached the world of fashion, as a designer crafted a gown for an elegant lady in *la mode au ballon*. Her fan

Montgolfier's balloon lifts off at the Palace of Versailles in 1783. (American Heritage)

displayed drawings, while pumpkin-shaped appurtenances festooned the hat, sleeves, and billowing skirt, though not the bodice.

"The balloon excitement was now building toward a peak," writes the aviation historian Tom Crouch. "Hair and clothing styles, jewelry, snuffboxes, wallpaper, chandeliers, bird cages, fans, clocks, chairs, armoires, hats, and other items were designed with balloon motifs." Party guests sipped *Crème Aerostatique* liqueur and danced the *Contradanse de Gonesse,* which took its name from the village where the *charlière* had met its untimely end.

Though there indeed was much talk of journeys in the sky, no person had yet made one. This was the next item on the Montgolfiers' agenda, and other people were urging them on. One of them, François Pilâtre de Rozier, was known for his public lectures on physics and chemistry, which resembled those of Jacques Charles. Rozier was well connected, holding the patronage of the king's younger brother, while his personal circle included the king's cousin.

Like Charles, Rozier became a balloon enthusiast at an early date. At the end of August, shortly after the flight of the *charlière,* he met with members of the Academy of Science and proposed that he should fly in a balloon built by Montgolfier. He failed to receive assent at first, but three weeks later the successful flight of the sheep, the duck, and the rooster made it clear that there soon would be a demand for aeronauts.

Another volunteer, François d'Arlandes, was a minor nobleman who had grown up near Annonay and had known Joseph Montgolfier for over a decade. He won an early promise from Étienne that when the time came for a manned flight, he, d'Arlandes, would be the pilot. He reminded Étienne of this promise in the wake of the flight at Versailles. Étienne not only took him on as a pilot but set him to work as a foreman, as he pursued his man-carrying project.

The launch site was a château in the Bois de Boulogne, west of the city. The place of construction again was the Reveillon wallpaper factory, and this time, both Reveillon and Étienne outdid themselves. The new balloon was considerably larger than its predecessors, being 46 feet in diameter and 70 in height, with a capacity of 60,000 cubic feet. A circular gallery of wicker, with a tall exterior wall, surrounded the orifice at the bottom, which was 15 feet across. A brazier hung near the neck of the balloon, adjacent to the gallery, and a pilot standing within it could feed its fire while in the air, to develop more lift. He did this with a pitchfork, pushing straw through a hole in the side.

The decorations were certainly the most elaborate to date, far surpassing those of Versailles. Reveillon started with his stylized gold bands and king's initial on a background of azure, and then went much farther. He added royal suns that recalled the Sun King of a century earlier. Friezes at the top showed fleurs-de-lis and portrayed the twelve signs of the zodiac. The bottom displayed painted draperies and curtains, along with eagles whose outspread wings were to bear the contrivance aloft. These embellishments were certainly pretentious; still, while they are far removed from our present taste, we can see that they were appropriate. They represented a salute to the first manned aircraft ever to fly.

Étienne conducted several tethered test flights during mid October, giving his balloon more than three hundred feet of rope. Rozier made out his will, said goodbye to friends, then climbed aboard for flights that proved successful. He had a live fire for his third ascent, and he needed it, for a wind blew the balloon toward the branches of a large tree. Undismayed, he added straw and wool to his burner and rose above the danger. There was time that day for two more flights, and Rozier carried a passenger on each of them. On his last ascent, his companion was the marquis d'Arlandes.

Rozier and d'Arlandes became the first men to fly freely, on November 21, with d'Arlandes setting down his recollections immediately afterward. D'Arlandes had charge of the brazier, but found himself repeatedly distracted by the view. Early in the flight, Rozier chided him: "You're not doing a thing, and we're not climbing at all." D'Arlandes apologized, tossed some straw onto the burner, then went back to sightseeing. Soon they were over the Seine, and Rozier again called to him: "There's the river, and we're dropping. Come on, my good friend, the fire!" When a new helping of straw surged into flame, they felt themselves "hauled up as if by the armpits."

Suddenly they heard a popping sound, followed by another. D'Arlandes looked inside the envelope—and saw that sparks from the heater had burned holes in the fabric. He dampened some smoldering edges with a sponge on his pitchfork, then discovered that threads were loosening within an important seam. "We've got to put down," he insisted, even though there was no open ground below, for they were still over the city.

Rozier assured him that there was no damage on his side, and when d'Arlandes looked more closely, he saw that the seam was holding and the holes were not growing larger or more numerous. He agreed that they could continue to sail on, and he still had plenty of fuel. They entered the countryside and soon let the fire die down, for they expected to come down soon. Then, dead ahead, they saw windmills. Another bale of straw lifted them clear of the danger, and they landed just beyond a pond. They had spent some twenty-five minutes in the air and covered five miles, while their supply of straw would have allowed them to fly considerably farther if they had wished.

Jacques Charles, with his hydrogen balloons, was also preparing his own manned flight. The royal family granted favor to him as well as to the Montgolfiers, for Charles received permission to make this ascent from the palace of the Tuileries. His new balloon was only twenty-six feet across, reflecting the great lifting power of his gas. Even so, it needed 9,200 cubic feet of hydrogen, ten times more than the *charlière* of August, and Charles addressed this problem by introducing an improved chemical generator. He used several barrels, each filled with iron filings and acid. When any of them needed recharging, this could be done while the others continued to work. The hydrogen flowed through pipes to a central enclosure filled with water, bubbling through the water before rising into the balloon. This washed the gas by dissolving some of its impurities. To keep the equipment from overheating, Charles diluted his acid.

The first manned balloon, as seen from the residence of Benjamin Franklin. (American Heritage)

He also introduced improvements that drew on lessons from the August flight. That balloon had continued to rise until it burst, and Charles saw that he needed a means to relieve internal pressure if an aeronaut rose too high. He installed a valve, operated by a cord, that could open to allow some of the gas to escape. Then, because a pilot might release too much, Charles decided that balloons should carry ballast. If a flight started to descend prematurely, or if it was falling rapidly and heading for a rough landing, an airman could toss some of this weight overboard.

Charles lacked the artistic touch of Reveillon, but his creation was attractive enough, with a spherical envelope striped vertically in yellow and red. He also introduced a gondola suspended by ropes, with the shape of a stylized ship's hull. Its stern showed fleurs-de-lis surmounted by a crown, and it might have ridden on a merry-go-round in a later age. He stocked it with a mercury barometer and thermometer, a telescope, and a set of maps.

Through his work, in the summer and after, he had had a great deal of help from two brothers, Jean and Noel Robert. Noel accompanied him, with the ascent taking place on December 1, only ten days after the flight of Rozier and d'Arlandes. Charles, ever the showman, had arranged for a large amount of publicity, which swelled the crowd to record levels. He again charged admission, with the choicest seats going for as much as $400 in present-day currency.

Charles and Robert, the two adventurers whose last names were first names, took their places within the gondola. Charles toasted the project by opening a bottle of champagne, with the two men lifting their glasses high. A ground crew had been holding the balloon with ropes; now Charles told them to let go, and they sailed into the sky. The crowd fell silent, caught up in astonishment.

They approached two thousand feet in altitude, as measured by the barometer. Charles allowed excess gas to escape through an "appendix," a long and narrow neck that he could open or close with his hand. He slowed his ascent, then tossed out small amounts of ballast to stay close to this altitude. The wind set the course; then, fifty-six minutes after launch, they heard the report of a distant cannon. It was at the Tuileries, signaling that they were lost to view.

They continued onward, with Charles navigating by barometer, releasing gas and then dropping ballast to stay close to his desired altitude. It now was late afternoon, and with the sun descending, it was time for the flight to descend as well. They were well beyond the city, over a clear extent of fields, and Charles allowed the balloon to sink slowly. His course threatened to take them into a row of trees, but he threw out a few more pounds of ballast and flew over them. They skimmed along the ground for a hundred feet, then came to rest. Their greeters included several dozen peasants—and two dukes, who had kept them in view while riding on horses.

There still was light in the sky, and Charles saw that by ascending alone, without Robert, he would lighten his craft and soar aloft with ease. It took him only ten minutes to reach nine thousand feet. He now showed that a balloon could allow an observer to make meteorological observations at high altitude, for he noted that his barometer had fallen by over nine inches, with the temperature having dropped from fifty to twenty degrees Fahrenheit.

He was above the clouds, and he later wrote of his "inexpressible delight, this ecstasy of contemplation":

The cold was sharp and dry, but not at all unbearable. . . . I stood up in the middle of the gondola, and lost myself in the spectacle offered by the immensity of the horizon. When I took off from the fields, the sun had set for the inhabitants of the valleys. Soon it rose for me alone, and again appeared to gild the balloon and gondola with its rays. I was the only illuminated body within the whole horizon, and I saw all the rest of nature plunged in shadow.[2]

These two flights, on November 21 and December 1, capped the events in aviation of this dramatic year. It now was clear that people could fly with the speed of the wind, and Benjamin Franklin, living in Paris as a diplomat from the nascent United States, wrote in a letter, "A few months since, the idea of witches riding through the air on a broomstick, and that of philosophers upon a bag of smoke, would have appeared equally impossible and ridiculous." He also looked to the future:

The invention of the balloon appears to be a discovering of great importance and what may possibly give a new turn to human affairs. Convincing sovereigns of the folly of wars may perhaps be one effect of it, since it will be impractical for the most potent of them to guard his dominions. Five thousand balloons capable of raising two men each, could not cost more than five ships of the line; and where is the prince who can afford so to cover his country with troops for its defense that 10,000 men descending from the clouds might not in many places do an infinite mischief before a force could be brought to repel them.[3]

This form of warfare awaited the paratroop attacks of 160 years later, but even as Franklin wrote those words, a mere two men in a balloon was already becoming out of date. Joseph Montgolfier, the original inventor, had not joined Étienne in Paris, but had remained close to home in Lyon. There, during the summer and fall, he proceeded with calculations and designs for a balloon that would be enormous indeed, with a diameter of a hundred feet. Its volume of 560,000 cubic feet gave it nearly ten times the hot-air capacity of the balloon of Rozier and d'Arlandes, which had been large enough. Joseph expected that the new one would carry up to a dozen people. He named it *Flesselles*, in honor of the chief officer of government of his city.

He built it of coarse sackcloth, which quickly developed holes during a preliminary inflation, late in December. Rozier showed up the next day and recommended rebuilding the top of the balloon, which received the most strain, using two layers of taffeta with paper between them. He also recommended cutting the number of passengers to six. Two weeks later, during another inflation, someone tossed in a bale of straw that had been soaked in alcohol. The sudden surge of heat further damaged the fabric, which split seams and developed new holes.

Rozier and Joseph Montgolfier were working in the open, and a few days later came rain and sleet. The envelope became soggy, and when Joseph tried to inflate it in order to dry it, they set part of it on fire. Water pumps put out the blaze in good time, and workers repaired the burned portion with new fabric and paper. However, the rest of the balloon was still sodden and wet, and when freezing weather blew in, it froze into stiffness. The ground crew thawed it anew, this time more gently, by using heat from charcoal burners. Then they inflated it slowly. An official poked his head into the swelling envelope—and saw blue sky through an array of new holes.

Nevertheless, everyone expected a launch. A large crowd had gathered, and four young men, all with titles of nobility, climbed aboard. Rozier objected that the balloon was too weak to stand the strain of carrying them, that only three men should make the attempt, and that he should be one of them. The four noblemen responded by drawing pistols and threatening to shoot, as they shouted to the ground crew to cut the restraining ropes. With this, Rozier leaped on board, followed closely by Joseph and by one of the latter's close collaborators. Rub-a-dub-dub, instead of three men in a tub there now were seven.

They cast off and began a hesitant ascent, with Rozier using the balloon's brazier to add as much lift as possible. They took nearly fifteen minutes to struggle to twenty-five hundred feet. Then a four-feet rip opened near the top, in the area that had been damaged by fire and repaired, and *Flesselles* began descending much more rapidly than it had risen. Rozier stoked the burner vigorously, while the sheer size of the envelope allowed it to act somewhat like a parachute. The landing was rough but caused no injuries. Nevertheless, those elegant noblemen had to make their way through mud produced by melting snow, to avoid having the fabric collapse all around them.

Joseph had financed this project in the fashion of Charles, by selling tickets. He designed one more balloon, financed by the marquis de Brantes, an enthusiast from Avignon. However, after that he made no further such effort. Étienne, with government funds, built a fourth balloon, *Marie Antoinette*. It flew in front of that queen at Versailles in June 1784, honoring Sweden's King Gustav III, a visitor who had expressed a wish to see a balloon ascent. Rozier again was the pilot, accompanied by a chemist, Joseph Proust. However, this was Étienne's last project. His grants came to 14,000 livres—$70,000 in today's money—and while this would pay for a king's amusement, it was nowhere close to what it would cost to develop balloons as a serious enterprise. The Montgolfiers proceeded with their careers, riding through the French Revolution amid little difficulty. But they made no further contributions to aviation.

New pilots now were taking to the skies, with Jean-Pierre Blanchard in the forefront. He had dreamed of flying machines and had tried to build one, with wings driven by springs; when he learned of the Montgolfiers, he found his calling. He became the world's first professional airman, earning his income through fees charged for his public ascents. He flew some sixty times, lived until 1809, and died in bed.

He launched this career in February 1784, selling tickets for his flight in a hydrogen balloon from the Champ de Mars. Just before take-off, a young cadet from the nearby École Militaire approached with sword in hand, demanding to ride aloft as a passenger. Rebuffed, he swung his weapon and wounded Blanchard in the hand. Blanchard did not scrub the mission, even though he was bleeding. He rode alone, and set a new altitude record of 12,500 feet.

He nevertheless concluded that Paris was not the place to hone his skills, and continued his activity in Rouen, capital of his native province of Normandy. He made two more public flights, in May and July, and then set a goal that was ambitious indeed. He would try to become the first man to fly across the English Channel.

He knew that a hydrogen balloon could make such a journey; the first manned version, flown by Charles and Robert, had covered twenty-seven miles during its flight of December 1, which was more than the distance from Dover to Calais. He left for England in mid August and quickly introduced himself to the small community of London men who shared his interest in ballooning. These included John Jeffries, an expatriate American who had spent his early life in Boston but remained loyal to King and Crown. He earned a good living as a physician, spending much time at theaters in Drury Lane and the Strand, while making himself familiar in the city's most fashionable brothels.

Difficulties with customs had prevented Blanchard from bringing his balloon from France, and he needed a sponsor of means if he was to resume his ascents. He found his initial angel in an anatomist, John Sheldon, with the two men making an initial flight in mid October of 1784. Jeffries was part of the large crowd of onlookers, and watched with enthrallment. "I resolved to gratify this," he later wrote, "which had finally become my ruling passion."

He arranged to meet Blanchard, and quickly agreed to meet the latter's expenses in return for the opportunity to accompany him on his next flight. This took place late in November; it was the first for Jeffries, and only the fifth for Blanchard. The launch was shaky, as they blew against a building and sent a chimney pot crashing to the street. But they recovered and flew for two hours, traversing the whole of London and proceeding eastward before landing near the Thames.

Now they were ready for the cross-Channel flight. They left London on December 17 and reached Dover two days later. Then, amid unfavorable wind and weather, they waited through Christmas and New Year's, while Blanchard's expenses also mounted. Their tempers rose as well, for it was becoming increasingly clear that the two men could not get along. Jeffries was appalled at the rising cost, while Blanchard hoped to make the flight alone, thereby winning sole glory. He went so far as to obtain a lead belt, with which he hoped to add so much weight that Jeffries would have to leave the gondola.

Finally, at six in the morning of January 7, 1785, Blanchard came into Jeffries' room and told him that the wind and weather were fair. Indeed, the day was beautifully clear; when they ascended, they were visible from the French coast. Liftoff came shortly after 1:00 P.M. "We rose slowly and majestically from the cliff," Jeffries later wrote. The Channel resembled "a fine sheet of glass." They gained altitude; the balloon expanded, and they valved off hydrogen. They released too much of this gas, and had to drop ballast. Their gas bag appears to have been leaky, for they dropped more ballast, until all of it was gone.

An hour into the flight, and still not halfway across, they began to throw overboard some of the items they had brought with them. By 2:30 they had jettisoned their food supply. Blanchard had built his gondola with silk-covered aerial oars, a rudder, and a hand-cranked propeller, all of which went over the side as well. A bottle of brandy soon followed. Nearing the three-fourths mark, they threw grapnels and rope into the water, then dispensed with the heavy clothes that they had worn, to guard against the cold of January. Blanchard threw in his trousers, leaving them with little more than cork life jackets. Still they failed to climb, remaining below the level of the cliffs of Calais. With only four or five miles to go, they felt that their only hope was to climb onto the balloon's ropes in an attempt to remain afloat once they hit the water.

Suddenly their luck turned, as a change in the wind carried them aloft once again. They crossed the French coast, still rising. They had done it; they had crossed the Channel! However, they still had to come down safely, and they needed something to throw overboard to control their final descent and landing. It occurred to Jeffries, a physician, that he and Blanchard both had a good deal of urine in their bladders. The gondola had air-filled sacs for flotation, and both men put them to an unintended use.

The wind blew them into a tree. Jeffries grabbed hold of a branch; Blanchard frantically valved gas. Then they worked their way from branch to branch until they could drop to the ground. They stood shivering in the cold, but a search party found them and gave them warm clothing. The hard part was finished; now came an extensive round of honors, including a visit to Versailles. They met the king and queen, and while in Paris, Jeffries soon found his way to other women of the city.

The ubiquitous Rozier, a veteran of the first manned flight more than a year earlier, expected to follow with his own cross-Channel voyage. By now it was clear that both hot-air and hydrogen balloons were capable of traveling long distances, but through very different means. Hydrogen balloons relied on valves and ballast, whereas the hot-air variety used an onboard heater and a fuel supply, to add lift and to control the descent. Rozier's new model sought to combine the best features of both, for it used a thick cylinder that held the hot air, surmounted with a hydrogen-filled sphere. It amounted to a two-stage balloon, for Rozier could control its altitude using hot air until he exhausted his fuel, then fly onward by relying on hydrogen with its valve and ballast. In overall appearance, it resembled the mushroom cloud of an atomic bomb. However, it showed the usual elaborate decorations on a field of blue, including paintings of Aeolus, the Greek god of the wind.

Rozier certainly needed help from such a source, for he wanted to fly from France to England, whereas Blanchard and Jeffries had ridden prevailing winds in the other direction. Those winds continued to prevail until June of 1785, five months after their flight, but in the middle of that month, conditions were finally to Rozier's liking. He took along an assistant, Pierre Romain, and launched in the early morning, with the weather still cool and the balloon developing its maximum lift.

Something went wrong, for shortly after takeoff, at around five thousand feet, the hydrogen-filled globe suddenly burst into flame. It may have ignited due to a spark from the hot-air burner, which could have started a smoldering fire at the top of the cylinder. Perhaps the spark was of static electricity, within a hydrogen valve that was built of copper and steel. The cylindrical hot-air section remained largely intact, but proved wholly inadequate as a parachute. The remains of the balloon fell to the ground, with Rozier perishing almost instantly and Romain following only a few minutes later. This was history's first air disaster, and the first aircraft to crash.

Despite its clear risks, the first two years of ballooning established the broad forms of this activity according to patterns that persisted through the nineteenth century and into the twentieth. The principal further innovation was the parachute, which might have saved Rozier and Romain. André-Jacques Garnerin made the first such descent, in October 1797. His parachute was attached to his car; he released his balloon and remained within this gondola as it descended from twenty-three hundred feet into a Parisian park. For use with parachutes, hot-air balloons remained in vogue, for they did not use costly hydrogen and did not fly far after the pilot bailed out.

For serious ballooning, hydrogen stayed in the forefront. An English inventor, Charles Green, cut the cost by introducing common coal gas, which is rich in hydrogen. In 1836 his balloon, *Royal Vauxhall,* took him and two companions from London to Germany's Duchy of Nassau, covering 380 miles and setting a record that stood for decades. For sheer size, no one could top *Le Géant,* built in 1863 by a famous Parisian photographer who called himself Nadar. It approached 200 feet in height, with a capacity of 212,000 cubic feet, and lifted a two-story gondola that carried fourteen people.

Balloons also made voyages of exploration and discovery. The meteorologist James Glaisher rode with an experienced pilot, Henry Coxwell, and claimed to have reached 37,000 feet on a flight from Wolverhampton in 1862. He didn't; they used no oxygen, and the historian Charles Gibbs-Smith writes that they may have reached "19,000 feet, or a bit higher." Thirteen years later, France's Gaston Tissandier tried to top this record by using oxygen. His equipment did not work well, as he and two companions passed out at around 25,000 feet. He regained consciousness on the way down, but the others were dead.

The century ended with the dramatic flight of Sweden's Salomon Andree, who flew from Spitsbergen in July 1897 with two other men, in an attempt to reach the North Pole. They went only one-third of the way before they had to set down on the ice, but salvaged their equipment and walked southward toward their base. They nearly made it, but all three of them died within sight of Spitsbergen, probably from eating the infected meat of a polar bear. The world learned of this in 1930, when hunters found their bodies, diaries, and photos.

Significantly, the balloons of these flights did not differ fundamentally from those of Charles and Blanchard. Only months after the balloon's invention, during the single day of December 1, 1783, Charles demonstrated that a hydrogen balloon could fly long distances and reach high altitudes. With these achievements in hand, the record flights and achievements of the subsequent century amounted largely to embellishments. Yet while the technology of balloons quickly matured, their flights also stimulated thoughts of true airplanes, powered perhaps by steam.

Airplanes of the Mind

2

THE RAILROAD, the steamship, and the telegraph were three of the pathbreaking inventions that distinguished the nineteenth century from prior eras. Significantly, no visionary anticipated any of them until their technical bases—steam engines, flows of electric current—were already in hand. Such engines and forms of energy flow simply were not part of the mental equipment of savants in the eighteenth and earlier centuries. But when they became available, their technical consequences soon spanned the world's continents and oceans.

Aviation was different, up to a point. Dreams of flight trace to medieval times, as when Roger Bacon declared, "Flying machines can be made, and a man sitting in the middle of the machine may revolve some ingenious device by which artificial wings may beat the air in the manner of a flying bird." Two centuries later, Leonardo da Vinci wrote at length of man-powered flight, giving particular attention to wing-flapping machines called ornithopters. Subsequently, other visionaries offered their own futuristic drawings and predictions.

It is tempting to see such imaginings as preludes to the airliners that fly every day from our airports. In fact, they had nothing to do with the eventual advent of aviation. Nothing. Their present-day counterparts are not the Boeing 747 and Airbus A-340, but the starships and X-wing fighters of *Star Trek* and *Star Wars*. Those speculations, amounting at times to outright fantasy, in no way foreshadowed flight as it eventually evolved. Leonardo, for one, was twice removed from valid aeronautical technology, for he did not publish his writings, and his ornithopters could not be made to work. Dreams of flight inspired daredevils who fashioned crude wings and jumped from towers, breaking their legs and sometimes their necks. But flight, like railroads and telegraphs, awaited an adequate technical base. When it appeared, with the discovery of hydrogen and the Montgolfiers' hot-air balloons, its consequences unfolded rapidly.

Visions and prophecies have their uses, for they can inspire people who will do the actual work. But the advent of a new engine offers even more inspiration, for its advocates can often envision its uses quite presciently. Indeed, at times one faces the problem of holding them back, for the history of technology is littered with predictions that never came true. Nuclear power too cheap to be worth metering, flights to Mars departing on the hour, and humanoid robots are familiar examples.

Nevertheless, between the early dreams of flight and its eventual accomplishment in the heavier-than-air machines of the Wright brothers, there was a long century during which serious people contributed to developing appropriate technical insights—often showing, in the process, how much had to be learned. Heavier-than-air flight, even with gliders, demanded far more than the cut-and-try techniques of the early balloonists. It needed a well-developed science of aerodynamics, and the man who took the lead in its formulation was England's Sir George Cayley.

He traced his descent to Osborne de Cailly, a lord of Normandy who came to England in 1066 with William the Conqueror. A thirteenth-century scion, Sir Thomas de Cailly, adopted a crest that depicted a family legend, whereby an ancestor had killed a lion with a battle-ax and torn out its tongue. A descendant, Edward Cayley, purchased the family estate, Brompton Hall, near Scarborough in Yorkshire, in 1622. His son William received the title of baronet from King Charles I in 1643; Sir George, born in 1773, became the sixth in succession to hold that title. On his mother's side, he claimed descent from Scotland's Robert I (the Bruce).

He was marked from birth for the life of a country squire, with hearty plowmen to till his crops and produce his income. His mother tended to make the family's decisions; when he was fifteen, she sent him to board with a tutor in Nottingham, Reverend George Walker, a man of scholarly repute who was a Fellow of the Royal Society. The attractions of Walker's home included his daughter Sarah, as she and young Cayley developed a budding mutual interest. She was quite intelligent and excelled him in mathematics. He set himself to compete with her, and soon surpassed her in this field.

He brought Sarah home to meet his mother, who did not like her. Mrs. Cayley decided to intervene by withdrawing George from the tutelage of Reverend Walker and sending him to a different tutor in London. It didn't work; George and Sarah stayed in touch by exchanging letters, as they anticipated a future together. Then in 1792 his father died, and George returned from London to inherit his title and landed estate. Three years later, he married his Sarah, and they settled at Brompton.

His interest in mechanics dated to his teenage years, for although he was a well-born gentleman, he spent much time in the farmers' village, where he formed a friendship with a watchmaker. His interest in aviation appears to date to 1796, when he constructed a model helicopter. It drew its power from a stringed bow made of whalebone, with the string winding around a shaft of wood. The ends of the shaft each held a cork, with feathers stuck in to act as propeller blades. The flexible bow pulled the string from both ends and rotated these propellers, with this small aircraft rising toward the ceiling.

In 1799, Cayley invented the airplane. The historian Charles Gibbs-Smith has taken the lead in crediting him with this. He did not offer a feasible and flightworthy design, but he was the first man in history to set down a general layout and get it right. The essence of a practical airplane is the separation of airframe and power plant, with the engine being distinct from the fuselage and wings. We see this today in aircraft design, as with the 747, which has its engines placed in pods below the wings. We see it as well in the structure of the industry. The companies that build engines—General Electric, Pratt & Whitney—are distinct from Boeing and Airbus, which build airframes.

The main line of speculative aeronautical design, dating to Leonardo, involved wing-flapping ornithopters. These merged the sources of lift and power, with movable wings providing both. Cayley had different thoughts, which he set down as an engineering drawing, and as an engraving on a silver disk.

The engraving shows nothing that we would easily recognize. It appears to show a man sitting within a large clamshell, with various attachments at the sides and rear. However, the bottom half of the clamshell is a cockpit somewhat resembling a rowboat. The top half is a large curved or cambered wing, seen nearly edge-on, and it is noteworthy that at this early date, Cayley already expected that his wing would show such curvature; it would not be a simple inclined plane. He had drawn this conclusion from examining the wings of birds. To the rear we see a set of vertical and horizontal fins, somewhat like the feathers of an arrow, to provide stability in flight. For propulsion, Cayley expected to use large oars or paddles, with his pilot rowing strongly. Not by accident did his cockpit look like a rowboat.

The engineering drawing presents a neatly rendered top view, and shows more. The wing appears as a large rectangle, broad in chord or distance from front to back, and somewhat wider in span. The arrangement of oars, paddles, and connecting bars suggests a modern rowing machine. A tiller steered the tail, which had a length that nearly equaled the wingspan.

It is difficult to overestimate the importance of these simple draw-ings, because for the first time they showed a clear understanding that mechanical flight would have to follow its own principles, rather than merely mimic the design of birds. To place this in perspective, we can imagine that people had tried for several centuries to build horse-drawn carts and wagons, designing them to ride upon articulated mov-ing wooden legs resembling those of a quadruped. Cayley, in a sense, invented the wheel.

Right at the start, he was well aware that these drawings did not represent the culmination of his work, but defined instead a point of departure for a program of research. Already the means existed to con-duct studies in aerodynamics. As early as 1746, the mathematician Ben-jamin Robins leaped two centuries into the future by discovering the sound barrier. More particularly, he found that the drag, or air resis-tance, of a body in flight increases markedly at velocities close to the speed of sound. When Chuck Yeager broke this barrier, in 1947, he relied on rocket power to overcome this sharp rise in drag.

How did Robins make such a discovery? He did it with a simple instrument called a ballistic pendulum. It used a block of wood sus-pended from a frame, free to swing upward when struck by a bullet. The bullet transferred its momentum to the block, which pulled a cloth tape measure to mark the height of its swing. This gave a measurement of the bullet's velocity.

Robins could calibrate his instrument by shooting at point-blank range, with the speed of the bullet increasing as he used more gunpow-der. When fired from a distance, the bullet lost speed as a result of drag, causing the pendulum to swing to a lower height. The loss of velocity, and hence the drag, were easily measured by noting the difference. When he shot his bullets near or just above the speed of sound, the markedly larger drag stood out clearly in his data.

Robins also invented another instrument, the whirling arm, that served in lieu of wind tunnels. A wind tunnel holds a model at rest and blows air past it, but during the eighteenth and nineteenth centuries, high-speed fans or blowers did not exist. The whirling arm rotated rap-idly through the air, with a model mounted to its end. A weight pro-vided the arm's power, pulling on a cord as it dropped, with the cord being wound around the arm's supporting shaft. The rotation rate was easy to measure, and drag produced by the model provided a countering force that made it turn more slowly.

Robins presented two papers to the Royal Society in 1746, titled "Resistance of the Air" and "Experiments Relating to Air Resistance." A civil engineer, John Smeaton, built his own whirling arm and used it to study windmills. His model windmill sails lifted weights, which grew heavier as his designs improved. His own Royal Society paper, in 1759, anticipated Cayley's curving wing by showing that a cambered surface gave more lift than a flat one. Smeaton, followed by the inventor Richard Edgeworth in 1781, also made measurements of the drag produced by square and rectangular sheets of metal.

During the first years of the new century, Cayley carried out three types of aeronautical experiments. He devised a whirling arm for his own use and revisited Smeaton's problem, working to determine a critical quantity: the speed at which a surface of one square foot produces one pound of drag. The drag of wings could be referenced to this measurement, and would increase as the square of the velocity. In turn, determination of drag was critical to learning the amount of power needed for flight.

"I have tried many experiments upon a large scale to ascertain this point," he later wrote. "The instrument was similar to that used by Mr. Robins, but the surface used was larger, being an exact square foot, moving round upon an arm about 5 ft. long, and turned by weights over a pulley. The time was measured by a stop watch, and the distance travelled over in each experiment was 600 ft." Averaging his data, he wrote that "I shall therefore take 23.6 ft. [per second] as somewhat approaching the truth." Smeaton had given 21 feet per second; the modern value is 27.2, showing that Cayley was the better experimentalist.

He also made measurements of lift, by placing his square-foot surface at an angle to the horizontal and arranging for it to lift a weight. At 21.8 feet per second, and at various angles, he found the following:

Angle, degrees	Weight supported, ounces
3	1.0
6	1.5
9	2.5
12	2.75
15	4.125
18	5.187

Whirling-arm studies represented one phase of his work. In a second set of experiments he built and flew gliders. He started by using a kite as his wing, attaching it to a pole and throwing it down a hill like a spear. It quickly dived into the ground, and he responded with improvements. He gave the kite a small upward tilt by installing a stick as a support; he also added vertical and horizontal tail surfaces. His device now flew much better.

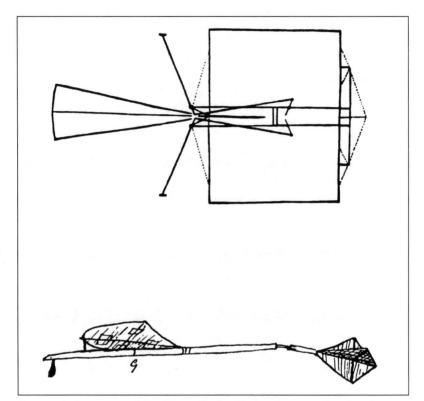

Aeronautical concepts of Sir George Cayley. Top, engineering drawing showing a top view of an airplane powered by oars. Bottom, side view of a glider.
(Art by Cayley, reproduced by Charles H. Gibbs-Smith)

His gliders grew in size and sophistication. The best of them used tail surfaces in a cruciform arrangement, angled slightly downward. This caused the glider to nose down. However, the wing was set at an upward angle, and responded to the rapid downward glide by developing considerable lift. This was the first such craft in the history of aeronautics.

Cayley's third research topic dealt with shapes of minimum drag. In his notebook, he considered that a dolphin had the appropriate form, and used it as a basis for his diagrams. He also conducted experiments, receiving a supply of gunpowder from the arsenal at Scarborough, along with the use of a six-pounder cannon. His country was at war with Napoleon just then, and he considered that by introducing ordnance of reduced drag, he could increase its range. His shapes were those of our modern air-dropped bombs, with streamlined bodies and cruciform fins. Wooden plugs helped them fit the bore of the gun.

"All these different shots were fired over the sea at Scarborough," he wrote,

> where they fell into a calm bay, and each experiment was noted by an old artilleryman conveniently placed for the purpose. My object at the time was to ascertain whether, by obviating as much as possible the resistance of the air, the range of cannon shot might be so considerably increased as to enable our line-of-battle ships to destroy the French flotilla then collected in the semi-circular basin at Boulogne, and yet keep out of range of the French batteries.

His best tests showed increases in range of one-fourth of a mile when compared to conventional cannonballs. However, they tended to wobble in flight, which cut the range and reduced the accuracy. The long-range shells of the future indeed used streamlined shapes, but relied on rifled gun barrels to make them spin for stability. Nevertheless, Cayley's views on streamlining were right on target. A hundred fifty years later, in 1954, the aerodynamicist Theodore von Kármán overlaid a Cayley low-drag shape on a modern airfoil, and showed that it "almost exactly coincides."

Having dealt with the important issues of lift, drag, general layout, and streamlining, Cayley now turned his attention to the difficult part of the problem: engines for propulsion. He knew only too well that the steam engines of his day were far too heavy, and placed his hope in an alternative, the air engine. Instead of raising steam by boiling water, it was to heat air, which would drive a piston by expanding within a cylinder. Once again, he was on to something important; the internal combustion engine, which in time made powered flight practical, was a remote descendant. But Cayley's flirtation with this field served chiefly to introduce him to the difficulties, which he set aside for the attention of other specialists.

Then, in 1809, he was stirred by a report that Jakob Degen, a clockmaker in Vienna, had achieved man-powered flight with an ornithopter. He hadn't; he had used a hydrogen balloon to lift much of his weight, with his flapping wings carrying only the remainder. By beating his wings rapidly, he reportedly rose to a height of fifty-four feet. Contemporary accounts tended not to mention the balloon, or to show it in illustrations, and this was no small matter. When a man in Ulm, Germany, duplicated Degen's equipment and tried to fly without the balloon, he quickly flopped from a tower into the Danube, and the best that could be said was that he escaped serious injury.

Nevertheless, Cayley thought that Degen was stealing his thunder. He had read of Degen's flight in *Nicholson's Journal;* he now wrote up and published, within that periodical, a three-part paper, "On Aerial Navigation." He wrote, "The whole problem is confined within these limits, viz.—to make a surface support a given weight by the application of power to the resistance of air." This statement covered helicopters as well as fixed-wing aircraft, and he declared himself to be "perfectly confident that this noble art will soon be brought home to man's general convenience, and that we shall be able to transport ourselves and families, and their goods and chattels, more securely by air than by water, and with a velocity of from 20 to 100 miles per hour."

He approached this noble art by returning anew to the issue of power. He believed that a man possessed the strength to "fly like a bird, and the ascent of Mr. Degen is a sufficient proof of the truth of this statement." He hoped for an engine with "the power of a horse and the weight less than that of a man," and suggested, but did not design, a steam engine of one horsepower that would weigh 163 pounds, including its water supply and fuel for an hour. Then, having satisfied himself that the problem of power might soon be in hand, he turned to the details of aerodynamics and airplane design.

He presented results from his work with the whirling arm, supplementing his conclusions with data from France. He also touched on his gliders, the largest of which was five feet long and loaded with a weight:

> I have myself made a large machine on this principle, large enough for aerial navigation. . . . It was beautiful to see this noble white bird sail majestically from the top of a hill to any given point of the plane below it with perfect steadiness, and safety, according to the set of the rudder, merely by its own weight descending in an angle of about 8 degrees with the horizon. . . .
>
> I made a machine having a surface of 300 square feet, which was accidentally broken before there was an opportunity of trying the effect of the propelling apparatus, but its steerage and steadiness were perfectly proved, and it would sail downwards in any direction according to the set of the rudder. Its weight was 56 lbs., and it was loaded with 94 lbs., thus making a total of 140 lbs., about 2 square feet to one pound.
>
> Even in this state, when any person ran forward in it with his full speed, taking advantage of a gentle breeze in front, it would bear upward so strongly as scarcely to allow him to touch the ground, and would frequently lift him up and convey him several yards together.[1]

Cayley introduced the topic of aircraft stability, starting with a discussion of parachutes. When Jacques Garnerin descended over Paris in

1797, his chute lacked a hole in the center, a modern feature that allows trapped air to escape. His chute could spill its trapped air only by rocking strongly from side to side, "which is said to have endangered the bold aeronaut." Cayley declared that rather than designing a parachute as an inverted cup, it should have the form of a cone of broadly obtuse angle, pointing downward. He showed that such a shape would be stable, whereas Garnerin's was not, and invited his readers to demonstrate this result with a cone of paper: "Place a small weight in the apex, and letting it fall from any height, it will steadily preserve the position to the ground."

Then, turning to airplanes, he declared that this shape of a broad letter V, "with apex downward, is the chief basis of stability in aerial navigation." By giving wings dihedral, having them angle upward when seen from the front, a designer "most effectually prevents any rolling of the machine from side to side. Hence the section of the inverted parachute . . . may equally well represent the cross section of a sheet for aerial navigation."

He also discussed stability in pitch, whereby an airplane would avoid nosing into the ground, or turning its nose upward and stalling. He argued that a vehicle could avoid this by placing its center of gravity directly below the wings' center of lift. Then, presenting an insight of considerable significance, he wrote that this center of lift "does not coincide with the center of its surface, but is considerably in front of it."

He then gave some comments on the practical matters of flight, including the use of the movable tail: "From a variety of experiments upon this subject I find that when the machine is going forward, with a superabundant velocity, or that which would induce it to rise in its path, a very steady horizontal course is effected by a considerable depression" of the tail surfaces. However, "when the velocity is becoming less, as in the act of alighting," the tail "must gradually recede from this position and even become elevated for the purpose of preventing the machine from sinking too much in front." This movement of the rear stabilizer would counteract a shift in the center of lift; in Cayley's words, "the centre of support approaching the centre of the sail," which would cause the craft to nose downward.

He also noted that craft with engines would need maximum power at takeoff, writing of "the absolute quantity of power demanded being so much greater at first than when full velocity has been acquired." He drew this conclusion from observations of birds: "Many birds, and particularly water, run and flap their wings for several yards before they gain support from the air. The swift . . . is not able to elevate itself from level ground." We see this in today's airliners, whose engines deliver peak thrust during takeoff before throttling back substantially for cruising flight.

Finally, he offered some proposals for the design of lightweight wings. He showed fabric stretched across a framework, with the frame also supporting a king post, or vertical strut. Wires, running from the ends of structural members to the post, bent and curved these members and gave the wing its camber. "Diagonal bracing is the great principle for producing strength without accumulating weight," he wrote, "and if performed by thin wires looped at their ends, so as to receive several laps of cordage, produces but a trifling resistance in the air and keeps tight in all weather." He gave a diagram of a wing that "contained 54 square feet and weighed only 11 lbs.," with two of them lifting a weight of 125 pounds.

Cayley wrote of all these matters at a time when his countrymen had won the Battle of Trafalgar in wooden warships powered by sail. The first true railroad line, the Stockton and Darlington, would not enter service for another fifteen years. Cayley thus was very much ahead of his time, and it didn't help that *Nicholson's Journal* had only a limited circulation. His three-part paper gave a solid foundation for the development of successful gliders, but over thirty years elapsed before anyone went further, even in speculation.

This happened in April 1843, when William Henson, a lacemaker in Somerset, received a patent for a design that he called the Aerial Steam Carriage. His patent included a fine set of drawings, and he had an active publicist, Frederick Marriott, who supplemented them with vividly imaginative engravings that soon appeared in such widely-read publications as the *Illustrated London News* and *L'Illustration* in Paris. The historian Charles Gibbs-Smith describes it as "the first design in history for a fixed-wing airscrew-propelled aeroplane of modern configuration." From the perspective of a century later, it was largely correct in its specifics.

Henson envisioned a rectangular wing with dimensions of 150 by 30 feet, built with spars and with ribs in the shape of an airfoil, and covered with fabric on both sides. King posts supported wires at both top and bottom, to provide this monoplane wing with structural strength. At the rear, the horizontal stabilizer had the shape of a bird's tail; it could expand or contract like a fan, and swiveled up and down to act as an elevator. A small vertical fin hung downward at its hinge. A boat-shaped hull served as the fuselage, and mounted a steam engine of 25 to 30 horsepower, which drove two 20-foot pusher propellers, each with six blades. Tricycle landing gear completed the layout.

Model of the Aerial Steam Carriage concept of 1843. (National Air and Space Museum)

Henson expected to provide the added power for takeoff by having his craft roll down a ramp. His engravings showed his airplane and ramp in a variety of locations; to illustrate travel to India, for instance, he had an elephant standing nearby. He took out full-page advertisements, stating that his invention could "fly to China in twenty-four hours certain," in an era when travel by sea to the Orient took up to six months. He tried to win support from Parliament, and when this failed, he set up the Aerial Transit Company and sought to raise funds by selling shares to the public. He also used the press to his advantage, planting a rumor that this airplane had already crossed the Channel.

In fact, he never got farther than building an unsuccessful model. He worked with a fellow lacemaker, John Stringfellow, and constructed a version with wingspan of twenty feet, powered by a small steam engine of their own invention. Between 1845 and 1847, they tried repeatedly to make it fly, but while it descended the ramp readily enough, it could not sustain itself in the air. Henson's role in the work ended as he got married and left for the United States, arriving in New York in May 1848. He made no further contributions to aviation.

Stringfellow, however, continued in his attempts to make a steam engine fly. He built a smaller model, of ten-foot wingspan, and fitted it with a new engine of Henson's design. He ran it along an overhead wire, neatly bypassing the need for its wings to carry its weight, while also sidestepping all issues of stability in flight. By giving the wire a gentle upward angle, he was able to claim that his airplane could climb under power. However, it never flew without that support.

The Aerial Steam Carriage received plenty of continuing attention during subsequent decades, for it combined dramatic illustration with the aerodynamics of Cayley. Its pictures and descriptions, printed repeatedly, served for many years to herald an age of flight. The poet Alfred, Lord Tennyson contributed as well, for while his "Locksley Hall" predated Henson's work, its lines captured the public response:

> For I dipt into the future, far as human eye could see,
> Saw the Vision of the world, and all the wonder that would be;
> Saw the heavens fill with commerce, argosies of magic sails,
> Pilots of the purple twilight, dropping down with costly bales;
> Heard the heavens fill with shouting, and there rain'd a
>   ghastly dew
> From the nations' airy navies grappling in the central blue;
> Far along the world-wide whisper of the south-wind rushing warm,
> With the standards of the peoples plunging thro' the thunderstorm;
> Till the war-drum throbb'd no longer, and the battle-flags were
>   furled
> In the Parliament of man, the Federation of the World.

Gibbs-Smith has hailed the Steam Carriage as "one of the most outstanding and influential aeroplanes in history." Nevertheless, it "was never built, and the model made from it could not fly."

Steam-driven flight indeed was a genuinely difficult problem, even with balloons. These could carry loads of some weight, but the steam engines of mid-century still lacked power for their poundage. The world saw this anew in 1852, as a wealthy Parisian, Henri Giffard, built a steam-powered dirigible. His gas bag had the shape of an elongated lemon, 144 feet in length and 39 feet across, with a capacity of 88,000 cubic feet. Filled with hydrogen, this bag could lift three tons. Its steam engine, rated at three horsepower, turned a propeller of 11 feet in diameter.

Dressed in style, with a top hat and Prince Albert frock coat, he started his motor and cast off his ropes. A mild breeze was blowing; he traveled downwind for seventeen miles, moving with the wind at seven miles per hour. Then he swung a large sail that served as his rudder and tried to come about. He made no headway; he had hoped to tack against the wind, but found himself pushed backward. Clearly, his invention was useless except in a dead calm.

Even so, the opportunity existed to break new ground. Cayley was well aware of Henson's ideas, publishing a critique of the design in the same month that it openly appeared. He declared that the long wing would break in flight, for its spar and strut-braced structure lacked strength. He suggested replacing this monoplane wing with a much shorter triplane and "to compact it into the form of a three decker, each deck being 8 to 10 feet from each other, to give free room for the passage of air between them." Cayley soon adopted the triplane for his own use, as he returned to the design and test of gliders.

He was getting on in years, as he turned seventy in 1843. But although he had turned to other matters since 1809, he was ready to blaze anew with novel ideas. His critique of Henson appeared in *Mechanics' Magazine* and was part of a longer paper that included a description of what we now call a vertical takeoff and landing craft. Drawing in part on the ideas of another inventor, Robert Taylor, Cayley showed a vehicle with four large multibladed helicopter rotors for use during liftoff. Once in the air, separate propellers would provide power for forward motion, while the main rotors would stop, their blades merging to form airfoils. Each airfoil would show a "rather slightly curved state, like a very flat umbrella."

In renewing his work with gliders, Cayley started with the simple monoplane type that had flown in 1804. To learn more about airfoils, he built a new whirling arm, with the intent this time of constructing a man-carrying craft. It was ready in 1849, amounting to a triplane wing with a boat-shaped gondola suspended below on struts. Both the wing and the gondola had cruciform tail surfaces, with the lower set being movable. The wing area was 338 square feet; the empty weight was about 130 pounds.

Cayley flew it several times unmanned, and also arranged for a young and lightweight boy to serve as its pilot. In a paper of 1853, he wrote that "a boy of about ten years of age was floated off the ground for several yards on descending a hill, and also for about the same space by some persons pulling the apparatus against a very slight breeze by a rope."

Cayley was no Henson; he lacked the will for publicity, confining his comments to his notebook and his published papers. Early balloon ascents had featured impresarios who arranged for large crowds to attend, but Cayley conducted his work in the seclusion of his country estate. In 1853 he was ready with a larger glider, of 165 pounds. Nearly eighty years old and still active, he persuaded a reluctant coachman to make the attempt. This was the world's first true manned flight in a glider, but what we know of it comes largely from a letter written in 1921 by his granddaughter Dora:

> I remember in later times hearing of a large machine being started on the high side of the valley behind Brompton Hall where he lived, and the coachman being sent up in it, and it flew across the

little valley, about 500 yards at most, and came down with a smash. What the motive power was I don't know, but I think the coachman was the moving element, and the result was his capsize and the rush of watchers across to his rescue. He struggled up and said, "Please, Sir George, I wish to give notice. I was hired to drive and not to fly."[2]

This was Cayley's last important contribution. He died in 1857, and we may summarize his work succinctly: His papers and writings laid the foundation for aerodynamics and for airplane design. Yet his personal modesty prevented him from creating public sensations, stirring premature hopes, mulcting investors of cash, or breaking anyone's neck.

Powered flight, with or without a pilot, remained an entrancing goal, one that proved to be achievable with a model several decades before the Wright brothers did it at full scale. The man who did it, Alphonse Penaud, used a rubber band for power, along with a propeller formed from a pair of feathers. His craft, which he called the *Planophore*, closely resembled the model planes that now are sold in every hobby shop. Its fuselage was a twenty-inch stick with the propeller pushing from the rear; the wingspan was eighteen inches. For stability, its center of gravity lay just aft of the leading edge of its monoplane wing. This wing had dihedral along with upturned tips; similar tips on the horizontal stabilizer served in lieu of a vertical fin.

Penaud was only twenty-one years old when he demonstrated it at the Tuileries, in 1871, before the Société de Navigation Aérienne. It stayed in the air for eleven seconds and flew 131 feet. His father was an admiral, which gave him hope of raising money through social and professional contacts, and he followed this initial success by developing and patenting a design for a full-scale biplane. However, he had a bone disease, which became progressively worse. His youth placed him at a disadvantage for seeking funds, while his illness robbed him of hope. In 1880, at age thirty, he committed suicide.

His competitors included Felix Du Temple, a naval officer. He had started with a model of his own, powered by steam. In 1857 or 1858 he achieved Stringfellow's goal, as this model took off under its own power, remained briefly in the air, and landed safely. This was the first successful demonstration of powered flight, and Temple followed with a full-size machine. Viewed from above, it resembled a large bird with outstretched wings, with a propeller in place of the beak. In 1874, with a man aboard, he tried to make it fly with a hot-air engine. It rolled down a ramp and was airborne momentarily, and that was all.

Thomas Moy, in London, obtained similarly minimal results the following year, with his Aerial Steamer. It was a tandem-wing craft, with a horizontal stabilizer that was a wing in its own right, for a total lifting surface of 114 square feet. This made it intermediate in size between the models of Stringfellow and the man-carrying glider of Cayley. A three-horsepower steam engine drove two large propellers that resembled fans, set between the two wings.

Moy was an engineer and a patent agent, with a background in ballooning. He spent a decade studying heavier-than-air flight and developing his airplane. It was unmanned; he arranged for it to fly at the end of a tether, circling the fountain at the Crystal Palace. It lifted six inches into the air, and *that* was all. It set a mark as the first steam-driven airplane to raise itself off the ground, but like the pseudo-flight of Du Temple, it had less to do with real aviation than Evel Knievel's motorcycle jumps of a much later era.

Aleksander Mozhaiski, a captain in the Russian navy, was another such jumper. He built a steam-powered monoplane with an engine crafted from an English design, and flew it near St. Petersburg in 1884. In a contemporary illustration it has the definite look of an airplane, with king posts and wire-braced wings, propellers fore and aft, and a smokestack belching black fumes. It carried a pilot, I. N. Golubev, and took off by rolling down a ramp that resembled a ski jump. It flew no farther than a hundred feet, and the best one could say was that it indeed was airborne, however briefly. Its main significance came in subsequent decades, when Bolsheviks pointed to it and declared that their countrymen had invented the airplane.

Next came two men of wealth, Clément Ader and Hiram Maxim. Ader made his fortune by installing telephones in France, and drew on his funds as he pursued an ongoing interest in flight. He made a significant contribution by inventing a lightweight steam engine of eighteen to twenty horsepower, and built his airplane, named *Eole*, as a monoplane in the shape of a bat. He made his attempt at a château near Paris in 1890, with *Eole* becoming the first piloted and powered airplane to raise itself from level ground without the use of a ramp.

But while it could take off, it could not fly. It reached an altitude of eight inches and stayed aloft for about 160 feet before descending, and Ader himself avoided claiming that he had solved the problem of flight. In the words of Gibbs-Smith, he had "only the most rudimentary conception of flight-control and of stability." He had no elevator or horizontal stabilizer; his craft amounted to a flying wing, a configuration that would tax the ingenuity of designers a half-century and more in the future. He nevertheless continued this line of development as he won support from the War Ministry. But his next airplane, in 1897, was less successful, for it did not leave the ground.

Hiram Maxim was a kindred spirit, having accumulated his own millions by inventing the machine gun. Like Ader, he knew how to build good steam engines. The road to improvement lay in high pressure, which boosted the power-to-weight ratio. Maxim's engine reached 320 pounds per square inch and weighed 9 pounds per horsepower, without fuel and water. This was a tenfold improvement over the engine of 1804 that Cayley had merely envisioned, without ever attempting to construct.

Maxim used two of them, each driving an 18-foot propeller, for a total of 360 horsepower. His airplane was immense, with a 110-foot span, a crew of three, and a weight of 8,000 pounds supported by 4,000 square feet of lifting area. It was a biplane; the wings were well separated and showed considerable dihedral, with elevators both fore and aft.

Maxim, like Ader, knew very little about flight control. However, he knew what he didn't know, and made no attempt at free flight. Instead he arranged for his machine to run along a track, with auxiliary wheels engaging guardrails to prevent it from rising into the sky. On his most successful attempt, in 1894, he indeed rose into the air, with his wheels and guardrails working as planned. Suddenly an axle broke from the force of lift, and a wheel fouled its rail. Maxim, at the controls, shut off power and came to a stop. He had spent £30,000 but did no more, except to flatter himself in later years that he had invented the airplane.

He hadn't, of course; to do so, he would have had to execute a controlled free flight of some duration. Even so, the work of Ader and Maxim showed that at the end of the century, the problem of power was well on its way to solution. Nevertheless, good engines alone were insufficient, for there still was much to learn concerning control. If anyone was to invent the airplane, well and truly, it would be necessary to absorb thoroughly the work of Cayley and his successors, and then to go a good deal farther. Cayley had laid the essential groundwork, but as late as 1900, no one really understood how to control an aircraft in flight. The first men to learn this skill were Orville and Wilbur Wright.

The Problem of Control   3

B<small>EFORE</small> <small>ATTEMPTING</small> powered flight, it was a good idea to start with gliders. Cayley did it that way, though Ader and Maxim did not. Nevertheless, two other leaders of the 1890s, Otto Lilienthal and Octave Chanute, also proceeded in this fashion. Neither got as far as building airplanes with engines, but both men invented hang gliders. More than seventy years before hang gliding became popular as a sport, it came to the forefront as a prelude to true aviation.

Lilienthal, born in Pomerania in 1848, developed an early fascination with the flight of birds, which he shared with his younger brother Gustav. He continued to hold this interest as he studied engineering and then fought in the Franco-Prussian War; his fellow soldiers in the infantry later recalled that he talked often of flying machines. Demobilized in 1871, he returned to Berlin and set up a small factory. This gave him his livelihood, while permitting him to pursue his studies of aviation on the side.

He held the conviction that the proper approach to flight lay in building ornithopters. To do so successfully, he knew he needed the strongest possible background in observations of birds. He learned that birds propel themselves by using their outer feathers; he developed tables showing the lift provided by wings with various amounts of curvature. He published his findings in 1889 in a book titled *Der Vogelflug als Grundlage der Fliegekunst* (Bird Flight as the Basis of Aviation), which quickly became influential within this nascent field.

Soon after, he began building a succession of gliders. He made no attempt to introduce movable controls; instead, he steered them by moving his body and legs. His first two designs didn't work, but he learned from his mistakes and crafted an increasingly successful series, beginning in 1891. He also had a stroke of good fortune when he learned that a canal was to be built near his home. He allowed the contractor to pile the excavated dirt on land that he owned, creating a hill fifty feet tall. He could take off in any direction from its top, depending on how the wind was blowing.

He also flew from hills near Berlin, making a weekly excursion every Sunday. As his designs improved, he achieved ranges as great as 1,150 feet. Most of his craft were monoplanes, with the plane of the wings at chest level. However, his No. 11 of 1894, which he regarded as his standard model, was a true hang glider that placed his entire body below the wing, for greater stability. It had a separate tail with vertical and horizontal stabilizers. He made some 2,500 flights in the course of five years, taking off by running downhill and into the wind. As few as three steps would see him airborne, with a seat supporting his weight. When landing, he pushed the wings to angle them upward, losing speed and dropping lightly to the ground.

Although No. 11 was his best, he remained open to new approaches. He built and flew a biplane. He considered the use of control surfaces: a movable tail, an air brake at each wingtip to produce drag for steering by making the craft turn in the air. He also built lightweight engines, though he did not fly with them. He did not plan to use a propeller; he continued to think of propulsion using flapping wingtips, an approach that reflected his continuing interest in ornithopters. Nevertheless, his strong base of experience in controlled flight placed him in a good position to become the first to fly under power.

He never lived to make the attempt. One day in August 1896, he was flying his reliable No. 11 when a sudden gust of wind lifted the nose and made him stall. He threw his weight forward to try to bring the nose down, but he did not succeed, falling off on one wing and slamming into the ground. He suffered internal injuries that included a broken back, and died the next day.

Much the same fate befell a Scotsman, Percy Pilcher, who was active at the same time. He had served in the Royal Navy and took a post in naval architecture at Glasgow University. He crafted a glider, spent some time with Lilienthal in Berlin, flew one of Lilienthal's biplanes from the artificial hill, and proceeded to improve his own designs. There were hills aplenty in the Highlands, and Pilcher introduced the use of a towrope to pull him into the air. He learned still more by working with Maxim as an assistant; his best flight, in June 1897, took him 750 feet.

Like Lilienthal, he built a small engine and tested it on a bench. However, he never got to fly with it. During a flight in September 1899, a bamboo rod in the tail broke and the tail assembly collapsed, causing his glider to dive into the ground. He died two days later.

Had they lived, either Lilienthal or Pilcher might be remembered today as the inventor of the airplane, with the Wright brothers as also-rans. With their deaths, Europe lost two of its leaders in aviation, with no one immediately at hand to carry on for them. Leadership in this field now passed to the United States, where Octave Chanute for some time had been active and vigorous.

Born in 1832, he was in his sixties during the 1890s. He had had a distinguished career in civil engineering, building a bridge over the Missouri River at Kansas City and serving as chief engineer of the Erie Railroad. Residing in Chicago, his projects also included the Union Stock Yards. He came to aviation after reading an article by France's Alphonse Penaud, in 1876. This led him into a careful study of the available literature. His friends included the editor of *Railroad and Engineering Journal,* who invited him to contribute a series of articles on the subject of flight.

The first of them appeared in October 1891, with new ones being published monthly through the end of 1893. The following year the complete series appeared as a book, *Progress in Flying Machines.* Along with Lilienthal's *Vogelflug,* it became a classic, for it offered an insightful survey of the attempts made to date, showing what had and hadn't worked. Chanute also entered into extensive correspondence with other inventors, including Lilienthal, Maxim, and Lawrence Hargrave, an Australian who invented the box kite.

Then in 1896, he decided that he could build successful gliders of his own. He set up a camp amid sand dunes on the southern shore of Lake Michigan, working initially with a Lilienthal-type glider built by an assistant, Augustus Herring. Chanute felt that he was too old to fly himself, and encouraged Herring to be a test pilot. A storm blew in and ripped up their tent; Chanute sent for a new one. A reporter from the *Chicago Tribune* learned what they were up to and wrote stories that attracted a steady stream of bothersome visitors. Chanute and his associates nevertheless went ahead.

The Lilienthal glider flew repeatedly but did not work well, finally being damaged beyond repair following a bad landing. Chanute by then had developed ideas of his own, and was ready to nurture a fondness for designs with a large number of wings. His next device, the Katydid, had as many as six pairs. It was a hang glider, like all the others of that day, and he hoped it would show a high degree of inherent stability. He wrote that "the wings should move automatically so as to bring the movable center of pressure back over the center of gravity, which latter would remain fixed. That is to say, that the wings should move instead of the man."

It flew acceptably, though for shorter distances than the Lilienthal model, and Chanute declared that he had learned more in two weeks of flight test than in years of studying other people's writings. He returned to Chicago with his group and proceeded to build a new glider that was considerably simpler in form. It took shape as a triplane, which he later converted into a biplane by the simple method of removing the bottom wing. He built it as a Pratt truss, a lightweight structure patented in 1844 that he had previously used in railroad bridges. This represented a real contribution, for subsequent biplane designs, including those of the Wrights, used the Pratt truss as well.

Chanute returned to the dunes in August, picking a location five miles farther down the coast, where the dunes were taller and the site was harder for the casually curious to reach. Photos of subsequent flights with the biplane have a distinctly modern appearance, as we see Herring and others skimming along the face of a dune or lifting into the air for a long glide. The beach and the sandy hills have not changed in the past hundred years, while the biplane design shows a simplicity that suits the mind of today. Herring set the record for this round of experiments, flying 360 feet in fourteen seconds. The glider also proved to be flyable in winds that topped thirty miles per hour. Some visitors found their way to the secluded camp, and by late September, Chanute had so much confidence in his biplane that he allowed these rank neophytes to fly with it.

Chanute, Pilcher, and Lilienthal together showed that good solutions were in hand for wings and for overall designs, with a pilot achieving control by moving the weight of his body. However, successful powered flight would call for more than scaling up the design and installing an engine. These hang gliders lacked movable control surfaces—ailerons, elevator, rudder—and hence could not grow in size. Already, Maxim had built a large machine that lacked such surfaces and therefore could do no more than lift itself from a track.

Only a pilot could exercise control in flight, but people knew by then how to build airplanes that would be inherently stable in the air, and advances in steam-engine design brought new opportunities for unpiloted models. The man who did the most in this area was Samuel P. Langley, the director of the Smithsonian Institution in Washington. Like Cayley, he was an aristocrat. He did not trace his background to the Norman Conquest, but his ancestors had come to Massachusetts soon after the arrival of the *Mayflower*. These forebears included the religious leaders Cotton Mather and Increase Mather, the latter being an early president of Harvard College.

He developed a strong early interest in astronomy, and worked with his younger brother to build telescopes with mirrors of his own design. This brought him appointments at Harvard and at the Naval Academy in

Annapolis, followed by a permanent position as director of the observatory at the nascent University of Pittsburgh. His work helped to broaden astronomy into the new realms of astrophysics, moving beyond a traditional concern with the positions of stars to embrace their study as physical objects. He specialized in studies of the sun, leading an expedition to the top of California's Mount Whitney and making observations at high altitude. He also invented the bolometer, a sensitive instrument for measuring the flow of energy at any wavelength.

However, Pittsburgh was no place for a first-class scientist such as Langley. It was an industrial town, where people with real brains were in short supply, and it didn't help that he was painfully shy. Though tall and commanding in appearance, he was unattractive to women; he never married, and he formed few close friendships. He therefore responded eagerly in 1887, when he received an appointment as assistant secretary of the Smithsonian. Later that year he became full secretary, or director, upon the death of his predecessor.

Already he was nurturing an interest in aviation. This dated to the previous year, when he had attended a meeting of the American Association for the Advancement of Science and read a paper on the flight of soaring birds. With help from William Thaw, a wealthy local philanthropist who had financed the Mount Whitney expedition, Langley built a large whirling arm driven by a steam engine. He concluded that one horsepower could lift two hundred pounds into the air, at a speed of sixty feet per second.

During 1887, with Washington as his new home, he also began experimenting with small models powered by rubber bands, in the fashion of Alphonse Penaud. He had no background in airplane design, but he learned what he could from other people's layouts, and he worked by trial and error as he sought success. It took him four years before one of his models flew well, and he never achieved distances greater than a hundred feet. Nevertheless, by 1892 he was ready to build lightweight steam engines, and he made his first attempts at powered flight.

He called his craft "aerodromes," from the Greek for "air runner," with the first of them being No. 0. Its design was so inadequate that Langley abandoned it before completing its construction. Nos. 1, 2, and 3, which followed, all proved to be so underpowered that they could not fly. Nos. 4 and 5 had better engines, but their wings proved to lack structural strength. By then it was 1895, and Langley had merely succeeded with his rubber-band models.

But during that year, he settled on a new configuration that seemed to hold particular promise. It was a tandem-wing monoplane, with wings of equal size set one behind the other. England's D. S. Brown had published this concept some twenty years earlier, and had shown that it was stable in pitch. Langley rebuilt Nos. 4 and 5 to this new design, redesignating the former as No. 6. He continued to work with tandem wings during subsequent years.

He launched his aircraft from a catapult atop a houseboat that he moored in the Potomac near Quantico, Virginia. The remote location gave him privacy; the aerodromes could take off into wind from any direction and fly over a flat river surface, devoid of trees. He also expected that a rough landing in water would do less damage than a similar crack-up on land. In May 1896 he was ready to try again. On the first attempt, with No. 6, a guy wire snagged an obstacle during launch and a wing collapsed. He brought out No. 5 and placed it on the catapult. As for what happened next, we have Langley's own report:

The signal was given and the aerodrome sprang into the air. I watched it from the shore with hardly a hope that the long series of accidents had come to a close. And yet it had.

For the first time, the aerodrome swept continuously through the air like a living thing. Second after second passed on the face of the stopwatch until a minute had gone by. And it still flew on.

As I heard the cheering of the few spectators, I felt that something had been accomplished at last. For never in any part of the world or in any period had any machine of man's construction sustained itself in the air for even half of this brief time.

Still the aerodrome went on in a rising course until, at the end of a minute and a half (for which time only it was provided with fuel and water), it had accomplished a little over half a mile. Now it settled rather than fell into the river with a gentle descent.[1]

Alexander Graham Bell, inventor of the telephone, was there with Langley, and gave his own description. Bell wrote that the model "rose at first directly into the face of the wind, moving at all times with remarkable steadiness, and subsequently swinging around in large curves of perhaps a hundred yards in diameter, and continually ascending until its steam was exhausted. At a lapse of about a minute and a half, and at a height which I judged to be between eighty and one hundred feet in the air, the wheels ceased turning."[2]

The craft that did this had a wingspan of 14 feet, with an engine that delivered a single horsepower. It weighed about 30 pounds—and on this first flight, it covered some 3,300 feet. Then, just to show that this was no fluke, Langley fished it from the water and launched it on a second flight, later that afternoon. This time it circled to the left, but it stayed aloft for about the same time and covered the same distance.

Late in November, he was back on the river and ready to try with a repaired No. 6. It did even better, for instead of circling it flew in a long gentle curve that hugged the shoreline, remaining in the air for a minute and forty-five seconds while covering over three-fourths of a mile. Here was something new and highly significant, for in contrast to Ader and Maxim, Langley had done what he set out to do and had achieved true powered flight. Moreover, this accomplishment represented work by the Smithsonian Institution, one of the nation's premier scientific organizations. Both in its prestige and in the extent of accomplishment, Langley's work topped anything done to date.

He had done what he could with models and small steam engines; piloted flight, in a full-scale airplane, clearly stood as the next goal. However, such a project lay beyond the resources of the Smithsonian. Then in April 1898, the nation declared war on Spain. The Spanish-American War lasted only a few months, but that was long enough for President William McKinley to take an interest in potential military applications of Langley's work. He appointed a committee, which recommended support. In December, Langley accepted an invitation from the War Department to build a man-carrying airplane, with a grant of $50,000. No one had yet flown successfully in a powered aircraft, but already the federal government was ready to get involved.

During the next several years, he worked closely with an assistant, Charles Manly, and placed particular emphasis on engines. He took full advantage of a century of technical advances in this area, but his powered craft, Aerodrome A, might have followed the designs of Cayley. He built it as a tandem-wing monoplane, with a movable elevator at the rear to control the pitch. To turn it, he installed a rudder like that of a ship. The wings had dihedral for stability, and he expected that this would keep his airplane on an even keel while the rudder did its work. His emphasis on intrinsic stability followed conventional wisdom, and drew on his experience with Nos. 5 and 6.

In Dayton, Ohio, Wilbur Wright was nurturing different ideas. He was part of a close-knit family that included Orville, sister Katharine, and father Milton, the latter being a bishop in the evangelical United Brethren Church. Another brother, Lorin, lived close by, with a wife and children of his own. The world remembers Wilbur and Orville for their bicycle shop, the Wright Cycle Company, which also was close to their home.

Bicycles were a serious matter during the 1890s. They gave people the mobility of a horse, at far less expense and inconvenience. With automobiles still in the future, they encouraged the paving of streets and roads while nurturing a generation of mechanics. The versions of that era already were safe and easy to use, differing little in appearance from those of today.

The Wrights came to bicycles by way of printing. They constructed their presses from scratch and got them to work, publishing a local newspaper and running off church and business publications. This gave them plenty of experience as mechanics, while they became acquainted with bicycles after purchasing their own in 1892. Interest in bikes was burgeoning by then, and they found themselves in demand by friends and neighbors in need of repairs.

They kept their print shop, but within a year their bicycle activities represented their main line of business. They started by setting up a repair service, offering parts and accessories as well, while selling a number of brands known for their quality. However, this line of business was attractive to others, too. As competition intensified, the Wrights soon found three other shops within two blocks of their own. They knew they needed something special to stand out in the crowd, and proceeded to build fine bicycles of their own design.

The experience of several years had given them a clear understanding of the versions that were already on the market, and they were certain that they could offer a superior model. They set up a small machine shop with a lathe, a drill press, and tube-cutting equipment. For power, they built a single-cylinder internal combustion engine, which turned an overhead shaft that drove their machine tools. They did not merely assemble components purchased from suppliers; they built their own, including the wheels. They were particularly proud of their dustproof oil-retaining hubs.

The bicycle business gave them a good living. It was highly seasonal, however, slumping markedly during the fall and winter, and this gave them time for other activities. Aviation drew their attention during 1896, with Langley conducting his two long flights in May, Chanute flying his hang gliders during the summer, and Lilienthal dying during August. Wilbur took the lead in learning what he could, as he proceeded to read the modest literature that was available in Dayton. Because Langley was at the Smithsonian, Wilbur was well aware that this was the place to go for more, and in the spring of 1899 he wrote a letter. He requested "such papers as the Smithsonian Institution has published on this subject, and if possible a list of other works in print in the English language."

Richard Rathbun, one of Langley's assistants, responded by having a clerk put together a package of pamphlets and reprints that included writings by Langley and Lilienthal. Rathbun also wrote a letter in reply that included further suggestions, including a publication of Langley's that could be ordered for one dollar, postage included. Wilbur assembled this library of recommended books, read them with care—and decided that the aeronauts of the day had overlooked the important topic of flight control.

As an experienced bicycle man, he was well aware that a bike demanded skillful steering, to keep its rider from falling over. Yet bicycles ran on solid roadways; would an airplane, flying in thin air, be any less demanding? Bikers had to turn the front wheel to maintain control, and Wilbur decided that the proper turning of aircraft could be the key to their control. He was not impressed with the idea of steering an airplane by using a shiplike rudder; bicycles relied on banked turns, and he expected that an airplane would as well.

As he wrote a year later, "My observations of the flight of buzzards led me to believe that they regain their lateral balance when partly overturned by a gust of wind, by a torsion of the tips of their wings. If the rear edge of the right wing tip is twisted upward and the left downward the bird becomes an animated windmill and instantly begins a turn," executing a controlled roll or bank.

One day in July 1899, working in the bicycle shop, he picked up a small cardboard box and idly twisted it in his hands. This was it! He visualized the box as a set of airplane wings, and decided that by twisting them as a unit, he could cause the wingtips on one side to angle upward while making the tips on the other side turn down. Here was a way to conduct a controlled bank, buzzard-style.

"We began construction of a model within a day or two," Orville later wrote. It was a small set of paper wings, stiffened with split bamboo, and it left Wilbur convinced that he could build a much larger set of wings that would both fly and twist for control. He built them with a span of five feet, with a small horizontal stabilizer in front; there was no rudder. He flew the assembly as a kite, with a control stick in each hand and with cords running to the top and bottom of each stick. He found that by using these sticks, he could make this kite rise or descend. More importantly, he could twist or warp the wings and cause the kite to bank to the right or left, then make it recover.

The brothers had funds for travel, time to experiment further during the slack season, and a new and highly exciting approach to flight. Wilbur, who continued to lead the effort, decided that he did not want to emulate Chanute or Lilienthal by building a new type of glider. Their glides had been too short; with only a few seconds aloft at a time, it had taken Lilienthal years to gain a few hours of total experience in the air. Instead, Wilbur decided to build a craft large enough for a man, and to fly it initially as a kite. Controlled at first from the ground and later by its pilot, while still tethered, it might stay up for hours at a time. Then, once proven, he or Orville could use it as a glider in free flight, and learn still more.

However, he could not do these things in Dayton; he needed a place where the winds blew strongly and continually. He wrote to the Weather Bureau and received a list of average wind velocities at 120 stations around the country. In addition to good winds, he wanted hills for gliding, soft sand that would cushion a fall, and plenty of solitude to avoid the curious. Kitty Hawk, North Carolina looked promising; it was on the Outer Banks, north of Cape Hatteras. He sent a letter to the local Weather Bureau representative and soon received replies not only from him but from the postmaster, William Tate, who extended a hearty invitation.

Wilbur made his way to Kitty Hawk in September 1900, with Orville following. Railroads carried Wilbur as far as Elizabeth City, on the mainland, where he found that the best way to reach his destination was in a fishing schooner whose owner never took a bath. "The sails were rotten," wrote Wilbur, "the ropes badly worn and the rudder post half rotted off, and the cabin so dirty and vermin-infested that I kept out of it." But the Tates welcomed him warmly, with his wife cooking a breakfast of ham and eggs. When Orville arrived, he brought a large tent, and the two men proceeded to camp on the dunes.

Their kite had a wingspan of seventeen feet, with its horizontal stabilizer in front. The brothers expected that this would avoid damage during a nose-high landing; it also gave a visual reference, forward of the aircraft, with which the pilot could see at a glance if he was climbing or descending. The forward location also contributed to lift while climbing. They built it as an assembly of prefabricated parts that could easily be shipped, and when Wilbur put it back together, Mrs. Tate allowed him to use her sewing machine to prepare fitted fabric for the wings.

Their tests continued to confirm the promise of wing warping as a method for control. However, they found that the lift was far less than they had calculated. After several weeks, having learned what they could, they returned to Dayton, leaving the kite in Kitty Hawk. Mrs. Tate promptly made good use of the wing coverings, which were of French sateen fabric. She sewed them into new dresses for her young daughters.

A larger wing was clearly in order, to provide more lift. The Wrights' design of 1901 doubled the wing area and increased the span to twenty-two feet, making it the largest glider ever constructed. It was too large to control as a hang glider, using Lilienthal's weight-shifting technique;

they knew they would have to fly it using aerodynamic controls, warping the wings and applying up- and down-elevator.

Wilbur and Orville reached Kitty Hawk just after a hurricane, with the Weather Bureau anemometer reaching ninety-three miles per hour before being torn away. The storm brought a week of rain, which created pools of water that were ideal for mosquitoes. "The sand and grass and trees and hills and everything were crawling with them," Orville wrote in a letter. "They chewed us clean through our underwear and socks. Lumps began swelling up all over my body like hens' eggs." They drove these insects away by burning tree stumps to produce smoke, and set to work with their airplane.

The brothers placed considerable emphasis on flying it as a glider, and soon found that it had some very forgiving flying qualities. They knew that Lilienthal had died following a stall, but when their own craft stalled, it did not dive into the sand; instead it mushed down slowly in a gentle fall. They concluded, correctly, that this was due to the forward horizontal stabilizer. Conventional thinking, dating to Cayley, placed this stabilizer in the rear, as a tail, but the Wrights would have none of this. Through subsequent years, they continued to put it in front.

However, the flight tests of 1901 left them discouraged and disheartened. Once again, the wings fell far short of developing their predicted lift. Even worse, wing-warping proved unreliable as a method of control. At times it tended to put the craft into a spin, or to turn in the direction opposite to that intended. On one flight, a wing tip dropped and Wilbur tried to level his wings. Instead of responding, the glider pitched into the sand, throwing him forward.

The problem of lift demanded the brothers' first attention, for until it was resolved, they would not be able to design good wings. They had used data published by Lilienthal, and now considered that he might have been wrong. As an initial test, the Wrights took a small bicycle wheel and mounted a flat plate to the rim, along with a model airfoil. The wheel, mounted horizontally, was free to turn so as to allow the forces on the plate and airfoil to balance. They mounted this rig to the front of a standard bicycle and took turns riding into the wind at full tilt. Using Lilienthal's data, they calculated that the airfoil should balance at a five-degree angle of attack. In fact, it developed so little lift that it required eighteen degrees, a major difference.

This simple experiment led the brothers to initial tests in a homemade wind tunnel, which again showed that Lilienthal was wrong. They responded by building a larger wind tunnel, sixteen inches across, with which they launched a comprehensive study of the lift and drag of wings. Lilienthal had worked with a whirling arm, and had used measurements that dated to John Smeaton in 1759, but the Wrights improved considerably on his methods. They devised ingenious supports for their model wings that enabled them to work both rapidly and accurately. They knew that they were pushing the frontiers of aeronautics, for in Orville's words, "Wilbur and I could hardly wait for morning to come, to get at something that interested us. *That's* happiness!"

This research gave them a solid foundation for designing the wings of their 1902 glider. They wanted more lift and less drag, and achieved these goals in part through a careful choice of wing cross section. They also made the wings long and narrow, which further improved the lift-to-drag ratio. In the final design, the drag was low indeed. Flown as a kite, it did not blow backward, but wafted nearly vertically, as if levitated.

The Wrights also tried to improve their control of turns. The 1900 and 1901 craft had lacked a tail, but for the 1902 model, they added a pair of fixed vertical fins set aft of the wings. The 1901 glider had tended to yaw rather than turn properly, in response to wing-warping, and these tail surfaces were to keep the vehicle pointing in its direction of flight.

They did not fly at Kitty Hawk itself, where the sand was flat, but at the Kill Devil Hills, several miles away. The hills were tall dunes that encouraged long glides. It took real effort to carry the craft up a slope, in hot summer weather, and the Wrights drew on their physical strength as they did this repeatedly. The new double tail helped, eliminating yaw and making the craft more controllable. But it did not solve the problem, for there still were times when the glider did not turn when banked, but sideslipped into the sand.

Orville suggested replacing the fixed tail with a movable rudder. This new control surface, working in concert with the wing-warping, proved itself in practice, for it eliminated the sideslips and allowed smoothly banked turns under all conditions of wind and airspeed. For the first time, the Wrights had a fully controllable craft that could fly well as a matter of routine. They ran off hundreds of successful glides during their remaining time on the dunes, staying aloft for over twenty seconds and topping six hundred feet in range. Orville wrote home and boasted, "We now hold all records!" With an engine and a good set of propellers, they would be ready for successful powered flight.

Meanwhile, what had Langley been doing? Drawing on his government grant, he gave a contract to a New York engine builder, Stephen Balzer, specifying twelve horsepower for a weight of a hundred pounds. It was to be of the internal-combustion type; Langley had done what he could with steam. Balzer's engine proved to lack power, and when Langley and his assistant Manly visited Europe, in 1900, they again found nothing suitable.

However, Manly was a good engineer in his own right, and he declared that he could work with Balzer to craft a custom-built motor that would serve the needs of the project. He built it within only a few weeks, working in the Smithsonian shops; it weighed 108 pounds and topped 18 horsepower. Langley had expected to use twin hundred-pound engines in his full-size airplane, each driving its own propeller, but Manly was convinced that a single unit could do the job. His second motor took shape as a five-cylinder radial that came in just above 200 pounds. When tested in January 1902, it delivered 52.4 horsepower. Here was a genuinely impressive accomplishment, representing the first really good aviation motor.

The Wrights needed an engine as well. In 1902 a number of people were building automobiles, but Wilbur and Orville found that the available engines all were too heavy for their power. This did not stop them; they had done everything else on their own, and having built their single-cylinder motor to run the power tools in their bicycle shop, they were certain that they could craft one for an airplane. When designed and built, it owed much to Charlie Taylor, an assistant whom they had hired in 1901 to run their bicycle business during their lengthy absences. Like the Wrights, he was an experienced mechanic, with skills and talents that complemented their own.

This engine came in at 180 pounds, but produced only twelve horse-power. This appeared adequate, according to the Wrights' calculations, but it took a while to get it to run properly. On the second day of testing, in February 1903, a bearing seized and the crankcase broke. It had been made of aluminum to save weight, cast in a foundry, and there was nothing to do but return to the foundry for a new one. It was May before the motor was running again.

Good propellers were important, to make the best use of the available power, and the Wrights thought they could learn from the screw propellers of ships. They found nothing useful, and fell back again on their aeronautical experience, visualizing a propeller blade as an airplane wing that whirled rather than traveling in a straight line. In June, Orville wrote a letter to a friend:

> . . . we worked out a theory of our own on the subject, and soon discovered, as we usually do, that all propellers built heretofore are *all wrong,* and then built a pair of propellers . . . , based on our theory, which are *all right!* . . . Isn't it astonishing that all these secrets have been preserved for so many years just so that we could discover them?[3]

Their airplane, the famous Wright Flyer, closely resembled the glider of 1902. To carry the weight of the motor, it was somewhat larger, with a 40-foot wingspan and a wing area of 510 square feet.

Langley's craft, Aerodrome A, was considerably larger, with twice the wing area. As with his earlier steam-powered models, he intended to launch it by catapult from a houseboat in the Potomac, with Manly as his test pilot. Unlike the Wrights, Manly had not learned to fly, for he had not practiced in gliders. Nor would he test his airplane in short hops, prior to attempting a true flight. The use of the catapult left him totally committed to succeeding on the first try, as if he was a naval carrier pilot in World War II. Nevertheless, there was method to this madness. The steam-powered models had shown inherent stability; Aerodrome A copied this feature. If all went well, Manly might merely go along for the ride.

These two independent efforts, of Langley and the Wrights, both had airplanes ready to fly in the autumn of 1903. Langley's went first, on October 7. The craft cleared the catapult and immediately began diving into the river. Manly grabbed his control wheel and threw the elevator to "full up" in an attempt to steady his vehicle. It did not respond, plunging into the water. Manly swam free and saved himself, but Aerodrome A was a wreck. Its motor and main framework proved to be salvageable, but Langley took two months before he was ready to try again.

The Wrights had reached Kitty Hawk more than a week earlier, and already were making new practice flights with the glider of 1902. The engine-powered Flyer demanded a good deal of ground testing, which began in early November. The motor ran rough and damaged the propeller shafts, and there was nothing to do but to send them back to Charlie Taylor in Dayton for repair. The refurbished shafts arrived two weeks later, and the Wrights worked to tune the engine and raise the propellers' revolutions per minute. After a week of this, one of the shafts cracked. Work stopped, and Orville returned to Dayton to prepare a new set of shafts made of resilient steel.

On December 8, Langley made another attempt, again with Manly as the pilot. Immediately after launch, the plane flipped onto its back; its tail and rear wings broke up while it was still in the air. Manly suddenly found himself under water with the aircraft on top of him, and with his jacket caught in the fittings. He exerted his strength and ripped the canvas garment in two, freeing himself, then swam under water until he was clear of the wreck. When he rose to the surface, his head hit a block of floating ice, and he had to dive anew. He finally reached the surface in clear water. Hauled aboard the houseboat, a doctor cut the cold and drenched clothes from his body, wrapped him in a blanket,

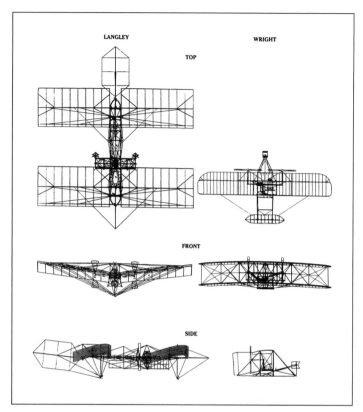

Top, front, and side views comparing Langley's Aerodrome A with the Wright Flyer. Langley's craft was considerably larger but could not be made to fly. (American Heritage)

and gave him a drink of whiskey. He responded with a loud and vigorous stream of curses.

Orville returned to Kitty Hawk on December 11; his new shafts were in place the next day. After that, it was a matter of waiting for a good wind. The Flyer was to take off from a rail built with wooden two-by-fours, which they called the Grand Junction Railroad, and Wilbur tried for a flight on December 14. He rose into the air under power, reached an altitude of some fifteen feet, stalled with the nose high, and pancaked into the sand some sixty feet beyond the rail. He was uninjured and the damage was repairable, but this certainly did not qualify as a successful flight. They would have to try again.

They made the needed refurbishments and waited again for the wind. It was there for them on the seventeenth, blowing at 24 miles per hour as measured by their anemometer, and this time Orville took his turn as pilot. In midmorning, with the wind gusting to 27 miles per hour, he threw a lever that cast off a restraining line and the Flyer began its run down the rail. It lifted forward, rose into the air once again—and when airborne, it proved very hard to control. It was quite sensitive in response to its elevator, darting up and down, in a wind so strong that he made headway over the ground at no more than 7 or 8 miles per hour. He remained in the air for 12 seconds, covering 120 feet, then came down a little too far and landed.

History records this as humanity's first successful piloted flight under power, but although the Flyer possessed all the elements needed for genuine success, this first excursion offered little improvement over Clément Ader's attempt in his *Eole*. The Flyer continued to show its unpleasant sensitivity in pitch during the second and third flights, with Wilbur and then Orville again at the controls. Their distances showed modest improvement, at 175 and 200 feet respectively, but on the latter, Orville stayed aloft only fifteen seconds.

But they were beginning to get the hang of it, and Wilbur climbed aboard to see what he could do on the fourth flight. This one left no room for doubt. He steadied the craft and flew it down the beach, maintaining good control as he continued onward, straight and true. Five, six, seven hundred feet; still he flew on. Then, approaching the one-minute mark, again the pitch sensitivity showed itself and he began to oscillate up and down. The flight quickly ended, but this was the one that counted. Fifty-nine seconds, 852 feet. He had done it; he had truly flown.

The landing had been somewhat hard and had caused minor damage, but the Wrights expected to fix it and fly some more. Confident now, they talked of trying for a really long excursion, perhaps all the way to Kitty Hawk. Suddenly, a powerful gust of wind took hold of the Flyer and sent it tumbling across the sand. Someone screamed; wires snapped, wood splintered, and the engine tore loose. Very soon, the Flyer had been wrecked as thoroughly as Langley's Aerodrome A. However, there was an important difference: this happened after it had shown what it could do.

If that wind had blown up a few minutes earlier, if it had damaged the Flyer prior to that fourth flight, we still would hail the Wright brothers as the inventors of the airplane. Langley ended his effort following his second failure, and no one else, anywhere in the world, was ready to compete with those brothers from Dayton. But we would not say that the first successful flight took place on December 17, 1903. During their first three attempts, the Wrights accomplished only slightly more than Mozhaiski, Ader, and Maxim, all of whom also made brief and poorly controlled excursions that ended prematurely. To gain real

First powered flight of the Wright Flyer: December 17, 1903. (National Air and Space Museum)

success, the Wrights would have had to build a new airplane and fly it under power for some time and distance, and they would not have done this until well into 1904.

As it was, though, they did enough on that December day to enable them to send a telegram to their home in Dayton:[4]

176 C KA CS 33 Paid.   Via Norfolk Va
Kitty Hawk N C Dec 17
Bishop M Wright
                    7 Hawthorne St
Success four flights thursday morning all against twenty one mile wind started from Level with engine power alone average speed through air thirty one miles longest 57 seconds inform Press home ##### Christmas   Orevelle Wright   525P

During 1904 and 1905, the Wrights advanced to new achievements. They abandoned the remoteness of Kitty Hawk and flew instead from a Dayton cow pasture that in time became part of Wright-Patterson Air Force Base. They did not match their fifty-nine-second record for time aloft until their forty-ninth flight, in September 1904, but they indeed succeeded in taming the pitch instability of the Flyer. Five days later,

Orville flew a complete circle, covered 4,080 feet, and stayed in the air for over a minute and a half.

Their third powered airplane, in 1905, did even better, establishing itself as the world's first truly practical aircraft. It remained tricky to fly; its pitch instability was greatly reduced, but had not been eliminated. Even so, they flew for increasingly large fractions of an hour. The best flight came on October 5, as Wilbur circled the field thirty times, stayed in the air for thirty-nine minutes, and covered over twenty-four miles.

On that day, Langley had less than five months to live. He had become a laughingstock following his second aeronautical failure, particularly because it took place near downtown Washington and not in the remote fastness of Quantico. He had spent his War Department money in full and then had tapped the Smithsonian for more; we thus could say that rather than inventing the airplane, he invented the federally funded cost overrun.

Nevertheless, he would not be forgotten. Uncle Sam takes good care of his own; the Navy's first aircraft carrier was named USS *Langley*, while the government's first center for research in aviation was the Langley Memorial Aeronautical Laboratory. It exists to this day as NASA's Langley Research Center. In addition, a unit called the "langley" entered use in astronomy, measuring the flow of energy received from the sun and thus commemorating his career in that field.

What of the Wrights? Though largely self-educated, they worked superbly both as engineers and as researchers, breaking new ground in wind tunnels, in studies of wings, in the design of propellers, as well as in their successful and original method of flight control, with its wing-warping and movable rudder. The aerodynamicist Fred Culick, who has studied their work, notes that as late as 1908, "no one else could execute proper turns. No one else knew how to make propellers correctly. Above all, no one else had pursued a comparable program: doing the necessary research, constructing his own aircraft and doing his own flying, so that he understood the entire problem."

The Wrights were more than mere tinkerers or bicycle mechanics. They were entrepreneurs, in the style of Silicon Valley, with the bike shop as the proverbial garage. Their success drew on years of hard work, but when it came, it was as dramatic as anything their descendants would achieve with computers, seventy years later.

Zeppelins

4

THE PASSENGER CABIN was carpeted and paneled in mahogany veneer, with inlays of mother-of-pearl, and with large sliding windows that provided views in all directions. Up to two dozen people could ride within at their ease, relaxing in lightweight wicker chairs, nibbling on chicken and ham while enjoying pâté de foie gras, caviar, and champagne, as well as wines from Bordeaux and the Moselle. The fare was 200 marks, some $42.50, for a flight of up to two hours. The time was the spring of 1911, with World War I still more than three years in the future.

Those coddled passengers were aboard the airship *Ersatz Deutschland,* which flew for only five weeks. But during the following year it was replaced by the *Schwaben,* which offered similar amenities while flying from its base in western Germany as far eastward as Berlin. In 1913 three new airships were in service, operating out of Frankfurt, Hamburg, and Leipzig. In the years prior to the war, this fleet carried more than 37,000 passengers, with nearly 1,600 flights. Every one of them was successful, with all aboard returning safely.

These airships were zeppelins. With their successors, they stand to this day as emblems of Germany's technical prowess, and as one of the most romantic inventions of the twentieth century. Yet their creator, Count Ferdinand von Zeppelin, was very much a man of the previous century. Born in Konstanz in 1838, he spent much of his career in the service of his native Württemberg, which until 1871 was an independent kingdom. He entered its army at age fifteen, and when war broke out, he hastened to the colors. With Europe being at peace, the conflict that attracted him was the Civil War in the United States, with the colors being the red, white, and blue of the Union.

He did not enlist, but accompanied the Army of the Potomac as a foreign military observer. He met briefly with President Lincoln; he then made his way to the headquarters of the commanding general, Joseph Hooker. He remained there during much of June 1863, at a time when Robert E. Lee was preparing to invade the North. He saw action, fighting a cavalry skirmish with troops of Jeb Stuart, and escaping capture only through the good speed of his horse. Then, only days before the Battle of Gettysburg, Zeppelin left Hooker and began a lengthy excursion through the Midwest.

In St. Paul, Minnesota, he met the aeronaut John Steiner, an immigrant from Germany who had made ascents for the Union army. They made a tethered ascent to an altitude of some seven hundred feet, and Zeppelin saw a ridge of hills that "forms a very good defensive position against an aggressor marching up through the valley." Steiner told him that balloons would be more useful if they could be made navigable. He also declared that an unpowered balloon might be steerable if it was long and slender and mounted a large rudder. The count later declared, "While I was above St. Paul I had my first idea of aerial navigation strongly impressed on me and it was there that the first idea of my Zeppelins came to me." He did not envision the *Ersatz Deutschland,* not in 1863, but within a decade his thoughts began to take appropriate form.

He returned home and became a cavalry officer, fighting against Prussia in the war of 1866 and then on the side of Prussia in the war against France of 1870. He advanced through the ranks, and in 1885 he was posted to Berlin as Württemberg's Ambassador Extraordinary and Minister Plenipotentiary. In 1890 he returned to active duty, commanding a Prussian cavalry brigade. He quickly fell into disfavor with the kaiser, for he resented Prussian domination, writing that this reduced his cherished king of Württemberg to "the role of a mere rubber stamp." He learned that he would not be promoted to command a division, and with this, he left the army and retired to his estates.

He now had the opportunity to pursue his old vision. As early as 1874, his thoughts had been fired anew when he attended a lecture and heard a suggestion that mail might be carried around the world by airship. He wrote in his diary, "The craft would have to compare in dimensions with those of a large ship. The gas compartment shall be divided into cells which may be filled and emptied individually." He thus appreciated that a successful airship would require heroic size, to provide enough lift to carry a large engine with enough power to make way against a headwind. Knowing the density of air in comparison to that of water, he already understood the central problem: to design a vessel the size of an ocean liner but of only a thousandth the weight.

After 1890, he set himself up as a full-time inventor. He spent that decade working on his first airship, the LZ-1, and in the course of those years, he found himself facing competition from France. His challenger was a wealthy Brazilian, Alberto Santos-Dumont, the son of one of that country's richest coffee growers. Whereas Zeppelin had been a fighting cavalry commander, Santos-Dumont was an effeminate dandy. He barely topped five feet and weighed 110 pounds; to compensate, he sometimes wore inch-high heels. His voice was high-pitched; he avoided the company of women.

But he was a man of courage, eagerly embracing both automobiles and balloons. On his first ascent, he rose over Paris and enjoyed a luncheon of roast beef, chicken, ice cream and cake, champagne, and hot coffee. "No dining room is so marvelous in its decoration," he told his friends at the Jockey Club.

Santos-Dumont purchased a gasoline-powered motorcycle with three wheels, thus gaining familiarity with the nascent internal combustion engine. He then set out to combine his two new interests by building a dirigible, powering it with an engine similar to the one that had carried him around the city on his cycle. It delivered three and a half horsepower, little more than the steam engine of Henri Giffard in 1852, but it had only one-eighth the weight. Hence his gasbag was much smaller, less than a hundred feet in length.

On Santos-Dumont's first try, in September 1898, the wind blew him into a tree. Two days later he was back in the air, and this time he showed that he could maneuver at will. For the first time, a powered airship responded to its helm! He put his craft into a dive, making people cry out in expectation of a crash. Then he pulled out and climbed anew. He made a circle; he did a figure eight. He flew over the housetops of Paris, still under complete control, and felt the wind in his face.

Suddenly Santos-Dumont saw that his gasbag had lost hydrogen and was contorting in its shape. He still had ballast; he lost altitude, but he expected to come down safely. He flew over an open field where some boys were flying kites, still descending. His long guide rope hit the ground and he called, "Take the rope! Run into the wind!" The breeze gave him extra lift, and he touched down lightly.

Zeppelin's turn came two years later, in July 1900. His LZ-1 was 420 feet long; it was by far the largest dirigible built to date. But its girders bent easily, and while it weighed thirteen tons, its two motors together had less horsepower than a Volkswagen Beetle. On its first flight, it stayed in the air eighteen minutes. In that brief time a winch used for control jammed, an engine failed, and the hull sagged at both ends. Two subsequent flights, made with a stiffened frame, showed mainly that the ship lacked the power to fly against even a mild breeze.

For Zeppelin, it was back to the drawing board, amid further news from France. In April 1900, at the Aero Club in Paris, the financier Henri Deutsch de la Meurthe announced that he would award a prize of

100,000 francs. The winner would fly from the grounds of the club to the Eiffel Tower and back, a total of seven miles, in half an hour. Santos-Dumont was the popular favorite, but while he found it easy to fly downwind and to circle the Tower, it was another matter altogether to return against the wind, and to beat the clock.

On his first try, in July 1901, he flew the course but arrived at the finish line eleven minutes late. Before he could land, the wind took hold of his craft and his motor failed. He wound up in a chestnut tree on the estate of Baron de Rothschild; rescuers found him nonchalantly enjoying lunch. On the second attempt, three weeks later, his dirigible plunged onto the Trocadero Hotel and his gasbag ripped apart. He leaped to safety on a window ledge, and firemen pulled him to safety amid cheers from a crowd. But on the third try, in October, he flew around the Tower and returned with thirty seconds to spare. Once again, he was the toast of Paris.

Another dirigible came from the engineer Henri Juillot, who worked for the brothers Paul and Pierre Lebaudy, the owners of a large sugar refinery. It came along too late to compete for the Deutsch Prize, but was larger than the airships of Santos-Dumont, with a length of 187 feet. It also was considerably more successful. On its first flight, in November 1902, it flew at 25 miles per hour. In June 1903 it set a distance record of 61 miles. Rebuilt following a forced landing, it stayed aloft for over three hours in July 1905, setting an endurance record. In the course of that single day it was airborne for more than six and a half hours, covering 126 miles. This drew the attention of the French army, which purchased it for military use. The Lebaudys went on to build a number of other airships, for France and for other countries as well.

Successful powered flight thus was a reality while the Wright brothers still were working with gliders, and by 1905, Count Zeppelin was in danger of becoming an also-ran. His LZ-2 of that year had stronger girders and more powerful engines, but its first flight proved to be its last. At an altitude of fifteen hundred feet, fighting a stiff wind, the craft went out of control and pitched like a bucking bronco. Both engines stalled; Zeppelin, riding what was now no more than an enormous free balloon, found that he had no easy way to bring it down. He managed to land it in a pasture after a wild flight of twenty miles, and local farmers helped his crewmen moor it to the ground. But that night a storm blew in and wrecked it beyond recovery. "An airshipman without an airship is like a cavalry officer without a horse," he lamented. "And I am both."

His chief engineer came to the rescue by building a homemade wind tunnel. With it he devised an arrangement of stabilizing fins that would

Workers prepare Count Zeppelin's LZ-2 for flight. (San Diego Aerospace Museum)

prevent the wild pitching. This refinement went into the next craft, LZ-3, and it achieved complete success. It carried eleven people for over two hours on its first flight, in 1906, and flew again the following day. The next year saw endurance flights lasting three, four, even eight hours. The last of these, in September, covered 220 miles. A week later came another milestone as the LZ-3 flew with the crown prince, son of the kaiser, as a passenger. Army officials already had shown their interest and the chief of the General Staff, Helmuth von Moltke, declared that such an airship could be superior to anything in service with the French.

By now Zeppelin's star was rising as rapidly as one of his dirigibles. Government officials offered to buy two of them if he could meet the goal of staying in the air for twenty-four hours while covering seven hundred kilometers along a predetermined course. The craft that was to do this, the LZ-4, made a warm-up flight in July 1908. It carried twelve people and flew from Lake Constance into Switzerland, then continued onward against a headwind to return to its base.

These flights raised tremendous public excitement, even awe. His dirigibles lacked windows that could give a sense of scale; seen across the water, near a floating hangar on the lake, they loomed as gargantuan structures of immense but indeterminate length. Their slow, majestic

The LZ-4 enters its hangar. From the outset, Zeppelin's dirigibles were as large as oceangoing ships. (National Air and Space Museum)

advance was something out of a Jules Verne novel. The impressiveness of such a craft can be gauged by recalling that decades later, an airship in the sky above Manhattan would still cause traffic to stop and heads to turn skyward. Nor was Zeppelin reluctant to show what he had; his flight over Switzerland carried a writer as a passenger and flew over such cities as Zurich and Lucerne. The twenty-four-hour flight was to cross major cities that lay along the Rhine, where crowds would turn out as if for an appearance by the kaiser.

That flight got under way in August, but after several hours it developed engine trouble. The ship flew on following an emergency landing near Mainz, but after passing Mannheim the front engine broke down completely. Its manufacturer's plant was near Stuttgart and early in the second morning of the flight, Zeppelin set the LZ-4 down so that mechanics from that company could make repairs. Then a storm hit and a strong gust of wind pulled the ship loose from its moorings, driving it into a clump of trees. Its hull was full of flammable hydrogen, which quickly ignited and reduced the craft to smoking wreckage.

The future British prime minister David Lloyd George came to the scene, and later recalled the reaction of the local people to the fall of their Icarus:

> Disappointment was a totally inadequate word for the agony of grief and dismay which swept over the massed Germans who witnessed the catastrophe. There was no loss of life to account for it.

Hopes and ambitions far wider than those concerned with a scientific and mechanical success appeared to have shared the wreck of the dirigible. Then the crowd swung into the chanting of *"Deutschland, Deutschland Über Alles"* with a fanatic fervor of patriotism.[1]

Some eighty years before the loss of the U.S. space shuttle *Challenger,* the burning of the LZ-4 aroused similar feelings of shock and of national hopes being violated. Zeppelin had a publicist, Hugo Eckener, who had been receiving news of the flight by telephone and sending bulletins to leading newspapers via telegraph. Now, learning of the disaster near Stuttgart, he sent out a further batch of wires, emphasizing that the loss of the LZ-4 was a major blow to the Fatherland.

The response was electric. From all over the country, people sent letters and gifts, many of which included money. This public outpouring brought Zeppelin a total of $1.3 million, turning the loss into triumph. He went on to set up a substantial airship company, including an engine-building division. Government officials, undismayed by the accident, ordered a replacement for the LZ-4 and purchased the LZ-3 as well.

Zeppelin now felt that he had every prospect of turning out airships for the army, much as if he owned a shipyard that was building cruisers for the navy. His new company proceeded to build another craft, the LZ-6, and he expected again that the government would buy it. This time, though, he met sales resistance. The War Ministry was disappointed with the speed and altitude of its earlier purchases and would procure no more airships until their performance could be improved. The LZ-6 thus represented an unsold dirigible for which no buyer was in prospect and whose cost and carrying charges had dipped deeply into the corporate coffers. The firm needed new income, and needed it soon.

Alfred Colsman, the business manager, proposed a solution: set up a commercial air service and offer flights to paying passengers. Zeppelin was reluctant. He was a count, a feudal aristocrat who disdained the idea of dealing with the public like a common tradesman. But the red ink in the company ledgers proved a strong stimulus. In October 1909 Colsman founded the Deutsche Luftschiffahrts Aktiengesellschaft (DELAG), or German Aerial Transport Company. It was the world's first attempt at an airline.

Zeppelin's enormous prestige made it easy to raise the necessary capital. Colsman quickly won the backing of Albert Ballin, Germany's most powerful shipping magnate. Ballin was the head of the Hamburg-America Line, his country's counterpart of Britain's Cunard. He agreed to advertise DELAG's service and to act as its agent. With this, passengers could buy tickets for a DELAG flight at the local Hamburg-America office.

Colsman met equal enthusiasm when he invited the mayors of large cities not only to build airship landing fields with hangars, but even to contribute to DELAG's supply of cash. Frankfurt, Düsseldorf, and Baden-Baden were the first. Soon they were joined by Hamburg, Leipzig, and Dresden, as well as Potsdam, close to Berlin. All DELAG needed now was an airship. The LZ-6 was undergoing modification in hope that the government still might buy it, but DELAG had plenty of money with which to order the LZ-7. Christened *Deutschland,* it entered service in June 1910.

There was no such thing as an experienced airship skipper; the *Deutschland* commander would have to learn his trade on the job. Colsman didn't realize what this would mean. For one of the earliest flights he invited two dozen journalists to join him as guests, with the craft flying from Düsseldorf, the first city to have a hangar ready. The captain took off even though he had received no weather report. He then headed downwind, though he should have proceeded in the other direction. Then, if there was trouble in flight, he would have been blown back in the direction of Düsseldorf instead of having to fight a headwind to return to the base.

The airship proceeded merrily toward a scenic valley. Then the wind strengthened. An engine failed; the ship now was unable to make headway toward Düsseldorf even with both remaining motors wide open. It drifted into a thunderstorm, which tossed it up to thirty-five hundred feet and then down to a crash landing in woods. Fortunately there was no fire and only one injury, when a crewman jumped to the ground and broke his leg. Colsman emerged from his cabin, and had the following exchange with the helmsman, named Marx:

COLSMAN: When do we proceed?

MARX: You'd better look at a railroad timetable to find that out. The ship is done for.

COLSMAN: (*in dismay*) Why, what do you mean?

MARX: Well, ordinarily the Teutoburg Forest lies within Deutschland, but this time *Deutschland* lies in the Teutoburg Forest.[2]

The ship had been lost after only six days in service, and this set a trend. The good old LZ-6 went into service with DELAG, hopes for a sale to the government having evaporated. It began its operations that August; three weeks later, it caught fire in its hangar. However, it was worth as much dead as alive. It carried insurance, and the check from Lloyds, some $68,000, helped pay for the *Ersatz Deutschland* ("Deutsch-

land Replacement"), the next to join the fleet. It entered service in April 1911, with Hugo Eckener as its commander.

In time he would become the most experienced and knowledgeable of Germany's airship pilots, but in 1911 his qualifications were only slightly less minimal than anyone else's. He had learned about dirigibles by writing about them as a journalist; he also was an amateur yachtsman, which meant he had some experience with wind and weather. For his new command, though, it wasn't enough. Five weeks after the new ship entered service, he was to take it out of the hangar for another flight. A gusty crosswind blew along the field; a load of passengers waited with tickets. Eckener put his trust in the fact that some three hundred men would be pulling the dirigible from the hangar with ropes; he thought they would keep it under control. But the wind took hold of the craft and piled it atop a nearby wall, breaking its back.

Eckener, properly chastened, laid down new procedures. He set up a weather-reporting service. He also ordered that no ship should fly unless the wind and weather were favorable. These changes worked and brought an end to DELAG's airship-of-the-month era. The next craft, *Schwaben,* joined the service in July and lasted nearly a year. Then, on a flight to Düsseldorf, it raced a violent storm and arrived in time to unload its passengers safely. But the gale-force winds caught it in the open and broke its structure, setting it afire.

That was the last of DELAG's disasters. A new ship, *Viktoria Luise,* named for the kaiser's daughter, was already in service. A sister ship, *Hansa,* joined the fleet during that summer of 1912 and replaced the lost *Schwaben.* Then in 1913 another one, *Sachsen,* entered operation. DELAG had found the winning combination and had every prospect of growing into a true airline.

It never reached that status prior to World War I; instead, it operated as an excursion service. It drew on the cachet of flight and of aerial sightseeing, offering the counterpart of the Grand Canyon air tours of a much later age. DELAG did not try to provide flights between cities, except on an experimental basis; instead it featured cruises that took off and landed at a particular field, flying in the vicinity for two hours at a stretch. In no way could it match Germany's passenger railroads, either in speed or reliability. Flight schedules were at the mercy of a day's clouds and wind, whereas the kaiser's Germany was definitely a place where the trains ran on time.

Nevertheless, the years prior to that war saw a host of technical improvements. Through those years and well into the future, they came forth under the direction of Zeppelin's chief engineer, Ludwig Dürr. He had joined the enterprise in 1899, at age twenty-one, a quiet man who quickly made his name by showing good sense and strong engineering talent. What was more, he won the respect of the workmen by showing skilled craftsmanship in the shops. When Zeppelin became the toast of his country, he let people know that Dürr had done the work. When the LZ-6 flew to Berlin in 1906, Dürr commanded the ship and was a guest of the kaiser.

Under Dürr's strong hand, the design of dirigibles took less than a decade to reach the threshold of practicality. His LZ-2 of 1905 was quite marginal; it still was underpowered, and with a top speed of only twenty-five miles per hour, it lost headway against no more than a brisk breeze. But the *Schwaben,* six years later, was another matter. It carried a reserve of power that nearly doubled the speed of the LZ-2, while it had a useful lift of seven tons, compared with three tons for that predecessor. Yet there was little in the *Schwaben* that represented a basic improvement over what was known in 1905. The advances during those years came mostly from practice and experience. They soon were supplemented by significant developments involving materials for airships, which offered greater strength, lighter weight, and better safety.

The first improvement involved the way hydrogen was held within a hull. Airship operators did not simply pump this gas into its cavernous emptiness, for this would have formed dangerously explosive mixtures with air. Instead, as Zeppelin had proposed in his earliest notes of 1874, the hull held a number of cells that could be filled and emptied individually. This meant that each of them could contain the gas in nearly pure form, which would give the most lift. It also meant that when a dirigible rose in altitude, the cells could expand within the rigid framework of girders and respond to the resulting drop in atmospheric pressure.

Zeppelin's early ships used rubberized cotton for these cells, gastight but rather heavy. The list of potential substitutes then was quite short, but he had one in mind: goldbeater's skin. This was the thin, delicate membrane that covered a cow's upper intestine; goldsmiths used it like tissue paper to separate sheets of gold leaf. It was available from slaughterhouses, but each sheet measured no larger than forty by ten inches. Zeppelin nevertheless sponsored experiments that showed how to fabricate gas cells of this lightweight skin, by laminating seven layers of it with a special glue.

The first such cell went into the *Deutschland,* and at first its usefulness appeared to lie merely in being lighter than the rubberized cotton. Then in 1912, further work showed that this cotton fabric could produce blue flames of static electricity when two surfaces rubbed together. This had evidently been the source of ignition for the hydrogen in both the LZ-4 and the *Schwaben,* and goldbeater's skin would henceforth be used regardless of its expense. Later designs used only two layers, gluing them to cotton fabric, and in this fashion it remained the standard material for making cells gastight.

A second new development involved the aluminum of the structural frames. The basic processes for its large-scale production dated only to 1886 and 1887, so for some time very little was known about its alloys. The LZ-1, built in 1899, had used it in the pure form, even though it then had only modest strength. In 1905 the LZ-2 used alloys that contained zinc and copper, but these were uncertain in strength and quality.

The breakthrough came in 1909, at a government laboratory near Berlin. The metallurgist Alfred Wilm was seeking a new material for cartridge cases, and found that an aluminum alloy containing copper, along with small amounts of magnesium and silicon, possessed unusual strength. The patent rights went to the firm of Durener Metallwerke, with the new alloy being named duralumin. It was little heavier than the pure metal, but had twice the strength; its tensile strength could exceed fifty thousand pounds per square inch. This was as strong as some steels; yet this alloy had only one-third their weight. This meant that airships could have lighter structures with no sacrifice in structural robustness.

The first ship to feature both these refinements was the LZ-26, built in 1914. Ludwig Dürr again was its architect, and with it, he showed that his craft truly could command the air. It lifted over thirteen tons, as fuel, ballast, and cargo, at a time when most airplanes could carry little more than a pilot. The LZ-26 also had plenty of power, reaching a top speed of over fifty miles per hour.

DELAG ordered it, but it never saw commercial service. By the time it was complete the war had broken out, and it was drafted for military service. The existing DELAG ships also joined the colors, and saw use as training craft. The speed of dirigibles such as the *Schwaben* had already convinced War Ministry officials to resume purchases; when the war began, in August 1914, the navy had one in service and the army had six. One of them, the LZ-21, raided the city of Liège in Belgium on August 6. As the historian Barbara Tuchman describes it, "The thirteen bombs it dropped, the nine civilians it killed, inaugurated a twentieth century practice."

With DELAG, Zeppelin and Colsman had shifted from military dirigibles to commercial versions. Now the shift in the other direction was far more pronounced. The government took over Zeppelin's company, treating it as a national asset and bringing rapid expansion. New designers came to the forefront: the aerodynamicist Paul Jaray, who produced streamlined shapes, and the stress analyst Karl Arnstein, who put the design of airship structures on a particularly sound basis.

In choosing the dirigible as a national priority, the German government assured that it would reach a high level of development, far exceeding that of the airplanes of the day. After the war, these craft then would be eminently suitable for the first airlines. In the meantime, though, there was a war to win. Only a few months after their divisions went charging into France, officials in Berlin gave their airships a particularly demanding role: strategic bombing.

The raids were highly dramatic, duels fought in the sky with all of London as spectators. The bombers came at night. Searchlights stabbed upward, their beams cutting through the air as their operators tried to catch an airship in their light. Their quarry was nimble and able to dodge away or hide behind clouds. Still, with dozens of beams slanting into the skies from various places in the city, several of them might converge on a target and hold it, often within range of incendiary shells. The British also had night fighters, mounting machine guns with phosphorus bullets. For what could happen next, we have the memoirs of Captain Ernst Lehmann:

> I was in the chart-room bending over the maps to set our homeward course when Gemmingen let out a scream. I looked back in the direction from which we had come and I saw, far behind us, a bright ball of fire. Despite the distance, which I estimated at thirty-eight miles, we knew that the blazing meteor on the further rim of the city could only be one of our airships. As we later learned, Fate had overtaken Commander Schramm's SL-11. The flaming mass hung in the sky for more than a minute; then single parts detached themselves from it and preceded it to earth. Poor fellows, they were lost the moment the ship took fire.[3]

The development of the airship then featured two contests. Within Germany, advocates of the aluminum-frame zeppelin had to contend against an alternative: dirigibles built with frames of plywood. These were the work of a Danzig naval architect, Johann Schutte. As early as 1909 he won the financial backing that allowed him to compete with Zeppelin, and his company, founded with this support, proceeded to turn out a succession of craft that were beautifully streamlined.

They reached higher speeds than the early zeppelins, and for a time offered strong competition. Schutte's SL-2, for instance, was flying months ahead of Zeppelin's LZ-26; it was nearly as large, had more power, and could reach fifty-five miles per hour when the LZ-26 puttered along at fifty-one. When the war came, Schutte received the same strong support from Berlin as Zeppelin, the government deliberately promoting their competition. But plywood in service proved to be less suitable than aluminum as a structural material. By war's end, Schutte joined his rival in specifying duralumin for his frames.

A second contest pitted the raiding dirigibles against British defenses. Safety lay in altitude, which defeated the ground-based antiaircraft fire while making life less easy for the fighter pilots. As fighter performance improved, the airships held their own. Early in the war, dirigibles rarely topped thirty-five hundred feet. By war's end, as Lehmann later put it, "fliers and airshipmen, bundled in furs and artificially protected from asphyxiation, were outclimbing each other at Mt. Everest altitudes."

The year 1917 saw "height-climbers," lightweight designs that were intended to carry their war loads at 16,500 feet. They often flew higher; the L-55 reached 24,000 feet, setting an altitude record for airships that has never been surpassed. This performance made such craft invulnerable, at one stroke overcoming the entire British air defense system. Nevertheless, they pushed the limits of the feasible.

The men were exposed to the open air, and lacked both heat and pressurization. They dressed in woolen long johns, heavy greatcoats, boots, scarves, and gloves. Some of them added sheets of newspaper for extra warmth. Even so, they experienced frostbite and stiffened joints. Compressed oxygen was available, but it often contained fumes of oil or glycerine, which left men feeling nauseous for days. Navigation was also a problem, for they flew above the clouds. At times they were fortunate to drop their bombs on the right country.

"Zeppelin, fly!" sang Germany's schoolchildren. "Fly to England! England will burn in fire!" Actually, it didn't, for the dirigibles did surprisingly little damage. During the war, the army and the navy commissioned over a hundred of these airships. They dropped only 196 tons in all areas of operation. The cumulative effort thus had no more punch, for the entire war, than a single medium-size bombing raid of World War II.

In England the raids killed 557 people, injuring over a thousand. But 500 airshipmen lost their lives while pressing their attacks, nearly matching Britain's fatalities. The damage came to $7.3 million, considerably less than the cost of Germany's airship program. As Winston Churchill might have put it, rarely in the field of human combat had so many paid so much for so little.

Even so, the technical achievements were far-reaching. They culminated in the world's first intercontinental flight, in November 1917. Its purpose was the relief of a force in Tanzania, then known as German East Africa. The headquarters of this force lay thirty-six hundred miles from the southernmost airship base, in Bulgaria, which was allied with Berlin. The airship L-59 was to make this flight, delivering fifteen tons of supplies.

Turkey was also allied with the Central Powers, which meant the L-59 could fly over friendly territory as far as the Mediterranean. A line of thunderstorms stood in its path but the ship plowed on through, its skipper undismayed by the extra weight of rainwater in the fabric of the hull. Africa came into view early in the second morning; the sun soon dried the ship. All day long it droned onward across the monotonous yellow desert. The Farafrah Oasis appeared below, with gardens and pools; it was marked on the chart and served to check the navigation. A camel caravan scattered in fright. They passed the town of Dechel in the afternoon, with mosques and houses of stone. Approaching the Nile, crewmen saw a flock of thousands of red flamingos.

The desert heat in the meantime was having its effect on the airship. It expanded the gas within the hull, some of which blew out through valves. Updrafts boiled from the sands into the sky, tossing the craft about and making some of the men airsick. Late in the afternoon they crossed the Nile at Wadi Halfa. The sun went down; the air cooled, and the ship lost lift. The captain was ready for this; he had ten tons of water ballast aboard, and now released forty-four hundred pounds.

A radio set was on board, and its operators were monitoring transmissions from the naval station at Nauen near Berlin. Just after midnight, with the ship 125 miles west of Khartoum, there was a message in code: ABANDON UNDERTAKING AND RETURN. ENEMY HAS OCCUPIED GREAT PART OF MAKONDE HIGHLAND AND IS ALREADY AT KITAUGARI. That was precisely the area to which they were headed, and the airship's senior officers concurred in a decision to return to Bulgaria.

Very soon there were new problems. Around three in the morning the craft dropped dangerously low, nearly striking a mountain. An additional three tons of ballast and ammunition went overboard, along with a case of wine and cognac that had been intended for the officers of the Africa force. But the following day they received a tailwind and reached the Mediterranean some twenty-four hours after the turnaround. Warships were scanning the skies with searchlights, but the L-59 slipped through unobserved. It passed Constantinople the following evening and a few hours later was over its base.

Ironically, the crew not only could have completed its mission, but then would have been on hand to share in a German victory. The order from Nauen had been based on a false report from a British radio station on Malta. Nevertheless, the L-59 had flown over 4,200 miles in ninety-five hours, and still had enough gasoline for another 3,750 miles. The distance covered was equal to that from Munich to Chicago; the total distance attainable would have allowed the crew to fly nonstop from New York to Tokyo.

At the end of the war, then, Germany's airshipmen and designers would have been in an enviable position except for being on the losing side. They soon learned what this would mean. Lord Northcliffe, owner of London's *Daily Mail*, offered a prize of £10,000 for the first nonstop flight across the Atlantic. After the L-59's achievement this would have been little more than a brisk outing for a zeppelin crew, but such records would not be permitted to Germans, not in 1919. The Inter-Allied Control Commission made sure of that. To add insult to injury, the British airship that would seek the prize, the R-34, had been designed by copying two German dirigibles that had been forced down in Allied territory during 1916 and 1917.

Nevertheless, Zeppelin's corporate directors tried to recover by reviving DELAG and operating it as a true airline. In 1919 they built a commercial airship, *Bodensee*. It represented quite a comedown from the glory days of the L-59 and the height-climbers, for it was smaller than the old L-26 of 1914 and had only about one-third the hull volume of standard designs that the company had been building late in the war. But its layout was clean and streamlined. With four engines delivering nearly a thousand horsepower, it set a speed record at eighty-two miles per hour.

The *Bodensee* was not entering service in the most propitious of times. Britain's wartime blockade had cut off German overseas trade; by 1918 the people had been reduced to wearing paper shirts and wooden clogs. But there proved to be enough business to assure full passenger loads. The ship could accommodate up to twenty-six people flying standard class, along with a single first-class seat in a private compartment for which DELAG charged double fare. The food wasn't up to the wine and roses of prewar days. But there was an electric galley and a buffet, along with bathrooms.

DELAG began by offering daily service between Friedrichshafen and Berlin, announcing 9 A.M. departures and 4 P.M. arrivals. This compared with the sixteen-hour travel time between these cities by rail, and the *Bodensee* often arrived ahead of schedule. It flew on 82 of 103 days in service during 1919, and included such extras as stopovers at Munich, sightseeing flights over Berlin, along with two trial flights to Sweden. The prospects were sufficiently promising for DELAG to lengthen *Bodensee* and to order a sister ship, *Nordstern*.

A number of military zeppelins were to be handed over to the Allies. But in June 1919, in a coordinated act of sabotage, their crews destroyed seven of the airships. The Inter-Allied Commission retaliated by seizing the two commercial airships, turning *Bodensee* over to Italy and giving *Nordstern* to France. These countries lacked experience with such craft, and owning them would help their governments catch up to the Germans. The Zeppelin company came close to going out of business, for a time surviving only by manufacturing aluminum pots and pans. Only in the mid 1920s, as the restrictions of the Treaty of Versailles began to ease, would this firm return to building dirigibles.

Meanwhile, what were the builders of airplanes doing? From the standpoint of long-range flight, they were hardly in the picture.

This became vividly evident in mid 1919, when Lord Northcliffe's transatlantic contest developed into a competition between British airplanes and dirigibles. The planebuilders were first to achieve the nonstop flight, on June 14. The equipment was a Vickers Vimy bomber, carrying a pilot and navigator; flight time was sixteen and a half hours. The route ran from Newfoundland to Ireland, over the narrowest part of the North Atlantic. This was not exactly a connection of vast commercial significance, and it didn't help that the airmen, Captain John Alcock and Lieutenant Arthur Brown, landed nose down in a bog. The flight had been at the limit of their capabilities, and the only reason they could make it at all was that they flew from west to east, a direction that gave them tailwinds.

Three weeks later it was the turn of the R-34, carrying not two people but thirty. It was essentially a copy of the German L-33 of 1916 design that had made a forced landing in England; it was smaller than the L-59, and lacked its extreme range. It took off from its base in Scotland on July 2, with its announced destination being Mineola, Long Island, close to New York City.

The ship was heavily loaded and its commander, Major G. H. Scott, flew much of the trip with its nose angled upward. This gave additional lift but also cost speed, while headwinds produced further delays. Its average crossing speed was only 33 miles per hour but the R-34 made it, landing in Mineola on July 6. The captain had not intended to set a new endurance record but that is what he did, staying in the air for over 108 hours and arriving with only 2 hours' worth of fuel in reserve. But just to make it look easy, he took off for a return flight on July 10. Helped this time by tailwinds, he made it back to England in a trifle over three days.

As the decade ended, then, planebuilders could think of themselves as if they were working with a collection of wheezy steamboats. The dirigibles, by contrast, were like great clipper ships upon the sea. Their builders had the advantage, and were likely to offer the best commercial air services. Planebuilders would have to play catch-up, hoping to take advantage of new technical developments, yet knowing that such improvements might give further advantage to the big airships.

The Red Baron 5

THE FIRST TIME Baron Manfred von Richthofen was shot down, he was flying as an observer over the eastern front in 1915. He was reconnoitering a force of Russian troops who were retreating, and who had set fires that produced a towering pillar of smoke more than a mile high. His pilot flew right into it, and as Richthofen later wrote, "Barely had the tail of the aircraft disappeared into the cloud than I noticed a swaying in the airplane. I could see nothing more, the smoke stung my eyes, the air was significantly warmer and beneath me I saw only an enormous sea of fire. Suddenly the airplane stalled and plunged spiralling downward. I could only grab a strut to brace myself; otherwise I would have been tossed out."[1]

The pilot regained control as they dropped out of the smoke, pulling up at around fifteen hundred feet in altitude. He then flew directly toward the German lines. However, he was in range of the Russian soldiers, who opened fire. The plane was hit; it came down and made a forced landing. Richthofen saw troops running toward them—who turned out to be Prussian. The aircraft was unflyable, but the commander provided Richthofen and his pilot with horses so they could return to their base.

Richthofen was accustomed to horses. Born in 1892, he had entered a military academy at age eleven, emerging in 1912 as a lieutenant in the cavalry. A year later, competing in a cross-country race, his horse stepped into a rabbit hole and threw him to the ground, breaking his collarbone. He remounted, continued onward for over forty additional miles, and finished the race.

In 1914, with the outbreak of the war, Richthofen led a cavalry force in France. They chased a group of French dragoons into a forest—and quickly found themselves in a trap, facing over two hundred riflemen. It was all very fine to talk of death or glory, but the situation called for retreat. Of the initial sixteen men in Richthofen's force, only he and four others got out on their horses. A few others came back on foot, after having had their mounts shot out from under them. He had shown courage and a cool head, but this was not the way to win an Iron Cross.

The war began much as in 1870, with columns of infantry on the march, accompanied by cavalry and artillery. Cavalry, with its dragoons and hussars, was to conduct sudden charges against enemy positions, with hoofs galloping and sabers flashing in the sunlight. In a matter of weeks, however, the fluid movements of battle in France congealed into the immobility of trench warfare. No-man's-land was no place for a warrior bold or a lancer riding his fiery charger. Not with machine guns close at hand.

Early in 1915, Richthofen was named the assistant adjutant of an infantry brigade. He found himself in a sector that by then was relatively inactive, amid rain, mud, and boredom. The only bright spot in his life was a week of leave at his home in Silesia, late in the spring. However, following his return, he found himself with an opportunity to do more than keep track of cheese and eggs. Cavalrymen had often acted as scouts, performing reconnaissance and observing enemy movements. Aerial observers increasingly were taking over that role, and Richthofen requested and received a transfer into aviation training.

He soon was back in action, not in a saddle but in the observer's seat of an airplane. In this role he survived being shot down, and he soon returned the favor. On subsequent missions, his plane carried a machine gun, and there came a day when his pilot succeeded in approaching a Farman biplane. "After I had fired off my entire cartridge case of a hundred rounds," Richthofen wrote, "I could not believe my eyes, as all of a sudden the opponent went down in a peculiar spiral. He fell and fell and in fact went into a big shell crater; we saw it, standing on its nose, with its tail up."

This did not count as an official kill, for it lacked independent confirmation. Nevertheless, though Richthofen was not yet a pilot, he had tasted blood.

It would be his last taste for a while, but he knew he wanted more. One day, traveling by train to a new duty station, he met the fighter pilot Oswald Boelcke. Glowing with youthful admiration, Richthofen approached him and asked, "Tell me, how do you really do it?" Boelcke replied that it was simple: "I fly close to my man, aim carefully, fire, and then, of course, down he falls." They formed a friendship, spending hours together as the journey proceeded, and Boelcke advised him to learn to fly a Fokker fighter. Richthofen arranged for a friend to give him lessons, and made his first solo flight in October. By early 1916 he qualified as a fighter pilot in his own right.

He fought in France; a neighboring squadron was under the command of Wilhelm Boelcke, brother of Oswald, and Richthofen hoped the latter would soon hear more of him. During a flight, Richthofen opened fire on a Nieuport scout and sent it into the ground, though again the kill was unofficial. He again was transferred to the eastern front and flew bombers, writing, "It is nice to fly straight ahead, to have a definite target and firm orders. After a bombing flight one has the feeling you have accomplished something."

Meanwhile, changes were occurring in both aerial equipment and tactics. Monoplanes had flown early in the war, but their structures, braced with king posts and wires, were too weak to enable them to compete against biplanes. The latter were stronger, faster, and more maneuverable, and quickly predominated. One type of French aircraft had its engine right below the fuel tank; when it was withdrawn from service, a German pilot lamented the decision: "They catch fire so easily."

Other problems arose from the need to shoot through a whirling propeller without cutting off the blades. Some aircraft designers bypassed this by building pusher types, with the engine at the rear, but this compromised performance. Britain's Royal Flying Corps had a song describing what could happen in response to enemy gunfire:

Take the cylinder out of my kidneys,
The connecting rod out of my brain, my brain,
From the small of my back take the crankshaft,
And assemble the engine again.[2]

The solution lay in mechanisms that synchronized the gunfire with the propeller's rotation, allowing the bullets to pass through safely.

Aerial tactics also saw change. Early in the war, combat pilots flew singly or in small groups. By 1916, however, emphasis was shifting toward teamwork, with aviators flying in wolf packs and relying on force of numbers. "Everything depends on sticking together when the squadron goes into battle," said Oswald Boelcke. "It does not matter who actually scores the victory as long as the squadron wins."

Boelcke by then was commanding his own fighter group, and was on the lookout for good talent. He had won the Pour le Mérite, Germany's highest military decoration; the name dated to 1740, at a time when French was the fashionable language of the Prussian royal court. This gave him a cachet that made him highly attractive to the young and ambitious. Richthofen later recalled what happened:

Suddenly in the early morning there was a knock at the door and before me stood the great man with the *Pour le Mérite.* I really did not know what he wanted of me. To be sure, I knew him, but it did

not occur to me that he had sought me out to invite me to become
a pupil of his. I could have hugged him when he asked whether I
wanted to go to the Somme with him.

Three days later I sat on a train and traveled across Germany
to my new field of action. Finally my fondest wish was fulfilled and
now the most beautiful time of my life began for me.[3]

The beautiful time began with hangar flying, as Boelcke assembled
his men and told them of his experiences in air combat. Soon his
squadron received new aircraft, and he began leading them in formation
flights. On one of these missions, in September, Richthofen closed on an
experienced British pilot, who took evasive action as his observer fired
at Richthofen with a machine gun. Believing that they had escaped him,
they headed for home.

Richthofen suddenly came up behind them and opened fire. "I was
so close to him that I was afraid I would ram into him," Richthofen
wrote. "Then, suddenly, the opponent's propeller turned no more. Hit!
The engine was shot up and the enemy had to land on our side." The
pilot, mortally wounded, guided his plane to a landing at a German airfield, with a highly exhilarated Richthofen following closely. He landed
as well—and saw that the pilot was dying and the observer was already
dead.

This was his first confirmed victory; his second followed in less
than a week, as he killed that plane's pilot as well. After a subsequent
success he wrote that, "the heart beats a little faster when the opponent, whose face one has just seen, goes roaring down from 4,000
meters." Yet the Germans had their own price to pay. During the first
four weeks of combat operations, Boelcke's squadron lost five of its ten
aircraft. In a letter home, Richthofen wrote that in six weeks "we have
had six killed and one wounded; two are washed up because of their
nerves."

Boelcke himself followed, in late October. This happened during
action between the squadron and several British fighters. Erwin Bohme,
one of the Germans, wrote of what occurred:

Boelcke and I had an Englishman right between us, when another
opponent pursued by friend Richthofen cut in front of us. During
the simultaneous lightning-quick evasive maneuvers, Boelcke and I,
obstructed by our wings, did not see each other for an instant and
that is when it happened.

How can I describe for you my feelings at that instant when
Boelcke suddenly appeared a few meters to my right, dived down,

I pulled up, yet we grazed each other and had to go back to the ground! It was only a gentle touch, but at such a furious speed it also meant a collision.

Bohme escaped without injury, but his undercarriage ripped into Boelcke's wing. Richthofen described what happened next:

> At first Boelcke went down normally. I followed him immediately. Later one of the wings broke away and he went rushing down. His skull was crushed on impact; therefore he died instantly. It affected all of us very deeply—as if a favorite brother had been taken from us.[4]

Boelcke at the time was his country's leading ace, with forty confirmed kills to his credit. Many of the men he had faced had been British; even so, a unit of the Royal Flying Corps flew over German lines and dropped a parachuted wreath with the message: "To the memory of Captain Boelcke, our brave and chivalrous foe."

Richthofen soon afterward was granted a short leave. He flew home, accompanied his mother at the wedding of a niece, then returned to the front. He resumed his aerial attacks with highly encouraging results, as he shot down a single-seater during morning patrol, then did the same to a second enemy airplane that afternoon, bagging two in a single day. Three days later, he did even more.

A British aviator flew down and attacked him, maneuvering so adroitly that Richthofen realized at once that this must be one of their best. He turned sharply out of the way as the other man opened fire, and dodged the stream of bullets. The attacker followed, and very quickly the two men found themselves chasing each other in a succession of tight circles, with neither able to gain an advantage or take aim for a burst of gunfire. They proceeded in this fashion for some time, banking steeply, as the wind carried them over German positions.

Richthofen's plane was faster, but the British craft could turn more tightly. Nevertheless, they both lost altitude, dropping from ten thousand to three thousand feet, and it was clear this would not continue for long. In Richthofen's words, "Mine climbed better and so I succeeded in getting above and behind the Englishman." That man suddenly broke away and ran for home at low altitude, zigzagging to make himself hard to hit. Richthofen followed, closed in—and both his machine guns jammed. Holding his control stick with one hand, he held a small hammer in the other as he banged away to try to clear the blockages. One of them unjammed, and he opened fire, shooting a bullet into the Englishman's brain. His plane dived straight into the ground, just short of No-man's-land.

The dead pilot proved to be Major Lanoe Hawker, who indeed was the best. He had won the Victoria Cross, Britain's highest decoration, and had been among the first to receive it for aerial combat. As a squadron leader, he discovered that the Germans tended to send their planes aloft at about the same time each day, and at the same altitude. By concentrating his forces and cooperating with antiaircraft batteries, he had increased the number of kills. Now he himself lay dead, and with this, Richthofen avenged the loss of Boelcke.

His own score continued to mount; early in January 1917 he had sixteen confirmed victories, the largest for any flyer who was still alive. During that month, he received his own Pour le Mérite. In earlier times, pilots such as Boelcke had been awarded this high distinction after as few as eight aerial successes. But while the standards were rising, Richthofen was up to the mark.

During that same month, he was given command of his own fighter squadron, and set out to build it into another elite force. Boelcke had shown him how, for his group had included not only Richthofen but Werner Voss, whose forty-eight confirmed kills represented the fourth-highest score for Germany's wartime aces. Richthofen, commanding his own team of eagles, now acted as a mentor to such experts as Karl Allmenroder and Kurt Wolff. They shot down thirty and thirty-three planes, respectively. Lothar Richthofen, Manfred's younger brother, followed him into the group and matched Boelcke by shooting down forty of his own. All four of these men joined Manfred in winning their own Pour le Mérite decorations.

Soon after taking charge of his squadron, Richthofen became the Red Baron. His aircraft had flown with standard color schemes of brown and olive drab, but he was willing to tempt fate by making himself instantly recognizable. He painted his airplane a flaming red, from nose to tail. His wingmates sought and received the same privilege, and Lothar noted, "The red color signified a certain insolence. Everyone knew that. It attracted attention. Consequently, one had to really perform." Individual pilots used other colors so they could recognize each other: white for the nose of Allmenroder's plane, green as trim for Wolff, yellow for Lothar. But when seen at any distance, they all appeared uniformly red, the color of a bullfighter's cape.

Early in March, Richthofen again was shot down. He was chasing an inexperienced British pilot who had shown his lack of judgment by breaking from his companions to head for home, and then by firing at long range, where he could not hope for accuracy. Richthofen calmly

Germany's Red Baron with his medal, the Pour le
Mérite. (*National Archives*)

closed in for the kill, opened fire—and suddenly heard a loud bang and smelled the heavy odor of gasoline. As his engine sputtered, he broke off the attack and headed for the ground, where he made a forced landing. Fortunately, his plane did not catch fire. He was behind his own lines, and an officer soon arrived, offering to drive him to headquarters in a staff car. The following discussion ensued:

OFFICER: Have you ever brought down a machine?

RICHTHOFEN: Oh, yes. Now and then, you know.

OFFICER: Indeed! Have you shot down, perhaps—two?

RICHTHOFEN: No. Not two. Twenty-four.

OFFICER: No, no, that's not what I mean. When I spoke of shooting down an airplane, I did not mean shooting *at* an airplane, not at all. I meant shooting *into* it, in such a manner that it falls to the ground, you see.

RICHTHOFEN: Quite so. That's what I mean by it, too.[5]

The man was quite nonplussed, but nevertheless invited his guest to join him at the Officers' Club. When they got there, Richthofen took off his flight jacket, which was badly stained with oil and gunpowder. As he did this, the officer noticed the enameled blue Maltese cross of the Pour le Mérite, which Richthofen wore around his neck. He stammered, "Perhaps I did not catch your name properly?" When the officer learned whom he had rescued, Richthofen received champagne and oysters, on the house.

He had entered that month of March with 21 kills to his credit; two months later, at the end of April, his score stood at 52. In that latter month alone he shot down 21, an average of one for each flying day. This matched that month's tally for the whole of Boelcke's former squadron, which remained a crack outfit. Richthofen's victories gave him a significant share of those of the entire German air force over the western front. During "Bloody April," as the British called it, the Royal Flying Corps lost 151 aircraft while German losses came to only one-fifth that number.

What caused this wild disproportion? In many encounters, the German fighters simply outclassed their opponents. Even Major Hawker lacked speed, which is why Richthofen had been able to pursue him and shoot him out of the sky. The British and French were building new aircraft, including the Sopwith Camel, known as much for its name as for its performance in battle. But for the moment, the British were continuing to fly with planes that dated to 1915. In the fast-changing realm of wartime aviation, many of them were already obsolescent.

Good pilots can often win even when flying less than the best, but the British carried a double handicap because many of their aviators were rank neophytes. Even possession of a Victoria Cross did not protect against this. Major Leefe Robinson had won this award by shooting down the SL-11 dirigible as it raided London, but in France, he swiftly discovered that he was out of his league. The historian Alexander McKee notes that he needed tutelage badly, but "was not even allowed to gain experience first under an expert. The first expert he met was a German. Leefe Robinson lasted precisely one half-hour."

British flying weather was often rainy, offering limited opportunity for extensive training. At the same time, the need for pilots was so great that the War Office recruited its pilots directly at the battlefront, with the men being veterans of ground warfare who hoped for more than the blood and mud of the trenches. Invitations from the recruiters often carried few appeals to King and Country, with one transferring infantryman recalling the words of his sergeant major: "If any of you wants to go to 'eaven quick, now's your chance. They're askin' for volunteers to learn to fly and become officers in the ruddy R.F.C. If any of you feels 'is old age isn't worth waitin' 'round for, step two paces forward out of ranks and I'll take the bloomin' idiot's name. But don't forget, it's a 'ell of a long way to fall—and you falls only once!"[6]

Within this cauldron, Richthofen found himself shooting fish in a barrel. As a squadron commander he could choose his prey, flying high above the action and looking for inexperienced stragglers. Yet even for him, there was no substitute for returning repeatedly to the dangers of aerial battle. He had an extended leave coming up, along with an invitation to meet the kaiser himself, and he wanted to come to this audience with a truly astonishing record of achievement. He succeeded, for on the single day of April 29, he shot down four aircraft. Moreover, he did it as a family affair, for he flew with Lothar as a member of the squadron, while his father, a commander serving near Lille, was on hand as a visitor.

He had whetted his appetite the previous day by downing a BE-2 from the Royal Aircraft Factory, a two-seater that was eight miles per hour slower than his own Albatros D-3. His father arrived by train early the next day and reached the airfield as the morning patrol was returning. Lothar greeted him: "Hello, Papa, I have just shot down an Englishman." Manfred took to the air and destroyed a French-built Spad S-7, killing its pilot. He did the same during an afternoon flight, dropping an FE-2, whose top speed of eighty-one miles per hour made it slow indeed. He noted, "The airplane burned to pieces in the air and the occupants fell out." It was his fiftieth victory, a nice round number that he had hoped to take to the All-Highest.

Still not through for the day, he and Lothar went out on evening patrol, with each of them bagging a BE-2. The squadron flew onward and soon encountered a dozen British fighters, with pitched battle ensuing. Manfred scored against a new Sopwith Triplane, an improved design that could reach 120 miles per hour, outstripping the 96 miles per hour of his own Albatros. The extra speed did not help, for its pilot died in the duel. On the next day, April 30, Lothar extended his streak by shooting down two more, for a total of four during those two days. Manfred wrote, "It is nice when one can fly together with his brother."

His leave began on May 1, and a friend flew him to Supreme Headquarters, near Cologne. The following morning was his birthday, as he turned twenty-five. He started by reporting for a meeting with General Erich Ludendorff, chief of staff of the entire army. Ludendorff was known as a cold, brusque man; he kept Richthofen waiting outside his office, then made no attempt at small talk. He asked about operations at the battlefront; Richthofen answered his questions, then was abruptly dismissed.

At midday, he met the kaiser, who noted his birthday and gave him a gift: a bronze and marble bust of His Majesty, so heavy it took two men to carry. They talked for half an hour, mostly about antiaircraft guns, for the kaiser had a consuming passion for ordnance of every variety. That evening, at a formal dinner, he met Field Marshal Paul von Hindenburg, Ludendorff's associate and the top army commander. Hindenburg proved considerably more congenial, as they talked of their days as cadets. They had attended the same military school, several decades apart, and indeed had lived in the same barracks.

Richthofen continued onward with further travels, hunting game in the Black Forest and returning home for a visit. Meanwhile, at the front, Lothar was in temporary command of his squadron, and during May it scored a significant coup in an encounter with Britain's Albert Ball. Ball was one of the war's top aces, with forty-four kills to his credit. He was a deeply religious man, fond of quoting the poetry of Kipling, and loved to play the violin. He lived in a tent close to the flight line, ostensibly to be close to his plane, while finding the privacy that kept his musical practice from disturbing his comrades.

He treated aerial combat as sport. In one encounter, he attacked two Albatros fighters and sent them fleeing, while he pursued until he was out of ammunition. He flew over their field and dropped a note within an empty machine-gun canister, inviting them to renew the fight the next afternoon. The Germans used the opportunity to set a trap, and when he returned as he had promised, he quickly found himself battling single-handed against five enemy fighters. Defying the odds, he stayed in the game until he again ran out of ammo.

As the Germans closed in for the kill, he put his plane into a stall and spun crazily downward as if hit and out of control. He pulled out and landed, then slumped forward as if wounded, with his engine idling. Three of his foes flew off in triumph, while two others followed him down, expecting to take him prisoner. They landed, approached him—and he suddenly shoved his throttle forward, taking off safely. He returned to his own airfield without a scratch.

On May 7, Ball was with a strong British force that tangled with Lothar's squadron. An Albatros chased Ball into a cloud, from which he did not emerge, receiving mortal wounds in a crash landing. A French farm girl tried to help him, but he died in her arms. He was barely twenty years old.

Six days later, Lothar came close to meeting the same fate, as ground fire struck him in the hip. Bleeding profusely, he fought off nausea and made an emergency landing before he blacked out. When he regained consciousness, he was in a field hospital. He had scored twenty-four aerial victories in little more than six weeks, but he needed over five months before he recovered sufficiently to return to battle.

Manfred came back from his furlough in mid June, a month after Lothar's misfortune, and quickly found himself with expanded responsibilities. Instead of commanding a squadron, he now was to lead a *Jagdgeschwader,* a fighter wing, comprising four squadrons and as many as fifty planes. His own group was part of the new wing, and retained its red war paint. His other new pilots went even further, with one of them recalling "green wings and yellow noses, silver wings with gold noses, red bodies with green wings, light blue bodies and red wings." British flyers called it the Flying Circus, both for its riotous colors and for its practice of moving from place to place along the front, to serve where needed.

On July 6, Manfred again was shot down. He encountered another Englishman, who demonstrated his inexperience by opening fire from a distance of nearly a thousand feet. Richthofen allowed him to blaze away, expecting him to merely waste his ammunition. Suddenly a lucky shot cut a deep gash across his scalp! As he later wrote, "I was hit! For a moment I was completely paralyzed. My hands dropped to the side, my legs dangled inside the fuselage. The worst part was that I was completely blinded. The machine dived down."

He remained conscious, and regained some vision while still in the air. He leveled out and made a bumpy landing, accompanied by two fellow pilots who came down to help him. Soon he was in a hospital, where doctors saw that the wound had cut to the skull and had caused a fracture. Even so, in his words, "the skull had not been penetrated. My thick Richthofen head had once again proved itself."

He was out of action for over a month. He returned to the air in mid August, went out with his comrades on morning patrol, and downed a Nieuport. But though his eye was sharp, his health still was weak; that single sortie left him exhausted, and he went straight to bed. He shot down three more during the next three weeks, raising his total to sixty-one. However, he was not truly his old self. His wound did not heal readily; he experienced throbbing headaches that did not go away, and now and then a bone fragment worked its way to the surface.

The Allies were flying with better equipment, and some of their pilots had survived long enough to develop genuine skill. In the course of only a few months, three of Germany's leading aces met their deaths. Karl Allmenroder was first, late in June. He had been named to command Richthofen's squadron in the new fighter wing, he received his own Pour le Mérite—and thirteen days later, he also died for his country. Richthofen wrote a letter of condolence to Allmenroder's father:

"I myself cannot wish for a more beautiful death than to fall in aerial combat."

September brought two further such losses. Kurt Wolff had been wounded in the left shoulder and hand during an encounter in mid July with a Sopwith Triplane, but had returned to the cockpit. He had succeeded Allmenroder as squadron commander, resuming this post following his recovery. Four days later, he tangled with a group of Sopwith Camels, and came off second best. Werner Voss, who had also risen to squadron command, received his own passage to Valhalla not long after. This dogfight showed again that it often took an ace to shoot one down, for the man who killed Voss, Arthur Rhys-Davids, ran up twenty-three aerial victories before meeting the same fate.

Better German aircraft were on the way; when Richthofen returned to the front following his convalescence, he had the pleasure of telling his men that they soon would receive new Fokker triplanes, which could "climb like monkeys and maneuver like the devil." He took one for his own use, but did not do much flying. He had become a national treasure; Ludendorff declared that he was worth three infantry divisions. Accordingly, he was ordered not to fly in combat unless it was absolutely necessary.

He returned to the air during the last week of November, amid a British offensive, and shot down two more. On the whole, however, from September 1917 until March 1918 he either was on leave or was flying a desk. But with spring approaching, he prepared to fight anew, as part of the strongest German offensive since 1914. For three and a half years, the kaiser's armies had been bogged down in their trenches, which extended across northern France from the Channel to the border with Switzerland. But events in the east now brought the dazzling prospect of total victory in the west.

From the outset, Germany had fought a *Zweifrontenkrieg,* a two-front war, with major forces operating in Russia as well as in France. However, while the western front quickly froze into immobility, the East remained a war of maneuver. In 1914, in their first joint command, Hindenburg and Ludendorff had crushed a Russian invasion in the Battle of Tannenberg, dealing a blow from which Moscow never recovered. That nation had a strong army, in numbers if not in good weapons or professional leadership, and the Allies eagerly awaited the "Russian steamroller." But the steamroller that counted proved to be German.

Protracted war places national governments under immense stress; the kaiser himself would fall amid revolution and flee to safety before the signing of the armistice. Czar Nicholas II was far weaker. When revolution broke out, in March 1917, he ordered a special train to take him

The Red Baron took his name from the red-painted fighters that he flew, such as this Fokker DR-1 triplane. (National Air and Space Museum)

and his ministers to St. Petersburg, in hope of restoring order. Railroad workers sidetracked the train and uncoupled the locomotive. With the Czar of All the Russias sitting in a coach on a sidetrack, the game was played out, and Nicholas abdicated.

A democratic provisional government took power, but proved unable to prosecute the war. Indeed, the country began to fall into anarchy, as a war-weary people clamored for peace at any price. Lenin, leader of the Bolsheviks, was in exile in Switzerland, and found himself in a position to reach for power in Moscow by promising peace to his nation, even if it meant betraying Russia to the Germans. Having made arrangements in Berlin, he rode across Germany in a sealed railroad car, arriving amid exulting crowds at Moscow's Finland Station. On November 7 he struck, overthrowing the provisional government. He went on to accept the Peace of Brest Litovsk, which surrendered one-fourth of his country's territory and population.

Having won the war in the east, Hindenburg and Ludendorff set the stage for final victory in the west by transferring forty-two divisions from Russia to France. Amid these preparations, Richthofen returned to the air. He quickly showed that he still was as capable as ever, racking up eight British planes in the course of five days, including three that he shot down on the single day of March 27. The Allies now were using the Sopwith Camel, but Richthofen found that it went down as readily as any other type. Of his seventeen kills during March and April, eight were Camels.

He added two of them to his scorecard on April 20, raising his total to eighty. These victories came only minutes apart, with both aircraft falling in flames. "*Donnerwetter!*" he said upon landing. "Eighty is a respectable number!" There was every reason to expect more; if he could avoid being sent back to a desk job, he might reach a hundred by summer. Amid such thoughts, he looked ahead to the next day's work.

Across the lines, a British force included two Canadians who really didn't belong there and who were present for action only because the pressing needs of battle gave them no alternative. Captain Roy Brown was a squadron leader with twelve enemy planes to his credit. He also had a bad case of ulcers, which he treated with brandy milkshakes and bicarbonate of soda, to little avail. His commander had urged him to spend a month in an English hospital, but he had refused, as he continued to stay at the front.

His pilots included Lieutenant Wilfred May, an old friend from his days as a student in Edmonton, Alberta. May had been posted to England for flight training, and as he told his fellow pilots, "I received orders to go to Scotland for a gunnery course. I arrived there one night and the following afternoon I was suddenly hustled back to London. My gunnery training was over!" This, too, reflected the desperate need of the British, hungry as they were for any warm bodies who could move the controls within a cockpit. Brown tried to help him by taking him up for familiarization flights over the front, but April 21 was to be his first day in combat.

The fight was spectacular, as fifteen Camels flew into a melee with twenty-five German fighters, including Richthofen's red Fokker triplane. Lieutenant May was under orders to fly above the battle and merely watch the action, but when a German plane flew underneath him without seeing him, he decided that the opportunity was too good to pass up. He gave chase; he opened fire—and his quarry led him into the thick of the fight. May maneuvered violently, firing nearly continually as he sprayed lead in every direction. This was a mistake; his machine guns were built to fire in short bursts, and it was the mark of an experienced warrior to use them in this fashion. Both of his guns jammed, and he was unable to clear them.

Lacking any semblance of combat experience, lacking the means to fight, he broke away and headed for home. Richthofen saw him as an easy opportunity, having accumulated his totals by picking off such stragglers. May soon found himself as a target, with gunfire crackling around him. He responded by zigzagging, sideslipping, banking—anything to avoid standing still and making it easy for his pursuer. "All I could do was try to dodge my attacker," he later wrote. "I noticed it was a red tri-plane, but if I realized it was Richthofen, I would have probably passed out on the spot."

Up above, Brown had been watching his men. He had his own orders, which called for him to come to the assistance of anyone who was in trouble, and when he saw the red Fokker pursuing May, he quickly gave chase. May's maneuverings allowed him to make headway only at modest speed, with Richthofen also throttling back to avoid outpacing him. Brown put his plane into a dive, flying straight for Richthofen and closing the gap that separated them.

May still was in the air, having dropped to low altitude. He was over the Somme River, with the Red Baron still in hot pursuit. "I was a sitting duck," he wrote. "I felt that he had me cold, and I was in such a state of mind at this time that I had to restrain myself from pushing my stick forward into the river, as I knew I had had it." Brown suddenly came up behind Richthofen, who stood in his seat and turned around to look at him. Brown opened fire, raking the Fokker with a long burst. One of his bullets cut through Richthofen's chest, piercing the heart.

The red triplane stayed aloft, losing altitude as it flew over a group of Australian antiaircraft gunners, who delivered their own shots. The airplane made a rough landing that collapsed its undercarriage, then slid to a stop. Australian troops approached it; an officer saw that the pilot was dead, and his men removed the body. The officer looked at his papers and exclaimed, "My God, it's Richthofen!"

The papers included a photo of an attractive young woman, and as his legend grew through the years, inevitably there was speculation that Richthofen had loved a sweetheart. This was never confirmed; family members insisted that he had deliberately refrained from such involvements, having no wish to leave a widow. The woman in the picture might have been a family member. Yet he indeed had found his true love, for he was enraptured with war.

Richthofen had waited impatiently for his Pour le Mérite, unhappy that the stakes had been raised so that it took sixteen kills to win this decoration, whereas previously it had taken only eight. He helped himself to patches of fabric from his downed British aircraft that showed their serial numbers; at his family home, an array of such patches formed a montage on a wall. He made a chandelier from an aircraft engine; he took the machine gun from Lanoe Hawker's plane and kept it as a trophy. He gloated over his triumphs, arranging for a jeweler in Berlin to honor each victory with its own silver cup. Larger cups marked the tenth, the twentieth, and so forth. Richthofen kept accumulating these prizes until his sixtieth, whereupon his supplier wrote that he could make no more, as he had run out of silver.

Richthofen nevertheless won the respect of combatants on both sides. The British particularly were fond of treating murderous battles as if they were cricket matches; their flight officers called him "the jolly old baron" and "the dear old baron." *The Aeroplane,* a British publication, saluted him as well:

> Richthofen is dead.
>
> All airmen will be pleased to hear that he has been put out of action, but there will be none amongst them who will not regret the death of such a courageous nobleman. Several days ago, a banquet was held in honour of one of our aces. In answering the speech made in his honour, he toasted Richthofen, and there was none who refused to join. . . . Anybody would have been proud to have killed Richthofen in action, but every member of the Royal Flying Corps would also have been proud to shake his hand had he fallen into captivity alive. . . .
>
> Manfred von Richthofen is dead. He was a brave man, a clean fighter and an aristocrat. May he rest in peace.[7]

As Australian officers prepared to bury him with full military honors, Captain Brown went to a tent where his body was open to view. "He looked so small to me, so delicate," he later wrote. "Blond, silk-soft hair, like that of a child, fell from the broad high forehead. His face, particularly peaceful, had an expression of gentleness and goodness." Brown turned and walked away: "I did not feel like a victor."

PART 2

Exuberance

Visions of Air Power 6

In August 1914, at the outbreak of the war, Germany's zeppelins loomed as a new and worrisome weapon. Britain had nothing similar in prospect. Within the Admiralty, there was concern that these airships could serve as eyes for the kaiser's fleet, offering views far more sweeping than could be had from a masthead. They also might observe the fall of shells in a naval battle, helping the Germans to correct their aim and multiplying the effectiveness of their guns. With the Royal Navy spread thin, guarding national interests that stretched around the world, it was essential to deny Berlin this potential advantage. Further, London's counter would have to be improvised on the spot.

It would have to involve sending airplanes to sea, and it was fortunate that for several years, both Britain and the United States had been conducting experiments. As early as 1910 an American stunt flyer, Eugene Ely, had flown a wheeled airplane off a platform mounted to a warship. A British pilot, Lieutenant Charles Samson, then repeated this feat during 1912. Meanwhile, other tests in the United States were showing that the seaplane would be the aircraft of choice. Its use of the open ocean would give all the room it could need for takeoffs and landings, while a pilot could abort a takeoff without plunging off the bows. If his engine failed in flight, which was a common occurrence, he could use the sea as an emergency airfield.

Accordingly, barely a week after Britain entered the war, naval officials undertook to build an initial seagoing air force. They commandeered three cross-Channel packets—*Engadine, Riviera,* and *Empress*—and ordered their conversion into seaplane carriers. Each received a hangar for four such craft, along with a pair of derricks. These would hoist the aircraft in and out, enabling them to take off and land in the ocean.

Months passed, and the German fleet stayed in harbor. But the zeppelins remained active, and because they could carry bombs or torpedoes, they still loomed as a threat. Accordingly, around Christmas, a British task force set out to launch an attack on a dirigible base near Cuxhaven. This took form as the first shipborne air strike in history, but its character was quite impromptu.

The morning was calm and sunny as sailors hoisted out nine seaplanes. Two of them failed to take off. The other seven took to the air, crossed the coast, ran into dense fog, and promptly got lost. One of them nevertheless succeeded in finding the base, and dropped bombs on the hydrogen plant. They missed.

The Germans meanwhile were counterattacking by sending out three seaplanes and a naval airship. All of them dropped bombs on the British vessels, and all of them missed. The British shot back with rifles and machine guns, generally missing as well. Then an escorting light cruiser burst a six-inch shell close to the airship, whose skipper decided to retreat. At the end of the day, all the British had to show for their work was to have damaged one inexpensive and easily replaced enemy seaplane.

A similar sense of the absurd marked the Admiralty's use of naval air power at the Battle of Jutland in 1916, the war's only full-scale naval engagement. One seaplane carrier lay at anchor in a remote reach of the main naval base, and missed the order to sail. The faithful *Engadine* nevertheless reported for action, and launched one of its planes. Low clouds prevented its pilot from seeing much, and very quickly he set down on the water, with a broken fuel line. The main contribution of *Engadine* to the battle was to take a damaged cruiser in tow.

By then, airships were raiding London itself. "Traffic is at a standstill," wrote a journalist as he described an attack. "A million quiet cries make a subdued roar. People stand gazing into the sky from the darkened streets. Among the autumn stars floats a long, gaunt Zeppelin. Great booming sounds shake the city. They are Zeppelin bombs—falling—killing—burning. Lesser noises, of shooting, are nearer at hand, the noise of aerial guns sending shrapnel into the sky. Suddenly you realize that the biggest city in the world has become a night battlefield."[1]

Britain responded with land-based fighters. Freed of the weight of a seaplane's pontoons, these repeatedly showed their value by shooting these raiders down in flames. This raised the obvious question of whether a ship might carry such aircraft, even though they had never been built for service at sea.

Already another seaplane carrier was in service, HMS *Vindex,* and was showing how to do it. In addition to its usual seaplane accommodations, *Vindex* carried a platform mounted near the bows, from which wheeled aircraft could take off. They could not return to land on the ship, however; they could serve only as one-shot weapons. But their pilots often could try to land ashore. Even when they couldn't, they could ditch alongside their ship. Air bags then would keep the plane afloat while seamen rescued the pilot.

Admiral Sir David Beatty, who had commanded his country's battle cruisers at Jutland, quickly endorsed this line of thinking. Following that battle, he became commander of the Grand Fleet. He declared that "provision of anti-Zeppelin machines" was most urgent, along with "ships to carry them." His eye fell on a battle cruiser, HMS *Furious*, that then was under construction, and he ordered its conversion for use as an aircraft carrier.

When commissioned, in June 1917, it offered a major step forward. It could reach thirty-two knots and it mounted a flying-off platform with a length of 228 feet. Because fighter planes could take off at speeds that were not much higher, they would have plenty of opportunity to gain the modest additional speed that would permit them to fly. In addition, this ship was substantially larger than *Engadine* and her sisters, carrying ten aircraft in a hangar.

Very soon the question arose: could a plane land on her deck, as well as take off? The aircraft of the day were so slow that a pilot might readily keep abreast of *Furious*, merely by having that ship head into a stiff breeze. Squadron Commander Ernest Dunning volunteered to try to land in this fashion, approaching from the stern and sideslipping past the funnel and bridge. He did it, and then repeated this feat. But when he tried to do it a third time, his plane went over the side and he drowned.

It was back to the shipyard for *Furious*, this time to receive a long stern-mounted platform for landings. But in sea trials, the vessel's funnel and superstructure set up severe turbulence and cross-flows of air, which made landings very difficult. Clearly, then, the Royal Navy would remain stuck with the one-shot use of sea-based aircraft as long as it continued merely to rig platforms to warships of existing type. To permit aircraft to land on carriers, these vessels would have to feature a purpose-built design.

Fortunately, the opportunity to build such a ship lay close at hand. In the wake of Jutland, the Admiralty had purchased the partially completed hull of an ocean liner, intending to convert it for use as a carrier. Its naval architects were quick to learn the lessons of *Furious*, for when that converted liner joined the fleet, as HMS *Argus*, it sported a completely unobstructed flight deck. Neither funnels nor superstructure broke its flatness, which extended 565 feet in length. The funnels were tucked away near the stern; when *Argus* was under way, it looked as if it was laying down a smoke screen.

Then in mid 1918, four years into the war, *Furious* vindicated its builders' hopes by finally conducting a successful air strike, the world's first. Seven Sopwith Camels flew from its deck, then set course for a zeppelin base near Denmark. They found two large dirigibles in a hangar and set them both afire with bombs. "It was one of the finest examples of nerve I ever saw," a German pilot later declared.

Admiral Beatty was delighted. He hoped for even better results from *Argus,* which could carry newly designed torpedo aircraft. Using such planes, he planned to attack the German fleet itself as it lay at anchor, in what would have amounted to a prelude to Pearl Harbor. But when the war ended, in November, *Argus* was still undergoing sea trials. Beatty's proposed carrier strike would be held over for the next meeting of arms.

Even so, the British achievements had been spectacular. At the outset, in 1914, they had nothing more than seaplane carriers converted from cross-Channel steamers. These had to stop in the water in order to hoist out and recover their planes. Those planes, in turn, could not take off if the North Sea was rough, which was often the case. *Furious* offered an advantage, for it could carry more aircraft. These were of the latest type, and could fly off with the ship under way in rough seas. But they could not land aboard ship, and hence were limited to one-shot use.

But by 1919, the Admiralty had overcome all these limitations. *Argus* now could embark a substantial force of torpedo aircraft with ship-killing power. It could recover as well as launch them, while under way, and could operate in a broad range of weather and sea conditions. There had been similar advances in their intended missions. Whereas the naval air force of 1914 had proved unable even to attack highly flammable dirigibles in their sheds, Admiral Beatty in 1918 was planning seriously to use *Argus* to strike at armored ships.

Even so, the British achievements had a strongly ad hoc character, for they had come forth principally in response to the threat from Germany's airships. This experience contrasted strongly with that of both the United States and Japan, which had faced no such threat and hence had done little to develop sea-based air power. With the zeppelins dead and gone, aircraft carriers lacked a clear mission. Battleships still commanded the sea, while submarines had emerged as commerce raiders par excellence. But no comparable body of naval doctrine existed for the carrier, to define its roles and missions in a future war.

This lack of doctrine did not discourage the carrier's advocates from envisioning sweeping roles for these warships; quite the contrary. Their lack of a settled mission encouraged far-reaching speculations. In 1919 Lord John Fisher, who had introduced the modern battleship, stated that "all you want is the present naval side of the Air Force—that's the future navy."

Two years later, it was the turn of Admiral William Sims, who had commanded U.S. naval forces in Europe during the war. Writing to Senator Henry Cabot Lodge, he predicted that carriers "will sweep the enemy fleet clean of its airplanes, and proceed to bomb the battleships, and torpedo them with torpedo planes. It is all a question as to whether the airplane carrier, equipped with 80 planes, is not the capital ship of the future."

These men were free to speculate, for they lacked responsibility for shaping their nations' postwar navies. Fisher was in retirement. Sims, who had made his name as a reformer, found few admirals who shared his views. His outspoken advocacy contrasted sharply with an unpleasant fact: during the war, nothing remotely resembling an aircraft carrier had gone to sea under the American flag.

Still, the Yankees were apt pupils of the British. Sims was one of several senior officers who had noted the Admiralty's strong interest in carriers, while serving overseas during the war. Their reports made it plausible that the United States too would build a carrier, if only to keep pace. Then in March 1919, the battleship USS *Texas* took part in a gunnery exercise that demonstrated vividly the potential advantages of naval aviation.

Battleships always looked impressive when they fired their big guns. Still, that was not the same as hitting the target, particularly when fighting at long range. Observers relied on specialized optical instruments for range finding, and watched through binoculars to correct the fall of shot. Then, in that 1919 exercise, an airplane carried out this function. Its observer was totally untrained. Yet this novice coached the guns on target with an average error of only sixty-four yards. The skipper of *Texas* described this as "many times better than was done by the ship's spotters," who had the benefit of long experience.

To advanced thinkers such as Sims, this exercise carried large implications. A modest number of aircraft, accompanying a battleship fleet in a general engagement, could vastly increase the number of hits and thus multiply these warships' effectiveness out of all proportion. Yet to do this, the Navy would have to achieve air superiority over the battle zone. This would be necessary not only to protect these spotters, but to deny

the enemy the advantage of spotting the fall of shot with its own aircraft. Hence a battle for air superiority was likely to precede the main
engagement. It then followed that aircraft carriers should be very large,
to carry a substantial force of planes. They also would have to be fast
enough to keep up with the battle fleet.

Nevertheless, no one was ready just then to build the eighty-plane
carrier of Sims's hopes. Under the lean appropriations of the postwar
years, the best the Navy could do was to convert an existing vessel into
a carrier. The ship was a collier, whose coal-carrying holds provided
ample space for a hangar deck. Still, it represented no more than a half
step into the future. Its speed of fourteen knots meant that it would not
be able to keep up with the battlewagons and cruisers in a fleet action.
But it would be invaluable for training, honing a force of pilots, flight
crews, and officers who would gain experience in aviation at sea. Then,
if the carrier was truly to come into its own, they would provide a
nucleus of skilled leadership.

This carrier, USS *Langley,* was to commission in 1922. Even so,
battleships still stood at the center of naval policy. They might receive
valuable support from carriers, but they had ruled the sea in the recent
war, and were expected to hold pride of place. With naval appropriations heading steeply downward, few large warships of any type were
likely to enter service. Yet ironically, this postwar climate of cutbacks
soon opened an opportunity to build the first truly large carriers. This
prospect arose as a result of the Washington Naval Conference of 1921
and 1922, which represented an early and successful effort at arms
control.

President Warren Harding convened this conference, hoping to head
off a naval arms race such as had marked the prewar years. The resulting treaty set limits on permitted numbers of battleships and battle
cruisers, with limits on carriers being thrown in for good measure. That
was not because negotiators lived in fear of carrier-based air strikes, not
in the early 1920s. It was because everyone knew that Britain had converted HMS *Furious,* a battle cruiser, to produce a carrier. It seemed only
too likely that nations might build carriers and then convert them in the
opposite direction; hence these ships also fell under the limitations. Significantly, there was no restriction on the number of aircraft they could
carry, which was what really mattered.

Just then, half a dozen battle cruiser hulls lay in U.S. shipyards in
varying stages of completion, as part of a wartime construction program.
All now were candidates for scrapping. It was true that in mid 1921 a
board of senior naval officers had pushed hard for construction of two
fleet carriers. But they had pursued the now-obsolete expectation that

USS Langley, *the Navy's first aircraft carrier, had a completely unobstructed flight deck.* (National Archives)

this wartime program would continue and reach completion. In the wake of the Conference, those proposals were likely to go on the shelf.

At this point the assistant secretary of the Navy, Theodore Roosevelt Jr., saw an opportunity. He persuaded the conferees to permit conversion of two of those hulls into carriers of particularly large size. The vessels that were farthest along were the USS *Lexington,* at Bethlehem Steel's Quincy Yard in Massachusetts, and the *Saratoga* at the New York Shipbuilding Company in Camden, New Jersey. These won selection for this new mission.

America now was building carriers, but hardly in a systematic or well-considered manner. All three of them, the *Langley* in commission as well as *Sara* and *Lex* abuilding, were converted vessels that had originally been designed to serve entirely different purposes. The latter two had come in through the back door, as a way to save two hulls that otherwise would have been scrapped. The carrier now had a role, but few admirals saw it as a war-winner. Instead it would serve as a battleship escort, providing air support to those kings of the sea.

What was more, at the outset there were serious questions concerning basic issues in large-carrier design. *Langley* had an unobstructed flight deck, making it virtually a twin of Britain's HMS *Argus,* but such a layout would not do for *Sara* and *Lex.* Their size and high speed demanded enormous power, and their engines would produce vast quantities of hot boiler gas. A flat deck, bereft of funnels or superstructure, would not allow these gases to flow upward through a conventional smokestack. Instead the gases would pass through long ducts on their way to exhausts at the stern. In turn, their heat would produce unbearable temperatures throughout much of the vessel. This had been the experience aboard HMS *Furious,* which received such internal ducting in the course of a refit. Jerome Hunsaker, a leader in aeronautics at Massachusetts Institute of Technology, reported that "she heated up like an oven. The whole after part of the ship."

There nevertheless was strong concern that a funnel would interfere with carrier landings. The British studied this problem by erecting a dummy "island," which included a bridge, on HMS *Argus.* This island amounted to a standard ship's superstructure, set to one side of the flight deck. When safe landings indeed proved possible, designers installed an island on another new carrier, HMS *Eagle.* This arrangement solved the heating problem, by returning to the short vertical ducts of standard practice. It also provided a larger hangar and offered a much more satisfactory bridge, with a view of the flight deck and a sweeping panorama of the surrounding sea. When *Eagle* joined the Royal Navy, in 1922, it established the definitive shape of future carriers.

In addition, a U.S. Army general, Billy Mitchell, was demonstrating the validity of Admiral Sims's views by the simple method of using bombers to sink a battleship. Within a military service that prized seniority, Mitchell had come up as a streak of brilliance. As a captain in 1912, age thirty-two, he became the youngest officer ever posted to the General Staff. He became the first American to see combat in the war, the first to win the Croix de Guerre. He commanded the Army's air branch in France, becoming a brigadier general through a battlefield promotion.

His enthusiasm for aviation predated the war, and while in France, he formed a friendship with Britain's General Hugh Trenchard, the commander of the Royal Flying Corps. Trenchard also commanded the Royal Air Force, formed in 1918 through a merger of the RFC and the Royal Navy Air Service, with the RAF operating as an independent service, coequal—at least on paper—with the British army and navy. He had bold thoughts that spurred Mitchell's imagination, for he envisioned air power as a mighty offensive force.

The two men had the opportunity to test some of their ideas in the crucible of battle, for some Allied offensives, late in the war, foreshadowed the powerful mechanized attacks of World War II. Machine guns ruled the battlefield during World War I, along with heavy artillery. They easily smashed every attempt at an offensive, while inflicting such horrors as sixty thousand British casualties in a single *day,* at the opening of the Battle of the Somme. But tanks proved immune to machine-gun fire, while aircraft, ranging far into the enemy's rear, helped to clear the way for their advance.

Mitchell returned to Washington after the war and soon became the number two man in the Army Air Service. However, he was not a man to deal with fools lightly; Trenchard had predicted that he would go far, "if he can only break his habit of trying to convert opponents by killing them." Having defeated his country's enemies in Europe, he quickly made new ones at home. As his fellow generals saw their battle-hardened divisions melting away amid postwar cutbacks, he offended them deeply by predicting that future wars might be decided in the air before ground forces even had a chance to fight. He also insulted the Navy by asserting that the nation could purchase a thousand bombers for the price of a single battleship. Admirals disliked him even more when he proposed that aircraft, rather than battleships, should provide the first line of defense for the nation's coasts.

He nevertheless drew considerable public interest, as he wrote extensively and gave interviews to newspapers. He also won support where it counted: in Congress. He believed that bombers could sink a battleship, and he had in mind Germany's *Ostfriesland.* Following the war, the nation had taken possession of several German warships, including that battlewagon. It was a twenty-seven-thousand-ton veteran of Jutland, having entered service in 1911; it continued to count as one of the most powerful vessels afloat. During that naval battle, it had taken eighteen hits from British shellfire, had struck a mine—and nevertheless returned home under its own power. Mitchell expected to do better.

The Navy had no wish to see such an aerial attack, but Senator William Borah, a supporter of Mitchell, proposed to cut off funds for shipbuilding until the question was settled. This brought the Navy around, and Mitchell soon learned that he indeed would be able to attack the *Ostfriesland,* along with other captured German warships. He already had his bombers, twin-engine Martin MB-2s that could carry a ton of high explosive. Indeed, all he needed was the bombs; the Army's biggest weighed eleven hundred pounds and he wanted new ones that came to a full ton. When a pilot dropped the first of them from an altitude of two thousand feet, at Aberdeen Proving Grounds, this man stated that "a pipeline straight to hell opened up below us, like a volcanic eruption. The plane was flying high in the air and the struts on the wings snapped all over the place."

Even so, such bombs were not substantially heavier than the largest naval shells. Mitchell's force had only a limited supply of them, and inevitably, many would miss. Mitchell responded by having them fused to detonate at depths of thirty to forty feet, rather than at the surface. He expected that each underwater explosion would produce a powerful concussion or pressure surge that might rip out the ship's bottom. If his ideas worked, a near miss might be even more effective than a direct hit.

The exercises took place during June and July of 1921. A captured submarine was first, as naval seaplanes attacked with 165-pound bombs. They straddled the target and then broke its hull with direct hits; it sank in sixteen minutes. Still, this hardly even counted as a warm-up. British aviators had attacked wartime subs in similar fashion, with those subs being free to escape by submerging; Mitchell's target had lacked this opportunity.

Three weeks later, he took another turn, this time against a destroyer. His planes came in with bombs weighing up to six hundred pounds, and it was all over in less than twenty minutes. Direct hits erupted aft of the bridge, severely damaging the superstructure as one funnel went over the side and the bridge crumpled backward. Mitchell wrote that when struck with his heaviest bombs, "it broke completely in two in the middle and sank out of sight."

The next target, five days later, was the armored light cruiser *Frankfurt,* displacing fifty-one hundred tons. Several preliminary attacks did little damage. Then Mitchell's Martin bombers flew in with their six-hundred-pounders. One of them scored a near miss close to the bows. The ship seemed to lift from the water, rolled violently, and began to sink. This air strike had started at 4:15 P.M.; at ten minutes to five, *Frankfurt* foundered.

This was impressive, but everyone knew it would count for little if *Ostfriesland* remained afloat. Navy officials expected this battleship to survive the bombing, and planned to sink it with shellfire from the fourteen-inch guns of USS *Pennsylvania.* No one expected it to go down easily, for it had watertight compartments along with a hull built with four layers of steel. Even if three of them were to fail, the ship could still remain afloat.

Preliminary attacks on July 20 used six-hundred-pound bombs. These had easily dispatched *Frankfurt,* but when used against *Ostfriesland,* they did little damage. On the following morning, Mitchell struck again, this time with eleven-hundred-pounders. This time the damage was considerably more extensive, but umpires inspected the vessel and concluded that it still was serviceable and able to return to port. "By Jove, we are not going to sink this ship!" a Navy captain exclaimed.

Air power in 1921: a phosphorus antipersonnel bomb strikes the mast top of a battleship. (National Archives)

The main air strike came shortly after noon, as seven bombers flew in with their two-thousand-pounders. The first of them missed by a hundred feet, splashing *Ostfriesland's* decks with thousands of tons of water and causing it to heel over before it slowly swung back. However, it was too far away to cause injury. The second bomb missed by three hundred feet and did even less. Then the third one struck the side armor, glanced off, and exploded in the water, again raising an immense plume of seawater and lashing the ship with a killing concussion.

This one tore a large hole in the starboard side. Three others followed within the next few minutes, all scoring similar near misses. Two of them fell off the port side, and a news correspondent said that the ship "rolled uneasily, plainly hurt." The bows rose from the water as the stern dipped under. The sixth bomb fell to starboard, lifting the stern. The battleship listed to port, settling by the stern as the bows, rising from the sea, disclosed a jagged hole. It rolled onto its side only twenty minutes after the first bomb fell; two minutes later, it sank below the surface.

Mitchell, triumphant, had not only proved his point; he had shown that an air strike could sink the heaviest battleships in mere minutes. A number of naval officers were on hand as observers, many of whom broke into tears. Even seasoned admirals and captains, veterans of the war, wept openly or hid their faces behind handkerchiefs. A newsman wrote that "the chins of navy officers watching, dropped. Their eyes seemed to be coming out of the ends of their marine glasses." General Charles Menoher, chief of the Air Service and Mitchell's superior, made his own comment: "I guess maybe the Navy will get its airplane carriers now."

Sara and *Lex* indeed entered service, as they ran up their commissioning pennants in 1927. Rated as sisters, they stood among the world's largest warships. Each of them displaced thirty-six thousand tons, more than *Ostfriesland,* and mounted a flight deck over eight hundred feet long. Each of them could carry more than eighty aircraft. In sea trials, they set world speed records for large ships by approaching thirty-five knots. In addition, these carriers had a commander whose driving force would match that of their engines.

He was Rear Admiral Joseph Reeves, who had headed the Tactics Department at the Naval War College. He wanted carriers to attack, not merely to reconnoiter, and he found his chance when he took command of USS *Langley* in 1925. Under his coaching, flight-deck crews learned to handle launches and recoveries swiftly and with a ballet-like precision. Reeves also placed firm emphasis on developing the ability to launch planes at night for an attack at dawn. In addition, he strongly supported development of a new tactic: dive bombing.

Reeves had come up as a battleship expert, and viewed carriers as a means whereby the Navy could build its strength without resorting to a costly program of battleship construction. Still, he held few illusions as to the relative merits of these two types of warship. Talking with officials at Boeing, he warned that their planes' bombs "won't penetrate deck armor." A force of three dozen carrier-based aircraft "can deliver eight tons of bombs, if they can get past enemy fighters. A battleship delivers eight tons of projectiles every time it fires a round from all its turrets, and it can keep on firing. A hundred rounds each from four two-gun turrets is eight hundred tons of steel. One battleship."[2]

He nevertheless was ready to show what his carriers could do, and he found his opportunity early in 1929, amid preparations for a mock attack on the Panama Canal. The operations plan for this fleet exercise called for carriers to escort battleships, whose heavy guns were to provide the main weapons for both attack and defense. Reeves approached his superior, Admiral William Pratt, and won permission to operate *Saratoga* as an independent striking force.

Cutting loose from his battlewagons, Reeves ran south toward the Galápagos Islands with only a single cruiser for an escort. Turning northward, he then proceeded toward Panama, running through the night at flank speed. Two hours before sunrise, he launched a strike of fifty planes. They achieved complete surprise, as dive bombers hurtled downward onto Miraflores Locks. A dozen Army fighters quickly took to the air, but the Navy men engaged them in dogfights, outclimbing and outmaneuvering their adversaries. All of them then returned to the carrier.

Saratoga did not "survive" this war game. In rapid succession it encountered defending battleships, a submarine, and the carrier *Lexington,* any of which could have sunk it. Still, this merely indicated that an attacking carrier would have to launch its assault from greater range. The important point lay in a decision by referees, who ruled that this raid indeed had knocked out the locks. That would have shut down the canal.

Here was a milestone: a carrier could strike unexpectedly at dawn, destroying a target of the highest importance. Admiral Pratt was astonished. "Gentlemen," he stated, "you have witnessed the most brilliantly conceived and most effectively executed naval operation in our history." The following year he became chief of naval operations. This put him in position to nudge the Navy further toward embracing this new form of warfare.

Unfortunately, Herbert Hoover was in the White House. He earned a curious naval distinction, for during his four years in office, not one new warship of any type received authorization. Carrier advocates held only the slender reed of a fourth such vessel, USS *Ranger,* authorized during Coolidge's final weeks in 1929. Amid the penury of the Great Depression, it was built to perform battleship escort only, rather than attack. Its complement of seventy-five aircraft was substantial, but at 14,500 tons it had less than half the displacement of *Sara* and *Lex.* At twenty-nine knots, it was also substantially slower. Yet *Ranger* might well have represented the future, for the Navy was planning to build four more of this class.

Still the idea of the attack carrier did not die, for new war games continued to confirm its significance. In a predawn strike at Pearl Harbor in 1932, *Sara* and *Lex* together launched 152 planes, catching the base by surprise and overwhelming its defenses. When *Ranger* joined the fleet, in 1934, operational exercises soon showed that it was quite unsuited to such a role. This opened the way, finally, for the Navy to accept that future carriers indeed should carry out offensive strikes. This principle guided it in pursuing new construction.

The New Deal by then was at the forefront, and in the impromptu fashion that had shaped carrier aviation to date, it opened a new opportunity to build such vessels. The instrument was the National Industrial

Recovery Act of 1933, which emphatically was not a naval measure. Instead it offered federal funds to relieve unemployment by stimulating industry. But the recipients of its largesse included the nation's ship-builders. In this fashion, without recourse to regular naval appropriations, the Navy succeeded in starting work on USS *Yorktown* and *Enterprise*. Rated at 19,800 tons, offering thirty-two-knot speed, they repaired the deficiencies of *Ranger*. They set the pace for a modest program of carrier construction that marked the prewar years.

The Army was also showing new interest in aviation. Its wartime Air Service became the Army Air Corps in 1926, with an agenda that included both bombers and fighters. Designs remained conservative; the biplanes that attacked King Kong atop the Empire State Building, in the 1933 movie, were among the Army's best fighters. Yet already new concepts were taking wing, and Boeing was in the forefront.

Its first important example, the B-9 bomber, made its initial flight in April 1931. It retained the open cockpits of World War I, both for the flight crew and for the machine gunners, for this was an era when aviators still liked to feel the wind in their faces. But it also introduced a host of improvements: all-aluminum construction, monoplane wing, engine enclosures that reduced drag, retractable landing gear. It proceeded to raise both eyebrows and speed records, as it showed a top speed of 186 miles per hour. Bombers all along had been the slowest of the Air Corps' aircraft, but the B-9 was five miles per hour faster than the best operational fighters of that day.

Nevertheless, it held pride of place for only a year. In 1932 the Martin Company introduced the B-10, which broke with wartime vestiges by introducing enclosed cockpits. With improved streamlining, it reached 212 miles per hour, for an increase of 14 percent over the B-9. The Air Corps clearly was getting a very good return for its investments, and with each year bringing a new round of innovations, its officials had ample reason to promote further design competitions.

The Air Corps' test center for new aircraft was at Wright Field in Dayton, Ohio, close to the cow pasture where Wilbur and Orville had honed their flying skills. In August 1934 it issued a set of specifications for a new multiengine bomber. The term "multiengine" generally meant two engines, as on the B-9 and B-10. At Boeing, however, work was under way on a four-engine airliner, as well as on the XB-15, a very large experimental four-engine bomber. Claire Egtvedt, a senior company official, flew to Wright Field and asked whether a new four-engine design might qualify. The answer he received was yes.

This Army procurement was not a design exercise involving paper airplanes. It was to feature real aircraft, built at the expense of the competing aircraft companies, which were to show their performance in actual test flights. Boeing was not in the best of shape, for in addition to the travails of the Depression, a law in Congress had forced it to divest itself of United Airlines, splitting up a profitable combination that had linked this Seattle planebuilder with a prime customer for its products. Nevertheless, late in September the board of directors voted to put up $275,000 to design and build the prototype of the new bomber. Within the company, it was called Model 299. The world would know it as the B-17.

Engineering drawings were in the shops by December; in July 1935 it was ready for initial trials. Newsmen saw it bristling with five machine-gun turrets, with one of them giving it a name that would stick by describing it as "a veritable flying fortress." It flew nonstop to Wright Field, covering 2,100 miles in nine hours, but when it arrived, almost no one was on hand to greet it. With its unheard-of speed of 233 miles per hour, it had arrived too soon; the Army's specialists didn't expect it until later in the day.

Four-engine aircraft were not new; the first of them had dated to 1913. However, designers had generally used the extra power merely to achieve large size and a heavy bombload. The B-17 doubled the bombload of the B-9 and B-10, but did not push to the limit, for it also used its lifting power to carry more fuel for longer range. The extra horses in its four motors also boosted its speed.

The Army competition matched Boeing's prototype against two twin-engine entries, the Martin B-12 and Douglas B-18. Flight tests evaluated speed, endurance, rate of climb, service ceiling, and landing characteristics. Other studies dealt with structure and design, engines, armament and onboard equipment, maintenance, and utility as a type. Then in October, Model 299 crashed and burned.

It was so large that its ailerons and other control surfaces carried locks, to prevent them from whipping in the wind. On that fatal flight, it took off with the tail surfaces still locked, which left it uncontrollable in the air. Two test pilots received severe burns and died soon afterward. The 299 had starred in all the evaluations, with only one item left on the list: utility as a type, which called for flights by operating commanders. But under the rules of the competition, the 299 now was ineligible. Moreover, Boeing was operating in the red, raising the prospect that the company might crash as well.

The Air Corps made its decision in time for Christmas. Douglas received the production order for its B-18. Nevertheless, Army officials agreed to place an order for fourteen of the new B-17s. With this, the Air Corps took its first hesitant step into the realm of heavy bombers.

During World War II, such bombers carried the war to the enemy's heartland, striking powerfully at German cities and industries while burning Japan into submission. Prior to the war, however, accepted doctrine envisioned no such role for these aircraft. Instead they were to serve for coastal defense, finding and destroying an enemy's capital ships while they still were far at sea. In 1938, two B-17s carried out an impressive demonstration of precision navigation by finding the Italian liner *Rex* while it still was seven hundred miles from New York. Already, however, air power was growing in scope and in frightfulness. The Nazis' Luftwaffe, in the Spanish Civil War, by then had carried out raids on Madrid and other cities, establishing precedents that would expand horribly in subsequent years.

The U.S. commitment to air power came piecemeal, in Navy decisions to build carriers, and in the Army's commitment to the B-17. When war came at Pearl Harbor, the nation had enough carriers, barely, to hold on until its titanic industrial strength could build more. In similar fashion, early experience with the B-17 and with a similar heavy bomber, the Convair B-24, gave the Air Corps men and equipment that supported its own rapid expansion. The United States was ill-prepared for war. Even so, its carriers and four-engine bombers existed in 1941 as forces in being. Greatly enlarged, these forces contributed substantially to the eventual victory.

Lindbergh

7

O<small>UT OF GAS</small> . . . lost somewhere over Illinois, far from a landing field . . . heavy fog below, at night, with no view of the ground. Charles Lindbergh faced this situation on an evening in September 1926, while flying along part of a scheduled route from St. Louis to Chicago. His only hope was to abandon ship, bailing out and trusting his parachute.

It had saved his life once before, during his flight training with the Army Air Service. In the course of a mock attack, he and a fellow pilot both dived to pursue their quarry. Their planes converged and collided; the struts of their wings locked them together, and both aircraft fell out of control. As these fighters plummeted downward, Lindbergh and his wingmate unfastened their harnesses and jumped clear, then used their chutes and descended safely. Now Lindbergh hoped to do it again.

As his engine sputtered and quit, he climbed over the right side of the cockpit and jumped into night and fog. He fell for a few seconds, pulled the rip cord—and then heard his plane's engine returning to life. It had nosed downward; residual gasoline had allowed it to restart. It flew into the distance, and he came down in a cornfield. Local people found the plane, two miles away; it had crashed, but with its tanks empty of gasoline, it had not caught fire. The mailbags were undamaged, and Lindbergh got them to a nearby post office in time for an early morning train to Chicago. His airplane was lost, but he was unhurt, and the mail went through.

He had come up as a farm boy in northern Minnesota. His father had served five terms in Congress; in 1913 young Charles had been present for the inauguration of President Woodrow Wilson. He nevertheless remained a farmer, piecing together a high school education by attending school intermittently, then flunking out of the University of Wisconsin after only three semesters.

By then he had a motorcycle, and had fallen in love with aviation. He went to work in an airplane factory, learned the rudiments of how to fly, and in 1923, at age twenty-one, he persuaded his father to cover the cost of buying his first airplane. The nation just then was awash in war-surplus aircraft and engines, and it didn't matter that he had no pilot's license; the law didn't require him to have one. He bought a Curtiss Jenny trainer for $500, with the dealer throwing in a brand-new engine and an additional gas tank. With this, Lindbergh became a barnstormer.

He slept in a hammock that he slung from the upper wing, and tried to help his father, who was campaigning for a Senate nomination in the primary election. They made a number of flights together in Minnesota, but the old man finished third at the polls. Charles resumed his aerial jaunts, carrying passengers at $5 each. Then he met a man who had flown for the Army, and who suggested that Lindbergh might do so as well. The idea appealed to him, for he knew that military pilots had the most powerful engines and the newest aircraft. The suggestion also touched his patriotism; he had missed the war, but hoped to fly for his country if there was to be another one.

He enlisted, and found that the training program was demanding indeed. It included ground school as well as flight training, and the washout rate was high; of 104 young men who were initially in his class, only 19 won their wings. Lindbergh, the college dropout, ranked first in the group. Army orders and regulations contrasted sharply with his recent life as a vagabond, but these strict rules appealed to him. He had come to view flight as an exercise in precision, both in navigation and in the care of his equipment, and military discipline complemented the discipline needed for success as an aviator.

He won a commission as a second lieutenant, and hoped for active duty within a squadron. But there was no opening for him, so he returned to his former life as a civilian pilot. The prospects looked good in St. Louis, where Lambert Field was becoming an important airport, and he went there in March 1925. He fell in with Vera May Dunlap's Flying Circus, with Vera May demonstrating her daring by skipping town with her hotel bill unpaid. He flew in an aerial wedding, with the bride and groom in one plane and the judge in another. He also made a Deaf Flight, which helped a hard-of-hearing patient by having him ride along as Lindbergh put the plane into a spin. Such flights were popular; people thought that these patients benefited by receiving a good shakeup.

Amid such balderdash, respectability lay just over the horizon. Two local fliers, Frank and William Robertson, were setting up an airmail company and offered him the job of chief pilot. They couldn't carry mail until they had a contract from the U.S. Post Office, but this came through in October. It was one of the first to be awarded; the route ran between St. Louis and Chicago. Then in the fall of 1926, with daily air-mail flights under way, Lindbergh's thoughts leaped across the ocean to Paris.

A New York hotel owner, Raymond Orteig, had put up a prize of $25,000 "to the first aviator of any Allied country crossing the Atlantic in one flight, from Paris to New York or New York to Paris," in a heavier-than-air craft. Orteig had set forth this challenge in 1919; in September 1926 France's top wartime ace, René Fonck, led a four-man crew that made the first attempt. Overloaded with fuel, their three-engine biplane ran off a Long Island runway into a gully and burst into flame. Fonck and a crewmate escaped; the two others died in the crash.

Everyone in aviation soon learned of this, as pilots on two continents talked about it and considered whether anyone might succeed where Fonck had failed. Lindbergh also found his thoughts stirred by news of a Wright-Bellanca, a new aircraft of superior design that represented a considerable improvement over his mailplane. "It could break the world's endurance record," he realized. If it carried the largest possible load of fuel, "I could fly nonstop between New York and Paris."

He won initial support from his boss Bill Robertson, and from Albert Lambert, who had built the local airfield. He determined that $15,000 would suffice to purchase an airplane and cover his expenses, and proceeded to talk to businessmen in St. Louis. The Robertsons had been encouraging them to use airmail to speed up their companies' correspondence, and at the brokerage firm of Knight, Dysart & Gamble, Lindbergh struck pay dirt. One of the partners, Harry Knight, was president of the St. Louis Flying Club. He brought in Harold Bixby, a private pilot who also headed the city's chamber of commerce. Together they agreed to raise the funds for the flight to Paris.

He contacted several aircraft manufacturers, but he had his eye on the Wright-Bellanca. Its manufacturer was willing to sell it—but reserved the right to select its pilot, who wouldn't be Lindbergh. This was unacceptable both to him and to his backers in St. Louis. Fortunately, there was an alternative: the San Diego firm of Ryan Aeronautical, which was willing to modify an existing design to give him what he wanted. The modifications included a forward fuel tank so large that it cut off the view to the front. Lindbergh had to look out through side windows, sometimes using a periscope.

Other aviators also hoped to cross the Atlantic, but during the spring of 1927, the contest turned into a demolition derby. The explorer Richard Byrd had flown across the North Pole, but during a trial flight, prior to his attempt at Paris, his plane crash-landed and injured three of his crewmates. Two other pilots, representing the American Legion, crashed during takeoff and died. Early in May, Charles Nungesser, another leading wartime French ace, flew westward from Paris—and vanished without a trace.

The transatlantic competition thus received extensive coverage as an ongoing news story, and Lindbergh stood out. Fonck, Byrd, and Nungesser all were famous; Lindbergh was an unknown barnstormer turned airmail pilot. Byrd was a Navy commander, while the French fliers had backing from their government. Lindbergh held only what he had been able to scratch up in St. Louis. His competitors flew multiengine aircraft and carried at least a copilot. He planned to fly alone and to trust to a single engine, a Wright Whirlwind of 223 horsepower. He had never crossed a body of water as large as Long Island Sound, but he expected to rely on his own navigation while traversing thousands of miles of open ocean.

He was ready in mid May, waiting only for clear weather. He had a busy day on the nineteenth, visiting the Wright plant and driving into Manhattan to see a current Broadway hit, *Rio Rita*. One of his colleagues suggested that they phone the Weather Bureau for a report. It had been raining; the tops of the city's tall buildings were hidden in mist. But the latest information stated that conditions over the ocean were clearing. With this, Lindbergh turned toward his hotel, hoping for some sleep before his departure. He didn't get it; just as he was drifting off, a member of his party knocked loudly on his door and woke him up. Too keyed up to sleep, he decided to start his day rather than take a chance on having the weather close in again.

His runway was nearly a mile long, but it was unpaved and soggy from the rain, and his plane, *Spirit of St. Louis*, was heavily loaded with gasoline. His propeller blades were set at an angle that gave the best performance in cruising flight, but was not the best for takeoff.

He started his engine and allowed it to run for several minutes to warm up. Then, as people pushed on his struts to keep him from bogging down, he started to roll. He rose into the air momentarily, settled back, and stayed on the ground to build up speed. He swooshed through large puddles of water, rose again, touched down again—briefly, this time—and then was in the air to stay. A tractor stood in his path; he cleared it by ten feet. Telephone lines lay dead ahead, ready to snare him like flypaper. He stayed close to the ground to gain still more speed, then pulled back on his stick and soared above them. It was just before 8:00 A.M., on the morning of May 20.

He navigated by using maps at first, crossing New England and watching for landmarks. He left the coast near Boston, setting his course

Charles Lindbergh with his Spirit of St. Louis. (*San Diego Aerospace Museum*)

by compass as he faced a flight over ocean of more than two hours before he would reach Nova Scotia. Bright daylight flooded his cockpit; the weather was perfect as he held his heading, entering Nova Scotia shortly after noon, crossing the coast only six miles southeast of his planned course. Here was the wild country of Canada's Maritime Provinces, with forests, lakes, marshes, and only a modest number of farms. He saw flocks of ducks and thought of deer, bears, and moose.

Cruising at close to a hundred miles per hour, it took him some four hours to reach open sea. He flew through rain squalls, altering his course to avoid the worst of them. Blue skies returned; he flew past Cape Breton Island and once again was over the ocean, bound now for Newfoundland. An hour later, he saw the dark water turn to dazzling white—an ice field! It stretched ahead into the distance as far as he could see, a surface covered with blocks of ice that lay motionless amid cracks and gaps filled with black seawater. He decided that he would land on the ice if his engine failed, build a fire with wood and engine oil from the plane, then pack his equipment on his back and try to reach safety by crossing the ice field on foot. He had a rubber raft, if he had to cross open water.

He reached Newfoundland in late afternoon. His navigation remained true; with twilight approaching, he found the coastal town of St. John's and dived across it. He already had made a considerable flight, having covered eleven hundred miles in eleven hours; yet only now was he leaving North America. He flew out to sea—and very soon he saw icebergs. They reminded him that he was well north of the shipping lanes; if he came down, he could expect no rescue.

Ahead lay night, trackless ocean, and every prospect of fog and storm. To cope with them, he had a turn-and-bank indicator, a cockpit instrument that would help him to keep from falling off into a spin while flying blind. He also expected to navigate by dead reckoning. He had plotted his course on maps, dividing it into segments that each were a hundred miles in length, with their own compass headings. His clock and airspeed indicator showed distance traveled; yet he could account only approximately for the wind, with its speed and direction often being unknown. Nevertheless, with fragile calculations that matched his fragile wings, he was prepared to stake his life.

Fog blew in; he climbed above it, reaching for altitudes where the stars shone clearly. He entered clouds that were too high to surmount; there was nothing to do except fly blind, in pitch darkness. Then he realized that the air was very cold. He pushed his hand out the window—and felt stinging pinpricks from freezing rain. He used his flashlight to look at his struts—ice! He maneuvered cautiously, found clear air, and saw the coating begin to thin. Then part of the sky grew slightly lighter as the moon began to rise. He had been in total blackness for only about two hours; now moonlight would help him steer around other clouds, if that was possible.

Halfway, and 2:00 A.M. in New York; no reason now to turn back, for Europe was closer. He was well into his second complete night of wakefulness; nearly forty-eight hours had passed since his last good rest, and he knew it might take until well into the next night before he could lay his burden down. His body craved sleep; he had never wanted it so much, or found it so impossible to attain. He had known lack of sleep on other nights, but never like this.

Dawn broke, slowly, but the brightening sky held heavy clouds that turned to solid fog. Glimpses of the ocean showed the whitecaps of enormous breaking waves. "The wind's probably blowing 50 or 60 miles per hour," Lindbergh later wrote. "It's a fierce, unfriendly sea—a sea that would batter the largest ocean liner. I feel naked above it, as though stripped of all protection, conscious of the terrific strength of the waves, of the thinness of cloth on my wings, of the dark turbulence of the storm clouds."

He flew for a considerable distance through fog, flying blind, relying on instruments amid featureless white blankness. Intermittent sunshine appeared, amid patches of blue, and here was the sight of land. To his north lay a coastline with purple haze-covered hills, clumps of trees, rocky cliffs. The pointed tops of spruce trees rose above a forest. Yet how could this be? He still was over the ocean, hundreds of miles from land! He was hallucinating, mistaking fog banks for land as a result of his extreme fatigue.

Twenty-four hours into the flight, and Lindbergh's eyelids willed to close. His *Spirit of St. Louis* was unstable in flight, and he was glad for this; when his attention wandered, the plane also wandered, and snapped him back to attention. Even so, his senses were gone. He slapped his face, repeatedly and hard; he felt nothing. He broke a capsule of ammonia smelling salts and held it right under his nose; he smelled nothing. Yet he still responded to fear of death. This kept him in a semblance of alertness, as he continued making rudder corrections to stay on course.

Flying now in clear weather, he looked down and saw a porpoise. He still was far out at sea. Then he saw a seagull, and another one some distance away. Signs of life, but still no sign of land; he knew that gulls could rest on the ocean. He flew onward—and saw a boat. Several of them, in fact; they were fishing boats! The coast could not be far away! He flew close to one of them, cut his throttle, and shouted, "Which way is Ireland?" There was no response, no one emerging from a cabin to point his arm. He continued on his course, into rain squalls that left the air feeling cool and fresh.

Something lay ahead; could it be land? This time it was no mirage, for he saw barren islands guarding a coast of fjords. He identified landmarks, studied his map—and found himself near Valentia on Ireland's southwest coast, less than three miles off course! Here was good fortune indeed; he had navigated with less equipment than Captain James Cook, a century and a half earlier, for Cook had used a sextant whereas Lindbergh did not. Yet with only his clock, airspeed indicator, and two compasses, he had found his path with accuracy that would do credit to a Boeing 747, fifty years later. Better yet, he had flown with a tailwind, and was two and a half hours ahead of schedule.

Here below him was a village. "There are boats in the harbor, wagons on the stone-faced roads," he wrote. "People are running out into the streets, looking up and waving. This is earth again, the earth where I've lived and now will live once more. Here are human beings. Here's a human welcome. I've never seen such beauty before—fields so green, people so human, a village so attractive, mountains and rocks so mountainous and rocklike."[1]

The craving for sleep left him; he now felt alert and fully awake. He had only six hundred miles to go, six hours to Paris, amid a clear afternoon and the prospect of good visibility at night. He reached the coast of France at sunset, crossing Cherbourg during twilight. A marked airway led to Paris, with flashing beacons, and the city was unmistakable; its lights extended for miles. He picked out the Eiffel Tower—it was an advertising billboard in 1927, with large illuminated letters that spelled out CITROËN—and then headed northeast to his destination, Le Bourget airfield.

He saw a dark patch of ground that might be the airport, but its pattern of lighting was all wrong. Part of it appeared aglow in floodlights, with a long string of lights reaching back toward Paris. Then he realized that he was seeing the headlamps of thousands of cars caught in traffic. He flew in, landed, started to taxi towards a hangar—and saw that the entire field was covered with people running to greet him. Some 150,000 had turned out, and Lindbergh quickly found himself engulfed in a tide of pandemonium.

Someone pulled off his flight helmet and put it on another man's head, turning him into a decoy and allowing Lindbergh to escape. The American ambassador, Myron Herrick, took him in tow, and allowed him to get his first sleep in three days. Very quickly, he found that literally overnight he had become the most famous man in the world.

He received a telegram from President Calvin Coolidge. He met heads of state: French premier Raymond Poincaré, Belgium's King Albert, and the British prime minister, Stanley Baldwin. At Buckingham Palace he was introduced to the royal family: King George V, Queen Mary, Prince Edward, who would later abdicate for the woman he loved, and a baby girl who in time became Queen Elizabeth II.

He returned to the States aboard the cruiser USS *Memphis*. As it entered the Chesapeake, it received an escort of four destroyers, two blimps, and forty airplanes. The number of aircraft doubled as *Memphis* entered the Potomac; the dirigible *Los Angeles* joined them as well. A quarter of a million people cheered Lindbergh, gathering on the Mall in Washington, D.C., as Coolidge presented him to the public.

Three hundred thousand more greeted him when he reached New York, entering Manhattan at the Battery. This was merely a prelude to his ticker-tape parade up Broadway, where 4 million people lined his route. Paper filled the air like a snowstorm; city workers swept up nearly two thousand tons. He tied up a loose end by finally getting to see *Rio Rita,* at a midnight benefit performance. Then it was on to a nationwide tour, where some one-fourth of the nation's population turned out to see him in parades.

His fame overwhelmed him. He couldn't pay bills with checks; they went uncashed, for they held his signature. He couldn't send shirts to a laundry, at least not under his own name; they never came back. The Army had found no place for him in its operational squadrons; now Coolidge announced his promotion to colonel in the reserves, while recruiting posters showed his face and declared, "Lindbergh the Bold—He Was Army Trained." He had flunked out of the University of Wisconsin; it awarded him the honorary degree of doctor of laws. A published list of his honors and awards filled ten pages.

What was behind the hoopla? His achievement was both impressive and undeniable, but Jackie Kennedy and Princess Diana would receive similar adoration in their day, for little more than being the wives of their husbands. Tall, slender, handsome, and modest, he entered a realm of the physically attractive whose fame fed on itself, and for whom public adulation rose toward worship. Yet there was more, for he came at a time when the nation wanted a hero.

Amid the prosperity of the 1920s, the United States was absorbing a considerable amount of disillusion. The war had brought no tangible advantage; rather than making the world safe for democracy, it had more plausibly made it safe for Bolshevism. It also had spawned inflation and a brief but sharp postwar recession. Amid a wartime surge of idealism, the nation had enacted Prohibition. As a result, speakeasies now were nearly as common as gas stations. Organized crime raked in the loot as it quenched America's thirst, then operated protection rackets that forced businessmen to pay up—or else.

Movies had their stars, with glamour manufactured in Hollywood. With their divorces, they deeply affronted people who cherished intact marriage. Married couples had formerly courted on porch swings or through walks in the park, but young swains now had automobiles, which often amounted to bedrooms on wheels. Flappers, with their cigarettes, shortened skirts, and bobbed hair, raised the concern that thirty years later would attach to juvenile delinquents. Other scandals included Teapot Dome, which set records for notoriety that stood until Watergate.

Facing a time of rapid change, the nation yearned for a vanishing past as it elected Republicans at all levels. It was a bad time to be different. Labor leaders, striking for higher wages in an era of high prices, were smeared as communists. An immigration law of 1924 drew on distaste for foreigners and imposed a strict regime of quotas. The Ku Klux

Klan swelled in membership, in the Midwest as well as in the South, and gained power within the Democratic Party.

Amid all this, the nation gave its heart to Lindbergh, the uncomplicated farmer who had virtually been born in a log cabin. He remained quiet and sincere, his head unturned by sudden fame. Wall Street money was at his command, but he continued to work as a pilot as he promoted the growth of aviation. Hollywood wanted him, but although he was highly photogenic, he turned down an offer of $300,000 from the producer Adolph Zukor and another offer of $500,000 from William Randolph Hearst.

"Unhappy the land that has no heroes," Bertolt Brecht wrote in his play *Life of Galileo*. "No," replied Galileo, "unhappy the land that needs heroes." Lindbergh was every mother's son; he embodied the old virtues, and his life held no trace of scandal. More significantly, holding no public record, he was an empty vessel into which the United States poured its hopes. The nation was not about to give itself over to a man on horseback, but its embrace of Lindbergh drew on that impulse.

Meanwhile, young Galahad wanted to get on with his life. He had dined with kings, but he personally was rather shy. He was close to his mother but had made few real friendships; his sobriquet of Lone Eagle covered more than his lack of a copilot. He had never even had a sweetheart. During 1928, however, he began to think of getting married. Plenty of women were ready to throw themselves at him, but he wanted none of that. He had already met his future wife, and she was in love with him.

She was Anne Morrow, the daughter of the ambassador to Mexico. Her father, Dwight Morrow, had been a senior partner in Wall Street's House of Morgan, taking this post following the death in 1913 of old J. P. himself. Morrow had been a classmate of Calvin Coolidge at Amherst; in 1925 Coolidge was president and had him chair a commission whose recommendations laid solid groundwork for the growth of aviation. Morrow met Lindbergh's mother in Washington, and soon began handling the financial affairs of her son. After Coolidge named him to the ambassadorship, Lindbergh made a nonstop flight from Washington to Mexico City, as a goodwill gesture. He then spent the Christmas season with the Morrows, as a houseguest.

Initially it was the older daughter, Elisabeth, who attracted him. In the fall of 1928, newspapers reported that they were about to become engaged. She went to Europe on a lengthy trip, and while she was away, for the first time in Lindbergh's life, he phoned for a date. This time, Anne was the one; she joined him for lunch, then he took her flying. Two further dates followed, as they found themselves feeling quite comfortable together. During their second evening together he asked her to marry him, and she said yes.

The nuptials took place in May 1929, two years after his flight to Paris. A baby boy followed, born in June 1930, with golden curls and a dimple in his chin that matched his dad's. The newlyweds built a home amid the wooded hills of New Jersey, a few miles from Princeton, and settled into their lives.

Early in the evening of March 1, 1932, Anne and a nursemaid rubbed the baby's chest with Vicks VapoRub, dressed him in a sleeper, and put him to bed in his crib. Charles came home and joined Anne for dinner. Somewhat later, the nursemaid went to check on the baby—and found that he was missing. She asked Anne, "Do you have the baby?" Anne, surprised, replied, "No." Charles didn't have him, either. He took his own look within the nursery and then looked his wife in the eyes: "Anne, they have stolen our baby."

The kidnapper had left a ransom note, crudely written and with many misspellings, that demanded $50,000 in small bills. Anne went into a daze, believing already that the child was dead. Charles called the police, who put out an all-points alarm. No arrests followed, and Charles agreed to pay the ransom, in cash, in exchange for information that would allow him to recover his little one. He drew encouragement as the kidnapper sent further notes that stated that the child was safe and was receiving proper care. The extortionist even returned the baby's sleeper, which gave further reassurance.

Lindbergh dealt with his own emotional pain by actively involving himself in the case, as if to rescue his son through his own efforts. At the suggestion of a senior manager within the Internal Revenue Service, he paid the $50,000 in gold-backed currency, with bills that carried a yellow seal. The country would soon be going off the gold standard, with these bills being withdrawn from circulation. Any of them remaining in use would be easy to spot, so that police could check their serial numbers against a list.

Then in May, ten weeks after the boy had vanished, two men drove along a road near the Lindbergh home. One of them walked into the woods to relieve himself—and saw a skull. It was the missing baby; his body had been in the open for quite some time, but still he was recognizable. Police showed his garments to the nursemaid, who identified them immediately. It was murder; he had died from a violent blow to the head.

The case remained open, but there were no suspects and no leads. Two years passed without further progress, until in 1933 President Roosevelt carried through his currency reform. He did it to fight the

Depression, not to help Lindbergh, but his action indeed made the gold-backed bills stand out. One day in September 1934, a teller in a New York bank checked a $10 note against a list of Lindbergh serial numbers, and found a match. Police traced it to a nearby gas station, whose owner stated that he had received it from a customer who had boasted of having a hundred more like it at home. The customer proved to be one Bruno Richard Hauptmann, who was arrested on the following day.

He was an illegal German immigrant who had committed serious crimes back home, and the evidence against him was overwhelming. Much of the ransom money turned up within his home. The kidnapper had used a ladder; wood from that ladder matched a plank in Hauptmann's attic. His handwriting and his misspellings showed interesting similarities to those of the ransom notes. He had worked as a carpenter and owned a set of woodworking tools, complete except for a three-quarter-inch chisel—which had been found outside Lindbergh's house.

No fingerprints or other evidence ever placed him personally at the scene of the crime, which raised questions concerning a possible accomplice. His legal defense was ineffective, and it didn't help that his attorney greatly admired Lindbergh while believing that his own client was guilty. Even so, New Jersey law defined first-degree murder broadly, and would have condemned him even if he had stayed in his home in the Bronx and had never crossed the Hudson. The jury found him guilty; in April 1936 he went to the electric chair.

Nevertheless, the trial of Hauptmann was also a trial for the Lindberghs, as it ripped open their emotional wounds. For nearly a decade, Lindbergh had lived amid a continuing media circus, which had focused in turn on his flight, his marriage, the kidnapping, and the court proceedings. He had not flown to Paris merely to make himself fodder for yellow journalists, and he loathed the press. He had seen reporters write lies when it suited them; he despised the sensationalism of the Hearst newspapers. The intrusions on his family's privacy had reached an all-time low when his baby had been found murdered. Someone broke into the mortuary, photographed the decomposing remains, then peddled prints of the photos for $5 each.

Anne had been pregnant at the time of the kidnapping; they now had a new baby boy. But during 1935, as legal appeals kept Hauptmann on the front pages of tabloids, the Lindberghs concluded that they would find neither peace nor privacy. The Morrows owned a guarded estate near New York that served as something of a haven, but the little boy already was being marked for the fate of his late brother. Photographers stalked him, on one occasion forcing to the curb the car of a teacher who was driving the boy home from school. Letters arrived, demanding money, threatening kidnap or murder.

At the end of that year, the Lindberghs responded by leaving the United States. They had the means to live wherever they wished; at first they rented a large house in the countryside near London, later purchasing another home on a tiny island close to the coast of France. They found surcease from the endless tides of sensation, and did not return to the States for over three years. Their social life touched the pinnacles, as they received frequent invitations from Lady Astor and met the king repeatedly at St. James's Palace. They spent evenings in long walks through the fields, and their marriage flourished.

Meanwhile, in Berlin, a U.S. military attaché was aware that the Germans were building a powerful air force, and decided that he needed a specialist in aviation to help him learn more about it. He decided that Lindbergh was the man he wanted, and broached the idea of a formal visit. Within a day, permission came from Hermann Goering, Hitler's top associate, who knew that it would be much to Hitler's advantage to welcome the Lindberghs as honored guests. They flew to Berlin in July 1936 and stayed for over a week.

In 1936 it still was possible to think well of Hitler. He had restored pride to his defeated people, and had brought work to the unemployed by building the autobahns and other public works. He was pursuing a major program of rearmament, but he argued that a powerful Germany was in the interest of Europe as a whole, for it would guard against the threat of Soviet Russia. His anti-Semitic laws already had stripped the Jews of many rights of citizenship, but the United States was hardly in a position to complain; laws of similar severity restricted black people in the South. Walter Lippmann, dean of U.S. journalists, had described a Hitler speech as "the authentic voice of a genuinely civilized people." The historian Arnold Toynbee expressed similar views, as did David Lloyd George, Britain's wartime prime minister.

Lindbergh's hosts showed him airfields and factories, warplanes in production, new and powerful engines. He and Anne also were present for the Olympic Games in Berlin, which the Nazis used as a showcase for a resurgent Germany. Lindbergh went on to visit Berlin repeatedly during the next several years, contributing to diplomatic reports that warned Washington of Hitler's growing strength. He remained the toast of officialdom; in October 1938, Goering personally presented him with the Verdienstkreuz, the Service Cross of the German Eagle.

Three weeks later came *Kristallnacht*, the Night of Broken Glass, as Nazi hoodlums conducted a nationwide pogrom against the Jews.

Roosevelt made a strong diplomatic response, recalling his ambassador from Berlin. Lindbergh would have been well advised if he had publicly denounced the Nazi terror and had thrown his decoration in Goering's face. He did no such thing, neither then nor subsequently. The Verdienstkreuz did not loom large in his thoughts; it was merely one more award, and he had donated them all to the Missouri Historical Society in St. Louis. However, this medal soon drew the attention of critics.

Lindbergh visited other countries as well as Germany, and he was not impressed. He found that both France and the Soviet Union were weak. The British seemed to be living in the past, holding on to King and Empire while Germany was charging ahead. War appeared imminent; he had seen Prime Minister Neville Chamberlain retreat in the face of its threat, conceding Czechoslovakia to Hitler. It was obvious that the Nazis wanted more, and would fight to get it.

Lindbergh returned to the United States in April 1939, hoping to help the nation build its defenses. His Washington contacts included the National Advisory Committee for Aeronautics, which sponsored advanced research; he also was on close terms with General Henry Arnold, who commanded the Army Air Corps. His personal observations of the state of aviation, in Germany and in other countries as well, made his counsel worth hearing. He even met Roosevelt, as he emphasized the importance of developing strength in the air.

The war began on September 1, as the Germans invaded Poland. Lindbergh quickly threw himself into a new cause as he insisted that the United States should stay out of it. He believed wholeheartedly that the great threat to Europe lay in Moscow, not Berlin, and that Germany held an essential role as a bulwark against Bolshevism. As the war spread, as the Nazis subjugated France and the Low Countries, he anticipated complete Nazi victory in Europe—and viewed the prospect with equanimity. He knew that a Nazi empire would offer protection par excellence against Stalin, whom he viewed as potentially the destroyer of Western civilization. It did not enter his thinking that the Nazis held that role as well, not potentially but in actuality.

His views can bear comparison to the policy of Henry Kissinger, the architect of détente during the 1970s. Kissinger accepted the permanence of the Soviet Union and of the communist regimes in Eastern Europe. He expected to deal with Moscow through diplomatic negotiations, while maintaining a strong military. Lindbergh expected that the Nazis would consolidate control of Europe—and that the United States could keep them at bay with its own armed might. This would create a standoff, wherein Washington and Berlin could attempt to deal with each other, again through diplomacy.

The threat from Moscow remained uppermost in Lindbergh's thoughts. He believed that an invasion of Nazi-held Europe would be futile, for the Germans were strong enough to repel it. Yet any war fought in Europe, aiming at Nazi defeat, would bring that continent to ruin, opening the door to reconquest by Stalin. He opposed giving assistance to the British, as they stood alone following the fall of France, for he argued that such assistance could draw the United States into the war.

Lindbergh was a thoughtful man who had traveled much, but his views laid him open to the charge of being a Nazi dupe, or worse. His view of Germany—that it was a bulwark against Moscow—represented his considered conviction. However, it was also a standard element of Nazi propaganda. He declined to condemn the crimes of the Nazis as they waged aggressive war, bombed civilians in cities, and slaughtered Poles and Jews. When a congressman asked him whether it would be better for Germany or Great Britain to win, he replied, "Neither."

Anne had won strong success as an author, writing the best-seller *North to the Orient* and following with *Listen! The Wind*. In 1940 she wrote *The Wave of the Future*. This wave, she asserted, involved new social and economic forces that Hitler and other totalitarians were using effectively, and that the democracies were not. These regimes' persecutions and mass murders, though reprehensible, were merely "scum on the wave." She came appallingly close to describing Nazism itself as the wave, and Roosevelt personally rebuked her, without mentioning her name, when he gave his inaugural address in January 1941.

In April, at a news conference with reporters, Roosevelt engaged in lighthearted banter as he described Lindbergh as an appeaser. This was no more than an ordinary political exchange, but Lindbergh took strong offense and quickly resigned his commission as a colonel in the Air Corps. This was another mistake; it showed he had a thin skin, which offers little protection when one is caught up in controversy. It did not escape his critics' attention that whereas he had held on to his Verdienst-kreuz in the face of *Kristallnacht* and much else, he had given up his officer's rank merely because he was miffed.

Following his flight to Paris, in 1927, he had toured the country and received its plaudits. Now he made another tour, speaking in thirteen public appearances. He addressed overflow crowds in New York's Madison Square Garden and in the Hollywood Bowl. Roosevelt, keenly attuned to what the nation would accept, pushed repeatedly for new laws that gave increasing help to Britain in its time of need. Lindbergh stood among his most effective opponents.

Early in September 1941, off Iceland, a German submarine attacked the destroyer USS *Greer.* The sub's captain had done this in error, believing the *Greer* was British, and the destroyer escaped without damage. Roosevelt responded by ordering the Navy to "shoot on sight" at any German or Italian ships in a new American Defense Zone, which covered an astonishingly large portion of the North Atlantic. With war now closer than ever, Lindbergh launched an attack on "the groups that were most powerful and effective in pushing the United States toward involvement": the Roosevelt administration, the British—and the Jews.

> Instead of agitating for war, the Jewish groups in this country should be opposing it in every possible way, for they will be among the first to feel its consequences. . . . Their greatest danger to this country lies in their large ownership and influence in our motion pictures, our press, our radio, and our government. . . . I am saying that the leaders of both the British and Jewish races, . . . for reasons which are not American, wish to involve us in the war. . . . We cannot allow the natural passions and prejudices of other peoples to lead our country to destruction.[2]

In warning Jews of "consequences," in describing their views as "not American," in declaring that they were "other peoples" who threatened to "lead our country to destruction," he was speaking words that might have come from his old companion, Hermann Goering.

That was it. His own views, so often marked by apparent Nazi sympathies, had long since cost him respect and support among the nation's opinion makers. He retained his following among the public, which remained bitterly torn over the issue of entry into the war. He had faced attack from prowar Democrats, but now even Republicans abandoned him. Wendell Willkie, their recent presidential nominee, described his speech as "the most un-American talk made in my time by any person of national reputation." Thomas E. Dewey, who became the governor of New York and the Republican nominee in 1944 and 1948, called it "an inexcusable abuse of the right of freedom of speech."

Three months later the question of war was moot; the Japanese had struck Pearl Harbor, and the United States was in to stay. Lindbergh was not yet forty years old; more than three decades of his life still lay ahead. But he had blundered badly in his public advocacy, not by opposing intervention but by acting like a Nazi fellow traveler. He fought in the war and continued to work in aviation, but he never again held the public limelight.

In time the controversy faded. He continued to stand as the Lone Eagle, the man of solitude who had flown to Paris. He had donated his *Spirit of St. Louis* to the Smithsonian, where it was on display; he was well acquainted with its curator of aviation, Paul Garber. There came a day when he asked Garber for a favor, and had it granted.

They waited until late in the day, while the halls of the Smithsonian closed and the crowds left the building. Then Lindbergh took a long ladder and placed it against the side of his *Spirit*. He climbed up, opened its cockpit door, and seated himself once again behind its instrument panel. He sat there by himself, alone once again, and soon was lost in thought.

8   Ships in the Sky

THE ACCOMMODATIONS offered far more than the cramped seats and reheated chicken of contemporary airliners. There was a lounge sixteen feet square, with four dining tables. It had carpets and drapes in burgundy, while large, outward-slanting windows gave superb views. A corridor extended to the rear, with ten staterooms. Each had a sofa that could fold down into a bunk; a second bunk could be slung over it, and this was the one that gave the best views through the adjacent window. A clothes closet completed each cabin's arrangement, while at the end of the corridor lay toilets and a bath. In this way up to twenty passengers could cross the Atlantic at their ease, aboard the dirigible *Graf Zeppelin*.

The *Graf* was a declaration that after a decade in the shadows, Germany's airship industry was back on its feet and was ready to take the lead in the new realm of passenger service. That decade had seen the Zeppelin works face outright destruction, for the Inter-Allied Control Commission had condemned its facilities to be dismantled. In 1921 the firm received a stay of execution, but only for the purpose of constructing the *Los Angeles*, which was intended for the U.S. Navy. That dirigible was part of Germany's war reparations and its builders took their time with it, knowing that upon its completion their facilities indeed would be destroyed. But in 1925, a year after the first flight of this airship, the Treaty of Locarno restored most German sovereignty and ended the threat. After that, Germany and the United States vied for the lead in the further development of large dirigibles.

In the United States, the Navy sponsored the work. With long coastlines to defend, to say nothing of important overseas possessions in Hawaii and Panama, its admirals faced the continuing problem of finding an attacking enemy fleet while it still was far at sea. Cruisers held that role and would continue to do so, but airships offered higher speed and the ability to see farther into the distance. Initial plans for a naval program took shape during the war, surviving severe postwar cutbacks.

The British already were active; their R-34 crossed the Atlantic non-stop in 1919, flying in both directions. They faced their own postwar retrenchment, and were happy to sell another airship, the R-38, to the Yankees. Its design drew on the German height-climbers, and was to reach twenty-two thousand feet. Unfortunately, these height-climbers were as fragile as eggshells. Some were so delicate that their structural frame could break merely by running a starboard engine full ahead and a port engine full astern. Moreover, the chief engineer of the R-38 lacked an adequate understanding of structural design. He did not know the specific forces that his craft would face in flight, and he tried to overcome his ignorance by designing this airship with safety factors that he hoped would suffice.

They didn't. During trials in August 1921, while over the city of Hull, England, the skipper gave a series of commands that put his ship through increasingly sharp turns. These imposed considerable stress on the aluminum framework. Suddenly the stress became excessive; the R-38 broke in two, with both portions catching on fire. Some of the gas cells had been contaminated with air leaking inward, forming danger-ously explosive mixtures. They blew up, shattering windows over a wide area. Forty-nine men were aboard; only five survived. It was the worst disaster to date in aviation history.

Even so, the U.S. Navy was not about to turn back merely because of this loss. It went ahead with a U.S.-built dirigible, *Shenandoah*, which made its first flight in 1923. Its design displayed very little originality, for it amounted to a strengthened version of a captured height-climber, the L-49. Still, in the wake of the R-38, its reliance on a German design seemed to promise safety. There was further hope of safety because its lifting gas was helium, not hydrogen. Being nonflammable, helium prom-ised to put an end to the danger of fire.

The availability of helium represented a fortunate mix of science and wartime urgency. It had been discovered in the sun before being found on earth. The British astronomer Norman Lockyer had seen its spectral lines in sunlight and suggested in 1868 that they were due to the new element, which he named for the Greek sun god, Helios. In 1895 the Scottish chemist William Ramsay isolated it in the laboratory; ten years later a Kansas chemist, H. P. Cady, found that it existed in nat-ural gas from certain wells. In time it became apparent that helium exists in quantity only within the United States, with most of the supply being concentrated within 250 miles of Amarillo, Texas.

During the war, Ramsay worked for the British Admiralty. In 1917 its officials proposed to the U.S. Bureau of Mines that the Yankees should make this gas available for use in British airships. After the United States entered the war, the Navy rushed two helium-separation plants to completion. The gas was chemically inert but easy to separate; these plants liquefied the major constituents of natural gas, methane and nitrogen, while the helium remained gaseous and could be pumped away. Some of it, compressed in steel cylinders, was ready for shipment from the New Orleans docks when the war ended. None of it got to England in time for use during the war, but these two plants, along with a larger one that reached completion in 1921, were ready to serve *Shenandoah* and its successors.

Early in its career, this dirigible showed that it indeed was a true ship of the Navy. It had been moored to a tall steel mast at its base in Lakehurst, New Jersey, where it was to show its ability to ride out a winter gale. As gusts topped seventy miles per hour, part of the crew remained onboard. Suddenly it pulled free, tearing a great hole in the bow and collapsing two helium-filled cells. Crewmen hastily dumped water ballast and gasoline tanks, and the airship managed to clear a nearby forest. Then the captain turned the nose away from the wind and allowed the craft to run with the storm.

He got five of the engines started, then proceeded to ride out the winds. The ship drifted as far as New York City, while the storm damaged the rudder. But after several hours the gale subsided and *Shenandoah* was able to limp home. It had held its own even though damaged, in a tempest that killed five people. During its hours of crisis in the air, not one airplane left the ground.

This proved to be little more than an interruption in a program of long-distance flights. It flew to St. Louis and returned, carrying forty-two people. It went to San Diego and onward to Seattle, then retraced this route on the homeward trip. It thus made a tour of the country that covered ninety-three hundred miles and twice crossed the nation with only a single intermediate stop.

Its hangar in Lakehurst was the largest single room in the world. Standing twenty stories high and with dimensions of 943 by 350 feet, it had room for six football fields—and for two full-size dirigibles. On returning to this base, *Shenandoah* had company, as it shared this hangar with the German-built *Los Angeles*. The latter had made its own long-distance flight, having flown the Atlantic nonstop from Friedrichshafen, with Hugo Eckener in command.

Unfortunately, *Shenandoah* lasted only slightly longer than the R-38. It met its end in September 1925, while on a tour of county fairs in

Ohio and other parts of the Midwest. Naval appropriations were lean during those years, and this tour was to demonstrate this airship to the public, thereby showing what people were buying with their taxes. The skipper, Zachary Lansdowne, urged his superiors to postpone the flight because September in Ohio could be dangerously stormy. He was overruled.

That put him in the gondola when violent weather developed around his ship, tearing it in two. That control car wrenched free, hurling Lansdowne and several others to their deaths. "No European designer could possibly imagine the violence of weather conditions in the American Midwest," Karl Arnstein, Zeppelin's chief structural analyst, later declared. The use of helium in *Shenandoah* had prevented a fire that might have killed everyone on board; as it was, twenty-nine of the forty-three men aboard managed to live through the crash. Nevertheless, the Navy now had purchased two dirigibles and had lost them both, along with nearly sixty lives. If large airships were to find a role, they would do so through the surviving *Los Angeles.*

This third one had the charm, avoiding accidents and remaining in active service from 1924 to 1932. Initial missions emphasized long-distance flights, interspersed with occasional tests that sought to broaden its operational uses. The Navy had a tender, USS *Patoka,* with a mooring mast; it had served *Shenandoah,* and *Los Angeles* moored to it repeatedly while at sea, receiving fuel and helium.

With *Patoka* amounting to an aircraft carrier for dirigibles, the question arose: could *Los Angeles* land on a real carrier? It made the attempt in 1928, as it tried to land on the deck of USS *Saratoga.* It encountered a downdraft and responded by releasing half a ton of water ballast, which soaked the landing crew on the flight deck. It touched down and proved hard to hold, for the carrier was rolling and pitching. Then a sudden upward gust lifted the airship and broke a restraining rope. Its commander, Charles Rosendahl, now had had enough; he broke off his landing and flew away. The Navy made no further efforts at combining dirigibles and aircraft carriers; these newest additions to the fleet went their separate ways.

Yet while a big airship could not land on a carrier, there was considerable interest in having it serve as a carrier. Fighter planes, launched and recovered from a dirigible in flight, might defend it against enemy air attack. They also might enhance its ability to find an enemy fleet, conducting the actual aerial search while allowing the huge and vulnerable mother ship to remain in the background, unseen and out of danger.

The core of the problem involved finding a way whereby an airplane in flight could hook itself to a support extending from the hull of *Los*

Angeles. This called for practice, for the air adjacent to the hull was quite turbulent. The method that worked best called for the aircraft to match speed with the dirigible while flying below it, in smooth air, and then to fly upward to engage its hook. Initial trials took place during the summer of 1929, with *Los Angeles* soon demonstrating this new skill before a crowd of a hundred thousand at the National Air Races.

A year and a half later, in 1931, *Los Angeles* played its intended role by participating in a major fleet exercise. The war game of 1929 had featured Rear Admiral Joseph Reeves's successful carrier-based attack on the Panama Canal, with this canal being the target for the new exercise as well. Reeves again was in command, directing a powerful force of battleships that was to clear the way for an amphibious landing. *Los Angeles* supported the defenders and had the task of finding Reeves's battle fleet while it was still at sea. This mock battle was important; the chief of naval operations, Admiral William Pratt, hoisted his flag aboard the battleship *California* and served as chief umpire.

Staging from *Patoka*, *Los Angeles* flew in a wide arc and spotted a large number of ships at a distance of thirty miles. They were Reeves's main body; this sighting gave the defenders their first reliable report, and led to a successful air strike by planes from their carrier, USS *Lexington*. However, Reeves had a carrier of his own, the USS *Langley*, which launched planes that intercepted the *Los Angeles*. This dirigible carried its own umpire, who ruled that it had been destroyed—and who shut down its radio while it was right in the middle of transmitting a message. Admiral Pratt then sent his own: "You are sunk."

Nevertheless, this exercise showed that a dirigible truly could serve as the eyes of the fleet. The "destruction" of *Los Angeles* demonstrated clearly that future airships indeed would have to carry their own airplanes, and the successors to *Los Angeles* soon did this. They were the *Akron*, named for the city where Goodyear Tire and Rubber had set up an airship-building subsidiary, and the *Macon*, the largest town in the district of Georgia congressman Carl Vinson, who controlled the Navy's appropriations. Dirigibles now counted as if they were cruisers; the new ones continued the practice of naming these vessels for cities, while battleships carried the names of states.

In addition, Germany was reentering the world of airships and once again was taking the lead, with its *Graf Zeppelin*. It had its start amid the same type of popular enthusiasm that had rescued its namesake, Count Zeppelin, following the loss of his LZ-4. Again a public subscription raised start-up funds, to a total of 2.5 million marks, with Hugo Eckener then prevailing upon the Weimar government to appropriate over a million more. In July 1928, on what would have been the count's ninetieth birthday, his daughter gave the new ship its christening.

It made two transatlantic trips during its first year, along with a winter trip to the eastern Mediterranean. During that voyage, passengers had the pleasure of eating breakfast over Crete and lunch over Palestine. Then, during August and September of 1929, *Graf* made a trip around the world with only three intermediate stops. No airliner then existed that could merely cross the United States with as few as three such stops, and *Graf* was the first passenger-carrying aircraft to girdle the globe. What was more, it did it in style.

The cuisine of each day matched its route. Over Germany, waiters served Rhine salmon; departing Japan, a dinner featured Kamakura ham. Printed menus resembled those of a luxury liner, showing scenes rendered by artists, such as a dirigible flying near Mount Fuji. The longest leg of the voyage extended for 7,000 miles, from Friedrichshafen to Tokyo. The ship flew over immense forests that stretched ahead endlessly. It demonstrated anew the ability of aircraft to reach the most remote outposts, for it dropped down for a close look at Yakutsk in eastern Siberia, a thousand miles from the sea and 750 miles from the nearest railroad. The skipper, Hugo Eckener, steered his ship along a narrow pass that led through mountains, and soon saw bright blue water: the Sea of Okhotsk. Following a stopover in Japan, he leaped the Pacific in a single bound, as he continued onward to San Francisco. It was enough to bring back the good old days, when the world stood in awe of Germany's aerial prowess.

More spectaculars followed: a flight in 1930 along a triangular route that included Brazil as well as New York, then an exploratory mission to the Arctic the following year. After that, the Zeppelin Company elected to concentrate on regularly scheduled passenger service. However, its transatlantic flights had shown that the proper destination was not New York. The ship lacked speed to make suitable way against the westerly gales, while rough weather over the North Atlantic threatened to limit the travel season. In addition, *Graf* was simply too small for the anticipated demand, for it could carry only twenty passengers. Hence, beginning in the summer of 1931, this airship initiated round-trip service to Brazil, where a colony of expatriate Germans provided a clientele.

The British took great interest in the exploits of *Graf*. Their empire and Commonwealth spanned the globe, including such far-flung states as Canada, India, South Africa, and Australia. Airships promised vast improvements over steamships, and in 1924 the Labour government of Prime Minister Ramsay MacDonald initiated a program aimed at building two very large dirigibles for long-haul commercial service. They were the R-100 and the R-101.

The Air Ministry took charge of their construction, and with the attendant government delays, the ships took five years to reach completion. The R-100 went forward within the privately held firm of Vickers, largely out of the limelight. By contrast, the R-101 was a project of the government-held Royal Airship Works. The public-affairs office of the Air Ministry gave it a blaze of publicity, while playing down the fact that it turned out to be seriously overweight. It was further burdened by the constant attentions of Lord Thomson, the secretary of state for air. He was a leading advocate of airships and a strong force behind the program. Yet he knew little about them, and readily dismissed the advice of his technical advisers if it conflicted with His Lordship's wishes.

The R-101 had serious flaws. Its gas cells were not held with stays within the rigid framework, but could billow back and forth. As they did this, they chafed against the girders, tearing holes that leaked hydrogen. If the ship pitched nose-down, the cells would shift aft, accentuating the motion and making it harder to restore a level attitude. In a storm, such pitching would be unavoidable. In addition, this dirigible had a sensitive valve that would release gas in response to even a modest tilt, compromising further its ability to stay in the air. Yet it lacked provision for the quick release of part of its water ballast. Helium would have improved its safety, but the United States had barely enough for its own needs and had none to export.

Engineers fixed the R-101's weight problem by cutting it in two and inserting a new gas cell for extra lift. But the chafing of these cells received only the quick fix of putting pads on parts of the framework. Test flights soon showed that this craft was reversing the usual airship practice, whereby a ship was heavy with fuel at the start of a mission but grew lighter as it burned its gasoline. Because of its leakage of hydrogen, the R-101 lost rather than gained lift during a flight.

In 1930 the R-100 made a successful round-trip to Canada, putting vast pressure on the R-101 to match this. Its goal was India, and Lord Thomson was eager to make the trip as a passenger. He hoped to be named viceroy of India, and while there he planned to attend to political business. But he had to be back in London before October 20, to attend an Imperial Conference. As Gilbert and Sullivan might have put it, the lordship that he held was the only ship he had ever seen, but on this point he'd never, never budge. "I must insist on the programme for the Indian flight being adhered to," he harrumphed in a letter to the Royal Airship Works, "as I have made my plans accordingly." Did this dirigible face danger? He declared publicly that "she is as safe as a house, except for the millionth chance."

The voyage was barely under way when it ran into wind and rain. At its best the R-101 was a fair-weather ship, but it continued across the Channel at low altitude. It entered France; near Beauvais it pitched down. The captain gave it full up elevator and momentarily halted this motion; then its nose went down again. A rigger went forward to drop ballast that couldn't be released from the control car. It was too late; the ship struck the ground and almost immediately was ablaze.

The subsequent court of inquiry put the blame on a ruptured gas cell in the bow, but its report wasn't important. What mattered was the list of the dead. They included Lord Thomson as well as the director of civil aviation, the director of airship development, the head of the R-101's design team, the ship's commander, along with forty-three others. Also among the deceased was Britain's airship program. The R-100 was still intact and ready for use, but it was sold for scrap. It fetched £504, less than a thousandth of its construction cost.

A similar disaster in 1923 had cost France its only large dirigible, *Dixmude,* a wartime zeppelin originally intended for the kaiser's navy. Following its loss, France left the ranks of the airship builders. With Britain's abandonment, Germany and the United States remained the only nations still active in this field. The dirigible was faltering, but not because its heavier-than-air competitors were flying higher and faster. Instead, the great airships were consuming themselves in masses of flame.

Nevertheless, both nations were ready to set their programs at full speed ahead. Germany treasured its Friedrichshafen construction facilities as an emblem of glory for *der Vaterland,* while the U.S. facilities in Akron were fully comparable. The U.S. arrangements dated to 1923, at a time when the German works still faced destruction following completion of *Los Angeles.* Zeppelin officials believed that they could find a future only through partnership with the Yankees. Paul Litchfield, president of Goodyear, responded by setting up a new company that purchased rights to Germany's airship patents and hired some of its most experienced engineers. These included Karl Arnstein, who had crafted the wartime zeppelins; he now became Litchfield's chief designer. He went on to create the dirigibles *Akron* and *Macon.*

It took time to build the Akron airship works, which featured an enormous hangar, larger than the one in Lakehurst. It took more time to secure the appropriations for the Navy's airship program. The *Akron* entered construction in 1929 and joined the fleet two years later, but did not stay in service long. In February 1932, while being taken from the Lakehurst hangar, a crosswind dashed its tail against the ground, causing damage that took two months to repair. As a result, it missed the major war game of that year, in which the carriers *Lexington* and *Saratoga* conducted a successful air strike on Pearl Harbor.

Akron had been built to carry scouting aircraft, and received six of them during that summer. A flight control officer devised a procedure whereby these planes were to fly to either side of their mother ship, sweeping a path a hundred miles wide when searching for an enemy fleet. Unfortunately, this dirigible did not live long enough to put this technique into practice.

In April 1933, only a year and a half after being commissioned, it went down in stormy weather off the New Jersey coast. The water was cold and the airship lacked life rafts, and seventy-three men died. The fatalities included Rear Admiral William Moffett, who headed the Navy's Bureau of Aeronautics. He had been the principal advocate of the airship program, and had been fond of accompanying his men during operational flights. This fondness cost his life, in a loss as serious as that of Britain's Lord Thomson.

Nevertheless, the Navy still had the *Macon,* which made its first flight later in that same month. It replaced *Akron,* much as *Akron* had supplanted *Los Angeles.* Like *Akron,* the new ship had been built to launch and recover fighter planes while in flight, and to use them to search large areas of ocean. However, it did not do this initially, for its skipper repeatedly used *Macon* itself to approach ships of the "enemy" during maneuvers. Time and again it was "shot down," showing repeatedly that its life expectancy was short when in the presence of a hostile force that included an aircraft carrier. Admiral David Sellers, commander in chief of the fleet, concluded that "the USS *Macon* has failed to demonstrate its usefulness" and that he was "decidedly of the opinion that further expenditure of public funds for this type of vessel for the Navy is not justified."

A new and aggressive commander, Herbert Wiley, took charge of *Macon* in mid 1934. He was one of only three men to have survived the *Akron* disaster, and he lost little time in shifting the emphasis to his onboard fighters. He refitted them for longer range and higher speed. He introduced a radio homing system that enabled them to take accurate bearings from distances approaching two hundred miles. He gave *Macon* the role of a radio relay station and command center, hiding it below the sea-level horizon of the "enemy" while using its altitude to stay in direct contact with its aircraft in flight.

Little more than a week after taking command, he intercepted the heavy cruiser USS *Houston,* which was taking President Roosevelt to

Hawaii. Everyone on the ship was astonished when they saw themselves being buzzed by fighter planes, for they were fifteen hundred miles from land, far out of range of such aircraft. Then *Macon* appeared. Roosevelt had been assistant secretary of the Navy during World War I, and he responded by sending Wiley a radio message: "Well done."

In November, during a fleet exercise, *Macon* used its planes to follow the carrier *Saratoga,* while remaining out of sight at a distance of sixty miles. Wiley did even more in February 1935, keeping *Macon* undiscovered as its aircraft tracked a battle force, reporting composition, position, course, and speed. By then he was looking ahead to that year's major war game. He expected to carry dive bombers, and to conduct a night attack against the carrier *Lexington.*

He never got to do it. His airship was approaching the California coast, late in the afternoon, when a severe gust of wind ripped away its upper fin. This brought structural damage that punctured three gas cells, making the ship highly stern-heavy. The crew dumped sixteen tons of fuel and water ballast, but they overdid it; with its engines running, *Macon* quickly rose to nearly five thousand feet. At this altitude, helium escaped through automatic valves, and when it began its descent, there was no ballast left to check its fall. It plunged into the ocean, only a few miles from shore. This time the airship had life rafts; the water was warm, and rescuers were close at hand. Of eighty-three men on board, only two lost their lives.

This latest disaster put an end to the Navy's dirigible program. *Los Angeles* remained available, but it had less than half the useful lift of *Macon,* and was far too small to carry operational aircraft. Indeed, naval analysts looked toward designs that would be even larger than *Macon,* operating as airborne aircraft carriers with a complement of nine dive bombers. These plans fell by the wayside, and the Navy abandoned thoughts of using airships to search for enemy fleets. It still needed aircraft that could do this, but this work soon fell to long-range flying boats such as the PBY Catalina of World War II. Admiral Sellers noted that up to forty such aircraft could be purchased for the cost of another *Macon.*

As the big dirigibles faltered within the United States, they took on new life in Germany. The *Graf Zeppelin* initially held the spotlight; by 1934, only seven years after Lindbergh's flight to Paris, published schedules were advertising round-trip flights to Brazil every fourteen days. The Nazis were now in power, and quickly turned to the *Graf* to show that they commanded the most advanced aeronautical technology. Only a few months after Hitler took over, swastikas sprouted on its upper and lower fins. Then in mid 1934 the propaganda minister, Joseph Goebbels, contributed 2 million marks toward the construction of a new commercial airship, *Hindenburg*.

It was planned as the first of a pair of sister ships that were to inaugurate the long-awaited service to New York. They were designed to use helium for safety, and were to be speedy as well. In the air, four diesel engines were to drive them at eighty-two miles per hour, thirteen miles per hour faster than the *Graf*. That earlier airship had accommodated only twenty passengers, but the new ones would carry fifty. *Graf* offered them no more than a single-deck gondola, but *Hindenburg* and its sister were to provide two decks. These would be built into the hull and hence would be far more commodious.

Passengers entered the ship on the lower deck and climbed a metal staircase, with a bust of the old field marshal at the top. Here on A Deck was the center of the ship's life. Promenades ran on each side for fifty feet; people could sit on a couch and watch the scenery through steeply slanting windows. Here too were the main public areas: a dining room three times larger than that of *Graf*, along with a lounge and writing room. Dinner tables were laid with linen, fine silver, and china decorated with the gold Zeppelin crest. The lounge included a baby grand piano, crafted of aluminum.

Behind them lay staterooms. These improved on those of *Graf*, for each had a washstand. Below, on B Deck, lay bathrooms as well as a shower room. There also was a smoking room that included a bar, as a legacy of the time when *Hindenburg* was to be filled with helium. Washington officials had refused to sell it, but even with hydrogen used in its place, the smoking lounge remained. It was fitted with an airtight door and kept under pressure to keep stray hydrogen from leaking inward. In addition, stewards took meticulous care to prevent passengers from taking lighters or matches with them.

The new airship made its first flight in March 1936. Soon after, with swastikas rampant on its tail, it entered commercial service and made ten round-trips to the United States during the rest of that year. These included a ten-hour "millionaires' flight," in October, in which six dozen of the wealthy and influential cruised to New England for a view of the autumn foliage. *Hindenburg* also made several flights to Brazil, accompanying the *Graf* as the latter continued its regular service. Back home, a new intercontinental airport opened at Frankfurt, close to a number of populous cities and ready to take over from Friedrichshafen as Europe's main airship center.

Both zeppelins put into this port for the winter, where *Hindenburg* received ten new staterooms on B Deck, raising its passenger capacity to seventy. Its sister ship was under construction in Friedrichshafen, with a first flight planned for August 1937. Officials of Germany and the United States met to form a consortium that would operate four transatlantic airships, two being under the American flag. Then, with the coming of spring, *Hindenburg* and *Graf* resumed service with flights to South America. On May 3 the former left Frankfurt on the first of eighteen flights to the United States that were scheduled for the year. It flew over Manhattan during the afternoon of the sixth, then headed toward its landing in Lakehurst.

Suddenly, Fate and Death reached up to engulf this pinnacle of human achievement. With shocking abruptness, a huge billow of flame erupted from its rear, growing and expanding as if the air itself was on fire. The stern lost lift and fell to the ground; as it crashed, a huge tongue of flame shot upward from the nose. The bow came down a moment later, with a mass of fire filling its interior and leaping into the sky. From amid this blazing inferno, a few survivors ran to safety.

A generation of Americans remembered the sobbing voice of announcer Herb Morrison, vivid as the newsreels that also were recorded at the scene:

> The back motors of the ship are just holding it, just enough to keep it from—it's burst into flames! Get this started, get this started! It's fla— and it's flashing, it's flashing terrible! Oh, my, get out of the way, please! It's burning, bursting into flames a— and it's falling on the mooring mast and all the folks agree that this is terrible, this is one of the worst catastrophes in the world. Ohhhhhh! The flames are climbing, ohhh, four or five hundred feet into the sky and it's a terrific crash, ladies and gentlemen, the smoke and the flames, now. And it's crashing to the ground. Not quite to the mooring mast. Oh, the humanity and all the passengers![1]

Astonishingly, sixty-two people of the ninety-seven aboard survived, many by jumping from the ship. The airfield was soft sand, wet from rain, which cushioned their impact. Nevertheless, the author John Toland reminds us that not all were so fortunate:

> A man suddenly darted out of the wreck. It seemed impossible that a human being could live in that heat. A flame licked after the man, knocking him flat on his face. Rescuers couldn't advance because of the heat. Helplessly they watched the man get up, toss his hands in the air, stagger a few feet, and fall again. Again he tried, half rising in the blistering heat. Then he crawled desperately a few more feet, but finally wilted and lay still. Ten minutes later two sailors, shielding their faces, dragged him out. He was as black as a burned stump.[2]

Demise of the Hindenburg. *(National Archives)*

Investigations ensued, whose findings were inconclusive. Static electricity was a favorite culprit, though some people spoke of sabotage. This meant that the world's premier airship had been lost, with no one knowing for sure how it could have been made safe.

Helium certainly now was more important than ever. When *Graf* returned to Germany on May 8, at the end of another trip to Brazil, Eckener refused to let it fly again. He then tried anew to win a helium supply from Washington, only to be told directly by Interior Secretary Harold Ickes, "Your Hitler is going to make war!" Just then it was the spring of 1938, the season of the Nazi annexation of Austria.

Nevertheless, the Germans gamely pressed ahead, as the sister of *Hindenburg* received the name *Graf Zeppelin II.* It took to the sky in 1938, appearing anew as a true ship of the air. It made flights within Germany that showed the flag, and the swastika, but did not enter commercial service. It flew reconnaissance missions over Great Britain during July and August 1939, in the weeks prior to the outbreak of World War II, but was far too vulnerable for any military use in the war itself. Early in 1940, Hermann Goering ordered the destruction of both the *Graf* and *Graf II,* scrapping them for the aluminum in their frames. With this, the zeppelin died in the country of its origin.

Hindenburg had perished in a blaze of hydrogen; even so, helium was no cure-all. The U.S. Navy used it from the start, in *Shenandoah*, *Akron*, and *Macon*—and lost all three amid storms and violent winds. On both sides of the Atlantic, then, the dirigible would live in memory as a gallant attempt that failed because it could not be made safe.

This is more than an impression; it gives an accurate summary of more than thirty years of operating experience. During those decades, a total of 161 dirigibles took to the air. Three-fifths of them met violent ends. Even when one deletes the losses due to action in combat, half of the remaining airships—60 of 123—were destroyed in accidents.

What caused them? Setting aside the war losses, the analyst Peter Brooks gives the following summary:[3]

Loss by fire		23
Burned in hangar	13	
Burned on ground	3	
Burned in flight	7	
Ground-handling and flying accidents		37
Coming out of hangar	3	
Landing	15	
Failed structurally in flight	3	
Lost in storms, at sea, etc.	16	
Total		60

Even if helium had been available from Day One, eliminating the risk of fire, a highly unpleasant statistic would have remained: 37 of 123 airships, some 30 percent, were lost due to their structural fragility.

One gains further perspective by noting that the complete airship fleet, all 161, accumulated some eighty thousand hours of flight time during those thirty years. Today, America's fleet of commercial airliners runs up that many flight hours every three days. If they were no safer than dirigibles, then a record of 37 lost in eighty thousand flying hours would bring a dozen airliner crashes every day. If this was the best that aviation could offer, there would be no such thing today as a commercial airline industry.

Moreover, the widespread use of helium would have acted to make dirigibles even less robust. That gas has less lifting power than hydrogen. It then would have brought the advent of oversize craft having particularly lightweight frames, like those of the World War I height-climbers. In turn, these would have been even more prone to structural failure.

This fragility was particularly significant during ground handling. The Germans assembled parties of several hundred people; at the command "Airship, march!" they walked it in or out of its hangar by pulling on ropes. The Americans used a rail-mounted mobile mooring mast at the bow, securing the stern by attaching it to additional rolling stock. Both techniques, though, relied strongly on avoiding sidewinds. The airships could not withstand more than about twenty miles per hour of crosswind without structural damage.

If there had been such a thing as safety in lighter-than-air flight, if the term "safe dirigible" had not proved to be an oxymoron, then these great ships might have developed into aerial cruise liners. Like today's Princess and Carnival cruise vessels, they might have carried a hundred or more passengers in comfort and luxury, offering unparalleled views of the world's scenic attractions. *Hindenburg* prefigured such a future with its millionaires' flight of 1936, and with its low passes over Manhattan. There might have been far more, if . . .

Lighter-than-air flight had a final chapter, during and after World War II, as the Navy turned to the blimp. This craft dispensed altogether with the rigid and vulnerable framework, amounting simply to an inflated gasbag with a gondola and engines. However, this frame was what had allowed the dirigibles to achieve their enormous sizes. Lacking it, the blimp was far too small and slow to offer the prospect of carrying passengers or of serving as an airborne aircraft carrier.

The blimp nevertheless found an important role in antisubmarine warfare. German subs posed deadly threats to the merchant shipping that was Britain's and the Soviets' lifeline. Escort carriers protected the convoys, with flight decks built on merchant hulls that carried modest numbers of aircraft. Long-range bombers helped as well. The blimps played their role by serving as aerial scouts, as crew members watched the sea for periscopes. Blimps had the endurance to accompany convoys on their long transatlantic voyages, and they proved highly effective. Not a single ship was lost to the torpedoes of U-boats while sailing under the protection of a blimp, and only one blimp went down due to enemy fire.

Even so, blimps remained in service for little more than twenty years. After the war, the Navy turned to airplanes for its antisub patrols, for these were faster and could cover more area. This drew on continuing technical developments in heavier-than-air aviation, which had already supplanted dirigibles for the tasks of strategic bombing, passenger service, and naval reconnaissance. The last naval blimp left active service in 1962.

The aerial cruise liner persists to this day as an attractive opportunity for a modern dirigible. New materials would replace the costly goldbeater's-skin gas cells with durable and inexpensive plastics. Stress analysis, conducted by computer, would assure improved strength; weather radar and satellite weather photos would protect against severe winds and dangerous storms. Yet the fundamental concept of the very large, rigidly framed dirigible remains so severely flawed that even with these modern improvements, no one has ever ventured to build a new one.*

The Goodyear Blimp remains in service, hovering over football games and carrying television cameras that show the play action. Hot-air balloons continue to fly as well, with propane burners replacing the braziers of two centuries ago that burned straw. Their owners gather from time to time, and as they rise into the sky, the air blossoms with brightly colored globes, as if it were a field of flowers. But apart from their reliance on propane, such balloons have seen only modest change since the heyday of the Montgolfiers.

There is a timelessness to lighter-than-air flight, which stands distinct from the quiet, graceful motion whereby one wafts slowly over the countryside. Though aviation has seen enormous advances, few of them have reached balloons, which continue to persist across the centuries. Similarly, any large new dirigible would look quite familiar to Count Zeppelin. It was the fate of the lighter-than-air innovators that while they pioneered aviation in a number of important forms, their balloons and dirigibles reached technical maturity early in their history. This left the airship with insurmountable deficiencies, in performance as well as safety, while the design of aircraft continued to progress. Indeed, so sweeping was the airplanes' eventual triumph that they relegated balloons to the world of hobbyists, while leaving the graceful dirigibles as nothing more than memories.

---

*Germans have recently built a new rigid-frame airship. However, it is little more than a large blimp, being far smaller than the heroic craft of the 1930s.

9

Night and Fog

AIRMAIL GOT OFF to a shaky start in the wake of World War I. Only a few mailbags spent any time aboard an airplane; the overwhelming majority went by rail. There was no night flying; mail moved by air only during daylight hours, then continued through the night on trains. Pilots navigated by following railroad tracks, swooping down to read a town's name from a water tower. When the weather closed in, they came down to low altitudes and continued onward, still following the tracks. This practice developed such nuances as keeping to the right, to avoid collisions with low-flying oncoming planes. Hazards of the business included running into a locomotive, or hitting a hill pierced by a tunnel.

"Map reading was not required," one of these pilots later recalled. "There were no maps. I got from place to place with the help of the seat of my pants. If it left that of the plane, when visibility was at a minimum, I was in trouble and could even be upside down." Another mail pilot was fatalistic: "I certainly had no wish to get killed, but I was not afraid of it. I would have been frightened if I had thought I would get maimed or crippled for life, but there was little chance of that. A mail pilot was usually killed outright."[1]

In 1920, Warren Harding won the presidential election. To Otto Praeger, who ran the airmail service, it was all too likely that the incoming Republicans would view his program as one more boondoggle to squelch. He resolved that during February, two weeks before Harding's inauguration, his pilots would fly at night in winter and would carry mail from coast to coast. They would take off at dawn, two from New York and two from San Francisco.

One of the New York pilots soon was forced down, while snow grounded the second at Chicago. A veteran pilot flew from San Francisco and died in a crash in Nevada. The fourth mail load made its transfer at North Platte, Nebraska, and a relief pilot, Jack Knight, took off to fly on to Omaha. His route had been publicized and as he bore through the night, he saw that people had lit bonfires to mark his course.

In Omaha he learned that his own relief had been unable to take off from Chicago. It was two in the morning and Knight had never flown the Omaha-Chicago route, but he was willing to try. He tore part of a Rand McNally road map off a wall and headed for Des Moines. Clouds closed in as he passed it, but he found railroad tracks and followed them toward Iowa City. Then he realized that he didn't know where the airfield was. He flew around the town, gunning his engine, and then saw a red flare. The ground crew had gone home but the night watchman had stayed, and had heard his motor. Knight landed and taxied; just then, his engine ran out of gas.

After that it was easy. His crew arrived and put gas in his tank, while dawn began to break. The weather still was bad, but now he could follow the tracks with ease. A few hours later he was in Chicago, where he found a relief pilot at last. The mail completed its run to New York, and Knight found himself hailed as a champion.

Still, while such bravura could save the airmail service from Washington budget cutters, it could not offer the promise of reliable operation at night. Two Army lieutenants took the next step. They were stationed at McCook Field in Dayton, Ohio, and they set up a lighted airway between Dayton and Columbus. It had rotating light beacons, flashing markers, and floodlights at airfields. With this, pilots could fly at night through all but the worst visibility.

In 1923 a successor to Praeger, Paul Henderson, began lighting airways across the nation. The effort featured lighthouses, 50-foot steel towers supporting revolving beacons of 500,000 candlepower that were fitted with 36-inch reflectors. These marked the main airfields, and could be seen a hundred miles away. Smaller beacons, visible for sixty miles, marked the emergency fields. Flashing acetylene lamps, spaced every three miles, defined the route.

The first such airway ran between Chicago and Cheyenne, Wyoming, in flat country where construction was easy. It covered the central one-third of the country. Flights could then take off from either coast at dawn, reach the airway by dusk, then fly through the night along its length and continue onward the next day. In initial tests, Henderson showed that his aircraft could beat the trains by two and even three days. He spanned the nation by extending his lighted airways across the Appalachians and the Rockies, and launched a scheduled coast-to-coast service. It began in mid 1924 and soon settled down to definite times of less than thirty hours eastbound and under thirty-six hours westbound.

The Commerce Department extended these lighted airways during the subsequent decade; its lines of beacons formed an eighteen-thousand-mile network by 1933. Again, though, pilots could see and follow these lights only when the visibility was adequate. When this was not the case, they continued to rely on the time-honored procedure of following the railroad tracks. They even did this at night, turning on landing lights. The steel rails, brightly illuminated, looked like ribbons of silver as they rolled past.

Radio also became useful for navigation, creating beamlike transmissions that fliers could follow from one transmitter to the next. It was not possible to produce a true beam like that from a searchlight; that would have demanded the use of microwave frequencies, which were beyond the state of the art. Instead the emphasis was on the clever use of existing low-frequency methods, with which it proved possible to offer a valuable service.

The key was the loop antenna, a rectangular circuit of wires rising vertically from the ground. It gave the strongest signal when facing the loop edge-on, as well as for some distance to the left or right. But there was little or no signal at right angles to this direction. German investigators had learned of this as early as 1908, and the firm of Telefunken had introduced a radio navigation system for the wartime dirigibles. It did not work well, particularly at long distances, and after the war the U.S. Army's Signal Corps asked the National Bureau of Standards to come up with something better.

A Bureau radio engineer, Percival Lowell, proposed to use two loop antennas set crosswise to each other. Along a line bisecting their angle, a receiver would pick up signals of equal strength from both of them. By transmitting alternately from each, the antennas would define a zone of equal signals known as the "beam." It lay along this angle bisector; if a pilot was "on the beam" he would hear the transmissions as a continuous hum. To either side of this bisector, though, one of the two signals would predominate, and the pilot would know that he had strayed from the beam's course.

Two Bureau physicists tried this for the first time in 1921. They rigged two large loops, supported by three masts, aboard a lighthouse tender in Washington Navy Yard. Then, using ground receivers, they found that the equisignal zone was about a mile wide, thirty-five miles from the station.

Then the Army took over, with flight tests at McCook Field. These added the refinement of placing the loop antennas at right angles to each other, thus marking out four equisignal zones that crossed like an X. The Army also added circuitry that made it possible to shift the orientation of these zones without moving the antennas. Also significant was the introduction of standard transmissions: a Morse-code *A*, dot-dash, from one loop and *N*, dash-dot, from the other. In the equisignal zones they merged into an unbroken buzz. Away from such a zone, however, the flier would hear either the dot-dash or the dash-dot predominating. He then would know that he was either to the left or right of the proper path.

This work brought the four-course radio range that remained a standard navigational aid until well after World War II. The first operational station was at Bellefonte, Pennsylvania, in hilly country where light beacons were often hidden in clouds and fog. Pilots of National Air Transport, an early airmail carrier, made a number of demonstration flights with it beginning in December 1927. A year later two other transmitters were on the air, at New Brunswick, New Jersey, and near Cleveland. The route from New York to Cleveland then had a continuous radio-marked course. Other stations, in operation by the fall of 1929, made it possible to fly on the beam from Boston to Omaha by way of New York and Chicago.

These stations were some two hundred miles apart; their beams had a range of around a hundred miles. A pilot flew along one by listening carefully to his earphones, until he momentarily lost radio contact within a zone of no signal, the "cone of silence," that spread skyward directly above a transmitter. He then followed an outward beam to its limit, then tuned his radio to the frequency of the next one.

All this assumed that the range signals were not drowned out by static. They had a tendency to do this, particularly during nasty weather when good navigation was most needed. Here too, though, it proved possible to make headway.

The planebuilder William Boeing had a brother-in-law, Thorp Hiscock, who got a group of pilots to make test flights at Arcata, California, which had a reputation as the foggiest place in the country. They wanted to try the use of loop antennas in flight. Such loops were used aboard ships for direction finding, and were known for receiving signals when conventional aerials, strung between masts, could not. In flight they also proved useful. Reception further improved when Hiscock's pilots attached bits of fine copper wire to their wing's trailing edges. The wire bled away the static electricity that interfered with reception. They did not lick the problem altogether; that required the use of VHF frequencies, years later. But they reduced the static sufficiently to make possible the use of radio in flight, at least much of the time.

Yet while pilots now could navigate in fog, it was another matter entirely to keep from spinning out of control. A flier would lose himself in the gray stuff but would continue trying to fly straight and level, relying on his seat-of-the-pants sense of balance. It wouldn't work; after a few minutes he would come down in a spin. The reason lay in the fact that just as an auto tends to wander off the road, a plane tends to start turning if left to itself. As it turns it banks; the wings are designed so that this happens automatically. In a banked turn, the downward direction continued to be toward the cockpit floor, even if the plane was virtually on its side.

As an airplane started to turn on its own, it dipped its nose and picked up speed. The pilot could sense an unbanked turn, the kind a car makes when rounding a corner, but not a banked one. However, he had no trouble noticing the increased airspeed, and he concluded that the plane was in a dive. He responded by pulling back the control stick—and with the plane actually in a turn, this steepened the turn and made things worse. Soon the engine was racing and the propeller was snarling—and still his seat-of-the-pants feelings urged him strongly to pull back some more.

If he broke out of the clouds and saw the ground again, thereby gaining the visual reference needed for orientation, he could recover and resume normal flight. If he didn't, if he continued to see neither the ground nor the sun but only the gray surrounding murk, it was almost certain that he would lose control and crash. The plane either would break up or would spiral-dive into the earth.

Even birds couldn't cope with fog. An Army flier tossed a blind-folded pigeon out of an airplane and saw it spin out of control. The bird could do no more than to let itself fall with wings held high, which amounted to bailing out. That settled it; if even a bird couldn't succeed, no pilot could fly blind if all he had was the seat of his pants.

Some airmen tried to sense their turns by hanging a watch from its chain within the cockpit, like a pendulum. It didn't work; in a banked turn the watch continued to point floorward. Others reasoned that a ship steers through fog by using its compass; why not an airplane? The problem was that a compass needle does not point to true north; left to its own devices, it would point steeply downward, to a location deep within the earth. This brought such forms of unpleasantness as "northerly turning error," whereby a pilot flying northward would turn right—and the compass would indicate that the change of direction was to the left.

Beacons, radio, and compasses all were important, but blind flight demanded more. It called for the gyroscope. The first published account of this device dated to 1852; the French physicist Léon Foucault introduced the name, which means "turn-seer." He conducted experiments, showing particularly how to attach a weight to its suspension so that its spinning rotor would align with the earth's axis of rotation. It then would act as a gyrocompass.

The gyrocompass soon emerged as an important focus for development. Mark Twain wrote, in 1877, that "there was a vast fortune waiting for the genius who should invent a compass that would not be affected by the local influences of an iron ship." Magnetic compasses became even less reliable when electricity went to sea, for a ship's motors and wiring produced localized magnetic fields. With the advent of submarines, after 1900, such compasses achieved total uselessness. These vessels' steel hulls screened out the earth's magnetic field entirely.

Gyros helped torpedoes as well as submarines, for in 1894 an Austrian inventor, Ludwig Obry, introduced a course-keeping system to steer the straight-running torpedo. The gyro came into its own with the new century, and the man that made it happen was Elmer Sperry, an American inventor and entrepreneur. He had carried through projects in a variety of fields: generators and electric arc lights, streetcars, mining equipment, electric autos and their batteries. He had achieved modest levels of success, for his companies had prospered. Still, people did not place him alongside the likes of Thomas Edison and Alexander Graham Bell, at least not then. But this began to change after the gyro entered his life.

He initially came to it with the view that a large installation, mounted in a ship, could make it stable against rolling. The gyro would swing and would counteract large rolls, allowing the ship to make much smaller ones. He drew support from the Navy, and launched a program of development. Meanwhile in Germany, the inventor Hermann Anschütz-Kaempfe was introducing the first practical gyrocompasses. Sperry believed he could build a better one, and learned again that the Navy was willing to help. In 1910 he founded the firm of Sperry Gyroscope Company, in Brooklyn, to pursue these two efforts.

Soon after, his son Lawrence introduced him to aviation. The young Sperry had come up amid a blaze of enthusiasm, building his own airplane inside the house, winning his dad's forgiveness after knocking down part of a wall to get it out, then installing a motor. His dad sent him off to prep school in Arizona before he could break his neck, but Lawrence nevertheless had no doubt as to what he wanted. In April 1912 he wrote home, "I want to enter the aeroplane business. I am very determined to go into aeroplanes and I think that you should help me get started."

The Navy was beginning to show an interest in flying boats, and the senior Sperry decided that Lawrence could help in developing a flight-control system. It was to improve on Obry's gyrostabilizer, for while that system kept a torpedo from changing course, Sperry's would control both pitch and roll. He already was prepared to use gyros as part of a control system, for his ship gyrostabilizer featured just such a system. It used a pendulum as a sensor, detecting incipient rolling and triggering an electric motor, to swing the big gyro preemptively before the rolling could begin to build up. In the airplane control, gyros themselves were to act as sensors by defining a stable reference. When the plane banked or pitched with respect to that reference, the system would activate servomotors that would move the ailerons or elevator, restoring the plane to level flight.

In 1914, Lawrence showed it off at an air show near Paris that was demonstrating new inventions for safety in flight. To the assembled crowd, well aware of the sensitive character of the airplanes of the day, his flight was astonishing. Piloting a two-man biplane, he flew low and took his hands off the controls, holding them high where everyone could see them. His mechanic then climbed onto the lower wing, making his way outward to a distance of several feet. The man's weight would ordinarily have upset the craft, but it flew onward, its ailerons deflecting automatically and its wings remaining nearly level.

Sperry continued to play look-ma-no-hands, standing up in his seat as his companion crawled rearward along the fuselage. The plane did not nose up, but again remained level. For a finale, both men abandoned their seats and walked outward onto the wings. The airplane now lacked a pilot entirely, but still it flew onward.

This caused a sensation. Officials at the air show awarded him a prize of 50,000 francs. William Cathcart, a leading aviation writer, hailed this achievement in the *Philadelphia Public Ledger*:

> The stabilization of the aeroplane is an accomplished fact. The human factor—to which in its history so many tragic deaths have been due—can now be entirely eliminated and replaced by an unerring apparatus, which will not let the aeroplane stray from any path the aviator may choose, which will guide it through eddies and gusts and over the dreaded "air holes" with serene unconcern for their existence.[2]

He was half a century premature; the gyros of the day tended to drift and lose stability, and the performance he anticipated was not achieved until the advent of inertial guidance. In addition, Sperry's system did not go far. The French tried to use it during World War I, but found that it was too heavy. It also interfered with the rapid maneuverings that could save a pilot in combat. Nevertheless, this 1914 demonstration indeed marked a milestone. It linked the gyroscope to the problem of aircraft control. It launched a line of development that led to important cockpit instruments and to automatic pilots. It also brought forth the Sperrys as leaders in this new field.

Elmer and his sponsors soon took the view that they could offer better advantages by building gyroscopic instruments. These would not activate a control system, but rather presented information to pilots. The turn indicator, invented in 1917, was an early result. This instrument amounted to an air-driven gyro mounted within an instrument panel to show a turn. It worked nicely—but after the aviator came out of the turn and took up a new heading, the needle stubbornly stayed at its new reading. Lawrence fixed that by attaching a spring to the gyro. Now it indicated rate of turn rather than the turn itself, deflecting more in a sharp turn than in a gradual one, with the needle then returning to the upright position.

This instrument soon became standard equipment in cockpits. A variant, the turn-and-bank indicator, incorporated a ball within a curving glass tube that resembled a carpenter's level; the ball stayed centered during a properly banked turn, but shifted position to indicate a sideslip.

During the 1920s, though, these instruments did not exactly take the world of aviation by storm, for pilots continued to trust their senses. Britain's Sir Sefton Brancker, a leader in postwar aviation, had put the matter plainly in 1917: "Instruments of late have become more reliable, and personally, I am the greatest believer in using them for training. After a little experience with instruments as a guide, any intelligent man will find himself working without them instinctively, and they will have tided him over many dangers in the early days."[3]

Flight experiments soon showed that blind flight was not so simple. Dual-cockpit aircraft made it possible to conduct tests, with one pilot under a canvas hood and the other in the clear for safety. These flight tests disclosed how blind flight led to spiral dives, and why no pilot could expect to avoid them by relying solely on the seat of his pants. Even so, the turn indicator offered no panacea. A man could indeed fly his proper course by keeping his eye on this instrument; as long as he did this, he could maintain his altitude as well. Nevertheless, the turn indicator went against all the feelings that a pilot honed and relied on. The aviation writer Wolfgang Langewiesche emphasized this vividly:

> In "contact" flight, when the airplane turns, things scream at you: the airplane is banked; the whole world is at a slant, and wheeling. But in instrument flight, when the airplane turns, nothing screams. Only a gauge sits there quietly, no longer like this ↑ but like this ↖.

And this quiet little signal must hit you like an electric shock. You must take action right away, without thinking, as if the instrument were part of your own nervous system.[4]

Few pilots could respond in this fashion. A common reaction was that the turn indicator wasn't something you could trust. It worked all right as long as you were in the clear, but when you flew into a cloud the thing went crazy and showed a turn.

To use the turn indicator successfully called for more than intellectual understanding. It demanded a knack. During the mid 1920s the word began to get around: some pilots had actually gotten the knack. One of the first was Charles Lindbergh, during his days as a mail pilot. He used the instrument twice while flying between St. Louis and Chicago, on occasions when he was caught in impossible weather. Both times he could do no more than climb to a safe altitude and bail out. But these experiences taught him the key: to absolutely believe the indicator and to disregard his own senses. He drew on this experience during his flight to Paris, in which he flew through fog and clouds for long stretches. Twice he started to fall off in a spin, but both times he recovered by trusting his turn indicator.

The thing could be done; blind flight indeed was possible. Even so, the turn indicator would not stand on its own, for by itself it offered too little information. At this point the Guggenheim copper barons came to the forefront. The wealthy Daniel Guggenheim had a strong interest in philanthropy, while his son Harry had flown in the war as a naval aviator. These influences led him to set up the Daniel Guggenheim Foundation for the Promotion of Aeronautics. It opened for business in 1926, with Harry as president.

Young Harry encouraged universities to build departments of aeronautical engineering, by providing grants to such schools as Caltech, MIT, and Stanford. He sent Lindbergh on a nationwide tour. He encouraged the growth of airlines by supporting California's Western Air Express, a predecessor of Trans World Airlines (TWA). In 1928 he turned to the problem of blind flight by setting up a laboratory at Long Island's Mitchel Field, close to Sperry's company in Brooklyn. His test pilot was James Doolittle.

To the general public, Jimmy Doolittle was the ultimate barnstormer. He had been the first to cross the country in under twenty-four hours, with a one-stop flight in 1922. He set a speed record of 233 miles per hour in a 1925 air race. He was the first to fly an outside loop, in which you nose over into a power dive and continue until you are flying upside down. Within the Army Air Corps, he had repeatedly come close to tearing the wings off aircraft.

Yet Doolittle was no Shipwreck Kelly, who won momentary fame by perching atop a flagpole for three weeks. He was a true aeronautical researcher. His Air Corps tests had given pioneering results on how a pilot blacks out when performing violent maneuvers. In turn, this work fed into studies at MIT, where Doolittle received M.S. and D.Sc. degrees.

Within the Guggenheim project, Doolittle wanted to do more than merely fly in clouds. He wanted to take off, fly a planned course, and land—all with a hood over his cockpit. Two test aircraft stood at his disposal, and he was welcome to equip both the planes and the airfield with whatever new instruments he thought would help. Radio was to offer part of what he needed, providing transmissions that would show the direction back to Mitchel Field and then indicating where he should start his descent. He expected to follow a sloping approach path that he described as "flying an airplane into the ground," relying on a strong undercarriage and heavy shock absorbers to permit a rough but safe landing. But he wanted other equipment as well.

He was dissatisfied with the altimeters of the day, which were accurate only to around a hundred feet. Through colleagues at the National Bureau of Standards, he learned that a German-born instrument maker, Paul Kollsman, had built an altimeter of surpassingly good accuracy. Kollsman had concluded that standard models had faulty gears, and he turned to Swiss watchmakers to fabricate his movement. His altimeter proved to be up to twenty times more accurate than a standard version, and soon was installed in the main research airplane.

Doolittle had turn-and-bank indicators, but he viewed them as insufficient, and he was displeased as well with the magnetic compass. He wanted a gyroscopic device that would show his angle of bank or pitch, along with a compass that would show no northerly turning error. He sought out Elmer Sperry, still going strong at age sixty-eight, who proceeded to have his son Elmer Jr. develop two new instruments.

The first was the artificial horizon. It featured a small airplane in the middle of a display, wings level, as well as a bar that represented the horizon. That bar was linked to a gyro; it would remain parallel to the real horizon. It would tilt to show a bank, or rise and descend to show pitching. Doolittle wrote that this instrument was "like cutting a porthole through the fog to look at the real horizon."

The second new item was a gyrocompass, with a gyro indicating direction with respect to a compass card. Doolittle could set the gyro while the plane was flying straight and level, by using his magnetic compass; under those conditions it would read true. The instrument then would show his actual direction even while turning or maneuvering, in circumstances where the magnetic type would be useless.

The main test came in September 1929. It featured a safety pilot who sat in a front cockpit while Doolittle sat in the rear one, under a hood. "I taxied the airplane out," he wrote, "and turned into the takeoff position on the radio beam. We took off and flew west in a gradual climb." He flew a course resembling an elongated racetrack, twice making 180-degree turns, then approached the field and landed successfully, all the while relying entirely on his instruments. The flight took fifteen minutes. The safety pilot held his hands up during both the takeoff and the landing, to make it obvious that Doolittle was flying blind.

After that, pilots installed these instruments as part of their arrays, and blind flight became increasingly routine. The new instruments also complemented the growing use of radio, which now provided weather reports and pilot instructions. Radio signals pierced clouds and fog with ease, enabling aviators to receive orders from the ground and to steer a true course. A law of 1930 encouraged its use by offering to pay a premium to airlines whose planes were equipped for two-way communication.

That same year saw the first radio-equipped control tower, at Cleveland Municipal Airport. It provided reports of weather and landing conditions to incoming pilots, kept track of traffic in the vicinity, and gave permission to land or take off. There was a certain casualness to it all; sometimes a controller would take an impromptu break for a cup of coffee, while at other times a pilot simply flew on in and landed. But within five years, some twenty cities followed Cleveland's lead.

By then, radio stations were transmitting weather reports throughout the entire country. Four-course radio range stations also blanketed the nation. Pilots then could navigate by following the beams, receiving weather information wherever they might fly.

After 1930, then, airmen could gain unprecedented advantages: two-way communications, weather reports, blind flying, all-weather navigation, along with air traffic control services near major airports. Nor were they optional; in 1932 the Commerce Department introduced pilot ratings that required proficiency in instrument flying and in navigating by radio. Yet with all these responsibilities crowding in on him, a flier could begin to resemble a juggler with too many balls in the air. How could he fly his plane, navigate, read a map, listen to the radio, and watch his instruments, particularly at the end of a long and fatiguing flight?

Again Sperry Gyroscope came to the rescue, with the first successful automatic pilot. It was a direct descendant of the gyrostabilizer of 1914.

That item of equipment had languished, and part of the reason had been that pilots expected to fly their planes themselves, rather than trust to a robot. But with their workloads increasing, aviators now could see real value in this robot, for it would amount to an extra man in the cockpit. Elmer Sperry Jr. took the lead in managing its development, and he carried it through.

A key problem lay in a gyro's tendency to drift. A gyro's spinning rotor was no delicate wheel as in a wristwatch; it had mass and heft. It needed pivots that could support this weight, and these pivots transmitted frictional forces to the rotor, causing it to shift position. In an autopilot, this could bring disaster. When a gyro drifted, it acted as if it still was properly aligned and responding to unwanted aircraft movements. It would cheerfully actuate the ailerons and other controls, flipping the plane onto its side or sending it into the ground without considering that it was wrong.

Hence it was essential to align the gyros continuously while in flight. The solution, ironically, lay with pendulums, which had proven worse than useless when used alone as a turn indicator. This defect now became an advantage, for the autopilot's pendulums would move only in response to gyro drift. This motion brought a corrective measure that restored the gyro to its appropriate alignment.

In 1933 this work received a powerful boost from the aviator Wiley Post, who was preparing to fly around the world alone. He visited the Sperry factory, saw a prototype of the autopilot, and insisted on having it installed in his plane, *Winnie Mae.* He went on to complete his flight in only eight days, and the autopilot was a mainstay. It took over the controls while he was navigating; it even allowed him to snooze while in flight. During 1934 it began to see use in airliners. It still lacked the accuracy to keep a plane on course for hours at a time. But it was just the thing when a pilot wanted to take a break for ten or fifteen minutes.

These commercial aircraft had to meet regular schedules regardless of clouds or fog en route, while carrying grandmothers and babies. The fact that they did this, by relying on instruments, shows that by the mid 1930s the problem of blind flight had reached a definitive solution. Then, following World War II, these efforts branched off in new directions.

The first involved landing approaches in poor visibility. Doolittle had made true blind landings, but only by trusting to the strength of his undercarriage. Postwar aircraft were too heavy to use his simple technique of blindly following a sloping approach path. However, it was very rare for visibility at an airfield to be truly zero. Usually the clouds were at least a few hundred feet up, even when it was raining. Radio offered a means to guide a plane through the murk, until a pilot could break into the clear and see the runway close ahead. He then could land in the usual fashion, relying on his eyes.

The arrangement that permitted this was the Instrument Landing System (ILS). In contrast to the low-frequency transmissions of the 1920s, ILS used high-frequency radio. Its transmissions indeed formed true beams, through the use of specialized antennas. One beam marked the glide slope for landing approaches, pointing above the horizon at a gentle angle. A second beam showed the direction to the airport.

ILS caught on quickly after the war. An early supporter was Tom Braniff, whose Braniff Airways was a rising force within Texas and the Midwest. His planes began using ILS in May 1947, with an early test taking place at San Antonio. The airport had a standard low-frequency radio range for instrument approaches, certified for a minimum ceiling of four hundred feet. The clouds were just below that level, and a DC-4, not equipped with an ILS receiver, had a pilot who wanted to land. San Antonio's ILS system was certified for a three-hundred-foot ceiling, and that made the difference.

A Braniff DC-3 approached, and flew in to land without delay. Its pilot later spoke of this: "The clouds were at almost exactly 300 feet, but we were able to get in. Shortly afterward, another Braniff DC-3 landed using the instrument approach. Its captain and I toasted ourselves at the airport lunch counter while the DC-4 crew raised Cain on the radio, wanting to know why we had been allowed to land."[5]

High-frequency radio, which gave the basis for ILS, also made it possible to overcome defects in the standard radio ranges used for navigation. Nick Komons, historian of the Federal Aviation Administration, has described them in vigorous and definite terms:

> The shortcomings of the four-course range were legion. Equipped with a loop antenna, it was an eccentric, unpredictable device highly sensitive to changing weather conditions, the rise and fall of the sun, the contour of the earth's surface, and the presence of conductive elements. As a result, phantom beams, shifting, bending, and multiple courses, signal reversals, static, and false cones of silence were an all-too-common part of flying by instruments in the 1930s. Coping with all the vagaries of this facility was hopeless. The facility could be refined and re-refined and still have serious shortcomings; they were intrinsic in the device.[6]

Chief among the problems was that the beams, or equisignal zones, often did not define fixed directions but broke up and wandered. One airline executive described them as "rotating ranges." The reason was that the loop antennas threw much of their signals skyward where they reflected off the ionosphere, particularly after the sun went down. These reflected transmissions then combined with those directly broadcast from the range stations, producing fluctuating areas of stronger signal that pushed the equisignal zones hither and yon. Nor was there much pattern in the wanderings; they depended on conditions in the upper atmosphere, which changed from one night to the next.

Other problems arose from the cone of silence, the zone of no signal that spread vertically from a transmitter in the shape of an inverted cone. It was an excellent waypoint marker because airmen could pick it up even at night and in bad weather. But if a plane was too low, it could miss the cone of silence entirely. There also were any number of vagaries within a radio receiver or its power supply, or in terrain surrounding a range transmitter, that might briefly interrupt a signal and produce a false cone of silence.

The cure involved nothing less than the outright replacement of the four-course ranges. The new system was Very-high-frequency Omnidirectional Range (VOR). It introduced transmitting stations that made it possible for a navigator to determine bearing or direction from a transmitter. Several such bearings, taken from VOR stations having known locations, yielded the position of the plane. A refinement of VOR added distance-measuring equipment, which placed a transponder or radio-return generator at individual VOR stations. A navigator then could bounce a radio pulse off the station; his equipment measured the signal's time of flight, thus determining his distance. Each VOR station then gave determinations of range as well as bearing.

VOR won quick support because it offered static-free reception through its use of high frequencies. The first hundred transmitters were in place by the end of 1947; the number approached four hundred by 1950. In that year the Civil Aeronautics Administration (CAA) began to designate specialized airways that were marked for VOR navigation. Pilots used individual stations as waypoints, flying from one to another and then on to the next one. In this connect-the-dots fashion, they could fly from coast to coast. A typical route, marked on a map, looked as if it ran from city to city, like a railroad. However, a VOR station was no larger than a small single-story house, with an antenna on the roof in the shape of a cone. Most of them were located in remote country. Pilots could not see them as if they were mountains or towns; they were visible only through their radio transmissions.

Radar, another postwar innovation, changed the very basis of flight on instruments. Since the earliest days of flight, pilots had followed the rule of see-and-be-seen, looking out for other aircraft in the fashion of motorists on a freeway. Flight at high altitude, well above the clouds, made this particularly easy at first. After 1955, people looked ahead to jet airliners that were to cruise at thirty-five thousand feet, in visual conditions par excellence.

Yet to knowledgeable specialists, this prospect was a thing of horror. With their high speeds, jetliners in no way would resemble cars on a turnpike. They would be more like the racers of Bonneville Salt Flats in Utah, which demand twenty miles of clear surface. The reason was that a jet pilot could no longer see another plane in time to avoid a collision. By the time he saw the other fellow, it would already be too late.

The CAA had a solution: positive control. Under this arrangement, airliners no longer would enter the air at will, to fly as their captains might wish. Instead they were to fly under the watchful eyes of ground controllers, who would follow them on radar and issue directives. In 1958 the CAA took the first step, marking out three transcontinental routes that featured positive control. Within them, visual flight was illegal. Over the next decade, as the use of radar expanded, positive control spread as well. It encompassed the whole of domestic airspace at airliner cruising altitudes, along with the low-altitude space near airports.

With positive control, aviation made a complete turnabout from its early beginnings. During the 1920s pilots had pressed on through clouds and fog, lacking instruments but trusting the seat of their pants. But positive control meant that aircraft would fly without visual references, even in clear weather. Indeed, they would be barred from the skies unless they carried appropriate equipment. Cockpit displays now meant everything. Flight crews still would look through the windshield during takeoffs and landings. But in the air, the outside world now was useful only for sightseeing.

Donald Douglas and His Airliners

10

Shortly after World War I, a planebuilder named Inglis Uppercu launched an airline. He started with a couple of leftover twin-engine flying boats that he had constructed for the U.S. Navy, and cast his eyes on Cuba and the Bahamas. Prohibition was about to go into force in the States, but these islands offered rum aplenty, along with much else. There was no shortage of boat service to these destinations, but Uppercu thought that some party animals would want to use his planes to get to their watering holes more quickly.

He began his operations late in 1919, flying from Miami to Bimini and from Key West to Havana. Soon he was going from strength to strength: winning an airmail contract for service to Cuba, buying back a dozen of his naval flying boats at one-third of cost, and adding new routes. He initiated a service down the East Coast from New York; travelers called it the Highball Express. He scheduled flights to Nassau during the winter tourist season, then moved some planes northward for the summer to offer a route from Detroit to Cleveland across Lake Erie. Bypassing Toledo, this cut a five-hour run by train to ninety minutes.

Then two accidents dampened his prospects. Another operator's flying boat came down in the Gulf Stream with engine trouble, and it was three days before rescuers arrived. By then only the pilot was still alive. He told a lurid tale of how his five passengers weakened slowly in the hot sun, one by one slipping from the aircraft to their deaths. Soon after, one of Uppercu's planes made a similar forced landing off Havana. It cost the lives of four people, including two children.

Traffic fell off rapidly, and Uppercu tried to get a bank loan to tide him over. He failed, declaring that "you cannot get one nickel for commercial flying." He had carried some 30,000 passengers in the course of four years, but in 1923 his airline went out of business. He had fallen afoul of a simple fact: the nation didn't need airlines and had little use for them.

For well over half a century, Americans had been traveling by train. The railroads had a quarter million miles of right-of-way in service, and offered both comfort and speed. Airplanes were faster, but not by much, and train stations were located downtown, where they offered particular convenience. Overwater routes such as Uppercu's provided modest opportunity for aeronautical entrepreneurs, but there weren't many of them, for the United States spanned the map as a solid continental mass. In addition, aircraft had a well-deserved reputation for being unsafe. As Uppercu learned to his chagrin, only a couple of well-publicized accidents could spook the traveling public and drive an airline into bankruptcy.

Nevertheless, it took less than a decade for airlines to emerge as going concerns. The Post Office led the way with its airmail routes, initially owning its aircraft and hiring the pilots. However, this smacked of socialism; it presaged a future wherein aviation would develop as a federal program. The Republicans in Washington would have none of this, and in 1925 they had Congress pass the Contract Air Mail Act. It provided that the nation's airmail routes were to go over to commercial carriers, which would serve particular connections under contract.

These carriers were not major enterprises with coast-to-coast service, such as the future TWA or American Airlines. They were more like Robertson Aircraft Corporation, which carried the mail from St. Louis to Chicago, numbering Lindbergh as one of its pilots. Even so, with airmail providing a steady source of revenue, this law encouraged the growth of start-up airlines that had considerably better prospects than those of Uppercu. These start-ups carried mail, not passengers; if they indeed carried paying travelers, it was merely as a sideline. But they provided day-by-day scheduled flights along marked routes, thereby laying groundwork for the passenger lines of subsequent years.

True airliners also entered the picture, with a Dutch planebuilder, Anthony Fokker, in the forefront. He was a streak of brilliance, setting up an airplane company in Germany as early as 1912, when he was not yet twenty-two years old. The Red Baron flew his fighter planes in combat. Then, after the war, Fokker turned his attention to the civilian world and built an eight-passenger airliner in 1924. By hanging two more engines below its wings, he converted into a trimotor. By then the automaker Henry Ford was showing an active interest in aviation, and his son Edsel bought this plane to carry the explorer Richard Byrd on a 1926 flight to the Arctic.

Ford had a chief engineer, William Mayo, who believed he could improve on existing designs. His work was just getting under way when Byrd flew in with his Fokker. Ford's people greeted him warmly and put his plane in a hangar for the night. Then, through the night, Mayo's staffers proceeded to make detailed measurements of the airplane, particularly of its wing. Only a few people knew about this, but those who knew were hardly surprised when the new Ford Tri-Motor proved to show a remarkable resemblance to Fokker's configuration.

This plane, the Tin Goose, entered service in the summer of 1926. It was built of aluminum, with a corrugated skin covering the fuselage and wings; this contrasted with Fokker's craft, which was of plywood. The Ford plane came in fourteen- and sixteen-seat versions. It was unattractive in appearance, with boxy lines and engines hanging in the open air. But it succeeded in the market, and spurred Fokker to build production trimotors of similar design.

The new airliners came along at a timely moment, for Lindbergh's flight to Paris touched off an aviation boom. In 1926, prior to his flight, only 5,800 people took to the air. A year later, at the time of his flight, the nation had only thirty aircraft that could even count as airliners, offering no more than two hundred seats. But in 1930, even with the Depression under way, the number of passengers soared to 417,000.

Railroads nevertheless continued to dominate; in that latter year they carried over 700 million travelers. Aviation occupied no more than a tiny niche, for while airline tickets cost more than first-class rail service (and vastly more than coach), the experience of flight was something that many people were glad to avoid. Trains offered a smooth ride along with the comforting familiarity of a locomotive's whistle and of cars that went clickety-clack over the rails. Airliners, by contrast, were harsh, noisy, and wearying.

Their cabins lacked soundproofing. This meant that passengers heard the roar of a trimotor's engines in stereo, one on each side as they blared at full volume. The engine in the nose transmitted its cacophony directly into the cabin. Propellers added their own noise, while the motors produced vibration as well, which passengers could not avoid. One traveler spoke for many others when he declared that "when the day was over my bones ached, and my whole nervous system was wearied from the noise, the constant droning of the propellers and exhaust."

Airsickness added further discomfort. The planes of the day had no hope of flying in smooth air above the weather; they flew right through it, turbulence and all. Passengers often became nauseous and threw up, even if they had not eaten the airline's food. The aircraft helpfully provided "erp cups," cardboard containers that a passenger could retrieve from a pocket in the seat directly in front. Some airliners also had windows that opened, allowing passengers to heave away. But if you stuck your head out to do this, you might find someone a few seats ahead with the same idea, and you could receive his blast right in your own face. Some people simply vomited on the floor; after a landing, planes often were hosed out.

In addition, the system of federal payments strongly encouraged airlines to carry mail, not passengers. The government offered up to $3.00 per pound, or $0.19 per ounce. Beginning in 1928, airmail postage came to $0.05 per ounce. An enterprising carrier thus could lay out a nickel per ounce of his own money and receive a clear profit of as much as $0.14 from Washington. Pilots thus had complete freedom to fill their mail compartments with telephone books, bricks, lead bars, even cast-iron stoves.

Passenger fares couldn't compete. In 1927 it cost $150 to fly from New York to Chicago, which was quite high. If a man and his luggage weighed two hundred pounds, that weight in mail would fetch up to $600, which was several months' wages for a typical worker. The system of mail payments also discouraged technical innovation. New designs carried risk, and existing aircraft were profitable enough. Their owners could make them even more so by tossing in a few more postage-paid lead weights.

A new postmaster general, Walter Brown, viewed these arrangements as an open invitation to abuse, and demanded reform. He particularly wanted to scrap the payments by weight and instead to pay the carriers by available space, offering up to $1.25 per mile. Airlines would qualify for the highest rates by flying the largest airplanes. This would encourage them to supplement their federal subsidy by using the extra space for passengers. Brown achieved this change with the McNary-Watres Act of 1930. When this act became law, the aviation industry found itself in a new realm, where existing rules no longer applied and where new and large airliners were suddenly in demand.

Brown wanted more. He regarded the existing system of airlines as an uncoordinated hodgepodge, which he expected to consolidate into a few strong carriers. Everyone still depended on mail for most of their corporate revenue, and Brown held the power to award routes and contracts. Indeed, the McNary-Watres Act strengthened his hand. He now not only could pick and choose among existing carriers; he could force mergers, enlarging strong companies while forcing weak ones to join the combinations that held his favor.

He wanted three coast-to-coast routes: a northern, a central, and a southern, each to be served by a single airline. The northern consortium took shape at about the time the Watres Act became law, featuring United Aircraft and Transport, an outfit owned by Boeing. Its routes extended from San Francisco to Chicago, connecting with National Air Transport for flights to New York. A Boeing man, Fred Rentschler, pushed through a buyout of National by purchasing a controlling interest in its stock. With this, Boeing's airline spanned the continent, holding airmail contracts every mile of the way. It took the name United Airlines.

Brown assembled the rest of his route map by exercising his newly granted legal powers. To create his central route, he forced a shotgun marriage between Transcontinental Air Transport and Western Air Express. This union gave rise to TWA. For the southern route, Brown used an existing firm, American Airways, as a nucleus. He arranged for this company to buy out three of its competitors, thus forming American Airlines. He also granted his favor to the nascent Eastern Airlines, which ran between New York and the vacationlands of Florida.

The nation now had four powerful carriers: United, TWA, American, and Eastern. They all had plenty of incentive to purchase new aircraft that could emphasize passenger service, and they had the financial clout to order them in substantial numbers. Boeing, joined at the hip to United Airlines, made the first move. During 1930 and 1931 its designers crafted the B-9 bomber, introducing the speedy twin-engine arrangement that soon became standard with the airlines. Its use of two rather than three engines was quite deliberate, for aircraft motors were increasing in power. Trimotors had offered safety, with three being better than two. But the new engines had enough horsepower to allow an airplane to fly safely with only one, if the other failed.

Late in 1931, Boeing brought a new look to aviation as its engineers started working on a twin-engine airliner, the Boeing 247. Only about six years had elapsed since the advent of the Ford Tri-Motor, but that was enough to bring sweeping change. The Tri-Motor had a boxy fuselage covered with corrugated aluminum; struts supported both the engines and landing gear. It made few concessions to streamlining; its wheels, struts, and engine cylinders hung in open air, and its speed was only slightly above a hundred miles per hour.

The 247 was different. Even to the modern eye, it *looks* like an airliner. It had a smoothly curving fuselage, nicely streamlined, with retractable landing gear. It lacked all trace of struts, while mounting each engine in a drag-reducing housing set within the wing. It carried ten passengers and cruised at 155 miles per hour.

It also made some headway in ameliorating some of the worst discomforts of flight. American Airlines gave each passenger a travel kit that contained chewing gum to equalize pressure on the ears during takeoff and landing, cotton to plug the ears against the noise, and ammonia to sniff when airsickness hit. The 247 did little against airsickness, other than flying faster to get people to their destinations more rapidly. But it did considerably more against noise and vibration.

An acoustics specialist, Stephen Zand, had begun to install soundproofing in airliners, which certainly needed them. With its nose-mounted engine and propeller blasting their cacophony directly into the passenger cabin, the Ford Tri-Motor reached 117 decibels, putting it on a par with a jackhammer. Even a boiler factory was quieter. The 247 dispensed with this front installation, receiving noise only from its wing-mounted engines, and Zand's acoustic-absorbing layers went far to muffle them as well. He reduced the interior level below 85 decibels, putting it on a par with heavy traffic in midtown Manhattan. Though loud, this was considerably more bearable.

The 247 certainly did not offer the gentle rustle of a library, but nevertheless was well below the threshold of pain. In addition, it diminished vibration with well-upholstered seats, which gave a considerable improvement over the unpadded wicker of a Tri-Motor. The problem of vibration did not go away; it remained a source of discomfort until the advent of the jets, a quarter century later. But the 247 was the first design to make headway.

The union between Boeing and United was quite cozy, and officials soon declared that the Seattle planebuilder would assemble sixty of these aircraft for United's exclusive use. This promised to give that carrier a major advantage over its competitors, which would have to wait two or three years before they could begin to receive their own deliveries. This was bad news for TWA, which relied on Anthony Fokker as its own planebuilder and which flew both Fokker and Ford Tri-Motors. The former was already in public disfavor, for a Fokker had crashed in 1931, killing the Notre Dame football coach Knute Rockne. The 247 now promised to make such craft obsolete as well.

This airline needed new planes of its own, and needed them soon. Jack Frye, a TWA vice president, set out to address this need by soliciting designs from several planebuilding firms. One of them was Fokker's own company, General Aviation. Another was a well-connected firm in Santa Monica, California, that carried the name of its founder: Donald Douglas.

He was from Brooklyn, where his father was a cashier in a Wall Street bank. He developed an early love of sailing, and followed an older brother by winning admission to the U.S. Naval Academy. But he also had witnessed flights by both the Wright brothers and the aeronautical pioneer Glenn Curtiss, and in time he decided that naval discipline was not to his liking. He dropped out and transferred to MIT, even though this meant throwing away his Annapolis credits and starting over as a freshman. An MIT engineering degree required four years, but he vowed to do it in two. He did, and graduated with distinction.

While at MIT, he fell in with Professor Jerome Hunsaker, a leader in aviation who introduced that university's first aeronautical courses. Douglas received his bachelor's degree in 1914, and stayed on to work as Hunsaker's assistant. A year later the planebuilder Glenn L. Martin lost his best designer and wrote to Hunsaker, asking him to recommend a replacement. Hunsaker recommended Douglas, who soon was heading to Los Angeles. Martin was startled at his youth—he was only twenty-three—but nevertheless hired him as chief engineer.

He took a leave of absence late in 1916 and went to Washington, working with the Army's Signal Corps. This experience also contributed to his education, for he learned about federal paperwork and its attendant delays, and left Washington a year later out of exasperation. Martin was glad to take him back, for by then the nation was in the war. Douglas quickly became involved with a twin-engine bomber, the Martin MB-1, which offered longer range and heavier bombload than existing British and French designs. Drawing on his Washington contacts, Douglas helped Martin win a production contract for these aircraft.

He had been working in Cleveland, but in 1920 he returned to Los Angeles, hoping to start his own aircraft company. The aviation industry was in a deep postwar slump, and Douglas had only a few hundred dollars to tide him over. But he arrived with a letter of introduction in hand, and set up an office in a barber shop on Pico Boulevard. He needed a financial angel, and found his man in David Davis, who wanted to become the first to fly nonstop from coast to coast. Davis staked him to $40,000, with the two men forming a partnership.

They rented a loft above a planing mill. Douglas recruited several of his associates from Martin, who worked with him as they crafted a plane called the Cloudster. It became the first to carry a load greater than its empty weight. Davis, along with Douglas's test pilot, then attempted the transcontinental flight in June 1921. They didn't make it; the engine quit and forced them to land near El Paso. Before they were ready to try again, two Army pilots beat them to it. Davis then lost interest, while the Cloudster ended its days flying beer to Tijuana. Still, it gave Douglas a basis for his later work.

His old friend Hunsaker had influence within the Navy, and rescued Douglas by giving him a contract to build three torpedo planes. With this support in hand, he won backing from other Los Angeles investors and moved to larger quarters within a converted movie studio on Wilshire Boulevard. These three aircraft amounted to prototypes; the Navy liked them, and ordered thirty-eight more.

Then the Army became interested. General Billy Mitchell wanted to dramatize the potential reach of air power by sending several aircraft on a flight around the world, even though they were to do this in a number of short hops. Douglas's torpedo-plane design had drawn on the heavy-lifting features of the Cloudster, and proved quite suitable for Mitchell's mission. The company modified several of these Navy planes, fitting them with particularly large fuel tanks, and christened them the Douglas World Cruisers. Four of them set out from Seattle in April 1924; two of them returned, late in September. After that, Douglas had no trouble in winning further military orders.

The company expanded anew, building a large manufacturing plant that adjoined the Santa Monica airport. Douglas renewed his old love of the sea as he purchased a sailing yacht, named *Cloudster*. The onset of the Depression brought little pain, for the company remained in good favor with the Army and Navy. It continued to pile up profits, which it paid out as dividends on its stock.

This ongoing success, along with Douglas's own shrewd eye for talent, enabled him to assemble a group of senior engineers that was without peer. It included John Northrop and Jerry Vultee, both of whom went on to found major planebuilding firms of their own. James "Dutch" Kindelberger and Lee Atwood, who also worked for Douglas, in time became president and chairman of North American Aviation. Frank Collbohm stayed with Douglas and founded the Rand Corporation, which provided high-level technical counsel to the Air Force and the CIA. Ed Heinemann, another Douglas designer, crafted dive bombers that won the Battle of Midway. Arthur Raymond showed similar leadership in creating the company's airliners, which ruled the skies for decades.

These airliners grew out of Jack Frye's letter, which arrived when the Boeing 247 still was months away from its first flight:[1]

August 2, 1932

Dear Mr. Douglas:

Transcontinental & Western Air is interested in purchasing ten or more trimotored transport planes. I am attaching our general performance specifications, covering this equipment and would appreciate your advising whether your Company is interested in this manufacturing job.

If so, approximately how long would it take to turn out the first plane for service tests?

Very truly yours,
Jack Frye

The attached page stated, "All metal trimotored monoplane preferred but combination structure or biplane would be considered." TWA's interest in trimotors reflected customer preference; people still liked the assurance of having extra engines if one were to quit. Biplanes also were still in service; one of them, the Curtiss Condor, had been the first to receive the soundproofing of Stephen Zand. But the 247, looming over the field of airplane design, now was redefining what it would mean to build a suitable airliner.

Frye's specifications called for "three engines of 500 to 550 h.p." However, Douglas and his associates were aware that more powerful engines were about to become available, making possible a twin-engine design that could match and even improve on the 247. They responded swiftly to Frye's letter; within days, Raymond boarded a train for New York, accompanied by the company's comptroller. They expected to discuss the terms of a contract, but when the conductor called "All aboard," Raymond did not even have a design concept in hand. He prepared his proposal during the trip east. Frye's specifications had called merely for "complete instruments, night flying equipment," along with "the usual miscellaneous equipment carried on a passenger plane of this type." But Raymond, responding to TWA's requirements, filled five pads of paper with handwritten notes before his train pulled into Penn Station.

The plane that resulted was the DC-1, the Douglas Commercial. Raymond's plans called for it to go the 247 one better, or rather two better, for it was to carry twelve passengers to the 247's ten. This followed Frye's requirements. It also proved wise in its own right, for the 247 entered service with United during the spring of 1933 and quickly showed that it was the plane to beat.

TWA had been providing coast-to-coast service using Ford Tri-Motors. Flight time was twenty-seven hours, with fourteen refueling stops. The 247 introduced both higher speed and longer range, cutting the flight time to twenty hours while reducing the number of intermediate stops to six. For the important New York-Chicago run, United offered departures at convenient times throughout the day, with a single stop in Cleveland.

Nevertheless, the 247 held this monopoly for only a single good year. TWA officials ordered twenty-five of the competing Douglas airliners, and Donald Douglas modified the design to make it even more attractive as a moneymaker. He did this by lengthening the fuselage by three feet, providing room for two more seats and thus boosting the plane's capacity by one-sixth. Those additional seats represented revenue for TWA and other airlines, with little increase in operating expense. This stretched version took the name DC-2, and was the one that went into production.

The first of them entered service with TWA in May 1934, and soon beat the 247 at its own game. It repeatedly set speed records from Newark to Chicago, while its longer range allowed TWA to introduce nonstop service on that route. This became the first leg of an eighteen-hour schedule to the West Coast, with only the two additional stops of Kansas City and Albuquerque. In addition, the DC-2 made it possible to work past lunchtime in Manhattan, fly out of Newark, and arrive in Los Angeles early on the following morning. TWA did this with its "Sky Chief" service, which departed at four in the afternoon and arrived at 7 A.M. the next day.

Even so, it was one thing for a stouthearted man to fly such a schedule and hope to do some effective work during the morning of his arrival. It was something else to try to get some sleep along the way. Soundproofing helped, and the comfortably padded seats stood in rubber mountings that helped further to reduce vibration. But the nausea of airsickness was as bad as ever, and airline food did little to help. Hot food was rare. Passengers subsisted on chicken salad, sandwiches such as cheese and egg salad, and, all too often, cold pickles.

C. R. Smith, president of American Airlines, was a strong advocate of making it possible for people to sleep in flight, in spite of the distractions. Railroads offered this service with their Pullman cars, and Smith had some of his airliners fitted out as sleepers, with berths that folded down. He started with the Curtiss Condor, which provided fifteen such beds but needed a tailwind to reach 120 miles per hour. He ordered his own DC-2s, which were much faster. But he found that the only way he could maintain his sleeper service was to fly them during the day and have their passengers transfer into Condors for the night.

The standard DC-2 was not well suited for use as a sleeper; its fuselage was too narrow to provide an adequate number of berths. But Smith saw that if he could get Douglas to widen the fuselage, it would accommodate fourteen sleeping passengers. Better still, such an airliner would carry twenty-one people in seats—and the revenue from their tickets promised a tempting increase in operating income. Smith broached the idea to Douglas in a two-hour phone conversation, offering to buy twenty of the new planes sight unseen. They took shape as the DC-3.

It launched its career in June 1936, flying from Chicago to Newark and breaking the four-hour mark with help from a tailwind. With this, American introduced its "Flagship" nonstop service between these cities, then went on to fly the DC-3 from coast to coast. TWA ordered its own DC-3s, complementing its earlier DC-2s, and other airlines quickly followed suit.

The new airliner offered undeniable advantages. The DC-2 had retractable landing gear, but the copilot had to pump the wheels up and down by hand. This called for brute strength, particularly when the mechanism froze in winter. It also had a way of jolting badly on landing. The DC-3 introduced hydraulics to retract the landing gear, along with better shock absorbers. Douglas also took the opportunity to introduce improvements in its adjustable propellers.

Better food also accompanied the DC-3. United Airlines took a while to receive them and put them into service, and its president, "Pat" Patterson, set out to attract the crowds by offering improved cuisine. He hired Don Magarrell, who had managed the menu on the liner *Leviathan,* and who soon invented airline food as we have known it ever since. An in-flight meal included a main dish, coffee with cream and sugar, salad in a paper cup, and dessert. Hot food came aboard in Jumbo Jars, thermos bottles two feet tall. American Airlines was already using them, serving stew, hamburgers, and on good days, steak or baked chicken. It wasn't the *Leviathan,* but it was a lot better than the cold pickles of earlier years.

Airlines rushed to purchase DC-3s, and it wasn't because of the landing gear and the Jumbo Jars. What made the difference was the operating economics. An airline paid about $800 to fly a DC-3 between Chicago and New York. This was only slightly more than the cost of a DC-2 over the same route, but with its additional seats, the DC-3 spread this expense over a substantially larger number of purchased tickets. This permitted lower fares.

"The DC-3 freed the airlines from complete dependence on mail pay," declared C. R. Smith. "It was the first airplane that could make money just by hauling passengers." It did this not only with its additional seats, but with high speed that enabled it to fly more miles during a day. It also cut the cost of maintenance. Like the DC-2 and the Boeing 247, it had only two engines compared to three in the trimotors, which meant much less machinery to care for. Moreover, the engines of the DC-3 had quick disconnects for easy removal and installation. A mechanic could replace a motor in only two hours. This helped the

DC-3 to spend less time on the ground and more time in the air, where it earned its money.

Although passenger service got its start amid the boom of the 1920s, the airlines truly came into their own during the Great Depression of the 1930s. During that decade, the number of travelers soared from 417,000 to 3 million. Much of this increase stemmed from the plummeting cost per passenger-mile, which plunged from 12.0 cents in 1929 to 5.1 cents in 1939. The DC-3 accounted for nearly all of this traffic, as it drove the competition from the skies. By 1939 some 75 percent of the nation's air travelers were flying in the DC-3; over 90 percent were in either that airliner or the DC-2. Together, these aircraft did far more than merely draw away the existing clientele. They generated much of the demand that they went on to serve.

Earlier designs had held well-deserved reputations for fragility. Knute Rockne's Fokker Tri-Motor, for one, had come apart in midair because it was made of wood; its glued joints had failed to hold. But experience in China showed that there was virtually no limit to what the Douglas airliners could withstand. One DC-2 ditched in a river and sank, after being badly shot up by Japanese fighters. Its owners fished it out of the water and returned it to service. A DC-3 had a wing blown off when attacked on the ground. No replacement wing was available, but it proved possible to mount a DC-2 wing, even though it was several feet shorter. The plane that resulted, called the DC-2½, flew successfully to Hong Kong, where it received its proper wing.

During the war, over ten thousand of the military version, the C-47, saw use. Their simplicity and rugged construction allowed them to operate in battle zones, carrying supplies, dropping paratroopers, evacuating wounded men. They had been built for a commercial world that often used grassy fields for want of paved runways; this allowed them to fly in and out of the hastily built airstrips that marked the Allies' advance. General Dwight Eisenhower placed these aircraft among the items of equipment that did the most to win the war, ranking them with the bulldozer, the jeep, the two-and-a-half-ton truck, and the amphibious armored "duck."

After the war, the nation found itself awash in used DC-3s. The armed services had no further need for them and willingly sold these surplus aircraft for as little as $25,000, payable at only a few hundred dollars per month. This made it easy for entrepreneurs to buy some, convert them to civilian use, and start a new airline. Newspaper stories told of wondrous four-engine planes, the DC-6 and Lockheed Constellation, that could cross the nation in a single leap. But airline executives were well aware that most routes had lengths measured in hundreds rather than thousands of miles, and on these, the DC-3 continued to shine. As late as 1958, on the eve of the jetliner, the DC-3 existed in larger numbers within the domestic fleet than any other type.

These planes also played starring roles during the Berlin airlift. That city lay deep within Communist-ruled East Germany, relying for its supplies on canals, a single rail line, and one highway. In June 1948, in a brutal ploy aimed at forcing the Allies out of West Berlin, the Soviet dictator Joseph Stalin blocked these routes of surface access. The city lay isolated, holding stocks of food sufficient only for a month, and of coal only for six weeks.

Two and a half million people lived within the blockaded areas, cut off from the fifteen thousand tons of goods they had been receiving daily. The Allies had held rights of access under international agreement, but if they were to attempt to enforce these rights by sending supplies under armed escort, the superior armed strength of the Soviets would bring their defeat. Still, the airways remained open, for Stalin knew that if he shot down American planes, that would bring war.

An airlift would at least boost West Berlin's morale; it might even supplement the available stocks. Yet no one had ever tried anything remotely on a par with supplying a large city entirely by air. West Berlin didn't need its full 15,000 daily tons, but it required at least 1,400 tons of food per day along with 2,000 tons of coal and kerosene in the summer, rising to 3,100 tons in winter. The U.S. Air Force had gained valuable experience during the war by running C-46 cargo planes from India to China. At the peak, in July 1945, that aerial supply line had delivered 71,400 tons—and the buildup to that level had taken three years. A truly successful Berlin airlift would have to aim for a hundred thousand tons per month and get there in weeks, not years, then rise again to double the China rate by winter.

General Lucius Clay, the U.S. military governor, looked at these requirements and did not flinch. On the day after the blockade began, he phoned General Curtis LeMay, the Air Force's senior commander in Europe. "Curt," he asked, "do you have any planes that fly coal?" LeMay was taken aback but responded immediately: "The Air Force can deliver anything."

LeMay had a hundred C-47s within Europe, and set the first of them to work on the next day. They carried eighty tons in thirty-two flights. The tonnage rose as the blockade continued into July, but everyone knew that the C-47 was inadequate, for it could carry no more than three tons. The plane that just might do the job was the C-54, with a ten-ton capacity. If these heavy-duty cargo aircraft could land in Berlin

C-47 cargo planes unload goods at Tempelhof Airport early in the Berlin airlift.
(U.S. Air Force)

at the rate of one every three minutes, around the clock, then the Air Force indeed could meet the city's minimum needs—barely.

The C-54 was a war baby. It had started its life as the DC-4, another Douglas creation that represented his first leap into the realm of four-engine design. Intended initially for civilian service, it made its first flight in February 1942, two months after Pearl Harbor, and promptly enlisted for the duration. The Army purchased over a thousand of them and used them to complement the C-47, for the C-54 had the range to cross the Atlantic. After the war, many of them became surplus as well, selling for as little as $90,000. But the Air Force held on to several hundred of them.

Just then, in mid 1948, they were scattered around the world: in Hawaii, Alaska, Japan, Guam, the Panama Canal Zone, and the continental United States. Many of them now were reassigned for use with the Berlin airlift, but it took time for them to arrive, and meanwhile the C-47s held the fort. Late in July, a month into the blockade, the daily tonnage was up to seventeen hundred, half the city's minimum summer requirement. During August, with more C-54s on hand, the tonnage soared anew. On August 12, the total reached forty-seven hundred tons, topping the winter requirement for the first time.

This speedup reflected new leadership as well. At the end of July, General LeMay turned the airlift over to a new commander, General William Tunner, who had shaped the wartime cargo lift over the Himalayas. Tunner cut time on the ground by arranging for mobile units to meet flight crews and provide them with coffee, paperwork, orders, and weather information. He set up a maintenance center in Bavaria; he installed radio navigation aids powered by generators on trucks. He broke ground for a new airport within the city, while building additional runways at the two existing airfields. As C-54s continued to arrive, he phased out the C-47s, which went out of service in October.

His pilots had to fly at night and in foul weather, and he ordered them all to fly on instruments, even in clear daylight. For landings in fog, he brought in Ground Controlled Approach, with ground controllers watching incoming aircraft on radar and issuing directions by radio. He gave each flight crew only one chance at a landing; if they missed, they had to return immediately to their home base. This gave each plane a clear slot, with no need to worry about the heavy air traffic.

German coal was a crumbly brown lignite, packed in surplus military duffel bags. It produced dust that fouled instruments, created electrical short circuits, gummed up hydraulic fluid, and wore away at aircraft control cables. Flour, leaking from its own bags, did the same. Aircrews learned to vacuum out the dust by running a wide hose from the cabin into the aircraft's slipstream. They did not eliminate the dust, but they made the problem more manageable.

The British joined the effort, bringing in flying boats. These had been built to land on salt water; they carried bags of salt to the city, and resisted corrosion. The British also contributed additional air bases in Germany. By October the daily shipments were up to 5,600 tons, and General Tunner now ordered "the maximum tonnage possible." On a day in April 1949, he orchestrated an all-out effort that featured close to 1,400 flights—nearly one per minute—and close to 13,000 tons of coal. One of his colonels described this single-day effort as the equivalent of a dozen 50-car coal trains.

It was clear that West Berlin not only could hold out indefinitely, but could resume an increasingly normal life. Moreover, with summer approaching, the city's need for coal was decreasing even while the airborne tonnages continued to increase. Stalin saw that he had lost the game; on May 12 he lifted his blockade. The airlift nevertheless continued through September, just in case, with the cargoes now building stockpiles for use if Stalin were to change his mind. When it ended, it counted some 277,000 flights, with close to a ton of material delivered for each man, woman, and child in West Berlin.

Few industrial leaders can look at a map of a continent and say that their products have shaped its internal borders. Donald Douglas was one of the few, for his aircraft saved West Berlin. It flourished through the subsequent decades as an outpost of freedom and prosperity amid the gray servitude of Communism. Then, when the Berlins and the Germanys reunited, it was not through Stalinist brutality, but through the decisions of the Germans themselves. They did this in 1990, forty years after the airlift. In turn, that airlift succeeded because of Donald Douglas and his airliners.

PART 3

War

The Battle of Britain 11

"WHEN THE German Messerschmitt plane dives on your car with all four machine guns chattering," wrote Ernest Hemingway, "you swerve to the side of the road and jump out of the car. And when the plane comes back to try to kill you again, and his bullets throw dust spouts over your back, you lie with your mouth dry. But you laugh at the plane because you are alive. He thinks your car is a staff car and he has a right to kill you. He does not kill you so you laugh. The Messerschmitt is too fast for good ground strafing."[1]

Hemingway was in Spain in 1938, writing about its civil war. That war pitted the Nazi-backed Nationalists against the Republicans, and the Nazis won. They did it in part with the aircraft of the Luftwaffe, which drew blood for the first time. Their bombers struck Barcelona, and Hemingway wrote of "murdered children with their twisted legs, their arms that bend in wrong directions, and their plaster powdered faces." They raided Madrid for three days straight; the dead lay in the streets; a photo showed one man on his back with his mouth open. The Nazis also bombed Granollers, far from the war zone, along with Lérida, Alicante, and coastal towns near Valencia.

Guernica was the worst. In April 1937, air attacks struck that town with a hundred thousand tons of high explosive, reducing its buildings to gutted shells of broken masonry. The Germans used incendiaries as well; their air strikes killed some sixteen hundred people. "Of course it was bombed," said a Nationalist officer. "We bombed it and bombed it and bombed it and *bueno,* why not?"

The world saw more horror in September 1939, when Hitler unleashed his army against Poland. This was blitzkrieg, lightning war, with fighters and fighter-bombers ranging far ahead of the main force as they cleared the way for rapid advance of tanks. Hitler received help as well from Stalin, who struck at Poland from the east, trapping that nation between two fires. The war ended after only four weeks, with the two dictators dividing up the conquered land. Across

German-occupied Poland, a long night of death and slavery settled upon the people.

The turn of France came in May 1940. On paper the combatants appeared evenly matched: 136 German divisions, 135 for the armies of the French, British, Belgians, and Dutch. Again, though, the German blitzkrieg gave the critical advantage. Only five days after the start of the invasion, on May 15, the French premier Paul Reynaud phoned Prime Minister Winston Churchill and cried, "We have been defeated! We have been beaten!" German tanks had already gained a decisive break-through, cutting off much of the Allied force; they reached the English Channel less than a week later. Paris fell on June 14; within days, the French government accepted a humiliating capitulation. The swastika now flew atop the Eiffel Tower.

Hitler had already conquered Norway, Denmark, and the Low Countries. In the wake of the French surrender, he held absolute sway over a European empire that extended from Scandinavia's North Cape to the Mediterranean and from the Atlantic to the borders of the Soviet Union. His allies included Spain and Italy, ruled by their own fascist governments. The British stood alone.

Would they accept an armistice? Churchill had neither active allies nor an adequate supply of arms. Nevertheless, he mobilized the English language and sent it into battle. He stood repeatedly in the House of Commons and delivered perorations that the world will long remember:[2]

> Behind the armies and fleets of Britain and France gather a group of shattered states and bludgeoned races. The Czechs, the Poles, the Norwegians, the Danes, the Dutch, the Belgians—upon all of whom the long night of barbarism will descend, unbroken by a star of hope. Unless we conquer. As conquer we must. As conquer we shall.

May 13, on taking office as prime minister:

> I have nothing to offer but blood, toil, tears and sweat. We have before us an ordeal of the most grievous kind. We have before us many, many months of struggle and suffering.
>
> You ask, what is our policy? I say it is to wage war by land, sea and air. War with all our might and with all the strength God has given us, and to wage war against a monstrous tyranny never surpassed in the dark and lamentable catalogue of human crime. That is our policy.
>
> You ask, what is our aim? I can answer in one word. It is victory. Victory at all costs—victory in spite of all terrors—victory, however long and hard the road may be, for without victory there is no survival.

June 18, in his most memorable of speeches:

> What General Weygand has called the Battle of France is over. The Battle of Britain is about to begin. On this battle depends the survival of Christian civilization. The whole fury and might of the enemy must very soon be turned upon us. Hitler knows he will have to break us in this island or lose the war.
>
> If we can stand up to him, all Europe may be freed and the life of the world may move forward into broad sunlit uplands. But if we fail, then the whole world, including the United States, will sink into the abyss of a new Dark Age, made more sinister and perhaps more protracted by the lights of a perverted science.
>
> Let us therefore brace ourselves to our duties, and so bear ourselves that if the British Empire and its Commonwealth last for a thousand years, men will still say, "This was their finest hour."

Churchill reinforced his words with deeds. The French fleet included a number of highly capable ships. Some of them were or soon would be under British control, but others were about to go over to the Germans. A British admiral led a powerful task force to the French naval base at Oran and called on the French to surrender their warships. They refused and he opened fire, destroying a battleship and forcing two other major vessels to run aground. Another attack, a few days later, seriously damaged another battleship.

Germany had posed no threat with her surface force. At the outbreak of war, in 1939, commander in chief Admiral Erich Raeder had written that his navy was "in no way equipped for the great struggle with England." His surface warships were "so few and so weak" that they could "only show that they know how to die gallantly." They now were even weaker, for action off Norway had severely damaged two German battle cruisers and a battleship. In the war with England, Hitler had no fleet worthy of mention.

Air superiority was another matter. To invade Great Britain, the Germans had to land and supply a seaborne force of at least thirty well-equipped divisions. To do this, they had to assemble a major fleet of barges in French or Belgian harbors. These would offer tempting targets for the Royal Air Force (RAF), which also would have every encouragement to strike at German stocks of fuel and ammunition. The Luftwaffe faced the task of protecting this amphibious force, both during the buildup and during the Channel crossing and landing. If its warplanes could do this, if they could win and hold air superiority, then Hitler would have his invasion and his victory.

Clearly, the Luftwaffe could not concede the air to the RAF and then gain control of it with a sudden thrust. Nor could the RAF relax its vigilance; it had to make the largest possible effort from the beginning. The key to the Channel and to both its coasts was the air above them, and control of it could not be won or lost during the invasion itself. It had to be won beforehand, in a preliminary battle that would precede the main clash of arms.

This meant that for the first time in history, the fate of a nation would depend on the performance of its air force. For the first time, the armies of contending powers would stand aside as they awaited the outcome of the aerial conflict.

Late in July, on the eve of the battle, the Luftwaffe had over a thousand first-line fighters, with another 500 in reserve. The RAF, weakened by its losses in France, held only 625 in the first line and 230 in reserve. In addition to their numerical superiority, the Luftwaffe had the advantage of being able to concentrate its aircraft against specific targets. The RAF could not achieve such a concentration, for it had to provide air defense over much of the country.

Nevertheless, recent experience in France encouraged the British to believe that they could stave off the German aerial assault. While Hitler's army advanced upon the Channel coast, the British and some French had fallen back on the port of Dunkirk, standing there late in May with their backs to the sea. As German tanks and infantry closed in for the kill, Hermann Goering, commander of the Luftwaffe and a great favorite with Hitler, persuaded his Führer to issue an order calling for the army to halt in its tracks. Instead, the Luftwaffe was to gain the honor of finishing off the trapped Allied troops.

Two days passed, during which it became clear that Goering's airmen would do nothing of the sort. Indeed, they flew into a hornet's nest, as the RAF put up fierce opposition. Hitler then rescinded his order, allowing his ground forces to resume their advance, but by then it was too late. The British and French had formed a strong defensive perimeter around Dunkirk, allowing most of their forces to escape by sea.

This evacuation was remarkable, for while British officials initially had hoped to take off only 45,000 men in two days, they held their pocket for more than a week and brought out 338,000. Hundreds of small boats converged on the town, along with larger vessels that included destroyers. The Luftwaffe pressed its attacks, sinking over one-fourth of the 861 boats and ships that participated in the sealift. But as the RAF continued to provide air cover, the Germans found themselves unable either to shut down the port facilities or to prevent the rescuers from proceeding with their work.

Churchill, speaking in the Commons, warned his nation not to make too much of this, declaring that "wars are not won by evacuations." He nevertheless pointed out that the RAF had triumphed in "a great trial of strength between the British and German air forces. Can you conceive of a greater objective for the power of Germany in the air than to make all evacuations from these beaches impossible and to sink all of the ships? They tried hard and were beaten back."

In mid July, Hitler made his decision. He issued Directive No. 16, "Preparation of a Landing Operation Against England":

TOP SECRET

Fuehrer's Headquarters
July 16, 1940

Since England, despite her militarily hopeless situation, still shows no willingness to come to terms, I have decided to prepare a landing operation against England, and if necessary to carry it out.

The aim of this operation is to eliminate the English homeland as a base for carrying on of the war against Germany, and, if it should become necessary, to occupy it completely.[3]

On the following day, the Army High Command allocated forces for the invasion, which now held the name Operation Sea Lion. Field Marshal Gerd von Rundstedt, who had commanded the main thrust into France, was to do the same against England. Six infantry divisions would embark from the Pas de Calais to landing points located between Ramsgate and Bexhill. Four additional divisions were to depart from Le Havre for objectives located between Brighton and the Isle of Wight. Three other divisions were to leave the Cherbourg peninsula for Lyme Bay. These thirteen divisions, numbering ninety thousand men, would form the first wave. A second wave was to follow, bringing the total force to forty-one divisions, including six armored, three motorized, and two airborne.

As plans for Sea Lion developed, so did plans for the occupation. In September the army's commander in chief, Field Marshal Walther von Brauchitsch, signed an order directing that "the able-bodied male population between the ages of seventeen and forty-five" was to be rounded up and sent to the Continent. This was unprecedented. Even Poland, the most harshly handled of Hitler's conquests, had been spared such treatment; yet for Great Britain, this was to be merely a beginning. The Jews were marked for their own fate, and there was more.

The Gestapo had its own orders, which provided for the utter extirpation of British literary and intellectual life. This secret police force had a list of some twenty-three hundred writers and thinkers who were to be arrested at once. The list included Virginia Woolf, H. G. Wells, E. M. Forster, Aldous Huxley, C. P. Snow, Noël Coward, Rebecca West,

Norman Angell, Bertrand Russell, Harold Laski, Beatrice Webb, and J. B. S. Haldane. Dangerous anti-Nazi and subversive organizations were to be crushed. These included the Boy Scouts, which the Gestapo viewed as a tool of British intelligence; its founder and leader, Lord Baden-Powell, was slated for arrest. The Nazis also listed foreign nationals who had found refuge in England. These included the pianist Ignace Paderewski and Sigmund Freud. Significantly, the list had been prepared well in advance and had not been updated to note that Freud had died in 1939.

To protect the British people, RAF Fighter Command expected to rely on the Supermarine Spitfire and the more numerous Hawker Hurricane. The Spitfire won a reputation as the plane that saved its country, but its principal adversary, the Messerschmitt Bf-109, was close to it in performance. The Spitfire was slightly better in speed and was more maneuverable. The Messerschmitt—an updated version of the fighter that had tried to kill Hemingway—had a superior rate of climb and held an advantage when entering a dive. It used a fuel-injected engine, built by Daimler-Benz, that accommodated a rapid pushover into diving flight. The Spitfires and Hurricanes used the Rolls-Royce Merlin, which was fitted with a carburetor. During a sudden pushover, with the plane pulling negative G forces, the carburetor would fail and the engine would quit. Pilots had to learn to avoid this.

Radar also helped. Scientists at Birmingham University had developed the magnetron, a powerful source of high-frequency microwaves that became the key to success. The magnetron was one of the war's outstanding inventions, and with great foresight, the British erected an array of coastal radar stations called Chain Home. They placed the rotating antennas atop tall steel towers that allowed them to cover the entire Channel and the French coastal areas.

These towers made poor targets for aerial attack, for they were small and hard to hit. At the same time, they were invaluable. General Adolf Galland, a fighter ace and a senior commander within the Luftwaffe, wrote of learning "that the RAF fighter squadrons must be controlled from the ground by some new procedure because we heard commands skillfully and accurately directing Spitfires and Hurricanes onto German formations. For us this radar and fighter control was a surprise and a very bitter one."

Goering waited for good weather and then launched strong and widespread air strikes on what he called *Adlertag*, "Day of the Eagle." Preliminary attacks, on August 12, put an RAF air base out of service and damaged two others that were close to the Channel. Strikes on radar stations damaged three of them while knocking out a fourth, on the Isle of Wight; it was out of action for eleven days. Raids continued through the next two days, with *Adlertag* proper on the fifteenth.

The two air forces fought five major battles that spanned five hundred miles. Goering sent some 800 aircraft to strike targets in the south of England, hoping to lure the RAF's fighters into the air where they could be destroyed. He also raided the north, expecting to meet little opposition, for he did not anticipate that the RAF had fighters in the area. He was badly mistaken; Sir Hugh Dowding, the head of Fighter Command, had seven squadrons at the ready. They fell on the German bombers, shooting down 30 of them; the overall losses for the day were 76 German planes to 34 of the RAF. For the week, the score was more favorable still: 134 British planes lost, 261 for Germany.

This disproportion was even stronger in pilots and aircrews. The Luftwaffe had a strong initial advantage, for Germany had recovered some four hundred of its airmen who had been taken captive after being shot down over France. By contrast, surviving RAF pilots were in prisoner-of-war camps, where they would remain. But when the air battles shifted to England, the situation reversed. Now the men of the Luftwaffe were lost for the duration when captured, whereas British airmen who bailed out could return to their squadrons.

In the wake of *Adlertag,* Goering elected not to emphasize further attacks on radar sites. He did not appreciate their importance, and believed that the air strikes of recent days had not been effective. This was a mistake; concerted raids would have knocked out more of them. However, Goering made a valid decision in pressing attacks on RAF airfields and command centers. This was one key to victory, another being to send bombers against aircraft and engine factories.

In addition to its radar stations, the RAF depended on over fifty thousand ground observers. They carried binoculars and portable telephones, and served as the main source of information about enemy aircraft flying overland. Their reports went to operations centers that were rendered bombproof by being placed fifty feet underground. Within such a center, commanders used telephones to give orders to operational squadrons. Each squadron had a base, often a grassy airfield with the planes lined up in a row. They often were ready for takeoff on two minutes' notice, or counted "at readiness" at five minutes. Pilots sprinted to their planes, parachutes on their backs, then gunned their engines and took off.

From August 24 to September 6, Goering sent a thousand planes a day, and the balance swung against Fighter Command. The Germans severely damaged five forward airfields along with six sector stations. The latter were communications centers that directed airborne fighters

Fighter pilots of the Royal Air Force run to their planes, to meet a German attack.
(*National Air and Space Museum*)

with radio commands, and were vital to the air defense of London. RAF losses exceeded production; the British counted 466 Hurricanes and Spitfires destroyed or seriously damaged, with only 269 new or repaired fighters entering the squadrons as replacements.

The supply of pilots was even more critical. Fighter Command had about a thousand such men on August 20, as Churchill spoke to Parliament and declared, "Never in the field of human conflict was so much owed by so many to so few." But during the fortnight that followed, the few became fewer, as 103 died in action and another 128 were seriously wounded, for a loss of nearly one-fourth. Some 50 new pilots were joining Fighter Command every week, but initially they could do little; a man had to fly four or five missions successfully before he gained the experience that made him effective. The need for new pilots became so severe that many replacements went directly from training units to the operational squadrons, often before they had completed their full courses. Matched against Goering's veterans, there was good reason to fear that these were the men who would die gallantly.

Air Marshal Dowding had followed a policy of keeping his frontline squadrons in combat for five or six weeks, then rotating them to the rear to rest while still remaining alert. Such rear squadrons had provided the fighters that shot down thirty bombers near Newcastle on *Adlertag*. However, Dowding no longer could do this; he had to keep his men on the line with their planes, even as they became fatigued. An Air Ministry report stated that "in three weeks more of activity on the same scale, the fighter reserves would have been completely exhausted." Goering then might have been able to gain air superiority, as an essential prerequisite to a successful invasion.

The fortunes of war often turn on small matters, and one such event occurred on August 23. Several German bombers were under orders to drop their loads on oil tanks and aircraft factories outside London, but they missed these targets and instead bombed the center of the city, destroying homes and killing civilians. Churchill viewed this as a deliberate Nazi atrocity. He had RAF Bomber Command on twelve-hour notice to strike in reprisal, which it did.

By Goering's standards, the initial British raid on Berlin was a minor affair. It featured eighty-one twin-engine bombers, and because that city lay under dense cloud cover, only about half of these aircraft managed to find it. Nevertheless, this attack came as a tremendous shock, for it was the first time bombs had fallen on Berlin. Goering had boasted of his air defenses, declaring, "The Ruhr will not be subjected to a single bomb." RAF bombers returned a few nights later in greater force, then came back a third time. Propaganda Minister Joseph Goebbels had his newspapers run headlines: COWARDLY BRITISH ATTACK! BRITISH AIR PIRATES OVER BERLIN! Goering responded by changing his list of targets, switching from direct attacks on the RAF to massive strikes against London. This had an important and unintended consequence: it gave the RAF an opportunity to recover.

The beginning of September brought the assembly of the invasion fleet. It did not include purpose-built landing craft such as the U.S. Marines relied on in assaulting Japan's Pacific islands. The Germans instead used merchant ships, self-propelled barges, and rivercraft. Hitler was eager to unleash them. On September 4, speaking to an audience of nurses and social workers, he said, "In England they are filled with curiosity and keep asking, 'Why doesn't he come?' Be calm. Be calm. He's coming! He's coming!"

An order from Army High Command set September 20 as the earliest date for the invasion fleet to sail, with the landings taking place on the following day. Again, though, the empire struck back. German naval headquarters warned that "the harbors at Ostend, Dunkirk, Calais and Boulogne cannot be used as night anchorages for shipping because of the danger of English bombing and shelling." On the thirteenth, British naval units attacked these ports as well as Cherbourg, while the RAF sank eighty barges in Ostend harbor. Subsequent strikes blew up an ammunition train and a five-hundred-ton ammunition dump, heavily damaged five transport vessels at Antwerp, sank or damaged eighty-four barges at Dunkirk. By the twenty-first, the date set for the invasion, one-eighth of the invasion fleet had been destroyed or damaged.

As reports of these losses reached Hitler, he vacillated. He had hoped to commit to the invasion on September 11, giving his forces ten days to prepare. But on the tenth, he chose to postpone his decision to the fourteenth. On that date, he decided to hold off his commitment for another three days. The seventeenth arrived, and Hitler elected to postpone Operation Sea Lion indefinitely. A subsequent order released the invasion vessels to their civilian owners, and British reconnaissance soon learned of this. Churchill responded characteristically: "We are waiting for the long-promised invasion. So are the fishes."

The RAF, together with the Royal Navy, had forced Hitler to call off his assault by sea. However, London and the nation still faced Goering's assault by air. If you had been in that city on September 7, and on many, many nights thereafter, you would have known the terror of a long, drawn-out, shimmering wail. It was the sound of a hundred air-raid sirens, reverberating through the streets, echoing off the broken buildings and deserted docks of the world's largest city.

The raids began late that afternoon as a wave of 320 bombers, well protected by fighters, flew up the Thames. They struck at Woolwich Arsenal and also hit gasworks, power stations, and docks and piers that extended for miles. Soon the entire waterfront area was in flames, while all railroads running southward were blocked. Senior commanders issued the code word Cromwell, which meant "Invasion imminent."

In a sense it was already under way, for this attack was the most devastating air strike ever delivered against a city, far surpassing Guernica. Early in the evening, after dark, a second wave of 250 bombers flew in, with further waves continuing to attack until dawn broke the next morning. When evening fell on the second day, 200 bombers returned, again keeping up their raids through the night. These first two nights took the lives of 842 people while injuring well over 2,000, with the attacks continuing through the week.

This was air war as Goering preferred it. It was all very well to strike at airfields and control centers, but his taste ran to mass murder, bombing civilians in hope of frightening the survivors into surrender. This did not happen; London remained defiant. People built their own air-raid shelters, following designs provided by the Home Department; many took refuge in subway stations, which were too deep for the bombs. When Churchill learned that individual people faced ruin from the destruction of their homes and businesses, he arranged for the chancellor of the exchequer to set up an insurance program that compensated their losses.

During the week that the Nazis were bombing London, they were not striking directly at Fighter Command, and that week was all the RAF needed to recover. On September 15, celebrated ever since as Battle of Britain Day, the two air forces fought one of the war's decisive battles.

In a daylight attack, some two hundred bombers crossed the Channel, escorted by a substantially larger number of fighters. The RAF was ready, having watched them on radar. Its fighters intercepted the enemy long before they reached London, shooting down some of the attackers and dispersing many others. Later that afternoon the Luftwaffe returned in even greater strength, and again it was routed.

A total of 277 bombers joined the attacks; 35 were shot down, for a loss of 12 percent. The Luftwaffe could not sustain this; its bombers had to go out day after day, and continued losses at such a rate would wipe them out. Goering responded by changing his tactics. *Adlertag,* a month earlier, had shown that he could not expect to conduct daylight raids unless his bombers had strong fighter escort. September 15 demonstrated that daytime attacks would bring unacceptable losses, even with such escort.

That evening, RAF Bomber Command conducted strikes of its own, mounting strong attacks against shipping in ports along the Channel coast. The raids inflicted particularly heavy losses at Antwerp. This, together with the demonstration that Fighter Command was still ready to defend London, drove Hitler to his decision two days later whereby he postponed Sea Lion indefinitely. In earlier centuries the British had held off the Spanish Armada and had kept Napoleon at bay; now they had saved their nation from conquest by an enemy that was far better armed and considerably more ruthless.

Nevertheless, England still was far from safe. Goering found himself limited to attacking after dark, but he proceeded to do this with a vengeance. For fifty-seven nights in succession, from September 7 to November 3, an average of two hundred bombers struck at London.

Courage in war takes many forms. For the American correspondent Edward R. Murrow, it meant transmitting by shortwave radio from the roof of the British Broadcasting Corporation building. The BBC was a prime German target; Murrow required Churchill's personal intervention before he could proceed. Night after night he went up there, beginning each report with his trademark, "This—is London." St. Paul's Cathedral stood defiant amid flames and smoke; he described it, while telling of carnage around Trafalgar Square and Westminster Abbey. His CBS office was bombed out three times; still he held his post. His words were meant for Americans, his message being one that many of his countrymen did not care to accept and were reluctant to believe: that Hitler's threat was imminent.

Bomb squads showed courage of their own. Some German bombs were duds; others had delayed-action fuses. All such ordnance, known as UXB (unexploded bombs), had to be defused. Disposal squads were well aware that if one of these munitions went off, they would die instantly, before knowing what had happened. They disarmed some of them by boring holes in the bomb casing to deal with the explosive charges. Churchill wrote that the people who did this "were gaunt, they were haggard, their faces had a bluish look, with bright gleaming eyes and exceptional compression of the lips." Some of them survived thirty or forty encounters before meeting their fate. Even titled nobles played their roles, with the earl of Suffolk forming a squad along with his private secretary and his chauffeur. They successfully disposed of thirty-four UXBs, but the next one blew up and killed the earl.

Churchill remained at his own post, as he continued to live at 10 Downing Street. One afternoon he heard a very heavy explosion in south London, perhaps from a large bomb with delayed action. He went to see what had happened, and found a crater some forty yards across and twenty feet deep. The people in that neighborhood were poor, and the bomb had leveled or badly damaged as many as thirty homes. Still they were not dismayed; they crowded around Churchill and his group, cheering, glad to see their prime minister, proud to be alive. As Churchill put it, "One would have thought that I had brought them some fine substantial benefit which would improve their lot in life. I was completely undermined, and wept." A woman said, "You see, he really cares. He's crying."

As the Luftwaffe pressed its aerial raids, its engineers introduced new methods for navigating by radio. They set up dozens of transmitters, each with its own call sign. Pilots determined their positions using direction finders, loop antennas that measured the bearings to several such stations. The British countered with stations of their own that received the German signals, amplified them, and retransmitted them from somewhere in England. A number of enemy aircraft thus were led astray; one bomber landed in Devonshire, with its pilot believing he was in occupied France.

Another navigational system resembled the four-course radio ranges of the United States. It relied again on paired transmitters whose signals overlapped to form a narrow beam. If a pilot flew to the left or right of this line of overlap, he would hear an intermittent signal, but when he was on the beam, the signals from both sides merged into a continuous tone. A second beam, with a recognizably different tone, could be set to cross the first, over a target city. The system worked in bad weather as well as at night; a bomber merely had to follow the first beam until its bombardier heard the sound of the second one. Then it was bombs away, without even having to see where they fell.

Such beams had a well-known tendency to wander, and the British encouraged this. They set up radio repeaters that strengthened the signal to the left or right of the true beam. An airborne navigator, seeking to merge the signals from both sides, would fly a wrong course and would intercept the crossing beam far from his target. One London family, sent to the country to escape the raids, was much astonished to hear a hundred or more heavy bombs falling on farmers' fields, ten miles from the nearest town.

Naval aviators also continued to fight for King and Country. The Royal Navy was eager to maintain control of the Mediterranean, and faced a powerful challenge from the navy of Italy. On November 11, aircraft from the carrier HMS *Illustrious* carried out a night attack on the main naval base at Taranto. Using flares to illuminate their targets, the British torpedoed three battleships and a cruiser, while inflicting considerable damage by bombing the dockyard. Of the twenty-one aircraft that conducted this strike, only two were shot down, with the rest returning safely to *Illustrious*.

The main theater of action nevertheless remained Great Britain itself, where it took more than electronic countermeasures to defeat the Luftwaffe. Goering continued to introduce new methods of radio navigation, which took time to foil. London continued to pay a heavy price. A strike on October 14 laid much of the Pall Mall district in flames, with at least five major fires burning. Other conflagrations roared in St. James's Street and Piccadilly.

The city depended on the Thames for its water supply, which threatened to spread widespread disease after German bombs destroyed the main sewage outfall. There was no alternative except to allow the city's sewage to flow directly into the river, and then to treat the water with chemicals. Underground shelters posed their own health hazards, for with the largest of them holding up to seven thousand people, there was reason to believe that they would offer fertile ground for the spread of influenza or diphtheria. This also did not happen, for London's people were sufficiently accustomed to one anothers' germs that they already possessed the needed resistance. As winter approached, with its chill and rain, there was fear of a glass shortage. The air raids had blown out many of the city's windows; in some instances, the blast of a single bomb sufficed to shatter panes along an entire street. Homeowners boarded up their broken windows with plywood, and carried on.

Unexploded munitions brought their own difficulties. When a bomb fell and failed to detonate, it was necessary to block off a substantial surrounding area until it could be defused. That could take a while, for such bombs tended to bury themselves in the ground, and took time to dig out. Delayed-action bombs, dropped into railroad yards, produced considerable congestion. Airfields, main thoroughfares, and important factories also had to be taken out of service.

The raids continued, with Goering now striking at important centers of aircraft and engine production. Coventry was one; the bombers came on November 14. Nine hundred years earlier, Lady Godiva rode through that town to protest an unjust tax, but now it faced outright destruction. A force of 469 bombers struck with six hundred tons of high explosives, along with thousands of incendiaries. Because Coventry was considerably smaller than London, it was correspondingly more vulnerable; its center was shattered, and the city as a whole was badly disrupted. Emergency reconstruction restored much of its life in less than a week, but four hundred people lay dead, with many more being seriously injured.

Another Luftwaffe force, its men specifically trained for the task, struck at the Rolls-Royce aircraft engine works near Glasgow. Birmingham, a city of a million people whose very name spoke of heavy industry, received raids on three successive nights. A total of seven hundred aircraft killed some eight hundred people, many of them children. All were buried in a mass grave.

Goering also struck heavily at ports: Bristol, Southampton, Plymouth, and particularly Liverpool, which received much trade from across the Atlantic. He continued to raid such industrial centers as Sheffield, Manchester, Leeds, and Glasgow. Then, four days after Christmas, these attacks reached a climax in London. The financial district, the City, took the brunt of it. At the outset, heavy bombs dropped by parachute broke the water mains that were essential for fire fighting. Nearly fifteen hundred fires broke out.

The radio war continued. The Germans introduced Apparatus X, a navigation method that again used crossing beams to mark a target, and that operated at high radio frequencies for better accuracy. British scientists found a way to defeat it, but it took two months to deliver the necessary equipment, and then additional months passed before its designers removed a technical error and made it effective. Goering's pilots used this system successfully to find their way to Coventry and to other cities, until Apparatus X was successfully jammed.

Germany responded with Apparatus Y, another high-frequency system that used a single beam along with distance-measuring circuitry. An aircrew could fly along this beam while keeping track of its range. They used it successfully in their raid against the Rolls-Royce plant near Glasgow, but the British had already anticipated that Germany would introduce such a system, and they responded with electronic countermeasures that worked at the outset. Very soon, British radio operators began to pick up angry remarks from German pilots, who learned that they were being led astray. The Luftwaffe continued to try to work with Apparatus Y, but in time it too was abandoned.

Often the Luftwaffe could find their targets even without electronic navigation. An initial group of bombers could serve as a pathfinder, dropping enough incendiaries to start a substantial fire in part of a city, to serve as a flaming beacon that guided the main force. Ironically, the German navigational transmissions proved quite helpful to the British. The Luftwaffe radio stations did not transmit continually, but only before and during a raid. Their crossing beams marked specific cities on particular nights, and the British put heaps of fuel in open country, with which they ignited decoy fires. These also led many attacking planes to drop their bombs far from any town. It even became possible to fool the Germans from start to finish, as deflected beams led them away from cities, to a beam-crossing point that lay above farmland, and with flaming piles of hay or coal directly below.

With the German beams supplementing British radar as an early warning system, British officials found that they could concentrate firefighting equipment in the threatened area, while warning the population in timely fashion. The beams also assisted the RAF in its use of night fighters, for they gave clear warnings of the time and location of attacks. The use of magnetrons, operating at high radio frequencies, led to the advent of airborne radar sets that guided British fighters to their aerial battles.

In May 1941, a year after the invasion of France, the Luftwaffe stepped up its raids. A particularly bad one came on May 10, when they dropped over seven hundred tons of high explosives and more than 86,000 incendiaries. Late in the month the Germans struck at Dublin, showing that the whole of the British Isles lay within the scope of their terror.

And then it was over. The Germans ceased their attacks, but not because the British had put up unbreachable defenses. The reason instead was that Hitler was preparing to pounce on the Soviet Union, and therefore redeployed his air force well to the east. Britain stood alone for an entire year, from the French surrender on June 22, 1940, to the invasion of the Soviet Union on June 22, 1941. During that year, Great Britain won the admiration of the world.

The Battle of Britain brought a clear British victory in the air. The RAF, aided by antiaircraft fire on the ground, shot down 1,733 German aircraft, for a loss to the enemy of nearly 3,000 airmen. RAF Fighter Command lost 1,017 aircraft, but only 537 pilots. In addition, during the critical year of 1940 the British actually outproduced the Germans in aircraft, 9,924 to 8,070.

Statistics told part of the story, but by far the more important part involved the human spirit and the will to be free. With Hitler at the height of his conquests, with France having capitulated in weeks after having held out for four years during World War I, Churchill and his people flung defiance in his face—and made it stick. They not only saved themselves; they offered hope at a time when the Nazis seemed beyond resistance.

"Do not speak of darker days," Churchill said in October 1941, when the Soviets were reeling under Nazi blows and the danger to England still was real. "Let us speak rather of sterner days. These are not dark days; these are great days—the greatest days our country has ever lived; and we must all thank God that we have been allowed, each of us according to our stations, to play a part in making these days memorable in the history of our race."[4]

Yamamoto Fights at Sea 12

IT WASN'T EASY to get into the U.S. Navy's codebreaking center at Pearl Harbor. It was located within a cellar, with locked doors at both the top and bottom of its flight of stairs, and with guards to check a visitor's papers before either of those doors would open. Two dozen people worked there, seeking to read intercepts of coded Japanese radio messages.

These people were individualists; their chief, Commander Joseph Rochefort, liked to work wearing slippers and a red smoking jacket. Within their windowless basement, file folders piled up on desks and chairs, spilled onto the floor, or accumulated atop a worktable of planks resting on sawhorses. They got away with this casual approach because their skills were unique. Only about forty people in the entire Navy had fluent knowledge of Japanese; many of them worked with Rochefort. He also directed the efforts of a number of skilled cryptanalysts. During 1942, as the Japanese tide surged across the Pacific, this Combat Intelligence Unit provided a key to their defeat.

Japan's naval commander in chief, Admiral Isoroku Yamamoto, had been in the Imperial Navy long before he became an adult. He had come up as a cadet at the naval academy at Etajima; in winning admission, he placed second in the entire nation on a standardized test. His working days had lasted sixteen hours; discipline involved plenty of slaps and blows. Through it all, he knew that he could be expelled, bringing lasting shame upon himself and disgrace to his entire family.

He graduated, and received his commission as an ensign. Sent to sea, he was present aboard a cruiser at the Battle of Tsushima Strait, in 1905. This naval engagement marked a milestone in the rise of Japan, for its fleet annihilated a Russian armada, in the first such victory ever gained by an Asian power. Yamamoto was knocked unconscious by a shell burst, and lost two fingers. Having thus shed blood for his emperor, he received strong respect from younger officers as his career proceeded, for he had fought at Tsushima and they had not.

Graduates of Etajima were known primarily for their willingness to die in battle, and not for originality in shaping naval doctrine. Yamamoto nevertheless found his own path to command. In 1919 he was posted to Harvard University to study English, and spent two years in the United States. On returning home in 1921, he became an instructor at the Navy Staff College. By then he had developed a strong interest in aviation. He learned to fly; he became convinced that airpower would become the key to control of the sea. He was on hand in 1923 when his navy received its first aircraft carrier, the *Hosho*.

He spent more time in the United States from 1926 to 1928, as a naval attaché in Washington. Working at the Japanese embassy, he won respect for his naval knowledge as well as for his excellent games of poker and bridge. He returned home as the first truly large carriers were joining the fleet: *Akagi* ("Red Castle") and *Kaga* ("Increased Joy"). Late in 1928 he became commander of *Akagi,* winning promotion to rear admiral a few months later. He rose to command the First Carrier Division. In 1934, at the London Naval Conference, he torpedoed proposed limits on Japan's naval strength, opening the way for its rapid increase. Serving in the Navy Ministry, he built a powerful air arm.

Then in 1936, a group of army officers staged a coup against the civil government, assassinating several of its leaders and attempting to murder the prime minister. Militarism and extreme nationalism, enforced by the sword, now became the order of the day. In 1937 Japan launched a war against China, conquering important portions of that country but soon finding itself trapped in a conflict that it could neither win nor end. At the same time, military leaders aligned themselves with Nazi Germany.

Yamamoto did not like this. He distrusted the Nazis, and when his colleagues spoke of new attacks that would widen the conflict, he knew that this threatened war with the United States. He had traveled widely, as other military leaders had not; he declared that "anyone who has seen the automobile factories in Detroit and the oil fields in Texas knows that Japan lacks the power for a naval race with America." These attitudes placed his own life at risk from the superpatriots. His appointment as naval commander in chief took him to sea, where he was beyond their reach.

He continued to speak against war with the United States. Meeting with Premier Fumimaro Konoye in 1940, he stated his view: "If I am told to fight regardless of the consequences, I shall run wild for the first six months or a year, but I have utterly no confidence for the second and third years of the fighting." Nevertheless, the general view was that six months to a year was more than Japan needed, for the Nazi conquests in Europe had presented Tokyo with a dazzling opportunity.

Japan needed rice, rubber, and oil. These resources existed respectively in French Indochina, British Malaya, and the Dutch East Indies. With France and the Netherlands under the German boot, and with Great Britain facing an imminent threat to its homeland, the time was ripe to unleash the forces of the emperor and conquer these lands. In July 1941 Japan took control of Indochina, including Vietnam.

President Roosevelt had already shown concern over Japanese aggression in China, and had placed an embargo on scrap iron and steel. Now he froze Japanese credits, thus extending the embargo to oil. The Dutch colonial governor in Djakarta did the same, thus cutting off Japan's oil imports from the East Indies as well. The Japanese government responded with an imperial war council, early in September, which set the agenda for the next wave of attacks.

The East Indies and Malaya were at the top of the list. The key to the latter was Singapore; hence this great British bastion was to be taken. Hong Kong also was to fall, for this British base lay athwart Japan's sea lanes. The U.S.-held Philippines also were close to Japan's shipping routes; Tokyo was not about to trust in Yankee goodwill, so those islands were also marked for conquest. To prevent the U.S. Navy from rushing to their defense, the plan called for eliminating much of its Pacific Fleet. Japan therefore would engage U.S. strongholds at Guam and Wake Island—and would strike the fleet at its home base in Pearl Harbor.

Yamamoto took charge of planning for the Pearl Harbor attack. His plan carried unprecedented daring, for it featured six aircraft carriers carrying 423 warplanes. Escorts were to include two battleships, two heavy cruisers, a light cruiser, nine destroyers, three submarines, and several tankers to refuel the other vessels while under way. This fleet was to remain at sea for ten days, crossing four thousand miles of open ocean. Yet because its route lay far from the shipping lanes, it was to achieve the advantage of surprise. If all went well, Pearl Harbor would receive no warning until aircraft emblazoned with the Rising Sun were directly overhead. Then, with U.S. Pacific forces either wiped out or under withering attack, as in the Philippines, there was reason to hope that Roosevelt would conclude a peace agreement that would give Japan a free hand within its new empire.

Japanese diplomats in Washington kept up a pretense of negotiating, while Yamamoto's warships slipped from their anchorages and assembled in the remote Kuril Islands. The fleet departed on November 26. At about the same time, U.S. intelligence sources learned that another powerful strike force, including troopships carrying five divisions, was heading southward. Admiral Harold Stark, chief of naval operations, responded with a message to his commanders in Hawaii and the Philippines:

> This dispatch is to be considered a war warning. Negotiations with Japan looking toward stabilization of conditions in the Pacific have ceased and an aggressive move by Japan is expected within the next few days. The number and equipment of Japanese troops and the organization of naval task forces indicates an amphibious expedition against either the Philippines Thai or Kra peninsula or possibly Borneo. Execute an appropriate defensive deployment preparatory to carrying out the tasks assigned in WPL 46. Inform district and army authorities.[1]

On its face, this message did not mention Hawaii, but it nevertheless merited strong action, for WPL 46 was the war plan. Admiral Husband Kimmel, commander of the Pacific Fleet, might have responded by sending his vessels to sea. He did no such thing, and there was more to his inaction than the vagueness of the threat and the strength of habits of peace. The naval historian Samuel Eliot Morison notes that although there was plenty of intercepted communications traffic, "every one of the Japanese messages decrypted and translated before 7 December was ambiguous. None mentioned Pearl Harbor. None even pointed clearly at Japanese intent to attack the United States anywhere. Thus, no clear warnings were sent to Hawaii because Washington saw no reason to anticipate an attack on Hawaii."

Japan held its secrets from the U.S. Army as well as from the Navy. On the very morning of the air strike, Army Chief of Staff George Marshall received a decoded intercept that left him convinced that Japan was about to do something serious. However, Marshall had no clue as to what specifically to expect. Nor did he know where to expect it. Accordingly, he sent warning messages to senior commanders not only in Hawaii but in the Philippines, Panama, and San Francisco.

On December 6, the assaulting fleet completed a refueling and increased speed to twenty knots, heading due south for Oahu. As noon approached, *Akagi*, the flagship, ran up the very banner that had flown at Tsushima in 1905. The seamen and aircrews cheered wildly. As the fleet approached Honolulu, some radiomen listened to that city's commercial stations. They heard popular music, showing that no one knew what awaited them.

The attacking aircraft took off from their carriers just after 6:00 A.M. As daylight broke, the sun sent shafts of light past clouds, as if nature itself displayed the Japanese national symbol. As they flew in, many U.S. sailors thought they were seeing nothing more than a particularly realistic exercise, as in the war game of 1932. One officer, Logan Ramsey, stood in his command center watching a color guard hoist the flag. A plane screamed as it dived overhead, and Ramsey said to a colleague, "Dick, get that fellow's number, for I want to report him for about sixteen violations of the course and safety regulations." Then they heard a bomb explode. Ramsey ran into a nearby radio room and ordered the men to send the message, AIR RAID, PEARL HARBOR. THIS IS NO DRILL!

Destruction was swift, particularly among the big battlewagons. The battleship *Arizona* took a bomb in the forward magazine. A powerful concussion ripped through the air; a massive detonation tore the ship apart, its superstructure leaning forward crazily. *Oklahoma* took on water and capsized. Other vessels also came under attack, with the destroyer *Shaw* exploding in an immense fireball. As the warships' tall masts continued to stand over shattered hulls, columns of thick, black, greasy smoke boiled densely into the sky.

Eighteen ships sank or received heavy damage, including all eight battlewagons that were at anchor. Six of them proved to be repairable, but *Arizona* and *Oklahoma* were total wrecks. Between them, they accounted for nearly two-thirds of the 2,403 people who died in the raid. Some three hundred aircraft were destroyed or disabled.

The strike force got away with almost no injury. Not a single Japanese vessel was even hit, let alone sunk, and only twenty-nine aircraft were shot down. Yet while the wound to the Pacific Fleet was deep, it was far from mortal, for the fleet's aircraft carriers were safe. *Enterprise* was at sea, returning to Pearl after delivering fighter planes to Wake Island. *Lexington* was away on a similar mission, delivering bombers to Midway. *Saratoga* was on the West Coast for repairs, while *Yorktown* had been detached several months earlier for duty in the Atlantic. These carriers proved critical during 1942.

Yamamoto himself had remained in Japan, sending subordinate commanders to direct the strike. It had succeeded brilliantly, and these men now faced the question of launching a second attack, this time on an enormous tank farm that held fuel oil. They elected not to go back, for they feared that the unseen carriers might even then be preparing to fling aircraft upon them. The Japanese commanders also considered that surviving land-based bombers might seek them out. In addition, U.S. gunners would be alert, and would take a heavy toll in Japanese airplanes. Still, if they had hit these tanks, breaking them open and sending their contents aloft in new plumes of smoke, then the remnants of the Pacific Fleet might have had to retreat to bases on the West Coast.

America was at war within a day, following a nearly unanimous vote in Congress. Yet the Nazis remained the principal threat, and Pearl Harbor raised the prospect that the United States might find itself in battle against the wrong enemy, on the wrong side of the world. Hitler solved that problem quite neatly; on December 11 he made his own declaration. In less than a week, the nation went from peace to war, with powerful adversaries on two fronts.

As the Rising Sun poured its baleful glare across the Pacific, Japan achieved its objectives in stunningly short time. In the Philippines, General Douglas MacArthur commanded a force of B-17 bombers. He failed to disperse them; the Japanese caught them on the ground, leaving MacArthur without airpower as troops stormed ashore near Manila. Off Malaya, bombers based in Indochina sank the battleship HMS *Prince of Wales* and the battle cruiser HMS *Repulse*. When news of this reached Singapore, the crowded bar at the Raffles Hotel, a principal social center, suddenly fell silent. British guns soon followed suit.

American comforted each other with hopeful lies. An Army pilot named Colin Kelly supposedly sank the battleship *Haruna*. He didn't. A naval engagement near Borneo was touted as an Allied victory. It wasn't. Marines on Wake Island were said to have radioed, "Send us more Japs." They certainly didn't, particularly after the island fell, two days before Christmas.

During the early months of 1942, about the only good news came in mid April as Jimmy Doolittle, now a colonel, led a reprisal raid on Tokyo itself. He used sixteen B-25 medium bombers, which had not been designed to fly from a carrier deck but did so anyway. They went to sea aboard the USS *Hornet*, with *Enterprise* providing combat air cover and with cruisers and destroyers as escorts. The air strike achieved complete surprise, with the bombers flying onward to the Asian mainland. The entire naval task force returned safely, and Roosevelt said that the bombers had been based in Shangri-La.

The Japanese knew that they had come from a carrier. They set hundreds of warplanes to defend Tokyo against a repeat attack, and officials listened to Yamamoto as he argued that the work of his navy was not yet complete. It was necessary to attack again, at Midway, northeast of Hawaii. This atoll was critical to America's position; the U.S. Navy would have to defend it. By sending a powerful naval group, Yamamoto expected to force a battle that would further cripple the Pacific Fleet. In Japanese hands, Midway would anchor a defensive perimeter far out in the ocean, thousands of miles from the homeland. It might even serve as a forward base for an invasion of Hawaii itself.

Action in the Coral Sea, northeast of Australia, set the order of battle. The Japanese wanted to capture Port Moresby on the south coast of New Guinea, from where they would threaten Australia. In the ensuing engagement, early in May, American airmen sank the light carrier *Shoho*. This was highly encouraging back home, for it was the first time the United States had sunk a Japanese flattop. More importantly, its loss led the Japanese commander to call off the landing at Moresby.

Larger carriers also took hits. *Lexington* sank, while *Yorktown* received severe damage from a bomb. On the Japanese side, two veterans of Pearl Harbor, *Shokaku* and *Zuikaku*, took their own war wounds. The former had its flight deck bent; it could not launch planes, and took two months to repair. The latter lost a large number of aircraft, which took over a month to replace. As a consequence, neither carrier would be present at Midway.

Meanwhile, American cryptanalysts were listening out. At Pearl Harbor, Joseph Rochefort and his colleagues were able to make headway because the intercepted transmissions used a standard naval code, JN-25. It was hard to learn much directly, for direct decoding rarely yielded more than about 15 percent of a particular message. Other insights came from experience. The name of one ship could suggest another usually with it. Particular communications officers had individual styles when transmitting; a man might change his call letters, but his personal quirks would remain recognizable, and would disclose his identity—and, by association, that of his ship or naval unit.

The sheer volume of message traffic told its own story, even when individual intercepts disclosed little. Early in May, it became evident that Battleship Division Three was communicating extensively with the First Carrier Force, as well as with certain troop transports. Those same transports were being ordered to Saipan, and Cruiser Division Seven was being ordered there as well. Rochefort concluded that a major operation was in the works, involving much of the Imperial Navy.

What was the objective? The entire Pacific was open. They might strike anew at Moresby, perhaps attacking New Zealand as well. They might head for Alaska, Hawaii, even the West Coast. Seizure of Samoa and Fiji would cut supply lines to Australia. Moreover, Japan was strong enough to throw a convincing feint in one direction while reserving its main force for a completely different action.

Nevertheless, the deciphered intercepts contained a number of references to a place called AF. Was this the target? Digging through the piles of decodes, staff members found other mentions of AF from March. Two flying boats had refueled from a submarine near French Frigate Shoals, an atoll lying between Midway and the main Hawaiian island group, and one pilot had spoken of passing near AF. The only militarily significant spot anywhere nearby was Midway, and Rochefort concluded that this was where the Japanese were heading.

The Pacific Fleet had a new commander, Admiral Chester Nimitz, who had replaced the hapless Admiral Kimmel. Rochefort was on good terms with Nimitz's intelligence officer, who arranged for Nimitz to send a senior staff officer to visit Rochefort's domain. This visitor came with the expectation of staying only for two hours; he stretched it to nearly four, and came away convinced that Rochefort had information of very great value. Nimitz agreed. He assigned another staffer to join Rochefort's group and to act as a devil's advocate, challenging the estimates and compelling Rochefort to back up his conclusions. With this, Nimitz became a firm supporter of the Combat Intelligence Unit.

Drawing on this support, Captain Jasper Holmes, a staff cryptanalyst, proceeded to trick the Japanese into disclosing the location of AF. A secure undersea telegraph cable ran between Pearl Harbor and Midway. With approval from Nimitz, Holmes sent a message to Midway directing its defenders to send an uncoded signal by radio: that the island's distilling plant had broken down and they were running short of freshwater. Two days later, a coded transmission from Tokyo stated that AF was running low on freshwater. An American station in Australia decrypted the message and signaled to Pearl Harbor, "This will confirm the identity of AF."

Now that Nimitz knew where to concentrate his forces, his next concern was to marshal as many carriers as possible. *Yorktown* drew particular attention; it had taken an eight-hundred-pound bomb amidships at Coral Sea that had killed sixty-six men and started a major fire. Its task force commander had stated that it would need a ninety-day refit. Nimitz, wearing hip boots, stood in the dry dock when it returned to Pearl and insisted that the ship must be made ready to fight in only three days. Some fourteen hundred workers turned to the effort, laboring around the clock to make the most essential repairs. Less than two days after entering dry dock, *Yorktown* left this dock, as hundreds of men continued their work. Nimitz made his three-day schedule with hours to spare, as this carrier put to sea carrying a full complement of aircraft.

The Battle of Midway had much in common with the Battle of Britain. Yamamoto, like Hitler, expected to seize the island with an amphibious invasion. However, before he could unleash such an assault, he first had to win air superiority in a preliminary engagement. He had shaped his fleet accordingly, with four powerful carriers in front. Behind them were seven battleships, one of which was his flagship and his headquarters at sea. Bringing up the rear was the invasion force, which had assembled at Saipan and Guam. It featured troopships, escorted by their own battlewagons and heavy cruisers.

Nimitz had no battleships, but he knew that if he could maintain air superiority—by sinking the enemy carriers or by inflicting very large losses on their aircraft—then he wouldn't need them. Despite the strength of those battlewagons, he knew that Yamamoto would retreat if he lost his air cover. In addition to *Yorktown*, Nimitz had *Enterprise* and *Hornet*. He also had an unsinkable carrier in Midway itself, home base to a powerful squadron of B-17s.

Despite the Japanese advantages in number of ships and in naval gunnery, Nimitz was prepared to fight at least the air combat on even terms. He had his own advantage, for he had a clear understanding of the Japanese order of battle, revealed in a decoded intercept of May 25. His own plans remained secret, for the Navy had protected the security of its own codes. Indeed, the Japanese believed that *Yorktown* had sunk at Coral Sea, along with *Lexington,* and they did not learn differently until the action around Midway was well begun.

At dawn on June 3, Yamamoto's carriers initiated the battle with an air strike against Midway proper. This was appropriate, for its bombers posed a significant threat. The carrier commander, Admiral Chuichi Nagumo, had led the strike on Pearl Harbor; he now learned that Midway required further softening up. Nevertheless, the initial air attack represented encouraging news to Nimitz's own commanders at the scene, Admirals Raymond Spruance and Frank Fletcher.

They knew that their carriers, rather than Midway itself, were Nagumo's true objectives. They also were well aware that his attacking aircraft could not raid the island and then fly on to launch an immediate strike against the American flattops. Rather, those planes would have to return to their own carriers, to refuel and rearm before returning to the air for the main attack. These activities would take time, and during that time, the carrier decks would be littered with fuel hoses, bombs and torpedoes, and aircraft with tanks full of aviation gasoline. Those decks would be tinderboxes; a single U.S. bomb might ignite a conflagration.

The two carrier fleets were some 175 miles apart, too far for an easy strike. Nevertheless, Spruance did not hesitate. He ordered the launch of nearly full deck loads from *Enterprise* and *Hornet,* which he commanded, reserving only a fighter force for combat air defense. Fletcher, commanding *Yorktown,* did the same. These admirals hoped that their aerial armada, comprising eighty-four dive bombers and forty-one torpedo bombers, would deliver a devastating blow.

It didn't. Nagumo's carriers were not where the Yankees had expected to find them, and the attacking force broke up into individual squadrons that set out in search of the foe. The leader of one *Hornet* group turned in the wrong direction, toward Midway, and flew right out of the battle. Other squadrons attacked piecemeal, in uncoordinated strikes that scored no hits but that cost both aircraft and pilots' lives. In one of the torpedo attacks, only a single pilot survived. In another, shortly after ten in the morning, a dozen planes flew in; only two escaped.

Following this last failed American attempt, Yamamoto and Nagumo stood on the brink of a victory that would exceed Tsushima, one that promised to echo down the rest of the century. Their aircraft were armed, fully fueled, and ready to strike. Senior Japanese commanders knew where to find Nimitz's carriers. At 10:20 A.M., Admiral Nagumo gave the order to launch when ready. *Akagi* turned into the wind, its aircraft on deck with engines running. The first of its planes took off; the others would follow within minutes.

Suddenly a lookout shouted, "Helldivers!" Three dive bombers plummeted downward, unopposed. The last American torpedo attack, minutes earlier, had achieved an impromptu coordination by drawing the defending Japanese fighters down close to the sea; they had not had time to return to their accustomed altitudes. One bomb exploded a few yards to one side, close enough to stave in *Akagi*'s hull. A second bomb sliced through the flight deck and exploded below on the hangar deck, setting off a fiery holocaust fed by gas tanks, bombs, and torpedoes.

Flames flared uncontrollably, quickly spreading to the planes on the flight deck. A third bomb struck the stern, amid a group of airplanes that were changing their armament. It detonated in their midst; the explosion jammed the ship's rudders, leaving it unable to steer. Fire engulfed the vessel as burning gasoline flowed freely. Crew members screamed in agony, their clothes and bodies afire. In an engine compartment, deep within the hull, other men died as the ventilator system sucked flames into the ship's interior.

Other dive bombers delivered similar attacks on the carriers *Kaga* and *Soryu*. One bomb struck a fuel tank on *Kaga*'s flight deck and sprayed the bridge with flaming gasoline, burning to death everyone who was there. A second bomb also hit the flight deck; a senior officer vaporized within its blast, and one of his colleagues had a thought: "Those who vanish like the dew will surely be quite happy." Other bombs struck as well, turning the vessel into a funeral pyre. As the flames spread, new explosions erupted. Ablaze along much of its length, it nevertheless remained afloat until a massive internal detonation finished it off.

Akagi and *Kaga* fell to the dive bombers of Spruance's command. A separate squadron, from *Yorktown*, took off later but arrived at the place of battle at nearly the same time. Hurtling downward onto *Soryu*, these aircraft set it ablaze as well. Within minutes its engines stopped. Fire reached a torpedo storage room, setting off a killing blast, and the captain ordered his men to abandon ship.

It had taken only a few minutes for Nagumo's attack aircraft to plunge America into war, by striking at Pearl Harbor. Now, again in only a few minutes, the fortunes of battle turned decisively against Japan. They held only one operational carrier, *Hiryu*, while the Yankees still had their three. The stricken vessels of the emperor lingered through the day, pouring columns of black smoke into a crystalline blue sky. Crew members tried to save *Akagi*, but early the next morning, Yamamoto ordered it scuttled. *Soryu* went down as well, its captain remaining aboard and calmly singing the national anthem.

Nevertheless, the fight was far from over, for *Hiryu* was still untouched. Bent on revenge, its skipper launched an attack on *Yorktown*, leaving it ablaze and dead in the water. Damage control parties put out the fires and relit the boilers. Then a second strike from *Hiryu* put two torpedoes into its hull. All power went out; the ship took on a severe list, and without power there was no hope of counterflooding to put it back on an even keel. The captain feared it would capsize, and like his counterpart aboard *Soryu*, he ordered his men to abandon ship. A Japanese submarine completed its sinking.

By the success of its attack, *Hiryu* now was marked for destruction, and dive bombers from *Enterprise* delivered the blow. Fires spread, raging out of control, and its captain and his admiral chose to go down with the ship. As the end approached and there was little more they could do, they gave themselves over to a ceremonious expression of friendship. "Let us enjoy the beauty of the moon," suggested the admiral. "How brightly it shines," the captain agreed. "It must be in its twenty-first day."

The action around Midway was about to enter its second day. The Americans held the advantage, but still could have lost the battle if Spruance sent his surviving carriers, *Enterprise* and *Hornet,* in pursuit of the Japanese fleet. Such a course would have delivered them into the waiting guns of Yamamoto's powerful battleships, which remained untouched. Spruance was wise enough not to do this, not to throw away his victory—which depended on his flattops' continued safety—by trying for more. He moved westward and sent out a final strike that caught two heavy cruisers, sinking one and severely damaging the second. Then he left the area, leaving Yamamoto to his defeat.

The Japanese heavy cruiser Mikuma *burned but remained afloat following the Battle of Midway.* (National Archives)

Yamamoto had spoken of running wild for six months, and he had been right; this battle took place almost half a year to the day after the attack on Pearl Harbor. He now went over to the defensive, abandoning plans to seize Port Moresby or to cut Australia's supply line by taking Samoa and Fiji. Nevertheless, Japan remained strong. Although Tokyo lost four carriers at Midway, it replaced those losses with new construction. Japan had started the war with eight carriers; at the end of 1942, it still had eight in service.

America was far less prepared. Prewar decisions had given the fleet only six full-size carriers, and had sharply limited the pace of new construction. The nation thus launched no new flattops during all of 1942. Moreover, as that year progressed, the Navy repeatedly ran short of luck, and of carriers. After losing *Lexington* at Coral Sea and *Yorktown* at Midway, *Wasp* and *Hornet* went down in the fighting around Guadalcanal. At that point the nation had only two such vessels in the entire Pacific, and for a time both were laid up for repair. With the Japanese holding their own in carrier strength, they enjoyed outright supremacy.

In turn, this supremacy sharply limited U.S. options. After Midway, Guadalcanal in the Solomon Islands, east of New Guinea, became the prize of battle. The stakes again were high; had the United States lost, Japan once more would have had the opportunity to seize Moresby and to threaten all of Australia. But in the action around that island, the Americans relied heavily on Guadalcanal's Henderson Field, another unsinkable carrier that countered the enemy's strength in naval aviation. Even then, it took six months to win.

Hence the decisions of the interwar years left the Yankees unprepared for the naval threat they would face. The country avoided outright disaster; it did not, after all, attempt to meet the Rising Sun with a fleet of *Ranger*-class carriers. But prewar policy allowed the Navy to achieve little more than bare adequacy. American carrier forces survived Pearl, held on to win at Coral Sea, triumphed at Midway, and then survived long enough to contribute to the hard-won victory at Guadalcanal. But they offered no basis for the eventual defeat of Japan.

Here lay a formula for stalemate. American troops secured Guadalcanal, further blunting Tokyo's continuing offensive threat. The Navy protected Pacific supply lines using surface ships, somewhat in the fashion of the Atlantic convoys. But U.S. forces could not advance up the Solomon Island chain, operating beyond the reach of aircraft based at Henderson. They could not threaten Japan's great bases at Truk and Rabaul. Nor could they advance into the central Pacific, sweeping across Japan's overextended ocean empire.

Popular history has it that the United States took the offensive immediately after winning at Midway, never ceasing until the emperor's minions surrendered in Tokyo Bay. It is true that early in August 1942, only two months after Midway, the Marines landed on Guadalcanal. However, the post-Midway offensive focused almost entirely on that island. The Marines secured it in February 1943, but then the stalemate set in, persisting through most of that year. The United States could not break this stalemate, and could not resume its offensive, until it had new and superior carriers.

And the United States built them. The turning point had come after the fall of France, for in mid 1940 Congress authorized eleven large flattops as part of a major naval expansion. These took shape as the *Essex* class, with these ships being so well built that some were still in service over thirty years later. They nevertheless took time to construct; not until mid 1943 did the first of them enter the fleet, under Admiral William Halsey. After that, though, the new carriers came forward in a surging wave.

They first saw action that November, as U.S. forces initiated a two-pronged offensive. One prong pointed at Bougainville, northwest of the Solomons and well along the route to Rabaul. The second was at Tarawa, where Marines opened a new theater of action in the mid-Pacific. In both these battles, *Essex*-class carriers provided air support. Then in 1944, they truly came into their own.

That third year of the war brought the great task forces, in which those carriers made their name. They operated as spearheads, leading a campaign of island-hopping that culminated, later that year, in the seizure of the Marianas. The duration of this offensive is significant. For nine months, from February to November 1943, the Pacific war lay in stalemate. But once the Navy had its new carriers it took only another nine months, to August 1944, before the whole of the Marianas were in U.S. hands. With those islands as a base, B-29 bombers flew repeatedly during the following year, to burn the enemy into submission.

From this perspective, the American experience with carriers echoed their experience with aircraft, tanks, and trained fighting men. When the United States entered the war, in none of these areas did it have enough. Still the nation held its own, launching limited offensives—a landing in North Africa, during the fall of 1942, coincided with the action near Guadalcanal—while relying on the protection of the oceans, as in former wars. Meanwhile, the country mobilized its titanic industrial strength. The United States won the carrier war as it won in those other areas, through production. That, rather than superiority at the outset, proved the key to victory.

When the Japanese surrendered aboard the battleship *Missouri*, in Tokyo Bay, Yamamoto was in his grave. His demise represented another success for Joe Rochefort's group of cryptanalysts, who had continued to read the message traffic. One day in April 1943, one of Yamamoto's staff officers sent a radio message to a number of base commanders:

> On 18 April Commander in Chief Combined Fleet will inspect Ballale, Shortland, and Buin as follows:
>   Depart Rabaul 0600 in medium attack plane escorted by six fighters, arrive Ballale 0800. Depart at once in subchaser to arrive Shortland 0840. Depart Shortland 0945 in subchaser to arrive Ballale 1030. Depart Ballale by plane to arrive Buin at 1110. Lunch at Buin. Depart Buin 1400 by plane to arrive Rabaul 1540.[2]

Within Rochefort's group, the intercept drew attention because of its large number of addressees. An experienced cryptanalyst, "Red" Lasswell, decoded the mention of the commander in chief, who was Yamamoto himself. He leaped to his feet and exclaimed, "We've hit the jackpot!"

Lasswell worked through the night to carry through the decryption. With help from colleagues, he got out nearly the whole of it, including the vital references to Ballale Island, off Bougainville. He passed the decode to Jasper Holmes, who discussed it with Edwin Layton, Nimitz's intelligence officer. Layton was well aware that by knowing Yamamoto's travel schedule, American forces might be able to find him and kill him.

Nimitz responded with a message to the South Pacific commander, Admiral William Halsey, directing him to do this. He added, "Good luck and good hunting." Halsey sent the order onward to Rear Admiral Marc Mitscher, commanding in the Solomons, with his own note: "Destroy the target at any cost." Mitscher quickly arranged a meeting with Major John Mitchell, commanding the Army's 339th Fighter Squadron, to plan the attack.

"Mitscher wanted to know if we could get Yamamoto by attacking his boat," Mitchell later recalled. "Yamamoto was going to travel between islands in a submarine tender. I told the admiral that I could hardly tell a submarine tender from a submarine, and in any case, even if we sank the right ship, Yamamoto might get away in a dinghy. I said the surest way to get him would be to shoot him down in the air." The admiral's plane was a twin-engine Betty bomber, which might be easy prey.

Mitchell's fighters were P-38s, twin-engine aircraft that could carry long-range fuel tanks. They did not carry onboard radar; to find the quarry, their pilots would have to search with their own eyes. They were to take off from Henderson at 7:30 A.M., then fly northwest for two hours at an altitude of fifty feet, navigating entirely over water and out of sight of islands that held Japanese coastwatchers. To plan the intercept, Mitchell recalls, "I had to back up all the times, from Yamamoto's landing time." The intercept had to take place well up the coast of Bougainville, away from a force of seventy-five Zeros that were based near Ballale. To estimate the Betty's speed, he had no intelligence information; he relied on his experience that such twin-engine bombers tended to cruise near 180 knots.

His squadron's navigational instruments consisted of only a naval compass, a wristwatch, and airspeed indicators. With these, Mitchell proceeded to guide his men across 410 miles of open sea. He relied entirely on dead reckoning to make the intercept. His course consisted of a series of legs, during each of which he maintained bearing and airspeed for a calculated duration, then turned to a new heading for the next leg. "It was hazy," Mitchell continues. "I didn't see a rock until we made landfall." Maintaining radio silence, they cruised at two hundred knots, just above the waves.

Meanwhile, Yamamoto was following his own schedule with similar precision. Ordinarily he and his staff wore dress whites, but for this field inspection, he decided on fatigues. Two of his aides failed to get the word, showing up at the Rabaul airstrip in dress uniform. Yamamoto considered whether to send them back to change, but this would have delayed his departure. He decided that it was more important to keep to his timeline—a decision that cost him his life.

Mitchell's navigation proved to be astoundingly accurate. "We came up to the coast of Bougainville within a minute of our planned arrival time," he said. His squadron, with sixteen P-38s, flew past Empress Augusta Bay. One of the pilots broke radio silence, saying, "Bogeys eleven o'clock high." The Americans were in excellent position to attack, facing two Bettys along with the six Zeros. A dozen P-38s climbed to fly cover at twenty thousand feet, with the enemy at forty-five hundred feet. Mitchell had chosen Tom Lanphier, a particularly skilled flier, to lead a "killer group" of four remaining fighters. Now he gave the order: "He's all yours, Tom."

Lanphier went in to attack the lead Betty, with his wingman, Rex Barber, close at hand. Three Zeros immediately jumped Lanphier, who broke away to meet them head-on. This left Barber free to pounce on the Betty's tail, and to deliver a withering fire. "I shot into his right engine," Barber recalls. "Into his fuselage, his left engine, then back into his right engine. He had steepened his dive; now he was at less than five hundred feet, and his right engine was smoking badly."

Meanwhile, Lanphier shook off the Zeros and approached the same Betty from the side. He fired; it went down into the jungle; part of a wing came off as it struck a tree. Barber had flown past this bomber, and as he looked behind he saw a pillar of smoke where it had crashed within the heavy growth.

The next day, Japanese searchers reached the crash site. They found the body of Yamamoto, dressed in his khakis, still wearing a white glove and holding a dress sword in his hand. He had taken two bullets, one of them in the left shoulder. The one that killed him had pierced the lower left jaw, exiting at the right temple.

His career, and his fate, mirrored those of Japan itself. He had trained at Etajima amid visions of glory in battle; he had shed blood at Tsushima. But when he died, it was not amid the roar of heavy guns on an admiral's flagship. It was in an inadequate twin-engine bomber, attempting to flee from the overwhelming superiority of the Yankees. He did not die a hero's death at sea; he perished amid distant jungles, on a remote island where Japan was losing the war.

"The War Is Over"   *13*

STRAFING TARGETS was one of several ways to make an air attack. You flew in close to the ground, as low as fifty feet; when you faced flak or machine-gun fire, your main hope was to get out of the danger zone before getting hit. Your fighter-bomber had machine guns of its own, .50-caliber weapons that converged at a range of 750 feet. Two hundred feet from the target, you pulled up and away, less than half a second from a fatal collision. If you had strafed an ammunition truck, its explosion would probably bring you down, anyway.

Low-level bombing had its own dangers, the most straightforward of which came from topography. The war in Italy was prolonged and deadly; much effort went into striking at the railroads, and one of the best ways was to blow a tunnel. Such a tunnel often presented itself as a small hole at the base of a granite mountain with a height of several thousand feet. You flew low above the track, dropped a thousand-pound bomb with a delayed-action fuse, and hoped it would skip into the tunnel's mouth, while you took quick evasive action to avoid crashing into the rock. If your aim was off, the bomb would ricochet off the mountainside, back toward your airplane, as you flew upward.

On flat ground, some of the most critical targets had defenses in depth. Among the most heavily defended sites was the complex of Romanian refineries at Ploesti, north of Bucharest, that provided Hitler with over one-third of his oil. It featured hundreds of flak guns, close to three hundred machine guns, and barrage balloons that dangled steel cables. These could slice off a bomber's wing. Air defense included 120 fighters of the Luftwaffe, supplemented by 200 in the Romanian air force.

Ploesti nevertheless had to be taken out, and a force of B-24s made the attempt in August 1943. They roared through the refineries between the towers of the cracking plants, as exploding oil tanks threw fireballs into the sky. Erupting storage tanks blew their lids into the paths of the aircraft. Airborne gunners, within the B-24s, exchanged fire with defending gunners in water towers, atop refinery units, and even aboard a railroad train that tried to keep pace with the slow-flying planes. Amid the billows of heavy black smoke, seventy-three bombers went down, nearly half of the attacking force. Another fifty-five received major damage.

For other targets, low-level bombing demanded great ingenuity. This was particularly true of two of Germany's great dams, the Moehne and the Eder. They were stoutly constructed of thick concrete, but the British scientist Barnes Wallis believed that they would be far less formidable if attacked with ordnance of proper design. Wallis was the top designer at the firm of Vickers, having carried through the structural layout of its R-100 dirigible. He also designed the Wellesley bomber, which set a nonstop distance record, and the Wellington, which for several years was the mainstay of RAF Bomber Command.

Barnes hoped to destroy those dams using the water-hammer effect, whereby a powerful underwater explosion could stave in a heavy wall. Such water hammers, produced by near misses, had sunk battleships. Barnes found that a charge of high explosive, detonating deep in a reservoir and very close to the dam's rear face, would shatter it. He devised a large, elongated bomb that would skip like a stone when dropped at very low altitude. If released at the right point, well behind the dam, it would sink against that face and blow it open.

This demanded the ultimate in precision flying, with aircrews maintaining specified speed and altitude while triggering their bomb releases just at the right moment. Standard airspeed indicators had enough accuracy for this purpose. For altitude, each bomber carried two fuselage-mounted lights that pointed downward and inward. At the proper elevation, sixty feet, their reflections touched, forming a figure-eight on the water below.

Achieving the right drop point was also simple. The Moehne, for instance, had two towers along its parapet, set six hundred feet apart. The bombardier squinted through an eyehole, looking past a handheld wooden triangle with two nails set wide apart. When the towers were in line with the nails, it was Bomb Away.

Squadron 617, trained as a team of specialists, raided the dams in May 1943. The Moehne had machine gunners, particularly within the towers, but the attacking Lancaster bombers had guns of their own, which spoiled the Germans' aim. When the dam cracked open, a wall of water rolled down the valley. In a nearby village, a priest heard the bombs exploding and rang a bell to warn the people. He was still at it when the thundering flood swept him away. The Eder Dam was easier, for it lacked defenses. This allowed the pilots to make repeated practice runs until they were ready. Then they. blew it apart.

Still, precision bombing was often a contradiction in terms. Sometimes the bombers simply missed. In Norway, an outfit called Norsk Hydro was producing heavy water that was essential for the German atomic-bomb program. A hundred forty B-17s struck this plant in November 1943, releasing seven hundred bombs. None hit the aiming point, and it took a commando to carry out the sabotage that denied this stock of heavy water to Hitler.

In addition, many targets resisted destruction, for the Nazis had plenty of slaves and quickly brought damaged facilities back on stream. Ploesti, for one, had abundant reserve capacity; the Germans maintained production and rebuilt the burned-out installations, while Allied bombers stayed away. Then, eight months after the initial raid, the bombers returned—and they kept on coming. Raids proceeded through the following four months, an average of about one per week, producing cumulative damage while denying Germany the opportunity to rebuild. Thirty thousand slaves tried to keep the damage under control, but in August 1944 there was very little left to hit, and production was down by 90 percent, according to intelligence estimates. Then the Soviet army took Ploesti, winning little of immediate usefulness but eliminating the need for further strikes. Still, it took twenty massive attacks by hundreds of heavy bombers to achieve this.

Cities also received such strikes. They began as ripostes to the Nazi terror in London, quickly escalating to levels of ferocity that Goering never matched. With this, the prime military objective became not the army in the field or the war industries that built weapons but a family's hearth and the pictures on its mantel. It was all very fine to destroy machine tools, but it was equally effective to kill the machinist who used them. If bombs maimed his children or dismembered his wife, if incendiaries reduced a cherished sweetheart to a charred corpse—well, it wasn't the Allies who had started the war.

Sir Arthur "Bomber" Harris, head of RAF Bomber Command, was a leading proponent of this use of air power. People called him Butch, for butcher. He was a forceful and thoroughly determined man who ridiculed suggestions that strikes at military targets alone could win the war. He derided their advocates as "panacea merchants, wanting to send a bomber to pull the plug out of Hitler's bath so he would die of pneumonia." He ordered that air operations "should now be focussed on the morale of the enemy civil population and in particular, of the industrial workers"—by deliberately seeking to kill them.

In pursuing this approach to war, in using Goering's own methods against him, Harris had the support of Churchill himself. In July 1940, Churchill had written a memo to Lord Beaverbrook, the minister of aircraft production:

> In the fierce light of the present emergency the fighter is the need, and the output of fighters must be the prime consideration till we have broken the enemy's attack. But when I look round to see how we can win the war, I see that there is only one sure path. We have no Continental army which can defeat the German military power. . . . But there is one thing that will bring him back and bring him down, and that is an absolutely devastating, exterminating attack by very heavy bombers from this country upon the Nazi homeland. We must be able to overwhelm them by this means, without which I do not see a way through.[1]

To implement such attacks, Harris favored using the largest possible number of bombers. This would do more than increase the destruction; he believed that it would minimize the losses, by overwhelming the defenses.

Harris took over Bomber Command in February 1942, and within days he conducted his first strike. The target was not a city, not yet; it was a large Renault plant near Paris that built some fourteen thousand trucks per year. His planes came in at night, with the moon nearly full and in clear visibility. A force of 223 bombers reached this plant and dropped 470 tons, with only one plane being lost. Production halted for an entire month and did not recover for several more. It was a solid success for British arms, and whetted Harris's appetite.

Late in March he struck Lübeck, Germany, with a bomber fleet of similar size, in his first significant raid on a city. Because it lay on an island at the mouth of a river, it was easy to find. It was lightly defended; it also was full of wooden buildings that ignited easily. Harris loaded more than half his bombers with incendiaries, and burned out nearly a third of a square mile in the city center.

Cologne came next. Harris had a front-line operational force of 416 bombers, but he wanted to show what a thousand planes could do. By drawing on his reserves and his training units, he mustered 1,046. As they crossed the North Sea, they formed a stream seventy miles long. This raid destroyed a square mile of built-up area, though the bombs spared the city's great medieval cathedral, with its twin towers.

A year later, with much experience having been gained, Harris issued Operation Order No. 173, classified Most Secret:

INFORMATION

1. The importance of HAMBURG, the second largest city in Germany with a population of 1½ millions, is well known and needs no further emphasis. The total destruction of this city would achieve immeasurable results in reducing the industrial capacity of the enemy's war machine. This, together with the effect on German morale, which would be felt throughout the country, would play a very important part in shortening and in winning the war.
2. The "Battle of Hamburg" cannot be won in a single night. It is estimated that at least 10,000 tons of bombs will have to be dropped to complete the process of elimination. To achieve the maximum effect of air bombardment this city should be subjected to sustained attack. . . .

INTENTION

4. To destroy HAMBURG.[2]

The second of several raids, during the early morning hours of July 28, 1943, was the one that carried through the annihilation of the city. "It was completely quiet," a woman later recalled. "No planes. No flak. It was an enchantingly beautiful summer night."

It was Harris's practice to drop high explosives and incendiaries in approximately equal tonnages. The former blasted homes and buildings into kindling; the latter set it alight. As the British airmen flew high above the burning city, they were awed at what they saw. One sergeant later declared that "it was as if I was looking into what I imagined to be an active volcano." There also were comments from a flight lieutenant:

The burning of Hamburg that night was remarkable in that I saw not many fires but one. Set in the darkness was a turbulent dome of bright red fire, lighted and ignited like the glowing heart of a vast brazier. I saw no streets, no outlines of buildings, only brighter fires which flared like yellow torches against a background of bright red ash. Above the city was a misty red haze. I looked down, fascinated but aghast, satisfied yet horrified. I had never seen a fire like that before and was never to see its like again.

Another sergeant saw similar views:

I was fascinated by the awesome and amazing spectacle. As far as I could see was one mass of fire. "A sea of flame" has been the description and that's an understatement. It was so bright that I could read the target maps and adjust the bombsight.

A flight sergeant:

> I was amazed at the awe-inspiring sight of the target area. It
> seemed as though the whole of Hamburg was on fire from one end
> to the other and a huge column of smoke was towering well above
> us—and we were on 20,000 feet! It all seemed almost incredible
> and, when I realized that I was looking at a city with a population
> of two millions, it became almost frightening to think of what must
> be going on down there.[3]

The chief of police, who indeed was down there, captured the event
in a single word written in his log: *Feuersturm,* or "firestorm." This was
a conflagration greatly intensified by a combination of well-concentrated
bombing and weather conditions. The evening had been warm and very
dry; the night was calm, with no wind. A layer of warm, still air covered
the city. When the fires started, they produced a powerful updraft.
Intense gales stormed inwardly from all directions, blowing with hurricane force, tearing trees from the ground by their roots, filling the air
with blizzards of red sparks. These gusts fanned flames into roaring
infernos that spread and combined, torching buildings that the fire-
bombs had missed. There was no way to fight this holocaust; firemen
had to let the affected city areas burn until all was consumed.

Air-raid shelters had saved many lives in previous raids, but now
some of them became gas chambers and crematoria. Carbon monoxide
entered them, killing people by silent suffocation where they stood.
When smoke came in as well, people realized that they were in imminent peril, and tried to escape to the streets. Sometimes they couldn't,
for collapsed brick buildings blocked their exits. As the temperature
rose within these underground rooms, bodies shriveled and desiccated,
with their fat melting into black, greasy pools. If there was enough oxygen and the heat was sufficiently great, the bodies would ignite, burning
until little was left except ash. Others remained recognizable, though
their faces were contorted by their dying screams, with mouths open
and lips drawn back.

A mother saved her teenage girl by wrapping her in wet sheets. "I
hesitated at the door," she recalled. "In front of me I could see only
fire—everything red, like the door to a furnace. An intense heat struck
me. A burning beam fell in front of my feet." Later, when both mother
and daughter were safe, the girl saw what looked like tailors' dummies
in the streets. This puzzled her, for she knew that this was not the garment district. Her mother grabbed her arm and said, "Go on. Don't look
too closely. We have to get out of here. Those are dead bodies."

A young man, close to the center of the firestorm, took a gas mask into his shelter. "Everyone became severely affected by smoke," he declared. "I heard people screaming but this became less and less; I believe they were suffocating. I never found my parents and was never sure where or how they died. Later, when their shelter was cleared, they found fifty-five bodies—at least they found fifty-five skulls."

Another woman tried to find safety in the company of her mother and aunt. They couldn't cross a particular street "because the asphalt had melted. There were people on the roadway, some already dead, some still lying alive but stuck in the asphalt. They must have rushed on to the roadway without thinking. Their feet had got stuck and then they had put out their hands to try to get out again. They were on their hands and knees screaming." She rolled down an embankment: "I think I rolled over some people who were still alive." She later identified the body of her aunt by recognizing her sapphire ring.

"The screams of the burning and dying people are unforgettable," declared a fifteen-year-old boy. "When a human being dies, he screams and whimpers and, then, there is the death rattle in his throat, not at all bravely and not as beautifully as in a film." A young woman tried to find her parents and saw more:

> Everything seemed to have melted and pressed the bodies away in front of it. Women and children were so charred as to be unrecognizable; those that had died through lack of oxygen were half charred and recognizable. Their brains had tumbled from their burst temples and their insides from the soft parts under the ribs. The smallest children lay like fried eels on the pavement. Even in death, they showed signs of how they must have suffered—their hands and arms stretched out as if to protect themselves from that pitiless heat.
>
> I found the bodies of my parents but it was forbidden to take them because of the danger of epidemic. All their precious little possessions they had taken to the basement were stolen. I had no tears. The eyes became bigger but the mouth remained closed tight.

Many of the dead lay facedown in the streets, one arm trying to protect the head, with the body withered to half its normal size. Within the burned-out districts, the roofless ruins of apartment buildings stood like stumps after a forest fire, interiors gutted, ground levels filled with broken bricks and the charred remains of personal belongings. Uncollapsed walls stood with empty windows gaping like eye sockets in a skull.

The fires died down, but the horror continued. A policeman on a motorcycle saw a young girl: "Her face was black with soot except for two streams of tears that were running down her face. She was dragging her little dead brother behind her; the right side of his face was already scraped smooth. She had been wandering around aimlessly for three days and two nights, I think." He took her to a first-aid station.[4]

This girl at least was among the survivors. However, this single raid took some 40,000 lives. Other attacks, during that same week, raised the total to 45,000; these dropped similar tonnages of bombs, but did not overwhelm the air-raid shelters by igniting firestorms. Nevertheless, the total of the dead approached the 51,509 British civilians who died under German bombing in the course of the entire war.

If Harris had been able to repeat his Hamburg achievement in other cities during the remainder of 1943, he might have gone far toward knocking Germany out of the war. However, Hamburg proved unique, not only in damage inflicted but in low RAF losses. The British flew under the protection of darkness, while the Luftwaffe air defense system relied heavily on radar. German defenders used their installations to vector night fighters that made interceptions. Over the city, attacking bombers faced radar-guided flak, helped at times by searchlights. But during the Battle of Hamburg, the RAF countered the radar as air crews dumped strips of aluminized paper from their planes. This countermeasure, known as "window," blinded the German radar by swamping the scopes with false returns. As a result, less than 3 percent of the raiders were shot down, most of them by night fighters. Flak proved almost totally ineffective.

Goering had feared that the British would overcome his radar in this fashion, and he responded with new tactics. The most important, named Tame Boar, continued to use ground-based radar to direct defending night fighters into the bomber stream. However, these fighters now were to carry airborne radar, which operated at wavelengths that were immune to window. As an interim measure, Goering also spurred the use of Wild Boar. It called on fighters to attack bombers as targets of opportunity, finding them in the night sky as they reflected whatever light was at hand: searchlights, bright flares dropped as target markets, the glow of fires in the city. Some Wild Boar pilots cracked up their planes when they failed to find their blacked-out landing fields. Nevertheless, these tactics were in use when Harris launched his next wave of attacks. This time the target was Berlin.

He carried out nineteen such strikes between August 1943 and March 1944. Bomber Command dropped over thirty-three thousand tons, again divided evenly between high explosives and incendiaries. However, Berlin was not Hamburg. It was vast and sprawling, which encouraged bombardiers to scatter their ordnance with little concentrated effect.

In addition, the city had broad streets, lakes, parks and open spaces, and tracts of forest, all of which acted as firebreaks.

Meeting with Churchill, Harris had declared that a properly executed bombing campaign would "wreck Berlin from end to end. It will cost between 400-500 aircraft. It will cost Germany the war." The raids scored at least one useful success by damaging an important tank factory. An attack in November struck the Kurfürstendamm, the city's most fashionable avenue; it ripped out the Kaiser Wilhelm Memorial Church, creating a postwar monument. However, the lack of a firestorm allowed the air-raid shelters to do their work. Some ten thousand people died under the British bombs during this campaign. This meant ten thousand empty chairs at family tables, but Berlin was the world's third largest city, with a population of over four million.

The Luftwaffe initially used Wild Boar quite effectively and inflicted heavy losses on Bomber Command, both in aircraft and in trained men. During the fall of 1943, Harris markedly reduced the losses by sending his aircraft over the target in denser swarms. But the new year brought new tactics as the Germans introduced Tame Boar. Their air defenses gained effectiveness, with the British loss rate topping 9 percent—72 heavy bombers shot down out of 793 dispatched—on the last major strike, late in March. This was beyond the limit of what Harris was willing to accept. He turned away from further raids on Berlin, striking instead at targets in France in preparation for the Normandy invasion.

An RAF attack on Nuremberg, also in March, showed conclusively that the Luftwaffe now was strong enough to take back the night. This city lay in southern Germany, requiring Bomber Command to face the full power of the defenses both when going out and when returning. Tame Boar pilots had an easy time of it, helped by clear skies and a half moon that made the bombers' contrails stand out. Some fighters mounted upward-firing guns called *schräge Musik,* "slanted music," the German word for jazz. A British gunner, who survived after being shot down, wrote that "it was obvious that we had encountered for the first time some form of aircraft that could fire vertically upwards with extreme accuracy because I saw the tracer in the cannon shells pass vertically upwards through all four engines and the wings."

Nuremberg was important; Hitler had tried to seize power there in 1923, and had used it to stage dramatic annual Nazi Party rallies. But overcast covered the city that night; few bombs hit important targets, with many falling uselessly in the countryside. Aircraft losses topped 12 percent, well above the rate at which Bomber Command was receiving new planes and aircrews. In addition, 545 RAF men died that night, more than had been lost by Fighter Command during the entire Battle of Britain.

The American experience was similar; in some important ways it was worse. Whereas Harris favored strikes at cities, conducted at night, the Yankees flew during daylight. Their commanders believed that their dense bomber formations would protect themselves with massive numbers of airborne guns. These leaders also had high hopes for precision bombing, which might take out specific factories. In practice, the American approach differed little from that of the RAF, for when bombs missed their aim points, which was often, they usually fell into nearby blocks of workers' apartments. Still, as one general told Churchill, "we shall bomb them around the clock and the devil shall get no rest."

A single airplane in flight is a lovely thing, a graceful yet purposeful instrument of human ingenuity and will. A force of B-17s, flying against the Reich, was a sight to take the breath away. They flew in echelons, above a base of billowing cumulus, showing tight V-shaped formations as they painted the sky with their vapor trails. Properly trained, these squadrons showed the tight precision of uniformed soldiers on parade. Single planes might fall behind their fellows to fly alone, but still they shared the overall intent.

The ball-bearing industry offered an enticing target for this power. The German war machine ran on frictionless bearings, which saw lavish use in aircraft, tanks, motor vehicles, submarines, electrical equipment, precision instruments, and factory machinery. These systems featured the world-renowned craftsmanship of that nation, which showed itself in extensive use of such bearings. A single flak gun used some fifty of them; a twin-engine bomber called for over a thousand. The needs were prodigious; in the single month of December 1943, the aircraft industry alone used 2.4 million such bearings. Moreover, nearly half of German bearing production was concentrated within the single city of Schweinfurt.

In August 1943, American commanders launched a heavy attack on both this town and on Regensburg, an important center of aircraft production. The bombers were to receive fighter escort as far as the German border; then they would be on their own. Both targets lay deep within Germany, not far from Nuremberg, but pilots were not to fly a round-trip from their bases in England. Instead they were to cross the Alps and continue onward to airfields in North Africa.

Luftwaffe commanders were well aware of the range limits of their P-47 escorts, and as these fighters turned back, they pounced. Their own interceptors then fought a running battle down the length of Germany. These aircraft formed up beyond the range of the bombers' machine

B-17 bombers over Germany, with escorting fighters tracing contrails at higher altitude. (U.S. Air Force)

guns, forged ahead using their superior speed, then turned and rammed full tilt in head-on attacks, their guns shooting hot lead and explosive shells. The B-17 could take astonishing amounts of battle damage. One had its plexiglas nose blown away, with power lines ruptured and engines riddled; still it came home. Another lost its right stabilizer along with much of its rudder; it also came back. Nevertheless, one-sixth of the attacking aircraft—60 of 376—were shot down. Sixty others were damaged and had to be abandoned in Africa, while others had to be scrapped. The total losses approached 150.

Clearly, the African bases were not capable of providing adequate repair, and commanders returned to flying round-trips out of England. The next strike at Schweinfurt came on October 14, a day that lives in memory as Black Thursday. Two hundred ninety-one B-17s set out; sixty were shot down. Moreover, the second Schweinfurt raid was part of an aerial offensive that cost more than two hundred American heavy bombers in only two weeks.

The U.S. Air Force accepts that with its losses on Black Thursday, the Luftwaffe regained air superiority over Germany. In addition, damage to the ball-bearing plants proved to be repairable. Albert Speer, Hitler's armaments minister, later acknowledged that a concentrated and continuing series of strikes at that industry indeed would have crippled it, with devastating consequences for the overall war effort. However, the two raids of 1943 were not enough.

How, specifically, did the Luftwaffe regain its ability to defend the Reich? Against the Yankees, it was a matter of mustering enough fighter power to overwhelm the bristling machine guns of the bomber formations. The British proved tougher, for they attacked in larger numbers and at night. Nevertheless, Tame Boar proved to offer the key to British defeat in the air. These German victories did not amount to outright denial of Hitler's airspace to the Allies. But by imposing losses, in men and aircraft, that the British and Americans could not long withstand, Goering restored safety in much of the Fatherland.

The Allies needed something new, and it took the form of a fighter, the P-51 Mustang. It offered considerable advantages over the standard P-47; indeed, it proved so excellent a design that even though it was piston-powered, it remained in service well into the age of the jets. It used a liquid-cooled engine that permitted a more streamlined fuselage, which reduced drag. It cut its drag still further with an innovative wing. These improvements gave it good fuel economy for long range, while boosting its top speed. It also proved more maneuverable than the P-47. It tended naturally to pull out of a high-speed dive, whereas the P-47 did not. Indeed, a story went around that one well-muscled pilot had bent his control stick in exerting the force needed to prevent his P-47 from crashing into the ground.

With the coming of the new year of 1944, British and U.S. commanders set up a system of long-range fighter escort that proceeded in relays. RAF Spitfires, short in range, covered the Channel and the North Sea. P-47s reached beyond the German border; P-38s extended the cover well beyond the Ruhr. The new P-51s, their range increased with extra fuel tanks, would accompany the bombers as far as Berlin. The B-17s received more firepower as well, for the new B-17G mounted extra guns in front, to defend against head-on attacks.

Having fortified their Flying Fortresses, U.S. commanders launched a new aerial offensive. A key event came in February, as over a thousand bombers carried out coordinated strikes on a dozen aircraft-production centers. The Luftwaffe could not defend so many targets, while strong Yankee fighter escorts gave further protection. Only twenty-one of the planes went down. This highly encouraging result suggested that fighter escort indeed could permit a renewal of the daylight attacks. The result was Big Week, which expanded the strikes on German industry as RAF Bomber Command joined in, along with American bombers based in Italy.

Big Week proved to be considerably bigger than the RAF raids on Hamburg. The new offensive dropped some twenty thousand tons of bombs, hitting such targets as Brunswick, Schweinfurt, Augsburg, and Regensburg. The Luftwaffe rose in force to defend these cities, inflicting a serious toll; in the course of that week, late in February, the Allies lost nearly four hundred bombers. However, their commanders were willing to take such losses, at least for a time, and the escorting fighters shot down some five hundred defending interceptors. Bombs wrecked many more, in factories and on the ground.

The ubiquitous Jimmy Doolittle was doing a lot; he now was a general commanding U.S. bombers based in England. He sent them back to Berlin in early March. His fighter escort had plenty of P-47s; some of them carried drop tanks for extra range. Doolittle put up everything that would fly, sending out 730 heavy bombers accompanied by 800 fighters. The losses again were harrowing, for 69 of those bombers did not return, while half of those that did sustained damage. Nevertheless, two days later Doolittle did it again, this time with 623 bombers escorted by nearly 900 fighters. The Luftwaffe, weakened by recent losses, shot down fewer than 40 bombers, which was a welcome reduction.

This proved to be the breakthrough; after March 8, the Luftwaffe failed to mount an effective defense of Berlin. This weakness showed itself as early as the ninth, when 300 B-17s raided the German capital— and not a single fighter rose against them. Two weeks later, Doolittle sent out 650 heavies. He lost 12, all to flak and none to enemy aircraft.

What had happened? The Luftwaffe had fighter planes galore, but the new aerial offensive was sharply reducing its roster of experienced pilots. The monthly losses during early 1944 were staggering:

Month	Percentage
January	12
February	18
March	22
April	20

There were old airmen and bold airmen, but now there were few who were both old and bold. There were plenty of warm bodies to fill seats in the cockpits, but increasingly these were ninety-day wonders fresh from their training courses, sent to face Allied veterans. Fighter escort turned bombers into bait that lured Germany's Siegfrieds, while the accompanying P-47s and P-51s shot them down.

With Big Week, and with the subsequent raids on Berlin, the Luftwaffe broke its sword on the armor of America's air defense. When

Goering saw that the bombers attacking Berlin now had escort from fighters, and that his own aircraft could not counter these new air attacks, he told his staff, *"Der Krieg ist vorbei"*: "The war is over."

It actually continued for another year, with the RAF and the U.S. Army Air Forces delivering a total of 363 strikes against this city. Other raids came from Soviet forces advancing from the east. Much of Berlin was pounded into rubble. Some 72 million cubic yards of debris had to be cleared, nearly as much as had been dug out within the main excavation of the Panama Canal.

Yet even near the end, on the eve of the Nazi capitulation, the city continued to function after a fashion. Two-thirds of its factories remained in working order, though workers often took hours to reach their jobs. Policemen remained on duty; postmen delivered the mail; garbage collectors made their rounds. Newspapers came out every day, while the city retained its electric power and telephones. The Berlin Philharmonic went through a season of performances. Subways still ran; department stores advertised sales; women visited laundries, dry-cleaning shops, and beauty parlors. Restaurants continued to draw crowds.

Not until late in the war did the air offensive strike major blows against German industry. Hitler had said, "Give me six hundred tanks a month, and we will abolish every enemy in the world." Tank production reached a thousand a month at the end of 1943, and rose to 1,800 per month in November 1944. Construction of aircraft peaked in mid 1944 at 3,750 per month. At war's end the Ruhr was turning out 30,000 tons of finished goods, every *day*.

It was as much as to say that the more the Allies bombed, the more Germany produced. It took time for the United States to build strength in the air; then it took additional time to battle the Luftwaffe, while losing and then regaining air superiority. Meanwhile, British and American commanders tended to overestimate the effectiveness of their raids. Reconnaissance aircraft took photos that showed bomb damage, but these did not readily translate into clear views of lost production. This optimism, stemming often from lack of experience, kept the Allies from driving home the frequent and repeated strikes that would indeed have brought devastating destruction.

At the same time, while failing to attack with crippling blows, the air raids made clear to the Germans that they needed more, and soon. These raids spurred them to do all they could to increase production in a number of important industries. To this degree, then, the air attacks actually were counterproductive, stimulating a far-reaching buildup while failing to destroy the new facilities.

Nevertheless, in several respects the bombing campaign indeed brought valuable results. Though it failed to break the morale of Germany, it helped morale on the home front, showing the British and American public that the Nazis were open to attack by air if not yet on land. Air support had played a role in land battles as early as World War I; now the strategic bombing of Nazi-held Europe raised this to new heights. The aerial offensive against Germany led the Luftwaffe to withdraw front line fighter units from the Russian front to the interior of the Reich. This helped the Soviet army to achieve tactical air superiority, and to press its ground offensive more strongly.

Air power played a vital role in the Normandy invasion, without which Stalin alone would have won the war. The German air defense effort absorbed a considerable number of men and production capacity, which otherwise might have been available to oppose the landings in France. In addition, air strikes in the Normandy area enabled the Allies to gain their own control of the air. Hitler had failed to invade England because he could not defeat the RAF, but at Normandy in June 1944, the shoe was on the other foot. When Allied troops saw an airplane, they could count on it being one of theirs.

Bombing raids contributed materially to the victory by shutting down much of Germany's oil industry. Germany itself lacked deposits of petroleum, but imported part of what it needed from Hungary and Romania. In addition, it was rich in coal, and with great ingenuity its chemists constructed an array of synthetic-fuel plants that converted this coal into oil. In March 1944, with the natural and synthetic industries largely untouched, they produced nearly a million tons of refined products.

In August, after Allied bombers had paid their visits, this total dropped to 345,000 tons. It remained at or below that level during subsequent months. The falloff in the flow of aviation gasoline was even more dramatic, for production dropped from 180,000 tons in March to only 10,000 in September. In turn, the shortage of petroleum devastated the German army.

Late in 1944 Hitler assembled a force of fifteen hundred tanks and unleashed them once again, hoping to bring back the good old days by driving to the Channel. His commanders lacked fuel for this Battle of the Bulge, and pinned their hopes on capturing an American supply dump that held 3 million gallons. When they failed to do this, their offensive ground to a halt and left them open to counterattack.

The Allies also helped their cause by shutting down much of Germany's transportation system. It relied primarily on railroads, with useful support from canals and inland rivers. Initial attacks hit these water-ways, cutting movement of coal by nearly four-fifths. This forced the Germans to rely more than ever on the railroads, which became targets in their own right. Freight yards, where trains were made up and disas-sembled, proved particularly vulnerable. They were large in area, mak-ing them easy to hit, and when well cratered it took time to restore them to use. Bulldozers would have helped to fill in the craters, but the Germans tended to rely on slaves with shovels, who didn't work very rapidly.

Between August and December 1944, car loadings fell by a third. Yards and sidings filled with freight cars that could not be formed into trains, and workers derailed them in large numbers to keep them from blocking rights-of-way. Within the Ruhr, steel output fell to one-third and then to one-fourth of normal levels. Railroad bridges and viaducts came under attack. One important viaduct was wrecked so badly that it was never rebuilt; the Germans constructed a bypass after the war.

With the coming of spring in 1945, the heartland of the Reich still was in German hands. The Soviets were preparing the ground offensive that would take Berlin, but they continued to stand to the east of that city. American and British forces were crossing the Rhine, but had not yet achieved their breakout. Nevertheless, air attacks had already left the Ruhr isolated, shutting down all but two of its eighteen exits. This industrial area strangled on its own production, for there was no way to move its finished goods to the fighting troops. Within Germany, freight car loadings fell to 11 percent of normal; only 7,000 of 23,000 locomo-tives were operating. Even before the main armies arrived, the air war had reduced Germany to a hollow shell.

It took time to build the necessary strength. Even by early 1944, four years after the Nazis had burst into France, the Allied bomber forces had struck telling blows only in Hamburg and a few other places. But during the final year of the war, their attacks brought results that were measurable from month to month. Bombers did not win the war; victory went to the ground troops. Nevertheless, the contribution of air power was decisive.

General Curtis LeMay   14

DURING THE mid 1970s a judge in California, Ralph Nutter, was known to his friends as a liberal. He had worked as an attorney for the American Civil Liberties Union. He was talking with several associates at a cocktail party when someone mentioned General Curtis LeMay. Nutter remarked, "I named my oldest child after him." Everyone around him fell silent.

LeMay, after all, was widely known as one of the nation's leading right-wing extremists. He had built the U.S. Air Force's Strategic Air Command into a powerful nuclear strike force, and had emphasized that he was ready to use it. During the Vietnam War, he had demanded that North Vietnam withdraw, "or we're going to bomb them back into the Stone Age." During the 1968 presidential election, he ran on a third-party ticket with Alabama's governor, George Wallace, who was widely known as a racist.

"How could you name your child after that son-of-a-bitch?" one of Nutter's friends responded. The judge replied, "I served under him in England during World War II. I was a navigator in his 305th Bomb Group. He was so tough on us, he trained us so hard and prepared us so well, I honestly don't believe I'd have survived to have a child if it weren't for Curtis LeMay."

LeMay was a contemporary of Lindbergh, being only four years younger, but his path to the cockpit was considerably more roundabout. He came from a working-class family; his father held jobs on railroads when he could get them, moving his family around the country and doing other types of work when he couldn't. The boy spent his high school years in Columbus, Ohio, and as he looked ahead to adulthood he knew that he wanted to fly. The Army seemed to offer the best prospect, but he could not simply volunteer; he needed a commission as a second lieutenant. To get it, he enrolled at Ohio State University, in his hometown of Columbus, and joined the Reserve Officer Training Corps (ROTC).

General Curtis LeMay. (U.S. Air Force)

He set his sights on getting a degree in civil engineering. His courses in this field, added to his military studies, gave him plenty to do. In addition, his family lacked money to send him to college, so he worked his way through by holding a full-time job at the Buckeye Steel Casting Company. This job kept him up past 2:00 A.M. six nights a week, and with his sleep getting lost in the shuffle, he took to dozing off during some of his more boring engineering classes. He flunked one course two semesters in a row, and was fifteen credits short of his degree when he received his commission.

Nevertheless, he graduated with honors in ROTC. His commission made him a reserve officer, not a member of the Regular Army—which put him at the bottom of the totem pole for selection as a flight-school cadet. He solved that problem by joining the National Guard, thereby winning higher priority for flight training. He put in his application, then waited to see if a vacancy would open up. When it did, later that summer, he finally was on his way.

No fanfare greeted him when he arrived by train in Riverside, California, to begin his pilot training. To get to the base he walked into town, found the post office, waited for a mail truck, and rode in the truck to the airfield. But military life suited him, and he showed his commitment by turning down a civilian job as a pilot that would have paid $1,200 per month. The Depression was under way, a time when many men were supporting families by earning that much in a year. LeMay nevertheless stayed with the colors, taking his Army salary of $187 per month (including flight pay), and sending much of it home to help his family.

He obtained a posting to Columbus that allowed him to finish his engineering degree. Returning to full-time military duty, he then volunteered for navigation school. This was something new; military pilots had been flying by the seat of the pants and had found their way by following the railroad tracks, like everyone else. But the new course gave LeMay a solid introduction to blind flight and the use of instruments. His engineering background helped him learn this material, as he took to navigation as an important military specialty.

He had been flying fighter planes. Now, newly married, he received an assignment in Hawaii, where he and his wife lived in a cottage on the beach. He proceeded to set up a navigation school of his own, knowing that this subject would certainly be important when flying over the broad Pacific. Then in 1936, on returning to the mainland, he switched from fighters to bombers. He learned that the B-17 was on the way, with the prospect of offering a true offensive threat. Such a threat would make bombers far more important than fighters. In addition, their long range strongly suited his background in navigation.

He became an operations officer, quickly acquiring a mentor in Lieutenant Colonel Robert Olds. Olds had flown bombers against the Germans during World War I, and had gone on to work with Billy Mitchell. He made it clear to LeMay that their duty was simple: to take care that at all times, their force would be ready for war.

Most of their fellow officers started their day at 8:00 A.M. Olds liked to come in at seven, and LeMay soon made sure that he was at his own desk when his boss arrived. Olds liked to ask questions: "What's the weather at Wright Field? You should know; your planes can fly that far." LeMay responded by making a point of visiting the Weather Room every morning. Olds also asked, "How many of your planes are ready to fly today?" The engineering officer kept track of that, and LeMay got him to come in early as well. This allowed them to know the status of their force as each day began.

The Army began to receive B-17s during 1937 and 1938, and LeMay served as navigator during a succession of pioneering flights. One mission featured cooperation with the Navy, in an attempt to find the battleship *Utah* at sea. The Navy provided incorrect information, giving locations that were off by as much as sixty miles, but LeMay found it just the same. This exercise tested the ability of the Army's bombers to defend the nation's coasts, by locating enemy ships while they still were out in the ocean.

A similar exercise, in May 1938, sent three B-17s to rendezvous with the Italian liner *Rex*. Its course and speed were known, and LeMay estimated an intercept time of 12:25 P.M. Heavy storm clouds lay along his path, but he flew into clear weather just in time to see it dead ahead. LeMay's navigation allowed them to intercept the *Rex* on the first attempt and at the calculated time, six hundred miles at sea.

Other flights took his bombers to South America, on excursions that showed the flag. These missions also showed that the B-17 could navigate with accuracy over long distances. A fifteen-hour nonstop flight covered 2,850 miles and took them from Miami to Lima, Peru; the bombers then crossed the Andes using maps from *National Geographic*. Other connections took these aircraft over the Caribbean, demonstrating anew the ability to fly over oceans. During 1941, with the United States not yet in the war, LeMay went to Canada and flew a B-24 as part of an impromptu airline, carrying high-priority people across the Atlantic to England.

Following Pearl Harbor, LeMay received orders that sent him to serve as executive officer of the 306th Bomb Group, at Wendover, Utah. The 306th didn't yet exist; at Wendover, there was a lot more that didn't exist. The town, population three hundred, lay in the Nevada desert, with the Bonneville Salt Flats extending off to the east. The planes lacked hangars and the men lacked barracks; they slept in tents. They ate canned rations and dug latrines by hand. Some loyal wives, including LeMay's, followed their husbands to Wendover, where they found rooms in a hotel. Still, this certainly was no beach in Hawaii.

Soon LeMay took over an outfit of his own, the 305th, and took it to California's Muroc Dry Lake for training. Muroc, the future Edwards Air Force Base, was out in the Mojave Desert, and was considerably worse than Wendover. Here there was not even a hotel; wives had to live in Santa Monica, waiting for the occasional plane flight that might bring their men for a single day of leave. Temperatures at Muroc reached 120 degrees in the summer, and LeMay had to order his mechanics to work at night; in daytime they blistered their hands. But there was plenty of time for training, and LeMay insisted that this was what they were there for. Some men failed to measure up and transferred to other units. The ones who stayed took to calling him Iron Ass.

At the outset, in June 1942, the 305th had all of four B-17s. In October it had thirty, and was ready to deploy to England. Its bombardiers had never dropped a bomb in anger; its navigators had flown only practice flights. They had left Muroc for Syracuse, New York; LeMay now led them across the ocean, with stops in Maine, Newfoundland, and Scotland. He told the men that they were representing their country and would have to get along with their British allies: "If you go into their pubs, don't get into any fights with them. But if you do, make sure you win."

Their base, northwest of London, proved to be chilly, foggy, and damp. The men had barracks now, with coal stoves, but found them overcrowded and underheated. Still there was plenty to do, for they needed a great deal of practice flying before they could bomb the Reich. They flew their first operational mission late in November 1942, a month after their arrival in England, striking Saint-Nazaire in occupied France. The group lacked experience, but right at the start, LeMay began to display the leadership that in time would make him Air Force chief of staff.

Enemy flak was something to fear. Conventional wisdom held that bombers were to evade it by making evasive maneuvers while approaching the target. LeMay didn't like the idea; he knew that such maneuvers would play hob with bombing accuracy. He had studied artillery in ROTC; he had intelligence information on German antiaircraft guns. He decided that his bombers could fly straight in, achieving much better accuracy, without sustaining severe losses due to flak.

He issued appropriate orders to his men—and took the largest risk by flying the lead plane in his formation. He then led sixteen bombers of the 305th as they joined with other units to carry out the raid. LeMay's group put twice as many bombs on target as any other group, with none of his planes being shot down. Within three weeks, every other U.S. bomber outfit in England was also making straight-and-level bomb runs, without evasive action.

LeMay believed strongly that he could cut his losses by flying in tight formations, where the bristling machine guns of the bombers would give good mutual protection. The B-17 showed its ruggedness during his initial missions, for one of them took 150 bullet holes but came home safely. Still, LeMay's formations helped as well; he lost only two planes during his first six aerial raids. In January 1943 his commanding general called a conference, seeking to standardize the choice of combat formation. LeMay's was the one adopted, for he was putting more bombs on target than anyone else, while taking the fewest losses.

While winning support from his superiors, he remained Old Iron Ass to his aircrews. As he ceaselessly drove them to learn more and to practice more, the word got around: stay away from him, he's the meanest bastard in England. Some of his men said that they looked forward to being put in a German prison camp, for they needed a vacation. Yet LeMay accepted that he could learn from them, and they could learn from each other. Following a mission, he had them all gather for a debriefing session, telling them, "If you think your group commander is a stupid son-of-a-bitch, now is the time to say it. And why."

Other commanders hosted similar sessions, but their men quickly learned that these senior officers really wanted agreement, not criticism. LeMay meant what he said. He didn't want his men to die because of mistakes that they made, or that he made. He listened willingly, rarely saying much in response, and visitors came away astonished at the level of candor that he encouraged. It complemented his strong emphasis on training. In addition, the unit's demonstrated combat effectiveness made it one to watch.

LeMay kept looking for ways to further increase this effectiveness. There were a large number of potential targets, each to be reached by a specific route, and no bombardier could hope to recognize them all. This meant that after fighting their way to a target zone, his men might miss due to their inability to recognize the aim point. LeMay set his staff to developing target folders, containing maps and photos of likely assignments. Their information came from British and American intelligence sources as well as from libraries, bookstores, and the British Museum. Specific teams of navigators and bombardiers studied specific folders in detail. Then, when the entire 305th received its orders, one of these teams often knew the day's target in detail—and was picked to lead that particular mission.

In June 1943, LeMay received a promotion by being named a wing commander. He also received new headquarters within the opulent country estate of a wealthy earl. Its main building had over a hundred rooms, richly decorated and joined by marble corridors. LeMay's personal suite included a large living room and a bedroom with private bath. He wasn't ready for such luxury, for his previous headquarters had been a muddy Nissen hut. Nevertheless, he knew how to use those rooms. He told his intelligence officer, "I want you to start target study classes in every group."

The men of these groups continued to live within their own Nissen huts, at the air bases. They always had too much mud and not enough coal. Latrines seldom were clean; hot water often was hard to come by, and their rooms were cold, damp, and stinking. They had plenty of blankets for their beds, but these tended to get wet in the fog and the rainy weather.

With the men asleep in darkness, a mission began when an operations officer came in and flipped on the lights. Amid the sudden brightness, he called off the names of the men who were to fly that day, then told them the time of the preflight briefing. They made their way to the briefing room amid early morning drizzle, chill, and dampness. Sitting on wooden benches, they dozed, chatted, smoked, or stared ahead and waited.

An officer pulled back a curtain, displaying a map crossed by a length of yarn. The target lay at its end, a classified destination that the men were not to divulge or discuss. The briefing officer presented details: flak, fighter defenses, aim points, return routes. An intelligence specialist displayed reconnaissance photos by projecting them on a screen. Others spoke as well: weather officer, group bombardier, group navigator. Then, at a command, the men all synchronized their watches.

B-17s generally flew at around twenty-five thousand feet, where the temperature was thirty below zero. These bombers were unpressurized and unheated, so the men dressed warmly. Boots lined with sheepskin. Woolen long johns; sometimes an electrically heated suit. Heavy outer clothing with a leather jacket. Mae West inflatable life preserver; parachute harness with its bulky chute; flak suit to protect the groin against shrapnel. Thick, heavy gloves. Leather helmet, often with a steel infantry helmet. Oxygen mask with hose line.

You took a leak before you took off, for you wanted full gas tanks and an empty bladder. Because you were still on the ground, you sweated freely, and as you crowded together with the flight crews, everyone stank of perspiration. Then came takeoff, with the planes lumbering into position and rising into the air at thirty-second intervals. During the climb to altitude, the hot sun beat through thinning air with the cloud deck well below, and you sweated some more. You wore your oxygen mask for hours, and it was damnably uncomfortable from perspiration that collected near your eyes. It stung and it itched, and you couldn't wipe it away because it lay beneath that mask.

Your pilot needed real physical strength to fly in formation, manhandling the controls in air made choppy from the planes up ahead. Flak appeared as small black puffs; a well-aimed shell could tear off part of the fuselage or send a wing plummeting amid a trail of flame. Enemy fighters attacked from the front and sometimes collided head-on. You knew that if your plane went down, you could try to bail out. If you succeeded, and you were over Germany, you'd spend the rest of the war in a prison camp. But at least you'd survive.

Plenty of your buddies didn't. Perhaps you had heard about the plane that slid out of formation when a German fighter put machine-gun bullets through the pilot's head. The copilot, splattered with that man's blood and brain tissue, went into shock. The aircraft still was flyable, and the navigator tried to bring it under control, but failed. The stricken bomber quickly attracted other fighters, who roared in to attack. Ten crewmen were aboard that B-17; two got out alive before it crashed.

Your bombardier took your plane in a straight-in approach to the target, shrugging off the flak, while onboard machine gunners fought like the devil against the fighters that continued to flash across the fields of view. The ball turret gunner had the worst of it, with his body and legs squeezed into a spherical enclosure on the plane's belly, and with the least chance of escaping if it went down. Then it was bombs away, knowing that if too many of them missed, you'd have to come back and do it again.

Homeward, through more flak, more enemy fighters. You picked up your own fighter escort, but by then you were already approaching England. Aircraft carrying wounded had priority when landing. At the base, people watched to see the planes return. An ambulance went out to meet them, but not all aircraft came back. Some, short of fuel, landed at other bases. Others, badly damaged, sometimes managed to ditch in the Channel. The rest simply were gone, shot down and lost. That night there were empty bunks in the huts, and empty places at the next morning's breakfast tables.

LeMay saw much of this at firsthand, for he personally flew his missions as a commander. He continued to do this until after the first Schweinfurt raid, in August 1943, when heavy losses made it all too likely that he would be shot down as well. But he now was on his way toward greater responsibilities, and he gained rank accordingly. He had been fighting his war as a colonel, but was promoted to brigadier general in September and to major general the following March. At age thirty-seven, he now was the youngest two-star general in the U.S. Army.

His new assignment took him to the Far East, to command an initial force of B-29s. This Boeing bomber was one of the war's great and costly gambles, but it was a gamble that the nation could not afford to lose. It was considerably larger and heavier than the B-17, with much longer range and a bigger bombload. However, it was being rushed into combat prematurely. It had been ordered into production before the prototype had made its first flight, and its engines had a tendency to swallow valves and catch on fire. No matter; people were on hand to try to deal with these matters, and meanwhile there was a war to win.

The new bombers flew out of bases in India and China. The latter location had no direct supply line; bombs and gasoline for its aircraft had to be flown in, over the Himalayas. It took seven round-trips across the Hump—seven successful round-trips—to carry enough fuel and ordnance for a single sortie by a single B-29. Certainly this was not the way to win an easy victory, but it offered priceless operational experience.

Characteristically, LeMay learned to fly the B-29 before taking command of his new force. On his first mission, in September 1944, he led 115 of the new planes and encountered Japanese fighters. They seemed to be no match for his fast bombers, and he said, "My first impression is that they won't be as tough as the Germans." He learned more in December, as he used incendiaries to strike at a major Japanese supply base. Most of its buildings were of wood, and LeMay was impressed at how easily they burned.

Already the war effort was preparing a new and much better B-29 base, at Tinian in the Marianas. A joint force of Army, Navy, and Marine units had taken the principal islands between June and August, with the Marines receiving most of the casualties. Navy Seabees, construction battalions, used bulldozers to put in runways, with the first attack on Tokyo taking place late in November. The distance was over fifteen hundred miles, the equivalent of striking at Moscow from a base near London. Every time a B-29 flew this round-trip, it covered the distance of a nonstop flight from Miami to Seattle.

The B-29s used standard B-17 day-bombing methods, striking at high altitude against specific targets such as steel plants. However, hard experience soon showed that this was not the way to proceed. The weather over Japan was cloudy much of the time, and suitable weather reports were scanty. Moreover, high-flying bombers often encountered the jet stream, with winds of two hundred miles per hour that played hob with bombing accuracy. This would not do; the head of the Army Air Forces, General Henry "Hap" Arnold, had staked much on the B-29, and he was eager to see it deliver results.

LeMay took over the force on Tinian in January 1945, and soon found himself being led to adopt the night-attack methods of the RAF's Bomber Harris. Flight at low altitude was an obvious possibility, to avoid the jet stream. Flak posed a clear danger, but as LeMay studied intelligence reports, he found good reason to doubt that Japan had anti-aircraft guns suitable for use against bombers at only a few thousand feet. "There was food for thought in this," he later wrote.

Now the logic of war drew him onward. Low-altitude flight would use less gasoline, for it would not be necessary for heavily loaded bombers to struggle up to the heights. Hence they could carry more weight in bombs, while lessening the strain on their engines. LeMay saw no danger in Japanese night fighters; hence he could remove his planes' machine guns and carry even larger bombloads. In turn, these loads could consist largely of incendiaries, with emphasis on a new type that used napalm. There would be high-explosive bombs as well, to chase away the firemen. He would not strike at discrete targets; his intention now was to burn down cities—if he could.

The destruction of Dresden, in mid February, showed that a sufficiently large force indeed could do this. Churchill himself ordered this attack; Harris responded with fourteen hundred bombers. They carried incendiaries, and for the first time since Hamburg, a raid sufficed to create a firestorm, killing some thirty-five thousand people. The next day, a U.S. force of similar size struck as well, with railyards as the prime targets. Clouds and smoke hid the city, but the Yankees dropped their bombs anyway, contributing to the general carnage.

Later that month, some sixty thousand Marines stormed ashore on Iwo Jima. This island had received weeks of continuous bombardment, from aircraft as well as from the Navy's heavy guns. It did little good, for the Japanese held an impregnable array of tunnels and caves, some extending five levels down. The Marines had to clean them out by hand; total U.S. losses came to nearly seven thousand dead and twenty-two thousand wounded. Only a handful of the defenders surrendered; most units fought to the last man, hoping to take as many Americans with them as possible.

Iwo Jima gave a foretaste of battles to come. Senior generals, along with the civilian leaders in Washington, accepted that Japan could only be defeated through invasion of its home islands—at a cost of up to half a million U.S. casualties. If air power could reduce this toll, by weakening the enemy, now was the time to do it. Ever since Billy Mitchell, airpower advocates had been touting the strength of their weapons. They had been persuasive enough to receive the B-29. But this new bomber was doing little to win the war, and now was the time for its advocates—notably General Arnold—to put up or shut up.

On February 19, LeMay received orders from Washington that directed him to place increased emphasis on using incendiaries to strike at cities. This order came less than a week after the destruction of Dresden, coinciding with the first landings on Iwo Jima. He responded with a preliminary attack on Tokyo that placed 453 tons of bombs within a single square mile. When he received the reconnaissance photos a few days later, he saw that this area had been reduced to ashes, with twenty-eight thousand homes and buildings destroyed. This was what he wanted. Now he knew what to do.

Two weeks later, on the night of March 9, he orchestrated one of the greatest man-made catastrophes in history. He sent 334 B-29s against Tokyo, with the first of them arriving shortly after midnight. A brisk wind was blowing as lead aircraft marked the city with fire, laying down a long swath of flame and then crossing it with another to form a blazing X. The wind grew stronger, while the main force turned additional districts into fiery furnaces. The updrafts were so intense that some bombers turned completely over.

Sixteen square miles burned to the ground. Nearly eighty-four thousand people died in the conflagration, over half of them suffocating from lack of oxygen. A million more lost their homes. Arnold was delighted, writing a letter that began "My dear Curt" and then continued: "As one of my first acts after returning to Washington after an absence of several weeks, I want to commend you and your Command on the superb operations you have conducted during the last month."

LeMay lost little time in giving Arnold further cause to cheer. During the next several nights he struck Nagoya, Osaka, and Kobe, burning out a total of sixteen additional square miles. Then he had to stop for the moment, for he had literally run out of bombs. Nevertheless, he now believed that his bombers alone might win the war. He expressed this view in a letter to his commander:

> I am influenced by the conviction that the present stage of development of the air war against Japan presents the AAF for the first time with the opportunity of proving the power of the strategic air arm. I consider that for the first time strategic air bombardment faces a situation in which its strength is proportionate to the magnitude of its task. I feel that the destruction of Japan's ability to wage war lies within the capability of this command, provided its maximum capacity is exerted unstintingly during the next six months, which is considered to be the critical period.[1]

It took awhile before he could repeat his successes of mid March. He had to wait for more bombs to arrive; he also received orders that diverted his aircraft to support of the Navy and the Marines, dropping mines into Japanese home waters and providing tactical bombardment for the invasion of Okinawa. Nevertheless, by mid June the devastated city areas topped a hundred square miles, which was five times the area of Manhattan. LeMay wrote that at the current rate, "it is expected to complete strategic bombing of Japan by 1 Jan 46." By the end of 1945, he expected to burn that nation to ashes.

Tokyo took the brunt of his attacks, with over fifty square miles lying in ruins. With factories as well as homes reduced to cinders, survivors

Tokyo in 1945 following the fire raids. Most trees were gone; standing buildings were burned-out skeletons. (American Heritage)

evacuated this city by the millions; its population dropped from over 5 million to less than half that level. And worse was to come, from an outfit called the 509th Composite Group.

The 509th was a picked unit. Its commander, Paul Tibbets, was a lieutenant colonel; his selection received the approval of no less than Arnold himself, who was a full general. Tibbets had led the first B-17 mission from England, had led the first bomber strike during the invasion of North Africa, and had piloted General Eisenhower to his command post. He also had served as a test pilot in the B-29. His new mission was to drop the atomic bomb.

The 509th flew out to Tinian while the bombing of Japan was rising toward its peak, but this group did not participate in the strikes. Its people kept to themselves, living within a cocoon of secrecy that was unusually strict even by military standards. Individual B-29s flew long-range missions and dropped single large dummy bombs painted orange, known as "pumpkins." They were full-size replicas of the plutonium bomb, though the men didn't know that. After dropping them, they executed unusual evasive maneuvers as they turned away. One bombardier from another group mocked them:

Into the air the secret rose,
Where they're going, nobody knows.
Tomorrow they'll return again,
But we'll never know where they've been.
Don't ask about results or such,
Unless you want to get in Dutch.
But take it from one who knows the score,
The 509th is winning the war.[2]

The last line showed no prescience; it merely played on a series of long-running advertising themes whereby food, oil, Lucky Strike Green, and much else was winning the war. Nevertheless, President Harry Truman had the responsibility of deciding whether to use the new weapons, and he made this decision amid clear warnings of anticipated casualties during the planned invasion of Japan's home islands.

In addition to Iwo Jima, the assault on Okinawa offered its own numbers, which were newer and deadlier. The Japanese had used kamikazes, suicide aircraft whose pilots had deliberately plunged them into naval warships. These attacks demonstrated anew the enemy's willingness to die for the emperor; they also killed over 4,900 Navy men. The complete butcher's bill came to 12,520 dead and 36,631 wounded, close to twice the toll on Iwo.

The planned home-island invasion was to take place in two steps. The first, Operation Olympic, was set for November 1; it was to seize Kyushu, the southernmost of the main islands. Operation Coronet was on the calendar for March 1, 1946. Its goal was to take and secure Honshu, the principal island, including Tokyo and other major cities. During July, Truman received estimates stating that the total casualties would run as high as 220,000, including 46,000 dead. He responded by authorizing a letter that went out from the office of General George Marshall, the Army's chief of staff:

1. The 509 Composite Group, 20th Air Force will deliver its first special bomb as soon as weather will permit visual bombing after about 3 August 1945 on one of the targets: Hiroshima, Kokura, Niigata and Nagasaki. . . .
2. Additional bombs will be delivered on the above targets as soon as made ready by the project staff.[3]

New estimates soon showed that Truman's casualty predictions were definitely on the low side. The medical staff of the Sixth Army, which had fought in the Philippines, estimated nearly four hundred thousand in Olympic alone, including some one hundred thousand dead. These were only the Army losses; the Navy could expect many more from kami-kazes held in reserve.

The Japanese knew that the next battle would fall on Kyushu, and were reinforcing its garrisons. American cryptanalysts were following this buildup by reading the message traffic. On July 24, General Marshall reported "approximately 500,000 troops" on this island, with a force of 680,000 expected on November 1. General Douglas MacArthur, who was to command the Army's divisions during Olympic, received a report warning that "this threatening development, if not checked, may grow to a point where we attack on a ratio of one to one, which is not the recipe for victory." Actually, Japan had 900,000 troops on Kyushu in early August, with more on the way. This was nearly fifty times its force on Iwo Jima.

So it was that on August 6, Tibbets flew to Hiroshima carrying a uranium bomb within his aircraft, *Enola Gay.* He had named it for his mother. His target was a city of considerable military importance; it was a major port of embarkation for troops reinforcing Kyushu, and was also home to Japan's Second Army. His copilot, Captain Robert Lewis, spent the time en route writing a letter home, adding, "There will be a short intermission while we bomb our target." Then he scrawled wildly: "MY GOD!"

It caught the people of the city unaware, for there were only three B-29s in the air, two of which carried observers. This looked like a reconnaissance or a weather mission, and did not trigger the air-raid sirens that would have sent people to their shelters. A blinding flash started fires across a wide area; a crushing shock wave flattened homes and buildings. Shards of glass riddled people's bodies, while their collapsing houses trapped them inside, with arms and legs broken. They died hideously as flames consumed them.

Some perished instantly, their bodies vaporizing and leaving only shadows on pavement. Others sustained burns from the flash that were worse than third degree, as skin died and weakened over large areas of their bodies. Moments later, the blast wave tore it loose. The dying then wandered in a state of shock, skin hanging like rags from their arms and faces, as they held their arms in front like sleepwalkers. One man stood naked, holding an eyeball in his hand. A man declared, "What made my blood run cold was that it looked like the eye was staring at me."

Radiation sickness struck many initial survivors, weakening them anew and killing them more slowly. One fourth-grade boy described how his mother lingered for nearly two weeks before she succumbed:

Mother was completely bedridden. The hair of her head had almost all fallen out, her chest was festering, and from the two-inch hole

Hiroshima, knocked flat to the horizon. (National Archives)

in her back a lot of maggots were crawling in and out. . . . Mother's condition got worse and we seemed to see her weakening before our eyes. . . . When we thought she had stopped breathing altogether, she took one deep breath and did not breathe any more after that. . . . At the site of the Japan Red Cross Hospital, the smell of the bodies being cremated is overpowering. Too much sorrow makes me like a stranger to myself, and yet despite my grief I cannot cry.[4]

"The world of the dead is a different place from the world of the living," writes the historian Richard Rhodes, "and it is hardly possible to visit there. That day in Hiroshima the two worlds nearly converged." The city had held a civilian population of some 290,000, along with 43,000 troops. By the end of the year, 140,000 of them lay dead, with another 60,000 dying during the subsequent five years.

So stunning was the blow, so sudden the shock, that it took time for officials in Tokyo to begin to grasp what had happened. Through August 6, all anyone knew was that they could not establish routine communications with the city, and no one understood why. Early on the seventh, a general received a report that made no sense to him: "The whole city of Hiroshima was destroyed instantly by a single bomb." American news reports already had trumpeted the tale of an atomic bomb. Japan had at least one first-rate nuclear physicist, Yoshio Nishina, who had conducted experiments with uranium and had considered what nuclear weapons might do to a city. Government officials flew him over Hiroshima, and as he later put it, "I decided at a glance that nothing but an atomic bomb could have created such devastation."

Truman already had issued an ultimatum, late in July, demanding "the unconditional surrender of all Japanese armed forces." The alternative would be "prompt and utter destruction." The prime minister, Baron Kantaro Suzuki, had responded with the word *mokusatsu,* "to treat it with silent contempt." This high-level rejection had brought the destruction of Hiroshima, and more devastation was at hand.

On August 9, just after midnight, the Soviet Union entered the war against Japan. This was totally unexpected, for diplomats in Tokyo had been sending out peace feelers through Moscow. The Soviets struck with 1.5 million men and 5,500 tanks, attacking Manchuria, which had been in Japanese hands since 1931. But many of its troops had been withdrawn for defense of the home islands, allowing these Soviet forces to advance rapidly against weak resistance.

On that same date, late in the morning, another plane from the 509th carried a plutonium bomb to Kokura, site of a major arsenal. Heavy ground haze obscured this target and the pilot, Major Charles Sweeney, turned away to Nagasaki, one of Kyushu's principal port cities. This bomb was more powerful than the earlier one—22 kilotons versus 12.5—but Nagasaki lay amid steep hills, which contained the damage. Even so, seventy thousand people died there by the end of 1945, with another seventy thousand perishing during the subsequent five years.

Early that morning, midway between these two events, the foreign minister called on Suzuki and demanded a meeting of the war cabinet. As this meeting proceeded, it quickly became clear that while civilian ministers were willing to accept Truman's terms of surrender, the military members insisted on fighting on. News of the catastrophe at Nagasaki arrived, making a strong impression on the minister of war, General Korechika Anami, who led the cabinet's diehards. He had refused to admit that the Hiroshima bomb was atomic. Now he told his fellow ministers that "the Americans appeared to have a hundred atomic bombs; they could drop three per day. The next target might well be Tokyo." But he did not budge in his demand for continued war, and the deadlock continued.

Suzuki adjourned the stalemated conference and convened a meeting of the full cabinet that afternoon. Again Anami stood by his guns, as he and his militarists continued to oppose a group of ministers who were willing to accept peace on Allied terms. Still Suzuki did not give up. He went to the palace and asked Emperor Hirohito to reconvene the cabinet meeting within the imperial grounds. He arrived just before midnight, and Suzuki asked an official to read Truman's terms to the group.

These terms had been on the table for over two weeks, and were far more lenient than what Japan had imposed on its own conquered peoples. War criminals were to receive "stern justice," but members of the armed forces were "to return to their homes." The Japanese nation was not to "be enslaved as a race or destroyed"; it was to give up its overseas empire, but would remain sovereign within its home islands. Japan was to "maintain such industries as will sustain her economy." The government was to guarantee "freedom of speech, of religion, and of thought, as well as respect for the fundamental human rights." The Allies would impose an occupation, but would withdraw their forces "as soon as these objectives have been accomplished."

At 2:00 A.M. on August 10, with the meeting still deadlocked, Suzuki did something unprecedented. He asked for a decision from Hirohito himself. This reflected the gravity of the moment; traditionally, the emperor did not speak, but merely hovered in the background. Hirohito now declared, "I give my sanction to the proposal to accept the Allied proclamation."

He did this with an important caveat: that he retain his throne. Truman's terms of surrender had left open the question of his postwar status. On this basis, at 7:00 A.M. the Foreign Ministry offered to accept Truman's provisions. Some twenty-four hours after Suzuki had initiated the previous day's meetings, peace was at hand.

Truman accepted the Japanese proviso, with Secretary of State James Byrnes stating that Hirohito's authority "shall be subject to the Supreme Commander of the Allied Powers." That is, he could keep his crown if he was willing to govern as a puppet of General MacArthur, the nation's postwar ruler. If he accepted this, the war indeed would end.

Hirohito agreed to host another cabinet meeting, which convened on the morning of the fourteenth. Again the ministers deadlocked on the question of war or peace. Then the emperor spoke through tears: "I have studied the terms of the Allied reply, and I have come to the conclusion that they represent a virtually complete acknowledgment of our position. In short, I consider the reply to be acceptable."

He then prepared to carry out another unprecedented act: for the first time, he would address his people, by radio. Never before had an emperor done this. He was said to possess the Voice of the Crane, which is heard as it flies unseen. Now, however, he went to a recording studio and made a record of his imperial rescript. Throughout the morning of the fifteenth, Radio Tokyo alerted its listeners to a "most important broadcast," which came at noon:

> Despite the best that has been done by everyone . . . the war situation has developed not necessarily to Japan's advantage, while the general trends of the world have all turned against her interest. Moreover, the enemy has begun to employ a new and most cruel bomb, the power of which to do damage is indeed incalculable, taking the toll of many innocent lives. . . . This is the reason why We have ordered the acceptance of the provisions of the Joint Declaration of the Powers. . . . We are keenly aware of the inmost feelings of all ye, Our subjects. However, it is according to the dictate of time and fate that We have resolved to pave the way for a grand peace for all generations to come by enduring the unendurable and suffering what is insufferable.[5]

World War II had lasted six years, with Japan's invasion of China dating to 1937. The war had been fought on three continents and across both the Atlantic and Pacific, engaging over a billion people. Still, when it ended, it did so in anticlimax. The Allied victory came in the shadow of the mushroom cloud. The bright hopes of peace dimmed within this shadow, which cast itself across the future. Yet there also was cause for hope. Humanity now held a new fire, which for good or ill might prove as portentous as its much earlier gift:

PROMETHEUS: I caused that man should cease foretelling doom.

CHORUS: To cure that malady what did you bring them?

PROMETHEUS: I set and placed within their hearts blind hopes.

CHORUS: This was a great gift that you brought to them.

PROMETHEUS: Beside that, I will add, I gave them fire.

CHORUS: Does mankind wield still that fervent flame?

PROMETHEUS: Yes, and 'twill teach them all their arts and skills.[6]

Germans Invent the Jet   *15*

WITHIN GERMANY, the University of Göttingen stands alongside England's Cambridge University as a center for human thought. Two centuries ago, its mathematician Carl Friedrich Gauss introduced research in his field in a form we pursue to this day. Its physicist Max Born was a founder of quantum mechanics; his graduate students included J. Robert Oppenheimer, who directed development of the atomic bomb. Göttingen also fostered work in applied science. Ludwig Prandtl founded the field of aerodynamics, and built up a center for experimental research in this new area.

Tradition marked this university. When a student received the Ph.D., custom required that he kiss the Goose Girl, a bronze statue that stood within a pool. Kissing the *Gänseliesel* meant getting wet, which was the point. Tradition also was at the forefront in the dueling societies, whose members were required to demonstrate Prussian strength by drinking until they dropped. The town was walled; university buildings dated to the eighteenth century but looked much older, displaying spires and gargoyles.

Yet events would show that one of the town's more important establishments was an auto garage. It stood along one of the cobblestoned streets, where a graduate student, Hans von Ohain, often took his car for service. He had received a fine education, with a strong emphasis on Latin and Greek; he was working on his Ph.D. in physics. Nevertheless, he was open to friendship with people who lacked this rarefied background. He soon found himself enjoying the company of Max Hahn, the chief mechanic at the garage. Together, they built the world's first turbojet.

The turbojet grew out of an earlier engine, the gas turbine. Specialists in aircraft propulsion were aware of its potential value, but they also knew that it could demonstrate this value only at high speed. Conventional piston engines worked quite well during the biplane era, when speeds were so low that jet engines would have been highly inefficient and hence not worth pursuing. But an annual race of high-performance seaplanes, the Schneider Cup, suggested strongly that the hottest aircraft were entering a realm where piston motors would falter.

Between 1921 and 1931, the Schneider record doubled, from 205 to 407 miles per hour. In 1934 an Italian entry raised this to 440 miles per hour. To Ohain, this meant that airframes capable of such speeds already were in hand. Yet propulsion for this Italian racer pressed the limits of the achievable, featuring two twelve-cylinder engines set back to back. Ohain considered that a gas turbine might offer lighter weight and vastly greater simplicity.

He developed his ideas further through discussions with investigators at Prandtl's aerodynamics center. Albert Betz, a colleague of Prandtl's, was directing the work, which aimed at building a rotating air compressor of high performance. Such a device could operate within a supercharger, to pump air into a piston motor for high-altitude flight, and Ohain saw that it could also supply air to his jet engine.

He drew up a design and arranged for his friend Max Hahn to build it, then placed it under test. An auxiliary motor set it spinning, and Hahn and Ohain hoped that it would operate on its own. They were disappointed. The fuel, gasoline, was supposed to burn within a combustion chamber, but instead it burned farther downstream, within the turbine that was supposed to drive the rotating compressor. "The apparatus resembled a flamethrower," Ohain wrote. He nevertheless found reason for hope, because "the flames came out at the right place with seemingly great speed." In addition, while the turbine failed to produce enough power to run the unit, it relieved much of the load on the drive motor.

Ohain now received interest and support from his professor, the physicist Robert Pohl. Within Göttingen's galaxy, Pohl was a star in his own right, working in electronics. Radios and similar circuits relied on vacuum tubes, but Pohl anticipated that these would give way to small crystals within which the motion of electrons could be precisely controlled. He conducted experiments; he initiated a line of research that culminated a decade later in the invention of the transistor.

He also was strongly involved in aviation, and had encouraged Ohain to pursue his own activities in engine research. By 1936 Ohain had gone as far as he could in his work at Hahn's garage, but he had convinced a willing Pohl that jet propulsion had a great future. Pohl now suggested that they seek support from industry, offering to write a letter of recommendation to the company of his choice. Ohain asked him to approach the planebuilder Ernst Heinkel, who held an active interest in high-performance designs. Pohl knew Heinkel personally, and sent off the letter.

Heinkel already had considered that rocket propulsion offered a potentially important path to high speed. He had recently met the rocket expert Wernher von Braun, and was helping him in his work. Jet propulsion offered another and perhaps more promising approach, for a rocket had to carry liquid oxygen in a tank, but a jet engine could use oxygen in the atmosphere. Hence it could stay aloft much longer. Heinkel invited Ohain to his home near the seacoast and found him to be "a very likeable young man, scarcely twenty-four years old, a brilliant scientist obviously filled with a burning faith in his idea." He hired Ohain, bringing in Max Hahn as well.

Ohain understood that his main problem was to arrange for his fuel to mix and burn rapidly within a compact combustion chamber. In his earlier engine, this had not happened sufficiently quickly; that was why the exhaust had showed flame, whereas it should have consisted entirely of hot combustion products. He decided that rather than continue working with gasoline, he would use hydrogen as his fuel, for he knew that it would mix readily with air and would burn almost immediately.

This engine made its first successful ground test in March 1937, delivering 550 pounds of thrust. "Hahn jubilantly called me up about one o'clock that morning," Heinkel wrote in his memoirs. "The unit had functioned for the first time. A quarter of an hour later I heard with my own ears that remarkable howling and whistling noise which made the whole workshop shudder." The psychological effect was enormous. Heinkel was a planebuilder, who had left engine development to such firms as Junkers and BMW. His company had no background in this area. Yet he had presided over the demonstration of an entirely new form of aircraft propulsion. Ohain, in turn, was free to pursue new research aimed at building a good gasoline-fueled combustion chamber.

This proof-of-concept demonstration complemented other Heinkel efforts that were building experimental rocket planes. As early as 1936, he had allowed von Braun to install an engine in an existing fuselage. Heinkel authorized a ground test, watching from behind a concrete wall. "A few moments later," he wrote, "a sinister red-and-white glow appeared at the tail of the plane and developed into a bright flame thirty feet long. Even behind the wall, we began to tremble as a result of the slipstream and the noise. About forty yards behind the plane some heavy steel plates were hurled into the air and tossed about."[1] This experiment left him convinced that rocket planes soon would become accomplished facts.

Flight tests followed. Heinkel donated a single-engine fighter, an He-112; von Braun installed a rocket motor at the rear, along with tanks for alcohol and liquid oxygen. The test pilot, Erich Warsitz, was to sit amid this propellant supply. The engine exploded during one of the tests, severely damaging the airplane, though Warsitz escaped unharmed. Heinkel gave the rocketeers a new fighter, which Warsitz took into the air in June 1937.

He took off under piston power, reached a normal flying speed of 190 miles per hour, then shut down this main engine and ignited his rocket. The plane leaped ahead, reaching 250 miles per hour using the rocket alone. Then a fire broke out in the rear of the aircraft, as leaking alcohol ignited. Warsitz brought the plane to a belly landing; a fire truck put out the flames and left the craft in condition to be repaired.

Only three months earlier, Ohain had successfully operated his hydrogen-fueled jet engine. Now Heinkel had achieved another milestone: for the first time, he had flown an airplane that used a propulsive jet in lieu of a propeller. Warsitz continued his test flights; Heinkel writes that when he took off using both piston and rocket power, he "shot almost vertically into the air." Warsitz also took off and flew with rocket power alone, again successfully.

In Kiel, Germany, an engineer named Helmuth Walter was also building rocket engines. He used hydrogen peroxide, which was tricky to handle but could be stored for long periods, whereas liquid oxygen tended to evaporate. Walter also found his way to Heinkel's office, and had one of his units installed in Warsitz's He-112. It again flew well. Heinkel then considered that because Walter's engines were compact and portable, they might help heavily loaded aircraft to ascend into the sky.

He tested this idea by installing two Walter rockets on a twin-engine bomber, loading it so heavily that it could not take off with its piston engines alone. The Walter units added extra power, enabling the plane to take off smoothly. Unloaded, the bomber "shot so fast and steeply into the sky with this rocket aid that the sight was truly awe-inspiring." Here was another important achievement. It showed that rocket engines could increase the capacity of existing warplanes, allowing them to carry more bombs or more fuel for longer range.

Walter had been receiving funds from the Air Ministry, which occupied a sprawling stone structure on the Wilhelmstrasse in Berlin. His contract officer, Hans Mauch, had a strong interest in advanced propulsion. Mauch took over this post in April 1938 and soon learned that Walter was working on a different type of engine, a ramjet. Soon after, Mauch learned that Heinkel was developing the turbojet of Ohain. Mauch visited Heinkel's plant in Rostock and saw that this planebuilder not only was crafting a flightworthy model, but was preparing to build a test aircraft, the He-178, that would use it for power.

Back in Berlin, Mauch circulated a notice stating that the government was seriously interested in jet propulsion. This brought a visit from Herbert Wagner, a senior manager in the airframe division of Junkers. Wagner had also tried to invent a turbojet, but like Ohain, he had also been stymied by the problem of rapid mixing and combustion. His engine ran at about half speed, with enormous fuel consumption, when fed with compressed air from an outside source. But as soon as this intake air was switched to atmospheric pressure, the engine power fell off and it came to a stop. Still, this showed Mauch that two major planebuilders—Heinkel and Junkers—had independently followed the same course and had encountered similar problems.

Another young engineer, Helmuth Schelp, was also stirring the pot. He held an unusually broad background, having studied engineering in both Germany and the United States. He also had worked in industry, having spent half a year at Daimler-Benz. He had recently completed an advanced course of study in Berlin that included independent research, qualifying him as a *Flugbaumeister,* "master of flight construction." This fitted him for a responsible position in industry or government, with assignments that were to be wide in scope.

His research had addressed the question: was there some natural limit to airspeed? He decided that this limit would result from the sound barrier, with a practical upper bound being Mach 0.82, some 625 miles per hour. He then considered how to propel an airplane at this speed. He decided the answer lay in building an air-breathing engine that would produce a propulsive jet. He knew of several ways to do this, but his calculations showed that the best approach was the turbojet.

He joined the Air Ministry in August 1937; a year later, he met Mauch. Schelp soon was regaling him with tales of jet-engine possibilities that were even broader than he had anticipated. Mauch responded by arranging for Schelp to join him as his assistant. At about the same time, Schelp's hopes for turbojets received new strength as he learned that Prandtl's research center in Göttingen had succeeded in building a compressor of particularly high performance. This meant that an important element of a jet engine was already in hand.

Up to this point, in the late summer of 1938, no one in the mainstream aeronautical-engine industry had touched a jet or rocket. These people had their hands full with piston motors for the coming war. The field of advanced propulsion belonged to talented entrepreneurs such as Walter and von Braun; to planebuilders at Junkers and Heinkel; and to academic researchers, including Ohain, Schelp, and Betz's group in

Göttingen. Nevertheless, Mauch and Schelp were well aware that this field would need the strong involvement of the big engine firms. Heinkel and Wagner had leaped into jet propulsion amid enthusiastic naivete, but professional engine builders understood the difficulties, while offering experience both in design and production.

During the fall of 1938, Mauch and Schelp visited Germany's major engine companies, dangling study contracts as a means of winning their interest. The firm of Brandenburg proved easy to persuade, for it had lost out in a consolidation of the industry, and was about to lose all its existing government contracts. BMW also showed interest, for it had been working on turbine-driven superchargers, and this experience carried over to jets. Junkers had been pursuing Wagner's engine within its aircraft division, which was independent of its engine division. However, the engine group entered the field as well.

With Brandenburg, BMW, and Junkers all pursuing studies, it was none too soon to look ahead to an operational fighter plane that could use their nascent engines. Within the Air Ministry, Schelp had a friend, Hans Antz, who shared his broad technical background and who also had qualified as a *Flugbaumeister*. Antz wanted to build such an airplane. He particularly wanted to work with the firm of Messerschmitt, which had distinguished itself with its Bf-109, the principal fighter of the Luftwaffe.

He approached the company's chief of development, Robert Lusser, and arranged to have him carry out preliminary design studies. Antz then returned with a specific order, calling for a jet fighter with one-hour endurance at 850 kilometers per hour, or 528 miles per hour. No military plane had yet reached 400 miles per hour, but Antz already was looking farther.

By 1939, then, plenty of people were talking about jet propulsion. However, no one had actually flown a jet plane. Heinkel and Ohain took care of that, using a gasoline-powered turbojet that delivered 1,100 pounds of thrust. The plane that was to fly with it, the He-178, had a length of only twenty-four feet and wingspan of twenty-three. Though small, it had received attention from some of the company's best engineers. Its engine was within the fuselage, and had long intake and exhaust ducts.

The flight took place at dawn on August 27, five days before the Nazis invaded Poland. Warsitz again was the test pilot, and Heinkel wrote about it:

> The plane was brought to the starting point and Warsitz climbed in. I grasped his hand and wished him "Happy landing." He started the turbine. The plane took off and rapidly climbed to 2,000 feet.

But something was wrong with the undercarriage. Warsitz did everything he could to retract it; then he gave up and flew with it at 1,500 feet in a wide circle around the field. With or without undercarriage, he was flying. He was flying! A new era had begun. The hideous wail of the engine was music to our ears. He circled again, smoothly and gracefully. Warsitz had now been three minutes in the air, but it seemed like an eternity. Calmly he flew around once more, and when six minutes were up he started to land. He cut out the jet unit, then misjudged his approach and had to sideslip. Sideslip with a new, dangerous, and tricky plane!

We held our breath, but the He-178 landed perfectly.[2]

At the Air Ministry and among the engine-building firms, an important development program was also taking to the air. Heinkel had used company funds, while the 1938 study contracts had been quite inexpensive. But when Mauch tried to push ahead toward development, he met strong opposition from his boss, Wolfram Eisenlohr. Within the Air Ministry, Eisenlohr headed the Power Plant Group. He viewed jet engines as long-range projects that would become useful only well in the future, if at all, and he did not want to divert industry resources from more pressing current concerns.

Mauch overcame Eisenlohr's opposition by going over his head. Mauch was on good terms with Eisenlohr's own superior, Brigadier General Ernst Udet, who headed the Technical Office within the ministry. Udet tended to support far-reaching developments; he liked jets, and personally gave Mauch the authority to proceed. Thus, by the end of 1939, Germany had a developmental program featuring two jet fighters and four different engines, all funded from Berlin.

Ernst Heinkel still was a planebuilder, but he hoped to emulate the firm of Junkers, which had separate divisions that built both airplanes and engines. He had hired Robert Lusser, the manager from Messerschmitt, who was crafting a twin-jet lightweight fighter, the He-280. Heinkel also had attracted members of Wagner's engine group at Junkers, who were pursuing a new turbojet design. Ohain remained active, with a separate engine project. Heinkel thus hoped to develop a fighter along with two different types of jet engine.

The firm of Brandenburg had saved itself by merging with BMW. Now they pursued a joint effort, the BMW 003, that was to use a BMW turbine within a basic layout from Brandenburg. Another engine, the Jumo 004, was in development at the Junkers engine division. Its designer, Anselm Franz, was quite familiar with the turbojet that Wagner had struggled to build. Franz saw that the new 004 could overcome its problems, by starting afresh and using a conservative design. Indeed, the 004 emerged as the only German turbojet to see service in combat.

Messerschmitt held the second jet-fighter project, the Me-262. It took shape under the strong hand of Woldemar Voigt, head of the preliminary design department, with its layout emerging during 1939. In its final form, it used two engines, mounted in pods attached to the wings' underside. This meant that the 262 could accommodate jet engines of the future, taking advantage of their increasing power. The design also featured swept wings. At that early date, engineers did not understand how to use wing sweeping to achieve high speed; the 262 swept its wings to correct a problem with its center of gravity. Even so, this helped the plane to achieve higher performance.

Progress initially was rapid. The He-280 flew as a prototype as early as April 1941, powered by two of Ohain's engines. During that month it set a world speed record, at 485 miles per hour. However, these engines lacked the thrust for the heavier Me-262. When the 262 made its first flight, also in April 1941, it used a piston motor. But development of its main engine, the Jumo 004, was also in hand.

It first ran on a test stand in October 1940, developing close to a thousand pounds of thrust. This was not far below the level of Ohain's engine in the He-178, but for the designers at Junkers, it was only the beginning. Problems with vibration delayed the move toward tests at higher thrust, but these problems came under control in mid 1941. In August it reached its rated thrust level, 1,320 pounds, and then did more. At year's end it was producing as much as 2,200 pounds, and was running in test for as long as ten hours.

The test pilot, Fritz Wendel, had set a speed record for piston-powered aircraft of 469 miles per hour in 1939, a record that was to stand for thirty years. He also had flown the initial tests of the 262 with its own piston engine. A year later, in March 1942, the 262 was ready for its first flight with jets. These were not yet Jumo 004s; they were BMW 003s, which were farther along in development. However, they were rated at only 970 pounds of thrust, half the level of the 004. Hence the 262 retained its conventional motor and propeller.

This combination of engines quickly produced misfortune. The propeller generated turbulence in the airflow entering the jets' inlets, cracking compressor blades in both engines. Both of them flamed out and shut down. With the aircraft now burdened by their weight and drag, Wendel found himself in imminent danger. He quickly showed his skill as a test pilot by drawing power from his pistons as he maneuvered to a safe landing. Clearly, though, the 003 was unsuitable; only the 004 with its higher thrust would do.

Germany's Me-262 jet fighter. (*U.S. Air Force*)

The 004 first took to the air in flight test during that same month of March 1942, mounted to the fuselage of a twin-engine fighter. Four months later, a 262 was ready for test with two of these engines as the sole source of propulsion. Its first flight under jet power took place on July 18, and Anselm Franz, designer of the 004, recalls this climactic moment in aviation:

> The engines were turned on and Wendel carefully brought them to full power. Now he released the brakes, the plane rolled, and he held her down to the ground. Suddenly this airplane left the ground and, propelled by those two 004 jet engines, as seen from where we were, climbed almost vertically with unprecedented speed until it disappeared in the clouds. At this moment, it was clear to me that the jet age had begun.[3]

The success of the 262 came amid a considerable pruning in the array of engine and aircraft projects that dated to 1939. Heinkel was first to feel the pinch. He had hoped to ride to glory on Ohain's achievements: first successful jet engine in ground test, first jet plane, first flight of a prototype jet fighter. However, his He-280 had much less range than its rival, the Me-262, and mounted fewer machine guns. The project was canceled in September 1942, two months after Wendel's successful jet-powered flight.

Moreover, in the field of engine development, Heinkel bit off more than he could chew. Even with the infusion of talent from Junkers, he had a technical staff of only fifty engineers, designers, and draftsmen. Virtually all of them were aircraft specialists; few, if any, had a significant background in engine design and development. Nevertheless, lacking both experience and numbers, this group set to work on two jet engines, while conducting studies on other novel forms of propulsion in the bargain. The effort simply was stretched too thin. Both engines fell by the wayside during 1942, with Schelp instructing Heinkel to put all his effort into a new Ohain engine, the 011. Heinkel also received a welcome enlargement of his staff, which tripled in number. Even so, he went through the war without ever flying another engine under its own power.

Meanwhile, what were the Allies doing? They also cherished a strong commitment to high-speed flight, but in no way did they abandon the trusted piston engine for the unproven turbojet. Instead they worked to improve their piston motors by using advanced superchargers. By pumping extra air to the pistons, these installations allowed conventional engines to deliver full power even at high altitude. The B-17, for one, routinely flew above thirty thousand feet, with the motors probably tolerating those conditions better than the flight crews. In addition, the thin air at these altitudes diminished drag, enabling both fighters and bombers to increase their speeds considerably. As early as March 1942, an Army Air Forces general boasted that the P-38 and P-47 were the "only two honest 400-mile-per-hour planes in the world." The Germans lacked good superchargers, but tried to leap past them by entering the realm of jet propulsion in one fell swoop.

In the United States, the lure of the supercharger was so potent that no inventor independently built a successful turbojet. The British were less single-minded, for Frank Whittle, an RAF flight officer, became his country's counterpart of Hans von Ohain. Working on a shoestring, Whittle designed and built a succession of experimental engines, won support from his government, and launched a program of development that in 1941 included two fighters and three types of turbojet. One of the new aircraft, the Gloster Meteor, arrived in time to see service in the war. Yet it was no match for the Me-262, being up to a hundred miles per hour slower. It was no faster than the P-51, and had considerably less range. The British did not even bother to send it to Europe, keeping it in England for home defense.

By contrast, Germany faced the press of urgency, as Allied bombing raids spurred thoughts of wonder weapons that might defend the Reich. The Luftwaffe's main fighter, the Messerschmitt Bf-109, had been selected for a frontline role in 1936. It held that status to the end of the war, with over thirty-three thousand being built. Nevertheless, the Allies had superior fighters in service as early as 1941, while the RAF carried out its first thousand-plane raid in May 1942. If the Me-262 could turn back such assaults, it would certainly merit a close look.

The program drew vital support from Major General Adolf Galland, who commanded the Luftwaffe's fighter force. He was an experienced combat ace who had scored ninety-seven victories, mostly against weak opposition on the eastern front. Still, this had sufficed to earn him Germany's highest military decoration. This was no longer the Pour le Mérite of earlier wars, but the new Knight's Cross of the Iron Cross with Oak Leaves, Swords, and Diamonds.

In May 1943 he personally flew the Me-262. He left its cockpit with wild enthusiasm, declaring that flying it was "like being pushed by an angel." He immediately sent a telegram to his superior, General Erhard Milch, the deputy commander of the Luftwaffe, and stated that this plane should enter production as soon as possible. Milch agreed, deciding that an existing Messerschmitt fighter program should shut down to free up the needed production facilities. Within days, Willy Messerschmitt, head of the company, received his orders. By the end of the year, he was to deliver the first hundred 262s.

This was easier said than done, for Messerschmitt was short of machine tools. He also needed nearly two thousand additional skilled workers, for he faced limitations similar to those of Heinkel. Nor did it help when in mid August, Curtis LeMay personally led a strike on the Messerschmitt plant in Regensburg, home of the 262. The destruction included jigs, frameworks used in assembling its wings and fuselage, and gauges that measured parts for acceptance.

But the biggest problems involved the jet engines. Early versions had made free use of heat-resistant alloys that contained nickel and chromium. However, these strategic materials were in short supply throughout the Reich. These shortages had discouraged the Germans from matching the Allies by developing turbine-driven superchargers to improve the performance of piston engines. These turbines, drawing power from a motor's hot exhaust, needed temperature resistance for long life in service, and this appeared out of reach with available alloys.

The Jumo 004 had initially been designed to obtain working units in the shortest time possible. However, production versions had to reduce the use of strategic materials to a bare minimum. Engineers at Junkers attacked this problem with a will, and achieved important results. They had built prototype combustion chambers using high-alloy steel. Now they turned to mild steel, a common industrial metal, with channels to cool it by using internal airflows.

Turbine blades offered greater difficulties, for they faced extreme stress from rapid rotation, in addition to high temperatures. Blades made with cobalt would have been best, but Germany's limited supply of this metal had long since been allocated for use in high-speed cutting tools. The best practical solution called for an alloy called Tinidur that still contained chromium and nickel, with the blades being hollow. This permitted air cooling while also reducing the amount of metal used in each blade.

As shortages continued to increase in severity, the supply of Tinidur became uncertain. Junkers's suppliers turned to another alloy, Cromadur, that used no nickel at all, replacing it with manganese. The final results were spectacular, for production engines delivered 1,980 pounds of thrust and weighed 1,650 pounds. But they used less than 5 pounds of chromium. Those built with Tinidur turbine blades needed less than 6 pounds of nickel, while those with Cromadur blades used no nickel at all.

Nevertheless, it took time to advance from the prototype versions to the production models. An Me-262 did not fly with production engines until October 1943. By then it was clear that these turbojets were in serious trouble due to vibration of the turbine blades. A professional musician came to the factory; he had perfect pitch, and succeeded in determining the vibration frequencies. This made it possible to introduce technical changes that cured the problem, but the solution was not in hand until December. Finally, around March 1944, Jumo 004 engines began to come off the production lines in quantity.

Production of complete fighter aircraft encountered its own delays. Messerschmitt's existing plants proved unsuitable, for during 1944 the Allies struck them repeatedly and hard. Nevertheless, assembly of these planes proceeded in underground mines as well as in a forest near the town of Augsburg, hidden beneath trees. Bombing raids slowed the buildup, but the company delivered 28 in June and 59 in July, ramping upward to a peak of some 300 per month in February 1945.

The 262 first saw combat in July 1944. Its speed was matchless; it reached 541 miles per hour, and no Allied fighter in service could approach this mark. The Luftwaffe tended to reserve it for use in elite squadrons. The first such group, Kommando Nowotny, entered the air battle early in October. Its commander, the Austrian ace Walter Nowotny, had scored 256 aerial kills and had won the Knight's Cross with Diamonds.

Allied generals initially doubted that they could counter this threat, fearing that only a jet could beat a jet. Yet the piston-powered P-47 and P-51 proved more than adequate to the task. American pilots faced the challenge with zest, for they had turned German airspace into a vast shooting gallery, and were eager to try their skills against the enemy's new superfighter.

In the air, the Me-262 was advanced indeed. But it spent very little time in the air, and on the ground it was a sitting duck. Its engines, built from inferior materials, had a rated life of just twenty-five hours, sufficient only for a few missions. As a consequence, many operational 262s had to stay out of action while awaiting new engines and major spare parts. They also had numerous accidents on the ground.

The 262 had other weaknesses. Although it was very fast, it lacked maneuverability, and Allied airmen learned that they could out-turn it. It also was vulnerable when flying slowly, immediately after takeoff and during a landing approach. It could fly for an hour, but Allied fighters had greater endurance, and could wait for their moment. When it came, a pilot would dive to gain speed, then catch up with his prey, with machine guns flashing.

The Allies introduced a tactic called "rat catching," placing combat air patrols over jet airfields. These often caught 262s on the ground or during takeoff. An American general, William Kepner, trained his men to use this technique systematically. When one of them saw a 262, he was to shout, "Jet!" If there were only one or two of them, his P-51s would maneuver to box them in, with a Yankee fighter turning toward them whichever way they went. Alternately, these fighters were to head for every jet runway within a hundred miles. As the Messerschmitts ran low on fuel and came in to land, they would find groups of U.S. aircraft overhead, loitering with intent to kill.

This strong Allied response meant that even for Germany's top guns, the life expectancy was brief. Major Nowotny, for one, lasted only five weeks before being hit; he died when his plane plunged into the ground. Kommando Nowotny had scored twenty-two confirmed kills, but had lost twenty-six of its own aircraft.

General Adolf Galland barely avoided the same fate. He had headed the Luftwaffe's fighter command, but he lost his job by speaking frankly about his country's dim prospects, at a time when the top Nazis preferred to beguile themselves with fantasy and wishes. Ordered to lead a fighter squadron, he responded by forming another elite group, JV 44. Ten of its members held the Knight's Cross; its top aces held as many as three hundred victories.

This outfit trained with another fighter group that had grown out of the remnants of Kommando Nowotny. It then entered combat during the last five weeks of the war, racking up fifty victories during this short existence. But Galland's number came up on April 26, when P-51s shot him down. He managed to land and then survived a strafing attack by P-47s, but he was wounded. He ended the war in a hospital.

There were times, very late in the war, when these jet fighters assembled in numbers sufficient to do damage. In January 1945, a group of them attacked a squadron of twelve American bombers and shot down every one. The first concentrated attack came early in March, as twenty-nine Me-262s struck at an American bomber force. This time the Yankees had better defenses. The Germans shot down only three bombers, along with six escorting fighters.

Three significant air battles marked the war's final weeks. On March 18, in one of the heaviest raids on Berlin, 1,221 bombers flew to that city, escorted by 632 fighters. Thirty-seven jets rose against this massive armada, armed with new air-to-air rockets. They downed 8 bombers, while losing 2 of their own. Two weeks later the Germans scored again, launching nearly 40 of them against a joint force of British and U.S. aircraft. In what counted as a successful day, they shot down 14 bombers and 2 fighters, with all of the German jets returning safely.

The Luftwaffe did even more on April 10, as their jets flew fifty-five missions against the Americans. This was the largest number of sorties flown in a single day. Again they scored, knocking ten bombers out of the sky. However, this time the attacking force was better prepared. It destroyed twenty-seven of the jet fighters, close to half the number that had taken off. This raised the imminent prospect that the Me-262 might prove to be little more than a one-shot weapon.

For the Luftwaffe, the final tally was highly disappointing. Conventional defenses, including fighters and flak, had downed 60 American bombers during each of the two major raids on Schweinfurt, in August and October 1943. At war's end the Eighth Air Force, comprising all American aircraft based in England, counted only 52 bombers lost to the jets, along with 10 fighters. This meant that the toll through months of aerial combat was less than that of bad individual raids. In return, Allied fighters shot down some 130 jets, while bombing destroyed many more on the ground. The tale of the Me-262 proved to resemble that of zeppelins in the previous war. Once again, rarely in the field of human endeavor had so many given so much for so little.

This was even more true for two other German wonder weapons, the Messerschmitt Me-163 and Heinkel He-162. The first of these was a rocket-powered fighter that used the hydrogen peroxide engines of Helmuth Walter. This fuel was so corrosive that it could literally dissolve a pilot's body. In addition, the 163 lacked all semblance of range;

it allowed a pilot to make only one or two passes at an enemy plane before having to break off and glide back to his base. But there was no denying its speed; as early as 1941, a test pilot flew it to 624 miles per hour.

Air Ministry officials, noting its deficiencies, initially rated it as "not good enough for combat operations." They subsequently relented, under the press of dire necessity, and an improved version entered operational service. But like the Me-262, it was too little and too late. Three hundred of these rocket planes were built, but they achieved only nine kills in combat.

The He-162 did even less. It was a true desperation weapon, a last-ditch effort meant to darken the skies with technically superior German planes, and it too fell short. This jet fighter used the BMW 003 engine, which had risen to achieve 1,760 pounds of thrust and was much easier to maintain than its rival, the Jumo 004. The He-162 was of simple design, with wings of plywood. Nazi functionaries fantasized that the teenage boys of the Hitler Youth would fly it in combat.

The plane went under contract in September 1944, very late in the war. Ten weeks later, in early December, a prototype made its first flight. Subsequent tests soon showed that this was no airplane for children; it was tricky to fly, demanding considerable skill. It went into production just the same, with fuselage assemblies being built in an underground salt mine. Some three hundred of them reached flight status, but the war ended before they could enter combat.

Nevertheless, the Me-262 was a true jet fighter, and the first such aircraft to promise significant advantage. General Galland took the view that it could have entered service eighteen months earlier if it had received higher priority, and could then have shown very considerable value in prolonging the Luftwaffe's air superiority over Germany. Yet such a commitment would have represented a decisive break with German wartime air policy, which emphasized continued production of existing designs.

Even if we regard German jet production as belated, it still stands out within an overall program that repeatedly failed to pursue novel concepts of known value. Germany built no aircraft carriers, though Japan, which was weaker, used them in substantial numbers. Germany conducted its air offensives using twin-engine bombers, while both Britain and America constructed huge fleets of increasingly capable four-engine types, which were much larger. The Germans failed to develop turbine-driven superchargers for their piston engines. They also held to the Bf-109, dating to the mid 1930s, as the Luftwaffe's frontline fighter; they failed to introduce advanced piston-powered models that could match the P-47 and P-51. Amid this general stodginess, the Me-262 offered an impressive contrast.

An early and far-reaching commitment to the 262 would have been unwise, for during the war, jet engines and fighters were in immature stages of development. They offered highly uncertain supports on which to rest the fortunes of battle. These uncertainties were particularly strong for the Jumo 004, which had to be built from second-rate alloys. The British and the Americans were more fortunate, as they learned jet-engine design through direct experience, in the course of their own wartime programs.

British engines amounted to variants of basic designs by Frank Whittle. In the United States, the firm of General Electric used this work as its point of departure, as it started with Whittle engines and went on to craft turbojets of its own. The Allies faced neither bombing raids nor shortages of strategic metals; their engines freely used the best metallurgy available. Yet neither nation built an operational jet fighter that saw service in the war.

The initial attempts—the Gloster Meteor, the Bell XP-59A in the United States—proved to lack the speed and performance for frontline action, and were kept at home. Then in 1943, with the Me-262 looming on the horizon, the Army Air Forces sponsored a crash effort that sought to match it. The contractor, Lockheed, built the XP-80, taking this program from an initial contract in mid June to first flight of a prototype barely six months later, in January 1944.

Nevertheless, both this fighter and its engine required much development before they could advance from sensitive experiments to rugged weapons suitable for a war zone. Flight tests brought a succession of crashes that destroyed eight of these aircraft and severely damaged four more, while killing six pilots. The dead included one of Lockheed's best, Milo Burcham, along with Richard Bong, whose forty wartime kills had made him the nation's ace of aces. At war's end the program was mired in technical problems and the plane was still not ready for operational use.

From this perspective, the German achievement appears all the more remarkable. The Me-262 had superb performance; it was not a premature effort that found itself superseded by the best piston models. Development of both this fighter and its engine went forward without bogging down. It went into production and entered service, rather than remaining as merely a prototype. It did not save the Reich, but it did what it could, flying for a Nazi Germany that by 1943 was beyond salvation.

PART 4

Blue Skies

Howard Hughes

16

Howard Hughes lived his life as a riverboat gambler, with a bottomless pot of money and a penchant for doing as he liked. He became famous as a Hollywood playboy with a starlet on each arm—and as a recluse who hid from his closest associates. During a decades-long involvement with aviation, he built a record-breaking racing plane that the Army Air Corps declined to purchase, and an enormous flying boat that flew only once. Yet his checkered career saw solid achievement.

He sponsored the Lockheed Constellation, an outstanding airliner that set the pace in commercial aviation until the coming of the jets. Within the company he founded, Hughes Aircraft, the scientists Simon Ramo and Dean Wooldridge led the Air Force into the modern era of electronics. Another of that firm's managers, Harold Rosen, introduced the communications satellite in the form we use to this day.

His father, Howard Sr., was a technologist in his own right who made a fortune in petroleum—but as a manufacturer, not a wildcatter. During the great Texas oil rush, early in this century, drillers often were stymied because standard drills, shaped like a fishtail, wore out quickly when grinding through hard rock. Howard Sr. invented a rotary drill bit with 166 cutting edges that quickly became an industry standard. He did not sell these bits, but leased them—at $30,000 per well. Protected by patents, they formed the basis for his enormously successful Hughes Tool Company. Then he died when his son was in his late teens, leaving him in charge of the firm.

Young Howard had an uncle, the novelist Rupert Hughes, who was prospering in Hollywood as a screenwriter and director. Howard promptly set out for that city, where he saw his main chance, and drew on his family fortune as he began to make movies as an independent producer. The first, *Swell Hogan*, was so bad that he refused to release it. The second, *Everybody's Acting*, succeeded at the box office and covered his expenses. The third, *Two Arabian Knights*, starred

William Byrd, who later became the cowboy Hopalong Cassidy, and Mary Astor. Its director, Lewis Milestone, went on to direct *Ocean's Eleven*, the first Rat Pack movie. *Two Arabian Knights* won an Academy Award in 1927, with Milestone as best comedy director. This success left Hughes in a mood for bolder adventures yet.

He had already discovered flying. Now he decided to direct and produce *Hell's Angels,* an epic about air combat in World War I. It was to do for that war what *Ben Hur,* thirty years later, would do for chariot racing. He sank more than $2 million into the effort, much of which went for an armada of forty-five planes and airships. Then came Al Jolson in *The Jazz Singer,* and talkies were suddenly the rage. *Hell's Angels* was ready for release, but it was a silent film, and Hughes knew he would have to reshoot much of it.

He needed a new leading lady; his former star, Greta Nissen, had a strong Norwegian accent and wouldn't do. He found what he wanted in the youthful Jean Harlow, the first of movieland's platinum blondes and certainly one of Hughes's greatest innovations. *Hell's Angels* made her career, launching her as a sudden sensation.

Offscreen, however, Hughes's troubles were multiplying. His wife, Ella Rice, came from the Houston family that had endowed Rice University. She divorced him in 1929 after four and a half years of marriage, taking a settlement that came to $1.25 million. Then the stock market crashed and the Depression rolled in. Hughes calmly went on shooting, even adding a few rudimentary color sequences, while splicing in scenes of a bomber crashing and a zeppelin burning.

The total expense came to nearly $4 million, making *Hell's Angels* the most expensive film ever made until then. Finally, in 1930, it reached the theaters. It did well, but left Hughes with a loss of $1.5 million. However, this didn't bother him, for the Hughes Tool Company, which he owned outright, continued to gush money.

He continued to work actively in Hollywood. His next success, *Scarface,* starred Paul Muni in the role of a thinly disguised Al Capone. The movies of the day were subject to nationwide censorship, and Hughes had to make substantial changes to win a seal of approval. Even then, a separate board of censors in New York refused its own approval. Hughes responded by suing them. Within a film industry that trembled at the censors' power, this was unheard of. But he won his suit, forced the New York board to back down, and released *Scarface* in a form that he regarded as acceptable. He went on to produce additional films, including the original 1931 version of *The Front Page.*

Then, with Hollywood at his feet, he shifted gears and took a major plunge into aviation. He had made no permanent commitment to the film industry, for while he had worked with great success as an independent producer, he had built no studio that would demand his continuing attention. Instead, his true commitment remained with Hughes Tool, which yielded the cash that had funded his filmmaking. Now, like a man about town with a new mistress, he turned his back on the movies and embraced his new romance.

He started by working as a copilot for American Airways in 1932. The job included such tasks as handling passengers' baggage. He used an assumed name, but people later remarked how much he looked like Howard Hughes. Then, dropping his secret identity, he returned to Los Angeles, where he had obtained an Air Corps fighter plane that he intended to fly as a racer. Fitted with a powerful engine, it won an air race in Miami in 1934. This success fired his hopes anew. He had made the world's best aviation film; now he wanted to build the world's best airplane.

He held no engineering degree; he lacked experience at the drawing board or on the shop floor. But he was quite prepared to hire people who had this background—and he was also prepared to respond intelligently to the best technical suggestions. The world of aviation was abuzz with ideas that could increase speed, and Hughes learned of them as he read journals and consulted with experts. His design skillfully synthesized such existing ideas, introducing fully retractable landing gear and rivets set flush with the fuselage to reduce drag.

The Depression had put many good planebuilders on short rations, but Hughes had money to burn. He pulled together a picked group of designers, engineers, and mechanics. They called themselves the Hughes Aircraft Company, introducing a name that would stick. The plane that they crafted was the Hughes H-1. Hughes himself served as its pilot and flew it to a world speed record of 352 miles per hour in 1935, over a measured course.

He then rebuilt it to carry enough gasoline for a cross-country flight. In 1937 he flew it from Los Angeles to Newark in seven and a half hours, setting a record that would hold for seven years. This feat won him the Harmon Trophy, awarded to the world's best aviator. He also met personally with President Roosevelt at the White House. But when he tried to pitch his design to the Air Corps, he found no interest. The plane was speedy enough, but it lacked features that would have made it suitable for combat.

Nevertheless, by now even the United States was too small to contain his vaulting ambitions. He purchased a two-engine plane from Lockheed and flew it around the world in less than four days. This achievement, in mid 1938, won him a congressional medal along with the Collier Trophy for progress in aviation. He also received a ticker-tape parade down Broadway, as more than a million New Yorkers lined the streets to hail the nation's latest hero.

With this, Hughes had reached pinnacles of success in two vastly different enterprises. Yet while he was daring and bold, he also was painfully shy. The magazine *Collier's* described him as "self-conscious with strangers and reticent with intimates." He felt out of place at parties: "When standing he inclines his head out and down and looks at the ground. Seated, he clasps his hands between his widespread knees and stares at his knuckles."

This shyness influenced his relations with women. He met one in New York; she told him she would be spending the summer on the coast of Maine. He responded by flying to her island in a seaplane and rowing to shore with another man. The young woman was with friends, and Hughes's companion invited them all to take a cruise on his yacht, which was one of the world's largest. Hughes himself was present but stood silently to one side, dressed in rumpled, grease-stained overalls and looking bashful. The women declined this invitation, and Hughes's task force disappeared over the horizon.

He also had a strong phobia about germs, which had drawn encouragement from his mother's robust emphasis on cleanliness. Hughes raised this concern to new heights, particularly during the mid 1930s, when he learned that he had caught syphilis from one of his paramours. This disease cannot be spread via toilet seats, or through similar casual contact. Nevertheless, Hughes stuffed the whole of his wardrobe and bed linens into padlocked canvas bags, and ordered them burned. He then scrubbed his home from top to bottom with strong lye soap.

In time this shyness would ripen into life as a recluse, while his obsession with germs broadened into an utterly debilitating mental illness. But these lay in the future; just then and for many years thereafter, what counted was his keen mind. Robert Rummel, who became his senior technical manager, recalls his

> consummate, unquenchable interest in airplane design. His questions concerning broad design concepts as well as details were crisp, comprehensive, and usually exasperatingly detailed. He wanted to know everything. Working with Howard required exhaustive preparation; but no matter how well prepared I might be, he would frequently probe areas requiring further study. And he had a memory that made the proverbial elephant look like a dunce.[1]

He made another bold move during 1939 as he purchased control of a major airline, TWA. Its president, Jack Frye, was in deep trouble over plans for a new aircraft, the Boeing Stratoliner. Frye wanted to place an order for these planes, but the nation's economy was in a slump and TWA had been losing money. Its chairman, John Hertz of Lehman Brothers, had refused to release the funds for this purchase. Lawsuits were flying, though the Stratoliner wasn't, and Frye knew that he could save the airliner only with a high-stakes gamble.

He already knew Hughes through their common involvement with flight. Frye offered to sell some of TWA's air routes to Hughes for cash, with Hughes receiving a return on this purchase by leasing them back to TWA. Characteristically, Hughes upped the ante, saying, "Why don't we buy TWA?" He proceeded to buy 12 percent of the airline's stock, giving him an interest as large of that of Hertz and Lehman. Now Frye took charge as he challenged Hertz to a proxy fight, a shareholders' election to decide whether Hertz should remain as chairman. Hertz had no wish to pursue the matter, and caved in. Hughes then bought more stock and told Frye to go ahead with the Stratoliner.

This airplane represented an early effort in the new field of four-engine airliners. Douglas Aircraft, the nation's leading builder of commercial aircraft, was preparing its own entry—the DC-4—and was winning interest from United and American Airlines. Yet it offered a very unspectacular design. Its cruising speed, two hundred miles per hour, would merely match that of the Stratoliner. Its cabin would be unpressurized, limiting it to the low and stormy altitudes that made passengers airsick.

Hughes expected to go much farther. In subsequent discussions with Frye, the two men developed a concept for a four-engine airliner that would be advanced indeed. Hughes would gladly have carried through the design and production with his own planebuilders, but now that he controlled TWA, federal law prohibited him from building equipment for his own airline. However, he had purchased his world-circling plane from Lockheed, and Frye now approached that firm anew. The airplane that emerged was the Lockheed Constellation.

In June 1939, Lockheed's chairman along with two principal designers, Hall Hibbard and Clarence "Kelly" Johnson, met with Hughes at the home of the latter and presented preliminary drawings. The next meeting brought in Frye, and took place at the Beverly Hills Hotel. The final design showed again that Hughes knew how to respond to good ideas from good people. Like the H-1, the Constellation broke new ground, as it set a pattern for subsequent high-performance airliners.

Its key lay in pressurizing the fuselage, sealing it with care so it could hold a comfortable internal pressure. The plane then could cruise at twenty thousand feet, far above the turbulent weather. For passengers, flying then might actually be pleasant. The rarefied air at that altitude would substantially reduce the drag. Yet the engines would put out full power, for they would mount superchargers, pumps to provide them with all the air they needed. The plane thus would win a dramatic boost in speed, cruising at 280 miles per hour. Its top speed of 340 miles per hour would exceed that of contemporary fighters.

Two years later, the nation went to war. The Army drafted both the Constellation and the DC-4 into wartime service—and quickly expressed a strong preference for the latter, which was farther along in development. It entered military use as the C-54. The Constellation also enlisted for the duration, as the C-69. In April 1944, Lockheed arranged for a test flight of this wonderplane, ostensibly for the purpose of delivering its prototype to the Army in Washington. But Hughes, a consummate showman, stage-managed the event to suit his purposes. Painting the plane in the vivid red color of TWA, he flew it from Los Angeles in under seven hours.

For Donald Douglas, builder of the DC-4, this flight presented a twofold challenge. It showed that the commercial Constellation could fly nonstop from coast to coast, something no other airliner could do. And the flight time stood a half hour under the transcontinental speed record that Hughes himself had set in 1937. The *New York Times* saluted this flight, calling it "an outline of the shape of things to come in air transportation."

Douglas responded by reinventing the DC-4. New and more powerful engines boosted its cruising speed above three hundred miles per hour, topping the Constellation. These engines also stretched the range by allowing the plane to carry more fuel. A pressurized cabin now was a necessity, and this cabin stretched as well, growing in length to accommodate more seats. The new plane was the DC-6. United Airlines launched its career in September 1944 by placing an order for twenty of them.

The stage now was set for one of the great rivalries in aeronautics. Douglas and Lockheed both had superb designs that could take advantage of continuing increases in the power of engines. Later versions of these planes stretched their fuselages anew while widening their wings for extra range. During the subsequent decade, each of these firms repeatedly introduced new and more capable models. In turn, this competition defined the progress of airliners until the advent of the jets.

Meanwhile, Hughes was returning to Hollywood. He had made no movies since 1932, but in 1943 he outraged the censors anew with *The Outlaw,* a tale of Billy the Kid. He introduced the buxom Jane Russell as Doc Holliday's girlfriend, named Rio. Then, when film rushes failed to display her bosom to appropriate advantage, Hughes drew on his knowledge of engineering design and fashioned a brassiere that gave suitable prominence to her charms. A subsequent review noted that it showed "greater exposure of Miss Russell than was customary."

By the standards of subsequent decades, *The Outlaw* was tame. She kept all her clothes on throughout; there was plenty of cleavage but no bare breasts, and much was left to the audiences' imagination. Perhaps the raciest moment came when she told a badly chilled Billy, "My body will warm you." Still, here too was an outline of the shape of things to come. As he had done with *Scarface,* Hughes milked the ensuing controversy for the maximum possible publicity.

He also sought greater prominence for his firm of Hughes Aircraft, as he worked during the war to build new facilities and to win a share of the national effort. At the outset, he decided that aircraft of the future would be built of plywood, not aluminum, and he pinned his hope on a newly patented process that bonded thin sheets of plywood to a wooden frame. He used this as the basis for the design of a fast twin-engine bomber, the D-2, which he pitched to the War Department. Its officials showed no interest, for they strongly preferred aluminum. Indeed, they dismissed Hughes Aircraft out of hand.

An internal memo, two months after Pearl Harbor, declared "that this plant is a hobby of the management and that the present project now being engineered is a waste of time." Though harsh, this assessment was close to the mark. Howard Hughes wanted to build new aircraft and contribute to the war effort—but he wanted to do it his way, as he had shown by insisting on the use of wood. Hughes Aircraft was more than just a hobby, but it definitely was an extension of his ego, a means through which he hoped to continue to stand out.

He found a new opportunity in a partnership with the shipbuilder Henry J. Kaiser. Kaiser introduced assembly-line methods and achieved rapid production of the Liberty ship, a standard cargo carrier. Nevertheless, German submarines took a heavy toll of such freighters during 1942. Kaiser, as ebullient as Hughes, responded by proposing to build a vast fleet of flying boats, enormous aircraft that would fly above the danger. Kaiser had no background in aviation, but a similar lack of background had not hampered his shipbuilding. When he fell in with Hughes, he expected this partnership would conquer the skies.

The view in Washington was far less sanguine, for federal officials were quite ready to ignore their plans outright. But political considerations intervened, for Kaiser had a solid record of success in shipbuilding while Hughes carried the glamour and hope of aviation. Their supporters claimed that this plan could win the war, which made it difficult to turn them down flat. Buoyed by popular enthusiasm, which drew again on Hughes's skill at public relations, the partners won an $18 million contract to build three of these aircraft.

The design called for an airplane bigger than today's Boeing 747. Its wingspan of 320 feet set a record that stands to this day, while its weight of two hundred tons made it three times heavier than any airplane in existence. Hughes Aircraft had no background in building small flying boats, let alone big ones. Howard Hughes nevertheless proposed not only to assemble this behemoth, but to draw on his experience with the D-2 by crafting it of wood. Wood was more difficult to work with than aluminum, but it was readily available whereas aluminum counted as a strategic material. As a result, this plane gained the sobriquet of Spruce Goose, though most of the wood in it was plastic-impregnated birch.

Time passed and the Goose refused to hatch, as Hughes spent much of the allotted funds to little purpose. The government responded by moving to cancel the contract. Hughes hastened to Washington, lobbied furiously, and won the right to build a single prototype. It still was far from ready at war's end, but two years later, in November 1947, it finally was in shape for test. Hughes took the controls, and with plenty of newsmen in attendance, it skimmed across Long Beach harbor. He lifted it into the air; it reached an altitude of seventy feet and flew for less than a mile before he set it back down on the water. It never flew again, but it did not disappear. For the rest of his life, Hughes kept it in a hangar, where he cherished it as the largest of his many trophies.

The D-2 went through its own cycle of hype followed by disappointment. Hughes modified its design, changed its construction from wood to aluminum, and won a contract to build a hundred of them in a photoreconnaissance version, the XF-11. Again the war ended before production could begin; again the War Department canceled his contract and left him with no more than a handful of prototypes. Then when Hughes once more indulged his penchant for serving as his own test pilot, his XF-11 crashed and nearly killed him.

He now had built four airplanes—the H-1, the D-2, the XF-11, and the Spruce Goose—with not a single one reaching production, even amid the wartime aviation boom. His Constellation was on its way to brilliant success, but he had left it in the hands of experienced professionals at Lockheed. One of his biographers later described him as an eternal teenager, full of enthusiasm for movies, airplanes, and girls. But with the war over, it was time to grow up. If Hughes Aircraft was ever to amount to anything, he would have to build it on merit, in the face of a deep slump in postwar aviation.

Yet the man had an inner solidity, an ability to attract good people and to pursue good ideas. He now drew on this native talent as he

Howard Hughes's "Spruce Goose," officially designated the H-4 Hercules. *(National Air and Space Museum)*

steered this company into another new area: military electronics. This again reflected his keen eye for promising directions in technology; Air Force general Elwood Quesada, who later headed the Federal Aviation Agency (FAA), said that Hughes was the first to see that military aircraft would need lots more than the pilot.

During the war, a number of scientists and engineers had worked on fire control—the use of electronics to aim and fire a plane's weapons—and on radar and automated systems. These people now faced a postwar world where they might have to turn to the civilian market, building television and hi-fi equipment, which was much less challenging. As had been true during the Depression, Hughes found them easy to hire. He was famous, rich, smart, and he was offering them an opportunity to continue to pursue their wartime interests. With Pentagon budgets dropping rapidly, few other firms cared to compete with him.

He needed a chief scientist; in April 1946 he hired Simon Ramo, who had built a strong reputation at General Electric. Ramo brought in Dean Wooldridge, one of the top people at Bell Labs. Hughes also assembled a stellar team of senior managers: General Ira Eaker, the Air Force's deputy chief of staff; General Harold George, head of the wartime Air Transport Command; Charles "Tex" Thornton, who went on to build Litton Industries as a leading conglomerate.

They started with a small Air Force contract to study airborne fire control. This quickly blossomed into an $8 million contract to build fire-control systems for a new interceptor, the Lockheed F-94. Hughes's scientists also took another study contract, dealing with guidance systems for an air-to-air weapon, and parlayed it into the highly successful Falcon missile. Fitted with an onboard radar, it homed in on target airplanes even in its earliest tests.

Then during 1950, in a major coup, Hughes Aircraft defeated General Electric, Westinghouse, and a number of leading airframe manufacturers, winning a competition for fire and navigational control in the F-102 fighter. That year saw the nation again at war, in Korea, and the Air Force needed all the advanced electronics it could get. With its head start, Hughes Aircraft walked away with a virtual monopoly.

In putting together his team of scientists and senior managers, Hughes had promised them a large measure of independence. But with his company growing explosively, these people needed his close attention, and this clashed strongly with his personal preferences. Hughes was no hands-on corporate leader; he preferred to go off for long periods, leaving his associates dangling. He had been doing this for years; when he told Jack Frye that he would buy control of TWA, he went away on his yacht and couldn't be reached for advice on how much to pay for the stock. In subsequent years, when Frye tried to reach him by phone, Hughes would go for weeks without returning a call, even when the matter in question involved millions of dollars.

His quirks also flourished, preludes to his outright madness. He now was often rumpled and disheveled, postponing haircuts for as long as possible. He rarely slept, and when he made phone calls, it was often at two or three in the morning. He made his business appointments in out-of-the-way places, at night, and if he showed up at all he would be as much as two hours late. Irrelevant detail could obsess him; in designing a passenger plane, he became so absorbed with the galley that all work on the engines was held up for months. The crash of his XF-11 had left him in considerable pain; his doctor responded with increasingly large doses of morphine, later switching him to another narcotic, codeine. It was the beginning of a serious drug addiction. Advancing syphilis produced further deterioration in his mental state.

The first genuine quarrel with his managers took place as Hughes Aircraft won the F-102 contract. A major expansion of staff and facilities was in order—and Howard Hughes insisted that it take place in Las Vegas. He owned land there, and hoped to dodge California state taxes, but Ramo and Wooldridge knew that they could not attract good specialists to work in what then was merely a small and remote city in the desert. They protested vigorously and persuaded Hughes to back down, as he agreed to enlarge the existing plant near Los Angeles. He then vanished. Soon after, when Harold George was waiting impatiently for an important decision, Hughes responded by demanding a detailed accounting of candy-bar sales in the company's vending machines. On another and similar occasion, George received a directive concerning seat covers for company-owned cars.

A longtime associate of Hughes, Noah Dietrich, stepped into this managerial void but proved a meddlesome hack. A buyout could have refreshed the firm with serious leadership, and Hughes received an attractive offer from Lockheed. He then rejected it, vowing he'd never sell. In mid 1953, Ramo and Wooldridge decided they'd had enough. They both were corporate vice presidents, but now they handed in their resignations. This sparked an exodus of talent that included George, Thornton, the directors of production and of research and development, the sales manager, and sixteen senior staffers who comprised an advisory council.

Hoping to save the situation, Air Force Secretary Harold Talbott flew out to meet with Hughes and bluntly told him to shape up. Hughes might have escaped by cruising on his yacht, but he made no attempt to hide, for he knew that Talbott had the power to cancel his contracts and to shut down Hughes Aircraft. Chastened, Hughes put the company in the hands of an executive board and gave its members the authority to make major decisions entirely on their own. This action gave new life to the firm; freed from Hughes's peculiarities, it now came into its own as a major corporation and defense contractor.

These peculiarities ranged beyond Hughes Aircraft; they also marked his ill-starred ownership of a major movie studio, RKO Pictures. Between 1933 and the end of the war, Hughes had made only one film, *The Outlaw*. During 1946 and 1947 he collaborated with the director Preston Sturges on two unsuccessful films: *Mad Wednesday* (originally titled *The Sin of Harold Diddlebock*) and *Vendetta*. Then in 1948, he purchased control of RKO for $8.83 million. Within months his high-handed decisions brought the resignation of RKO's president and its studio chief, the highly regarded Dore Schary. Production plummeted. RKO had released 28 movies the year before Hughes bought it, but made only 11 in 1952. The staff fell from 2,000 in 1948 to around 500 four years later, while losses approached $20 million over the same period. In 1952 Hughes sold control to a five-man syndicate—whose members forfeited over a million dollars in cash as they handed it back to him. RKO still held valuable rights to old movies that could be shown on television, and Hughes finally sold the film division of the company for $25 million in 1955.

Nevertheless, Hughes Tool Company continued to gush cash for his ventures, while he retained control of TWA as his crown jewel. The jet age was at hand, and he clearly intended that his airline would stand in its forefront. During 1956 he placed orders totaling $375 million for jet airliners and engines. This was the largest purchase in the history of commercial aviation, and Hughes expected to pay for it by relying on his personal assets, which topped the half-billion mark. *Fortune* magazine described him as "the proprietor of the largest pool of industrial wealth still under the absolute control of a single individual."

Of course, these assets did not exist as cash; they represented the value of his corporate empire, which included extensive real-estate holdings. But all profits from Hughes Aircraft were earmarked for a medical foundation that Hughes had established in 1955. Hughes Tool remained the centerpiece, returning an estimated gross profit of $60 million during 1956, on revenue of $120 million. What was more, the bulk of Hughes's jet-age obligations would not fall due until he took delivery of the aircraft, during 1959 and 1960.

Noah Dietrich, his chief financial officer and the most knowledgeable of his lieutenants, insisted that the cash flow of Hughes Tool would fail to suffice and that Howard Hughes would have to arrange outside financing. He refused to do this, fearing loss of his absolute control, and as their disagreements grew in intensity, Dietrich resigned. He had worked for Hughes since 1925, but now he too had had enough.

Then Hughes Tool went into a slump, as a glut of oil brought a falloff in drilling, and in demand for its bits. In June 1959, unable to pay for some Boeing 707s he had ordered, he sold six of them to his principal rival, Pan American World Airways. In October, facing imminent bills for delivery of Convair 880 airliners, he sent armed guards into the Convair plant to prevent company workers from completing their assembly. Since he was one of Convair's biggest customers, the company made no attempt to oppose him. While these planes remained undelivered, he would not have to pay the amounts due.

These measures addressed immediate problems, but during 1960 he finally agreed to seek $165 million in financing. Negotiations were in a delicate stage in July, when Hughes provoked a disagreement with the president of TWA, Charles Thomas, who promptly resigned. Thomas had held the confidence of Wall Street, and when he left, its financiers stiffened the terms they would offer to Hughes. Now, to receive his loan, he would have to surrender control of TWA, much as he had given up control of Hughes Aircraft in 1953. Hughes delayed as long as possible before accepting these terms, but he knew the alternative was bankruptcy for TWA. On the last day of 1960, the airline passed out of his hands. Nothing could have been more galling to him.

By then he was entering the full throes of his madness. Facing business pressures during the late 1950s, he lived for a time in a room used for showing movies. He talked at length on the phone with lawyers and bankers, but he also spent much time rearranging Kleenex boxes in various patterns, or sitting in the bathroom. Prolonged use of the drug codeine had brought on severe constipation, and he sat on the toilet continuously for as long as twenty-six hours.

His fear of germs was constant. To avoid them, he wrote out memoranda running to several pages that set forth protocols for such matters as opening a can of fruit or taking an item from a cabinet. He spent hours cleaning his telephone, repeating the cleaning procedure again and again. He ate and drank only milk, Hershey bars, pecan nuts, and bottled water, which an aide delivered each day in a brown paper bag and presented in a formal ritual.

He wore the same white shirt and brown slacks for weeks. Then one day he set them aside and went about naked. He took to urinating on the floor of his bathroom, but he refused to allow janitors to clean it up, coping with the odorous mess by spreading paper towels on the floor. He had plenty of flunkies who catered to his every whim. These were former truck drivers and construction workers, blue-collar types who knew very well that by ministering to Hughes, they could assure themselves of lavish salaries and expense accounts. He also had plenty of support from attorneys and accountants.

In 1958, suffering a true mental breakdown, he threw tantrums and babbled incoherently. He recovered, but during the 1960s his mind, health, and appearance continued to deteriorate. He ate little; though more than six feet tall, by 1970 he weighed less than a hundred pounds. His hair rolled down his back; his beard trailed onto his chest, and his toenails were so long that they curled. He usually went about naked, and on many days the most he could do was to travel between his bed and bathroom. He seldom washed or used shampoo, and he had an extremely foul odor. He required enemas; after receiving one he often defecated on his bed, where his aides sometimes found him lying in his excrement.

Yet amid his obsessions, his personal filth, and his drug use, he retained a keen mind that continued to deal lucidly with the business matters that concerned him. He remained a man to reckon with. He bought a controlling interest in Northeast Airlines in 1961, and held it until he sold his holdings in 1965. He also fought doggedly in the courts to regain control of TWA. This effort failed, but the airline prospered under its new management—which caused its stock to rise sharply. Hughes owned 78 percent of the outstanding shares, and when he sold them in 1966, following the failure of his attempts to regain control, he walked away with a check for $546,549,171.

In 1968, hoping anew to own an airline, he offered to buy Western Air Lines. It was no more than a regional carrier, but it brought gamblers to Las Vegas, where his interests had burgeoned. The stockholders voted narrowly to accept his offer. But by a margin of 13 to 11 the board of directors voted no, well aware that he had brought TWA close to bankruptcy. His attorneys responded with a lawsuit against the dissident directors, seeking to hold them personally liable for any damages the airline might sustain due to their failure to honor the stockholders' mandate. That did it; six of the dissidents caved in, and once again Hughes had what he wanted. Renamed Hughes AirWest, the airline remained part of his empire until his death.

Even so, these successes paled by comparison to what might have been his. At Hughes Aircraft, the manager Harold Rosen had introduced the communications satellite in the form we use to this day. Bell Labs had laid the groundwork, building Telstar, the first such spacecraft, and launching it in 1962. But Telstar flew in low orbit, which was easy to reach. Rosen wanted to use geosynchronous orbit, at an altitude of 22,300 miles. This orbit was hard to attain, but it would allow a satellite to remain fixed in position within the sky, by circling the earth every twenty-four hours. Ground stations then could be simple, for they would not have to track moving spacecraft.

Test satellites built by Rosen, called Syncom, reached their high orbits in 1963 and 1964. An improved commercial prototype, Early Bird, entered service a year later. Just as Hughes Aircraft had grabbed an early lead in military electronics after the war, this venture now opened its own opportunity as the world prepared for the routine use of such spacecraft. A global consortium, Intelsat, pursued a strong interest in geosynchronous orbit—and found that only Hughes Aircraft had pertinent experience. This firm went on to establish itself, during the 1970s, as the world's premier builder of communications satellites.

Though Hughes by then had deteriorated alarmingly, only a few of his closest aides knew the pathetic details—and they weren't talking. To the nation at large, and to most people within his corporations, he remained a mystery man, a glamorous recluse who was rich beyond belief, pulling strings behind the scenes, ready perhaps at any moment to astound the world by drawing a billion-dollar rabbit from his hat. His secretiveness, his wealth, and his mystique all suited the CIA, which had secrets of its own.

The floor of the Pacific is carpeted with nodules, football-size and smaller, that are rich in manganese, nickel, cobalt, and copper. These metals appeared ripe for the taking, and the Los Angeles firm of Global Marine, which specialized in offshore oil drilling, had a particular interest in finding ways to tap this wealth. Hughes Tool contracted with this firm and arranged to build a large deep-ocean drilling ship, the *Hughes Glomar Explorer,* with the announced intent of launching seabed mining as a major new industry. Experts questioned whether seabed mining was economically feasible, but Hughes's involvement stilled the doubts. The oceanographer Jacques Cousteau said that "we had to treat it seriously because we all knew that Howard Hughes does not involve himself in uneconomic undertakings."

Actually, Hughes was working as a front for the CIA. A Soviet sub had sunk in 1968; intelligence agents hoped to raise it, thereby recovering its codebooks and weapons manuals. The *Glomar Explorer* was useless for economical ocean mining, but following its completion in 1972, it indeed found the sunken sub and tried to raise it with a grapnel. *Time* magazine reported that its hull, weakened by collapse under pressure, "cracked into two pieces . . . the aft two-thirds, including the conning tower and the coveted missiles and code room, slipped back into the seabed." The *Washington Post* added that the CIA then attempted "to raise the sunken boat piece by piece." Some bodies of crewmen were found and reburied at sea, but the CIA did not disclose whether it had successfully recovered other valuable nuggets.

This operation, called Project Jennifer, showed that the CIA was well aware of Hughes's faltering condition—and would continue to draw on his remaining sparks of lucidity. He indeed remained rational at times; as late as 1972 he held a press conference, talking with newsmen by telephone, and held his own for two and a half hours. But as death approached, he continued to decline.

From his fingers and toes, long yellowed nails extended in grotesque spirals. A malignant tumor formed a red mass of tissue that grew out of his scalp. Many of his teeth had decayed into rotten black pegs, which hung loosely within infected and pus-filled gums. Prolonged drug use had covered his kidneys with scar tissue. Bedsores festered along his back, with the bare bone of a shoulder blade poking through his withered skin. Needle marks carpeted his arms and thighs, clustering hideously around his groin. Moreover, because he had built up tolerance to his drugs, there was enough codeine in his system to kill a normal man.

When he died, in April 1976, X rays taken at the autopsy showed hypodermic needles that had broken off within his arms.

Who was he, this rare mix of money, talent, and psychosis? At his best, prior to 1950, he was far more than a venture capitalist who put up funds to support other people's ideas. He had ideas of his own, good ones, and he won the involvement of highly capable people when he refrained from meddling in their work. In this fashion he gave a valuable push to commercial aviation, led the Air Force into a new era of electronics, and built Hughes Aircraft as a major firm.

But the key to it all was hands-off management. His staffers indeed could do well, but only when he left them alone. He then saw Hughes Tool win new strength, while gaining such successes as the Constellation, the Air Force's electronics, and Project Jennifer. When he involved himself personally, as with his wartime aircraft and in many of his business dealings after 1945, his quirks and obsessions came to the forefront and cost him control of Hughes Aircraft, RKO, and TWA. Yet while RKO ceased to make movies after 1957, Hughes Aircraft and TWA went on to reach new heights after he relinquished control.

He worked in an era of large opportunities, when aviation and electronics were expanding into new realms. It was an era when corporations still could belong to their owners, not to stockholders with their cautious boards of directors, and in this time a man like Hughes could still work as a generalist. Building on his father's Hughes Tool Company and its oil fortune, he expanded by turns into movies, aviation, and electronics. In each of these areas he did memorable and even pathbreaking work. His life saw much publicity, great achievements, compelling dreams—and, overriding all, an enormous madness. Though Howard Hughes long ago became pegged in the public mind as an eccentric recluse, there remains a grandeur about this man.

Jack Northrop 17

There is generally an enormous gap between aeronautical engineering and flight as a subject for poetry and art. The artist deals exclusively with soaring metaphors and human emotions. The designer, while crafting wings and fuselages with the exquisite care of a sculptor, works from calculations and technical principles. Poets may admire an airplane's grace, but have little to say regarding its structural design. Engineers, creating that design, build it along functional lines, paying little heed to the merely ornamental.

Yet one leading engineer, Jack Northrop, spent his career working to bridge this gulf. His goal was elegance; he sought to reduce the airplane to its simplest and most natural form. He believed this form would be a flying wing, amounting to an enormous boomerang. It would feature nothing more than a wing, lacking all semblance of a fuselage or tail. What was more, he came astonishingly close to making it a mainstay of Air Force power. Yet he failed in his quest, as the world of aviation passed him by. This failure broke him and left him with an enduring bitterness.

This passion and drama, during his adult years, contrasted markedly with the ordinariness of his youth. Born in Newark, New Jersey, in 1895, his family spent part of his childhood in Nebraska, which he later described as "a pretty dreary place to live—flat country, either too cold or too hot and very little to see." California proved far more inviting, and the Northrops soon settled in Santa Barbara.

The young Jack found his pathway into aviation within that town, but in a rather casual way. Close to the beach there stood an auto garage and an airplane shop, which together filled a small building. The airplane outfit was the work of two brothers, Allan and Malcolm Loughead, who pronounced their name "Lockheed." In due time it grew into that aircraft company. In 1916, the youthful Northrop was a frequent visitor; he had graduated from high school three years earlier.

271

He had no university degree and never would get one. As he later recalled, "I had a little experience as a garage mechanic and I worked for a year as a draftsman for an architect, and I worked for my father who was in the building business, and this sort of qualified me to design airplanes." The Lougheads' work was very much a matter of proceeding by guess and by golly; they were actually constructing an aircraft without engineering drawings. When Jack Northrop joined them, his high school physics and algebra already qualified him to do stress analyses, in an elementary but still useful fashion.

America soon entered World War I, which brought new business for the Lougheads, but Northrop's world remained fixed within Santa Barbara. He joined the Army—which quickly sent him back home to help build flying boats. Then in 1918, out of the Army and self-supporting, he married his high school sweetheart, Inez Harmer. So far as he and Inez were concerned, life promised the simple happiness and modest prosperity of their parents, with no thought of renown in the wider world.

Already, though, he was pursuing the search for elegance that would mark his career. This came to the fore immediately after the war, as he set out to design his first complete airplane. He listened with great interest when the Lougheads' foreman, Tony Stadlman, described a captured German Albatros fighter that he had seen on display in San Francisco. The Red Baron, Manfred von Richthofen, had flown it in combat, and Northrop was aware that its fuselage amounted to a shell of molded plywood. He adopted this feature in designing his own plane, the Loughead S-1.

This construction technique was demanding. Most planebuilders were assembling their fuselages through the simple method of building a framework and covering it over with fabric. By contrast, Northrop had to fabricate a carefully shaped concrete mold, soak plywood in water to make it flexible, then force it against the sides of the mold by inflating a balloon. But this approach gave new freedom in design, yielding a gracefully curved fuselage shaped like a torpedo. It broke decisively with the boxy, angular forms that represented the norm.

Unfortunately, the early postwar years were very bad for the aeronautical world. In the wake of World War I, the nation was awash in war-surplus engines and aircraft. Many were both inexpensive and high in quality, for they had survived the ruthless aerial competitions of combat. Few people cared to order new designs, and with little new business coming in, the Loughead enterprise folded in 1920.

Northrop went back to architectural drafting and spent the next three years working with his father, but in 1923 that business folded as well.

He made his way to the Los Angeles area and found new work in aviation, joining a hole-in-the-wall outfit run by the planebuilder Donald Douglas. Douglas was struggling like everyone else, but at least he had a project: the Army's World Cruiser aircraft that flew around the globe in 1924. Northrop soon was designing bits and pieces of these planes.

Still, this was not enough for him. The Loughead S-1 had given him a taste for designing aircraft that were entirely his, and he now was ready to go beyond its design. Though possessing a streamlined fuselage, its biplane wings had offered nothing new. But after 1920 another wartime planebuilder, Anthony Fokker, introduced monoplanes that featured single strong wings made of wood. Other designers stuck with their biplanes, well aware that they worked. But the venturesome Northrop believed that he could break new ground by combining a Fokker wing with a molded fuselage. This combination represented his next step in the pursuit of elegance.

Working in his spare time, he prepared blueprints for his new plane, the Vega. "It was a radical design," he later declared, "far removed from the more conventional types that Douglas was building, and I felt he would not be interested." By contrast, Allan Loughead was highly interested. He too had left aviation and had become a real-estate developer, but he felt that the new Vega would offer him a route back into aeronautics. What was more, a Los Angeles venture capitalist named Fred Keeler was ready to back this enterprise. Still, whereas in Santa Barbara everyone had known the name of Loughead, in other cities it invited such mispronunciations as Loghead or Loafhead. Keeler therefore insisted on using the phonetic spelling, and late in 1926 the Lockheed Aircraft Company opened for business.

Northrop set to work within a rented shop in Hollywood, but the design was almost too strange even for Loughead. The monoplanes of 1927, such as Lindbergh's *Spirit of St. Louis,* all had at least a few external struts to brace the wings. The Vega would have none. "Allan kept insisting that we must put some brace struts on, whether they had anything to do or not," Northrop later recalled. "He felt that nobody would buy the airplane unless there was something that could be seen to hold the wing up. I finally won out." The first Vega was ready in mid 1927, just in time for the boom that followed Lindbergh's flight to Paris.

It was an immediate hit. With a 220-horsepower engine it cruised at 135 miles per hour, at a time when few civilian planes were topping 100. More powerful motors boosted this speed to as much as 170. The newspaper magnate William Randolph Hearst ordered a Vega. So did the pilots Amelia Earhart and Wiley Post. The plane found work as an airliner, carrying six passengers, and it also set records. Wiley Post's model,

Winnie Mae, reached fifty-five thousand feet. Later, it led the field in a race from Los Angeles to Chicago. At the 1927 National Air Races, it took a Vega to beat a Vega. Lockheed built five a month from mid 1927 through 1928, then continued production at a slower rate during subsequent years.

At Lockheed, Northrop now was the man of the hour. He could look ahead to new designs that would build on the Vega, creating it anew in aluminum rather than wood, while adding the latest forms of streamlining. Yet his hopes now ran far beyond such pedestrian notions. He saw a clear goal: "to build an airplane where there was nothing but the wing, where everything was included in it—powerplant, passengers, every function that was necessary."

The flying wing already was a well-established concept in aeronautics. Germany's brilliant Hugo Junkers, a planebuilder par excellence, had hailed it as the plane of the future, and had directed his own efforts toward its realization. It offered the ultimate in elegance, for by eliminating fuselage and tail, it truly reduced the airplane to its minimal essentials. Yet to build it represented a first-class technical challenge, for this wing, unassisted by tail surfaces, would somehow have to achieve stability in flight.

No one had built a practical version, not even the famous Junkers. Yet if Northrop could succeed, he might have more than an elegant design; he might break ground anew. Lacking the weight of a fuselage and tail, a successful flying wing would greatly stretch its range. Alternately, it might offer unparalleled power in lifting heavy loads.

As with so much else in Northrop's life, his vision of the flying wing had developed during his years in Santa Barbara. Within that coastal town, he had drawn inspiration from the seagulls. They were mostly wing, with minimal bodies, and he had decided on his own that an all-wing aircraft would offer the natural way to fly. He had done little to realize this vision, keeping it as his personal hope. But with the Vega in hand, having made his reputation as a pathbreaker and an innovator, he was ready to try.

Yet to Allan Loughead, he might as well have proposed to power a Vega with gossamer moonbeams. Worse, Northrop soon found himself working with a new manager who was quite ready to tell him how to design airplanes. A few weeks later he quit. The wealthy Hearsts quickly came to his rescue, staking him to a new company, Avion. He then went forward with two projects: the flying wing that he would build for love, and Alpha, an all-aluminum follow-on to the Vega, that he hoped to build for money.

The flying wing came out of the shop with a wingspan of thirty feet and with room for a pilot and a ninety-horsepower engine. It proved awkward in flight and Northrop realized he did not know how to control it, so he compromised. He mounted tail surfaces behind the wing, supported by two long booms. That made it easy to handle during takeoff and landing, while its wing provided a particularly fast rate of climb. Then, having done what he could for the moment, he turned to the Alpha.

This was a conventional airplane, but it had all the trimmings. He built its wing and fuselage using a structural design of his own invention, achieving great strength with light weight. He reduced its drag considerably by enclosing the engine within a cowl. For additional streamlining, he mounted the landing gear within aluminum "trousers" that resembled stubby wings. Cruising at 140 miles per hour, it carried mail rather than passengers, and Northrop built no more than seventeen of them. But when it made its first flight, in March 1930, it offered a clear demonstration of what now was possible.

By then the Depression was under way and his company was running short of cash. The planebuilder William Boeing responded by arranging a buyout. Northrop hoped to continue working near Los Angeles, but in 1931, with the Depression deepening, his corporate management decided to cut costs by combining his operation with an existing firm in Kansas. He had no wish to return to the Great Plains, not after his childhood in Nebraska, so once again he cut loose.

This time he set up a subsidiary of Douglas Aircraft, just in time for his structural designs to see use in the DC-1 and then in the DC-2 and DC-3. He crafted wings for all three of these airliners, drawing on a form of construction that he had used with success in his Alpha. It relied on crisscrossing ribs and longitudinal members that formed a framework resembling an egg crate. In tests, a steamroller drove over it without damage.

Northrop's life held many satisfactions. He was happy with his wife and their three children. He was quiet and modest, winning his employees' loyalty by showing a sincere respect and personal concern. He also was well aware that his lack of an engineering background had posed no handicap. To the contrary, he had repeatedly grasped opportunities that others had overlooked.

Even so, he still found himself in the same old bind. He held a substantial interest in his Douglas subsidiary, but he was working entirely on aircraft of conventional type. He wanted more; in his mind, conventional engineering amounted to "inventing rubber gloves to use with a leaky fountain pen." In the words of his longtime colleague and biographer, Ted Coleman, "he still was not at ease with himself, did not consider himself fully successful. For a reason that he could not understand, there was a continuing frustration in not being his own boss, in not being able to make the important decisions himself."

His chance came in 1938, when Donald Douglas bought out the whole of his interest. This left him flush with cash, and he soon secured more through a Wall Street financier, LaMotte Cohu. Together they proceeded to launch Northrop Aircraft. It built airplanes of conventional type; its P-61, a twin-engine night fighter, served with valor in the Pacific war. But some funds went into pursuing Northrop's own inventions. In particular, he pursued his road not taken by returning to the flying wing.

The first of them, the N-1M, took to the air during 1940 and 1941. It was definitely an experimental model, built of wood so that Northrop could readily tweak its design. Still, in learning about its aerodynamics, he no longer was flying blind. He now had the counsel of Theodore von Kármán, the nation's leader in this field, who was only a few miles away at California Institute of Technology. Flight tests showed that to make this plane stable in the air, its wings required sweepback, which moved its center of gravity in an advantageous fashion. The N-1M was underpowered, but the test pilot, Moye Stephens, succeeded in reaching altitudes of four thousand feet.

Meanwhile, across the Atlantic, the Nazis were unleashing their military forces upon an unready Europe. In January 1941, while Britain stood alone, a planning group within the Army Air Corps first considered what the United States might do if England were to fall. The planners decided that the United States might still attack Germany by building intercontinental bombers, able to make round-trip flights from the East Coast. That August, when President Roosevelt met with Prime Minister Winston Churchill, they agreed that the United States indeed would develop such aircraft.

The goal was simple to define but hard to achieve: "10,000 pounds for 10,000 miles." Such a bomber was to carry a five-ton war load across the Atlantic to Berlin, then return home without landing or refueling en route. Here indeed was a leap into the future; not until well into the 1950s would airliners fly the Atlantic nonstop and one-way, let alone make round-trips. But Northrop believed that a flying wing could do it. Along with designers in other companies, he expected to meet this goal by using piston engines of unparalleled power.

The increasing speed and performance of aircraft, during the 1930s and 1940s, paced the development of such power. Air-cooled engines of the 1920s had used a single row of cylinders that extended outward from the hub, like spokes of a wheel. However, this basic arrangement could accommodate only limited increases in horsepower before a motor's physical size would get out of hand. The solution lay in the twin-row engine, with two banks of cylinders set one behind the other. These designs entered service during the 1930s. The B-12 bomber was among the last new models to use single-row motors; the Boeing 247 airliner, dating to 1933, was one of the first to install twin rows.

When the Army Air Forces went to war, its airmen flew to battle using engines of this type. These powered the principal fighters and bombers of the era. The next step upward in power called for a four-row engine, which Pratt & Whitney developed. Earlier engines from that firm had been named Wasp, Twin Wasp, and Double Wasp; this one was the Wasp Major. It had twenty-eight cylinders; studded as it was with cylinder heads, it looked somewhat like a corncob. It made its first runs on a test stand in the spring of 1941, but it indeed proved waspish, for its development in no way went smoothly. It encountered a number of problems that took time to resolve, even under the press of wartime urgency. As a result, despite its early start, it did not qualify for service until the end of 1944. Still, it was worth waiting for. It delivered 3,500 horsepower at takeoff, as much as a diesel locomotive. Among operational engines, its nearest rival offered only 2,200.

Boeing, builder of the B-29, was quick to show what could happen by replacing that bomber's existing motors with the new Pratt & Whitney engines. The plane that resulted, the B-50, retained the fuselage and wings of its predecessor, making them nearly identical in appearance. But the performance differences were enough to make a general feel like a kid in a candy store. The bombload went up by 40 percent, from 20,000 pounds to 28,000. Cruising speed jumped from 220 to 300 miles per hour, while the service ceiling leaped from 32,000 feet to 40,000. And if this was what a planebuilder could achieve when constrained merely to modify an existing airframe, what might happen if designers could let their imaginations roam free?

The Air Force was in the process of finding out, for during 1941, only months after the meeting between Roosevelt and Churchill, it had set in train a pair of bomber projects that were to use the Wasp Major. One of them, the XB-35, went to Northrop. It indeed amounted to no more than a bare wing, having neither fuselage nor tail surfaces. In appearance it resembled an enormous boomerang, 172 feet in span. He had no experience in building conventional aircraft of such size, let alone unconventional ones, and he had been validating his theories with only the small twin-engine N-1M. It was an enormous step up to an intercontinental bomber, but the War Department was willing to give him a chance. It helped that Theodore von Kármán stayed on as a consultant, with one of his former students, William Sears, as Northrop's chief of aerodynamics.

The War Department also contracted with the firm of Convair, in Fort Worth, Texas, to pursue a second effort. This was the XB-36, which offered less risk because it used a standard layout with fuselage and tail. But there was nothing standard in its size, for it pressed the limits. It was twice the weight of a B-50 and nearly three times as heavy as a B-29, with much of this tonnage residing in the vast lakes of fuel that would sustain its long range. It mounted six Wasp Majors, and when one of these planes flew overhead, you could feel the ground shake.

As the war progressed these projects lost priority, for it became obvious that Britain would stand. They also encountered their share of technical problems along the way, though both of them took to the air during the summer of 1946. By then there was much interest in a next-generation bomber, and these efforts showed that even in the realm of piston-powered aircraft, there still was plenty of room for ingenuity. The XB-35 appeared particularly tantalizing. Lacking both fuselage and tail, it weighed only 206,000 pounds fully loaded, compared to 357,000 for the XB-36. But it was to fly the same mission, carrying 10,000 pounds for 10,000 miles. Its reduced weight allowed it to get along with only four Wasp Majors rather than six.

The turbojet had burst upon the scene, and there also was interest in a jet bomber. Five projects were under way, at five different companies, and these were not merely design studies; they called for full-size flying prototypes. Two of them, the North American B-45 and the Boeing B-47, reached production. The B-47 proved to be particularly significant, for it showed the shape of things to come. It introduced the basic shape of large jet aircraft, featuring swept wings, swept tail surfaces, and engines mounted in pods placed on struts below the wing. Decades later, new airliners continued to follow this basic layout with only modest change.

The XB-47 made its first flight in December 1947 and went into initial production the following September. It cruised at 560 miles per hour and had greater range than the B-29, which still was in service as the Air Force's principal weapon. The B-47 lacked the range of an intercontinental bomber, but it could carry the atomic bomb. Its pilots cherished it as a hot rod, with the speed and performance of a fighter.

Jack Northrop was ready to challenge this one as well. In 1944 he held a contract to build thirteen preproduction models of his flying wing as the YB-35. Late in that year he proposed to enter the jet age by replacing its four Wasp Majors with eight turbojet engines from General Electric. This raised the prospect of a jet bomber that would introduce the radical design of a large flying wing, while relying on an airframe that already was well along in development. The Pentagon accepted his proposal and gave permission to convert two of his YB-35s into the jet-propelled version, the YB-49. This made its first flight in October 1947.

This meant that immediately after the war, three programs offered different routes toward the bomber of the future. The XB-36 promised long range by using a plethora of pistons in a conventional design. The B-47 lacked its range but had jet speed. Northrop, with a foot in both camps, expected to beat the XB-36 at its own game with the elegance of a flying wing. He also expected to raise its speed by installing jets of his own.

The XB-36 made its first flights during 1946, and this program quickly flew into serious trouble. Already it had encountered lengthy delays and cost overruns. In December the head of the Strategic Air Command, General George Kenney, reported that the operational B-36 would have a range of only 6,800 miles when flown in wartime. He declared that this range "is not sufficient to permit the B-36 to reach and return from profitable targets in Europe and Asia from bases in the United States or Alaska."

His colleagues responded by placing their hopes in a new super-charger, a type of pump that would force more air into the plane's engines. It then would fly at higher altitude where drag would lessen, increasing the range. But in April 1948, Air Force officials learned that the new supercharger was a flop. It would not yield the ten-thousand-mile range. The B-36 was already in production, but its cancellation now appeared imminent.

No such difficulties had attended Northrop's YB-35, while his jet-powered YB-49 had gone forward in straightforward fashion. With the B-36 in serious trouble, Air Force thoughts turned to Northrop's alternative. Late in June, General Joseph McNarney paid him a visit. He was the man who signed the purchase orders for Air Force planes, and he had such an order among his papers. It directed Northrop to build thirty RB-49s, a version to serve for photoreconnaissance. "The order is only a drop in the bucket," McNarney added. "Convair's Fort Worth bomber plant, owned by the government, will be made available to you for production of the RB-49. In large numbers."

This plant featured a vast enclosed hall that had been used for wartime bomber production. It now was building the B-36. Northrop had his own production facilities, in Hawthorne, California, but these were too small to turn out the RB-49 on an adequate schedule. This Air Force decision meant not only that he had the superior airplane, but that Convair, his principal rival, would sign on to carry out its production.

Jack Northrop's flying-wing bomber, the YB-35, accompanied by a Northrop P-61 fighter. (Northrop Grumman)

At the personal level, the stakes were higher still. The search for elegance had been his great passion and the leitmotiv of his career. Its pursuit had repeatedly led him to introduce pathbreaking advances. Early on, he had built the Vega, a monoplane with a simple, strong, and well-streamlined wing. It had broken decisively with the strut-and-wire biplane. Then, because future aircraft would necessarily be of aluminum, he had developed all-metal wings of particular quality. That had led to the DC-2 and DC-3, which had lifted commercial aviation into an era of spectacular growth.

Now, still in his early fifties and at the top of his form, he was ready to build true flying wings as instruments of national power. This represented the capstone of his career, and it meant even more. It would show that Jack Northrop was the great planebuilder of recent decades, the man whose work had repeatedly opened the most fruitful paths in aeronautical design. At the convergence of those paths would stand the flying wing.

However, he faced an immediate problem in negotiating the formal arrangements whereby Convair would carry through production of his bomber. Two meetings between officials of the two companies, during

July, brought no agreement. Then on July 16, the Air Force secretary, Stuart Symington, hosted a third meeting.

"There are too many aircraft companies," he announced baldly. "The Air Force cannot afford to support another large aircraft manufacturer. We're going to have to cut one down." He looked right at Jack. "I want Northrop combined with Convair."

Jack was stunned, but kept his cool. "Mr. Secretary," he replied, "what are our alternatives to this move?" Symington answered, "You'll be goddamn sorry if you don't." General McNarney, who was also present, quickly responded: "Oh, Mr. Secretary, you don't mean that the way it sounds." Symington responded, "You're goddamn right I do!"[1]

Northrop Aircraft still held its production contract, but Jack had to respond to Symington's demand. He met with Floyd Odlum, the financier who controlled Convair, but was unable to agree on terms for a merger. And while he contemplated his company's demise, the B-36 was coming back to life. During the second half of 1948, a series of spectacular flights showed that it indeed could serve as the Air Force's main bomber.

As early as May, a long test flight had shown that this aircraft could top nine thousand miles in range. Subsequent tests confirmed this. Then in early December, a B-36 flew out of Carswell Air Force Base, near Dallas, bound for Honolulu. Its crew carried a ten-thousand-pound bombload and dropped it into the ocean off Hawaii, then returned to base.

President Truman meanwhile was preparing to hold the entire Defense Department to a total budget of $14.4 billion for fiscal year 1950, which would begin in mid 1949. The Berlin airlift was under way, but Truman did not fear war, for he believed that the Soviets would back down. He refused the strongest of Pentagon entreaties for more money. Symington had to live within this budget and yet had to build up his heavy-bomber force to meet the threat from Moscow. To do this, he prepared to cut back production of bombers and fighters that were less than vital, freeing up funds for aircraft that could carry the war to the enemy.

He set up a review board to advise him on procurement policy. The long flight to Hawaii of the B-36 was timed to influence its findings, and had the desired effect; the panel recommended stepping up its production. Symington received its report just after New Year of 1949. On January 11 he announced a series of cancellations—which included Northrop's thirty flying-wing RB-49s.

Meanwhile, the Navy was pursuing its own strategic hopes. Its focus of attention was the USS *United States,* a planned sixty-five-thousand-ton carrier that was to be the first of a new class. These were to embark large aircraft that could carry the atomic bomb. But by early 1949, congressional leadership was turning decisively to the Air Force as the nation's strategic power. In March it became quite clear which way the wind was blowing, for Secretary of Defense James Forrestal stepped down. He had been Secretary of the Navy during the war years; the new defense secretary, Louis Johnson, had made his name as a big-bomber man. In April the Navy held a ceremony to lay the keel of the *United States,* but a few days later, Johnson ordered its cancellation. With this, the triumph of the B-36 was complete.

Jack Northrop continued to hold to his hopes. He sent a YB-49 on a nonstop flight from California to Washington, D.C., at an average speed of 511 miles per hour. But he was a mile short and, literally, a day late. The previous day, a B-47 had flown in from the state of Washington at 607 miles per hour. This actually beat the previous coast-to-coast record that had been set in a jet fighter, a P-80A. It also drove home a point that was already clear to the Air Force: the flying wing was neither fish nor fowl. It lacked both the speed of the B-47 and the range of the B-36.

Its disadvantage in speed, even with jet engines, stemmed from the fact that it was really no more than a piston-driven airframe of 1941 vintage. Indeed, the B-49 had been nothing more than an expedient, to which the Air Force had turned in a moment of desperation. In the subsequent words of von Kármán, it "was doomed to failure because it appeared at the wrong moment in aviation history. Northrop had insisted that the crew, fuel, and everything else had to go into the Wing. This load made the wings thick, which is all right at speeds of three hundred to four hundred miles per hour." But at higher speeds, "the Flying Wing was unsatisfactory."[2]

Still the B-49 did not go gently into that good night. Plenty of people were wondering why the Air Force had so suddenly embraced the B-36, when a few months earlier it had stood on the brink of cancellation. Talk of a Northrop merger had not gone unnoticed within the industry, and rumor had it that Symington was misusing his post as Air Force secretary to advance his personal interests by selling out those of the United States.

These rumors held that Symington was seeking to build a "General Motors of the air" by pushing the firm of Curtiss-Wright, as well as Northrop, into a merger with Convair. Symington then was to head this enlarged corporation. He supposedly had favored the B-36, not because it was the best airplane available, but because its continued production would provide business for his company.

In May 1949, Congressman James Van Zandt, a member of the House Armed Services Committee, blew the lid off. In a spectacular speech, he leveled accusations against both Symington and the B-36. His committee responded by authorizing a searching investigation. If Van Zandt could support his allegations, the B-36 would stand in discredit and Symington would stand open to criminal charges. The B-49, in turn, might win a new lease on life.

However, this bill of particulars proved to rest on nothing more than a scurrilous document prepared by one Cedric Worth, an aide to a Navy undersecretary. Worth, in turn, had worked from nothing more than newspaper columns and industry gossip. The House held its hearings during August, and Air Force officials were ready for action. Telling testimony came from General Curtis LeMay, who had succeeded General Kenney as head of the nation's bomber force. LeMay was known both for being hard to please and for an unvarnished integrity. He stated that he had personally recommended stepping up B-36 production, based on the plane's merits. When Van Zandt responded with mere newspaper clippings, it was clear that Symington would receive complete vindication.

There remained the matter of giving more speed and altitude to the piston-driven B-36, to allow it to outfly enemy fighters. Under Moscow's imminent threat, this meant taking the aircraft as it was and adding some bells and whistles in a hurry. These took the form of four jet engines in two pods, one mounted beneath each wing. They provided further power during heavily loaded takeoffs, and they offered more. In July 1949, a B-36D with the new equipment reached fifty thousand feet and a top speed of 435 miles per hour. This appeared adequate to allow it to survive in hostile airspace, by flying at night and using electronic countermeasures to blind the radars of enemy interceptors.

The intercontinental bomber indeed had become the cornerstone of national defense, but its incarnation as the B-36 was worth only two cheers. That airplane now had ten engines, "six turning and four burning," and its jets and piston motors each burned a separate type of fuel. Maintenance problems were horrendous; mechanics said that the B-36 demanded a week of attention for every hour of flight. Lacking jet speed, it could only serve as an interim bomber, waiting for something better that could supersede it.

The Air Force was preparing to move decisively toward all-jet bombers, which might have offered yet another opportunity for the B-49. It didn't. Symington's immediate hopes lay in the B-47, which was faster than the B-49 and mounted six engines rather than Northrop's eight. The standard B-47 had a range of only four thousand miles, but by 1949 the Air Force was showing strong interest in midair refueling, which would stretch its range at will. The B-52 was also in development, as a particularly large jet bomber slated to replace the B-36 during the 1950s.

After the B-36 gained the jet engines that boosted its own performance, Air Force interest in the YB-49 dropped from minimal to zero. Northrop had eleven YB-35 airframes parked outside his plant in Hawthorne, waiting for their turbojets. They all were Air Force property, and in December 1949 the order came down to scrap them. The work took three months, using cutting torches and axes, and Jack Northrop could watch from his windows. Down below, trucks carted away dismembered pieces of the vision that had stood at the center of his life.

All this came to him as a hideous crisis of the spirit. He still had a company to run; the Korean War, which broke out in mid 1950, boosted Air Force demand and ended talk of a forced merger. Yet his hopes had focused on his flying wings, and their loss took the heart out of him. This loss carried over to his personal life, for he divorced his wife Inez, who had been his high school sweetheart, and married his secretary. He stayed at the helm of Northrop Aircraft for a while longer but retired in 1952. He was fifty-seven years old.

He never got over it. Never. As late as 1980, he made headlines by charging that Symington had tried to force him into the merger, and had canceled the B-49 out of spite when he refused. The chairman of Northrop, Richard Millar, had also been at that 1948 meeting with Symington, and he corroborated Jack's tale.

Yet those charges amounted to no more than a rehash of those of Cedric Worth in 1949, which had rested on mere rumor. There was good reason for the merger: to cope with the budget crunch. Indeed, far from acting spitefully toward Northrop Aircraft, Symington favored that firm. In March 1949, following the RB-49 cancellation but prior to Cedric Worth's charges, Symington gave Northrop a contract to build the F-89 fighter. It remained in production until 1957.

Certainly, Symington at the time had some very large fish to fry. He was Air Force secretary during 1948 and 1949, at the time of the Berlin blockade with its attendant threat of war. Amid this threat, constrained by Truman's limited budgets, he had to prepare to attack the Soviet Union with means that were already in hand. The scope of his concern lay far beyond the B-49, beyond even the whole of the aviation industry. It was nothing less than the weighty burden of a public official who knows that if he makes a mistake, the nation may be destroyed. Against this background, his peremptory treatment of Jack Northrop appears as a demand that Northrop was to shape up and get his plane into production by the quickest possible means, placing America's interests above those of his company.

Northrop's outlook could hardly have been more different. He still was an artist, obsessed with the merits of his flying wing. In the words of his biographer Ted Coleman, "Jack firmly believed that if something is efficient and beautiful it is right, a principle that guided Northrop throughout his professional career." For a brief moment his path had coincided with that of Symington, who had breathed life and promise into Northrop's vision. Yet they could not long travel together, for while Northrop cherished the flying wing as a love nearly won, Symington was concerned only with its value in the face of his preparations for war.

That value, again, was not large. Advancing technology, which had brought the flying wing to the brink of realization, now was passing it by. Its limit was one of low speed, for while it could lift heavy loads and achieve long range, its thick wing created drag that restricted its top speed to little more than 500 miles per hour. In operational service, it would have amounted to a slower counterpart of the B-47, with two additional engines in each airframe.

Yet the flying wing would not be entirely forgotten, for it possessed an important virtue: its shape made it nearly invisible to radar. During subsequent decades, advances in jet-engine design improved their fuel economy, raising the prospect that they could power a flying-wing bomber with particularly long range. New types of electronic flight control also came to the fore, easing the problem of stabilizing such craft when in the air. The day came, thirty years after the demise of the B-49, when the Air Force again turned to aircraft of this type.

In April 1980, Jack Northrop was old and feeble. He needed a wheelchair, while a stroke had robbed him of the ability to speak. Yet he could still see and hear, and his keen mind was as active as ever. So it was, in this last springtime of his life, that an old friend drove him to visit the Advanced Systems Division of his old company. It had kept its independence, and had grown; it now had divisions and plants all over the Los Angeles basin. And he was about to see a secret, for the facility he was visiting was the firm's center for preliminary work on new Air Force projects.

He saw plans for a bomber of the future, the B-2. It was to be a stealth aircraft, able to avoid being detected by radar. He saw that it would be built as a flying wing, and he smiled with pleasure. His concept would fly again. Once more the Air Force was reaching to accept his ideas, and to use them as a foundation for the nation's military strength. Moreover, his own Northrop Corporation was to build these airplanes.

He died the following winter, just a few weeks after his old friend Donald Douglas, convinced that his vision had been vindicated.

18

Chuck Yeager

I<small>F YOU DRIVE</small> northeastward from Los Angeles, into the Mojave Desert, you can visit the dry lakes of Edwards Air Force Base. These lakebeds extend for miles, flat as a pool table, providing some of the world's best landing fields for high-performance aircraft. You can look across the hard, desiccated silt, with distant mountains that turn blue and merge with the sky. Amid that cerulean vastness, unflecked by cloud, you may see the white chalk line of a vapor trail. With a little imagination you can hear the deep roar of a rocket engine. And you may think of the test pilot Chuck Yeager.

He grew up in Hamlin, West Virginia, amid the hills of that state. It was located on the Mud River, not far from the towns of Hurricane, Nitro, Sod, and Rumble. Career opportunities in the area have been described as "coal mine, moonshine, or movin' on down the line," and the Yeager family preferred the first of these. His father drilled for gas in coalfields; his brother did this as well. Sometimes all they had for dinner was corn bread and buttermilk, but Chuck could shoot a rifle by the time he was six. He brought home squirrel and rabbit, sometimes before heading for school in the morning. He went barefoot when he could, and spent much time in the woods. The Yeagers kept chickens, hogs, and a cow; they had apple butter and blackberries in season.

This was his world; he felt at ease here, treasuring it as his home for years after he had gone elsewhere. The war took him from Hamlin, as he enlisted in the Army and qualified for flight training. He met his wife, Glennis Dickhouse, while at flight school in Oroville, California. She was working as a social director; he asked her to arrange a dance for about thirty young men. She responded with annoyance: "You expect me to find thirty girls on three hours' notice?" He replied, "No, you'll only need to come up with twenty-nine, because I want to take you."

He went to England and flew eight combat missions before being shot down over occupied France, east of Bordeaux. Local farmers helped him hide from the Germans, then turned him over to members of the Resistance, who took him to the Pyrenees. Along with another downed airman, he hoped to cross those mountains into neutral Spain. A German patrol found them and fired a burst using dumdum bullets, blowing off his buddy's lower leg. Yeager applied a tourniquet and carried the unconscious man over a mountain to safety, then left him at the side of a road. Spanish police found him within an hour or so and took him to a hospital. Yeager found his way to a small hotel and soon was in the hands of the U.S. consul.

Back in England, he was eager to return to the war. However, he faced an inflexible rule that marked him for Stateside duty. This rule protected members of the French underground, for if the Germans captured an escaped pilot, they would torture him until he told what he knew about them. By then the Normandy invasion was under way; elements of the Resistance were fighting openly, leaving them with few secrets to betray. Yeager insisted on returning to combat, taking his arguments up the chain of command until he met General Eisenhower, the supreme commander. Ike requested an exception on Yeager's behalf, and the young West Virginian soon was back in the cockpit of a P-51.

He was flying bomber escort over Bremen when he shot down five enemy planes, becoming an ace in a day. He destroyed two of them without firing a shot, as he frightened one man and caused him to collide with his wingmate. Both men bailed out; their planes crashed. Yeager shot down three more with gunfire. Then, during another mission, he brought down an Me-262 jet fighter as it was coming in to land. Two weeks later he downed four Focke-Wulf FW-190 fighters, again in a single day. At war's end he had thirteen and a half kills to his credit.

This was impressive enough, but what really gave him an opportunity was that he had survived being shot down. Airmen who had been prisoners of war, or who had evaded capture, received the right to select an assignment at the base of their choice. Yeager had married his Glennis early in 1945, and he wanted to stay close to his home in Hamlin. Using a map, he found that the closest base was Wright Field, in Dayton, Ohio. Housing was tight, and Glennis soon was pregnant. She moved in with her in-laws, who were glad to help, for Chuck was away much of the time.

Wright Field was the Army Air Forces development center, the place where the hot new planes first took flight. Yeager spent much of each day in the air, flying over two dozen different types, including captured German and Japanese fighters. He qualified as a test pilot and flew the P-80 jet fighter repeatedly. As he racked up his flight hours, the nation's aviation researchers were preparing to leap beyond the jet into an era of rocket planes.

The basis for this work lay in an unfortunate tendency of the fastest aircraft to lose control and crash at high speeds. This problem had appeared during the war, when pilots put their piston-powered P-38 and P-47 fighters into steep dives. They didn't always succeed in pulling out, and those who did told of violent buffeting that made control nearly impossible. Yeager himself experienced this in his P-51. "My controls froze," he wrote. "I nearly bent that damned stick straining to pull out."

This resulted from "compressibility," which occurs in airflows close to the speed of sound. Flow over a wing speeds up; it can become supersonic even when the plane is not. This airflow slowed at the rear of the wing and produced a shock wave. This shock, riding atop the wing, created violent turbulence in the flow behind the wing—which was the flow that struck the tail surfaces. The severely disturbed flow brought strong buffeting, an intense shaking that made it hard to use the elevators. This wasn't good; the pilot needed those horizontal control surfaces to pull out of the dive. Worse things sometimes happened, for the horizontal stabilizer amounted to a wing in its own right; a shock could form on it as well. When that occurred, elevator effectiveness could completely disappear.

The federal government had a research organization, the National Advisory Committee for Aeronautics. It had wind tunnels that might have studied these matters, but they were inadequate. A NACA aerodynamicist, John Stack, held the view that only a supersonic experimental airplane could give the necessary data. He called a conference on high-speed flight and asked representatives of the Army and the Navy to pursue such a project, with NACA conducting the flight test program.

At Wright Field, the engineering manager Ezra Kotcher had been nurturing similar ideas. He won permission to proceed, and launched a search for a contractor that could design and build this research aircraft. He had little success at first; this new plane might point to the future of aeronautics, but the war was on and most companies were immersed in the present, building conventional bombers and fighters in large numbers. However, Kotcher found support at the firm of Bell Aircraft. It had failed to win a major contract; it could provide manufacturing space and technical specialists, and its management was willing to try something new.

The airplane that resulted was the Bell X-1. Its fuselage had the shape of a .50-caliber rifle bullet, which was known to go supersonic smoothly. Its builders fitted it with a rocket engine of six thousand pounds thrust, enough to drive the plane nearly vertically. A B-29 was to carry the X-1 aloft, with the rocket plane hanging from its bomb bay. Its pilot would light the engine as it fell away, head for the wild blue yonder, then glide down to a landing on the lakebed, without power. If he failed to do this, he would crash.

Edwards AFB, then known as Muroc Air Base, was the test site. Its dry lakes offered landing fields that were far larger than the runways of Wright Field. Located within the remote Mojave, it also was well suited to secrecy. In addition, its location placed it close to the big aircraft companies of southern California. This was not important for the X-1, which was built by firms on the East Coast. But officials at Wright Field expected to move their flight testing from that center to Muroc, and to fly increasing numbers of prototype aircraft that indeed came from nearby corporations.

Test pilots were ready to light their burners and punch holes in the sky, but they also knew how to fly with meticulous care. Many had engineering degrees, working in their cockpits as engineering experimentalists. Yeager had never been to college; he held only a diploma from Hamlin High School. But his piloting skills were unsurpassed. He also had a close eye for the details of engines and aircraft systems. The head of flight test, Colonel Albert Boyd, also found himself highly impressed with Yeager's ability to stay cool when under heavy pressure. "Above all, I wanted a pilot who was rock-solid to stability," he later wrote. "Yeager came up number one." Boyd selected him as the main test pilot for the X-1.

During 1946, events in England raised the stakes. The firm of De Havilland had built an experimental jet plane, the DH-108. Its test pilot, Geoffrey de Havilland Jr., was the son of the company's founder. He put the plane into a dive, trying to go supersonic. He reached Mach 0.94, less than fifty miles per hour short of his goal. Then the buffeting became so severe that the aircraft disintegrated in midair and killed him as it broke up.

Was there truly a sound barrier, a brick wall in the sky that would destroy any airplane that came too close? There was only one way to find out. A civilian pilot, Slick Goodlin, made initial flights in the X-1 under rocket power, reaching Mach 0.82. Then Yeager took over, making his first flight in August 1947. He flew his planned mission, including an unauthorized slow roll. Then he began descending, still with half his propellants onboard, gliding faster than jet fighters could fly at full power. He leveled off above the main runway—and hit his ignition. A blast of flame shot him upward; he reached Mach 0.85 at thirty-five thousand feet before coming in to land.

Colonel Boyd replied with a blast of his own: "Reply by endorsement about why you exceeded .82 Mach in violation of my direct orders." The program called for a step-by-step advance toward Mach 1, and Yeager had broken the rules. He replied, "The violation of your direct orders was due to the excited state of the undersigned and will not be repeated." He indeed had taken a chance; on that first flight he already had exceeded the speeds that had been studied in wind tunnels. However, after that he stuck to the plan.

He flew to Mach 0.86 early in October, and experienced buffeting from shock waves. It felt "like I was driving on bad shock absorbers over uneven paving stones." He went faster and saw his ailerons vibrating from these shocks. A few days later, he reached Mach 0.94. He pulled back on the controls—and nothing happened! "The control wheel felt as if the cables had snapped," he later wrote. A shock on the tail surfaces had destroyed his elevator effectiveness.

The builders of the X-1 had used rocket power to give it more thrust than it needed; it could accelerate while climbing. This was far safer than diving, for if anything went wrong, Yeager merely had to shut off the engine in order to slow down. He came back from this flight convinced that he could go no faster, for how could he fly without an elevator? The flight engineer, Jack Ridley, saw a way out. Designers of the X-1 had anticipated this elevator ineffectiveness, and had arranged for the entire horizontal stabilizer to pivot. This created a moving tail that could substitute for the elevator.

Yeager went up on Friday, October 10, and took it to Mach 0.94 once again. It worked! The movable stabilizer gave him the control he needed, and he knew he could do more. In keeping with Colonel Boyd's cautious approach, he accelerated to Mach 0.96, as indicated with his onboard machmeter. He remained in control. Then, amid the cold of high altitude, his windshield iced over and left him unable to see. A project engineer, Dick Frost, was flying a chase plane, a P-80, and talked him down to a safe landing on the lakebed.

Engineers reduced the flight data and concluded that Yeager had actually reached Mach 0.997 at forty thousand feet. This convinced everyone that supersonic flight was within reach. They set Tuesday the fourteenth as the date for its attainment, then went off to enjoy their weekend.

On Sunday evening, Chuck and Glennis went out to spend a few hours at Pancho's Fly Inn. It was a bar and grill that included a swimming pool and a dude ranch; it was one of the few places nearby where people could go for a good time. She had grown up around horses, and after dinner, they walked over to the corral and went out for a ride in the desert. Returning to Pancho's, they ran a race. There was no moon and although Chuck had very keen vision, he failed to see that the gate was closed. He hit it and tumbled to the ground. When he got up, his ribs hurt like the devil.

Glennis wanted to take him to the base hospital, but he knew that this was a good way to be grounded. The next morning, she drove him to see a civilian doctor in the nearby town of Rosamond, who told him he had two cracked ribs. The doctor taped them up, which eased the pain, and Yeager drove to the flight line for a chat with Ridley. Despite his injury, he was ready to fly the X-1 and to take it supersonic, with only Ridley knowing about his ribs.

Ridley agreed that once in the cockpit, he would be able to work the switches and controls. However, he also had to climb in and lock the cockpit door by pulling hard on a handle, and he couldn't do that. Ridley decided that with a short length of broomstick, Yeager might be able to exert enough leverage to succeed. He found a broom in the hangar, cut off a ten-inch length, and invited Yeager to climb into the cockpit to try it. Yeager did this, two or three times, and it worked. They left that bit of broomstick within the plane, as an unauthorized but essential item of equipment.

Like the other flights, the one of October 14, 1947, took place early in the morning, before the temperature got too hot for comfort. Yeager and Ridley took positions within the B-29 mother ship. They climbed down a ladder; Yeager slid into his seat within the X-1, with Ridley pushing the door against its frame. Yeager locked the door by using his broom handle; it worked perfectly. When the B-29 pilot asked if he was ready, Yeager replied, "Hell, yes. Let's get it over with."

He dropped away like a bomb, lit his rocket engine, and headed for the sky as the acceleration forced him back within his seat. At Mach 0.88 his plane began to buffet. He changed the setting on his movable stabilizer, and it smoothed right out. He reached Mach 0.96, as indicated on his cockpit instrument, and saw that the ride became more comfortable as his speed increased. He radioed to Ridley, "Elevator effectiveness regained."

His machmeter only went up to 1.0. As he continued to accelerate, its needle reached 0.965—and then tipped off-scale. In Yeager's subsequent words, "We were flying supersonic! And it was as smooth as a baby's bottom. Grandma could be sitting up there drinking lemonade." He said, "Hey, Ridley, that machmeter is acting screwy. It just went off the scale on me."

Chuck Yeager lights his rocket engine and heads for the sound barrier in his X-1 research plane. (U.S. Air Force)

"Fluctuated off?" Ridley replied.

"Yeah, at point nine-six-five."

"Son, you is imagining things."

"Must be. I'm still wearing my ears and nothing else fell off neither."

"I was thunderstruck," Yeager later wrote. "After all the anxiety, breaking the sound barrier turned out to be a perfectly paved speedway. I sat up there feeling kind of numb, but elated. After all the anticipation to achieve this moment, it really was a letdown. It took a damned instrument meter to tell me what I'd done."[1] He had reached Mach 1.06, seven hundred miles per hour. He glided in and landed. Fire trucks rolled up, and he hitched a ride back to the hangar with the fire chief. His ribs still ached, but the warm desert sun felt wonderful.

This was probably the most significant flight since Lindbergh's to Paris. The Air Force of 1947 had plans aplenty for supersonic jet fighters and guided missiles, but it needed confirmation that they could fly without meeting the fate of the De Havilland DH-108. Now this confirmation was in hand. In the course of that single morning, the speed-limit signs went down and a new era of flight came into view.

Nevertheless, the work was classified, and Yeager received no ticker-tape parade down Broadway. In June 1948 the Air Force finally took the lid off the news, and then the honors and awards started to roll in. He met General Hoyt Vandenberg, the Air Force chief of staff. He received a one-pound medal of solid gold from the International Aeronautical Federation. He went to the White House and shook hands with President Truman, who presented him with the Collier Trophy, the most prestigious award in aviation. *Time* magazine put him on the cover less than a year later.

None of this turned his head. He put the Collier Trophy on a workbench within his garage and used it to store nuts and bolts. He continued to cherish his ties to Hamlin, where people admired him—and remembered him as he had been. "When I had Charlie in the third grade," his teacher told *Time*, "he was a little slow. He used to sit in school daydreaming, and I always suspected he had his fishing pole hidden out back somewheres."

He now was the toast of the Air Force, but he continued to work as a test pilot. He won no promotion; he was a captain, with a captain's salary, and stayed at that rank for seven years before he became a major. Commercial opportunities beckoned, and he went to Colonel Boyd's executive officer, hoping to earn enough on the outside to buy Glennis a fur coat. He was turned down; his achievement was all in the line of duty, and that was that.

Officially, he still was assigned to Wright Field, holding only temporary duty at Muroc. This meant that Glennis could use the base hospital only in an emergency. When she gave birth to a baby girl, she did it in a tiny fourteen-bed hospital in the nearby town of Mojave. His family also was ineligible for housing on the base; they had to find what they could within the civilian market, even though there was very little in the desert. They had two young children, but they had to make do with a one-bedroom adobe house on a ranch, thirty miles from Muroc. They had no washing machine; Glennis did the laundry, including the diapers, in the bathtub, then hung it out to dry.

The Air Force sent Yeager on the rubber-chicken circuit, where he made after-dinner speeches to a host of Kiwanis and Elks clubs. His hosts usually were chamber of commerce types who needed careful instruction to understand what he had done, but that too was part of his duty. He continued to fly. He flew the XF-92A, an experimental fighter that introduced the triangle-shaped delta wing for improved supersonic performance.

He did not hold the limelight at Muroc, but participated in the standard activities of flight test. This included flying chase, accompanying an experimental aircraft as an aerial observer. Yeager brought the same standard of excellence to this work that he had upheld when flying the

X-1. Thus, in the summer of 1951 he flew chase during flight tests of the XF-91, a jet fighter that incorporated a rocket engine for an additional boost.

He flew an F-86 fighter and was flying formation with the XF-91 before its pilot, Carl Bellinger, even was airborne. This was superb airmanship right at the outset. Fire broke out within the XF-91, and Yeager saw it before the warning light went on in Bellinger's cockpit. Yeager then said, "I hate to tell you, but a piece of molten engine just shot out of your exhaust, and you'd better do something quick." Bellinger's cockpit filled with thick black smoke, but Yeager calmly radioed commands that brought him to a safe landing. Yeager landed as well, and was right there as Bellinger leaped to safety. The plane was in ashes by the time the fire trucks arrived, but Bellinger climbed onto the wing of Yeager's jet and held on to the fuselage as Yeager taxied up the lakebed.

It was all in a day's work, but this pointed up the fact that the experimental planes of that era were unproven and inadequately developed, and highly dangerous. Yeager himself might easily have died in his X-1, for only two weeks after his flight through Mach 1, his craft experienced a massive electrical failure as he fell away from his B-29. It stemmed from nothing more than a spot of corrosion on a battery terminal, but it left him without a radio, and without the means to ignite his rocket engine.

There he was, heavy with a full load of fuel. He couldn't dump his propellants in the usual fashion; he needed electricity to do this as well. He couldn't glide in and land; his landing gear could not stand the weight, and his plane would break on impact and explode. He lacked an ejection seat, and he knew that if he climbed out through the cockpit door, the plane's sharp-edged wing might cut him in half.

Fortunately, project engineer Dick Frost had anticipated this problem, and had installed an auxiliary valve with a supply of compressed nitrogen. Yeager worked the valve by hand and succeeded in blowing out much of his fuel and liquid oxygen. He couldn't learn anything from his cockpit instruments, which also needed power, and lack of electricity meant that he had to depend on the weight of his landing gear to get it lowered. He made a hard landing, but coasted safely to a stop.

There were plenty of other ways for a test pilot to die. Everyone knew about out-of-control crashes, but one man lost his life from nothing more than having a cockpit canopy come down on his head. People treated rocket propellants with due respect, but the real hazards sometimes involved dangers that experts didn't know about. One of the worst stemmed from nothing more than gaskets in the rocket systems. It was also one of the most elusive.

The gaskets were made from Ulmer leather, which was impregnated with substantial quantities of carnauba wax and a chemical, tricresyl phosphate. When a gasket was mounted between flanges and compressed, this chemical tended to separate, forming a gummy residue within a tank. It became highly explosive when exposed to liquid oxygen, detonating with nothing more than a light tap. The builders of early rocket-powered aircraft didn't know this; they specified Ulmer leather for gaskets as a matter of course. By the time investigators learned of its danger, a succession of explosions had killed a test pilot and a flight crewman, destroyed four rocket planes and two mother ships, and brought a two-year delay in the high-speed flight test program.

When Muroc Air Base became Edwards Air Force Base, the new name honored Captain Glenn Edwards, who had died in a crash of Northrop's YB-49 flying wing. Within the base, it became customary to name avenues and streets for dead test pilots. Friends of the late deceased often drove across Fitzgerald Boulevard and continued past Popson Avenue to Lilly Avenue. This gave occasion to remember the men who had died aboard such craft as the X-5 and the Douglas Skystreak.

One test pilot, Joe Wolfe, had driven around in a Model A Ford. He was killed; they named a street for him, and his widow sold the car to a colleague, Neil Latham. Latham died; they named a street for him, and his widow sold the car to Yeager. Yeager held on to it until he left Edwards, then sold it to another test pilot, Pete Everest. Everest passed it on to his friend Iven Kincheloe, who died trying to eject at low altitude from an F-104. They named an Air Force base for Kincheloe; his widow sold that car to Robert White, who flew the X-15 and lived to tell about it. That made three dead out of six owners, which at Edwards was par for the course.

The X-1 had been an Air Force project, and had reached Mach 1.45. In 1951 it had done what it could, with Yeager's craft, named *Glamorous Glennis*, being marked for the Smithsonian. The Navy now took center stage with its own research airplane, the Douglas Skyrocket. It was larger than the X-1 and could carry more propellants, raising the prospect of a contest for speed that the Air Force was in no mood to lose.

The Skyrocket's pilot, Bill Bridgeman, was a true naval aviator. He had been at Pearl Harbor on the day of the Japanese attack. He fought his war by flying bombing missions in the Pacific, then joined Douglas as a test pilot. His love of the sea carried over to his personal life, for he spent his spare time as a beach bum, living in a shack just north of Santa Monica. He was surfing long before the sport caught on; he also enjoyed water skiing, sailing, and chasing fish underwater with a spear gun.

Yeager had set the X-1 speed record in March 1948. Bridgeman topped it in May 1951, reaching Mach 1.7, and during the summer he went for more. He reached Mach 1.85 a month later even though he had to shut down his rocket engine, for his plane rolled violently, swinging its wings through arcs of 160 degrees in less than two seconds. He decided that he could prevent this by flying higher, and on August 7 he set a record for the Navy at Mach 1.88, attaining 1,238 miles per hour at 66,000 feet. A week later he did it again, setting an altitude mark of 79,494 feet.

The Air Force was ready to fight back, for it had two new models of the X-1 that had been built to hold more propellants. It lost both in quick succession, due to Ulmer leather explosions, though the accident investigations failed to determine this and pointed erroneously to other possible causes. This left the Navy in command, with NACA conducting flight tests using the Skyrocket. Its prime pilot, Scott Crossfield, had much to do without breaking records, for the Skyrocket had proved prone to "supersonic yaw," with the nose turning sideways and the plane skidding obliquely through the air. Like Bridgeman's uncontrolled roll, this was a form of high-speed instability that had to be understood if supersonic aircraft of the future were to fly safely.

Yeager was not impressed. As he later put it,

> Each time a new X research plane was delivered, the Air Force would fly it first, milk it dry of data, then turn it over to NACA. We did that with the X-3, X-4, and X-5, completely exhausting their capabilities. NACA would poop around with an X airplane for two or three years after we were done with it, acting as if they were discovering secrets of the universe. I thought that some of their pilots were the sorriest bunch in aviation.

His disdain extended to Crossfield: "He was a proficient pilot, but also among the most arrogant I've met. Scotty just knew it all."[2]

Crossfield had plenty of skill; perhaps he failed to win Yeager's favor because he indeed was good enough to challenge Yeager. One day, flying an F-100, Crossfield saw a fire-warning light and shut down his engine. The plane lacked flaps for extra lift at low speed, forcing him to make a dangerous high-speed landing without power. He did this flawlessly, gliding onto the lakebed and rolling up past the flight line. However, he had no brakes. He kept on rolling, as he frantically tried to stop, and crunched his plane's nose through the side of a hangar. Afterward, Yeager said that whereas he had punched through the sonic wall, Crossfield had broken through the hangar wall.

But during 1953, Crossfield became the man to beat, for in mid October he flew the Skyrocket to Mach 1.96. Hugh Dryden, the head of NACA, clamped secrecy on this achievement and told Crossfield to stay below Mach 2. This reflected interagency agreements that Dryden had negotiated, whereby NACA was to receive data from the flights, but the Navy or the Air Force was to set the records. Crossfield, naturally, had no intention of complying with this restriction. Prior to joining NACA he too had been a Navy man, and he pulled strings within that service's Bureau of Aeronautics. Within a week, Dryden agreed that the Skyrocket indeed could try for twice the speed of sound.

Crossfield made his run on November 20. He arrived before day-break, weak from a recent case of the flu, with the weather being cold and blustery. Mechanics loaded hydrogen peroxide into the Skyrocket, a dangerous and volatile fuel that was to drive its turbopumps. Something went wrong; the peroxide burst out of a pipe and flew into the face of a crewman. Another man had the presence of mind to grab a fire hose and douse his face and clothing with water. They got him to a doctor; with his clothes removed, his arms and legs were bleached white.

This accident brought a delay, but soon the B-29 mother ship was airborne with Crossfield's rocket plane hanging from its bomb bay. He dropped away and lit his engine, knowing it would burn for little more than three minutes. He flew a calculated trajectory that had been care-fully shaped to yield the highest speed, rocketing upward and then pushing over into a shallow dive.

This airplane had not been designed for such speed, and the ground crew had stretched its capabilities to the limit. They had waxed its sur-face, taped over its open apertures, and chilled its alcohol fuel to fit a few more pounds of it into the tank. "The Skyrocket was performing like an Olympic champion," Crossfield later wrote. "She held true on her spectacular dive. The rocket engine burned several seconds longer than usual—207. The Mach meter needle edged past 2.0 and hung at 2.04. WE HAD MADE IT! I had become the first man to fly at twice the speed of sound."[3]

This was not a physical milestone such as Mach 1, marked by important changes in aerodynamics. It was simply a nice round number that people could brag about. His actual mark proved to be Mach 2.005, or 1,327 miles per hour.

The fiftieth anniversary of the Wright brothers' first flights lay only four weeks away, and this speed record had been set accordingly. Cross-field was the guest of honor at a ceremony in San Diego, where he accompanied the movie star Esther Williams. She wore a tight-fitting gown of gold lamé. When her turn came she leaned over the mike to display her best features, then said, "You know, I've been getting a lot of static all night long about sitting next to the fastest man on earth. But I don't believe it. He hasn't laid a hand on me yet!" Crossfield responded quickly, for as he later recalled, "I reached over and swatted her on her beautiful behind. And my wife never did forgive me for that."

Yeager was not about to let that record stand without challenge. As Ridley remarked, "We'll take 'em on Mach 3." They now had a rocket plane that was suitable for this task, the X-1A, and again they had their eyes on the calendar. The fiftieth anniversary was on December 17; the television networks had special programs ready to go on the air, with Crossfield receiving plenty of attention. Ridley said, "Aw, shit. All that fuss for a guy who's gonna be the second fastest." He and Yeager planned to beat that record on the twelfth.

Yeager laid groundwork with preliminary flights, reaching Mach 1.9 on December 8. On the twelfth, he started his day before dawn, driving his Ford Model A and getting in a couple of hours of duck hunting before reporting for work. He stopped at the base firehouse for a sweet roll and coffee, leaving his ducks in the fire chief's refrigerator. He drove to the flight line, climbed aboard his B-50 mother ship, stepped down into the cockpit of his research aircraft, and proceeded with his preparations for the flight.

He was about to fly on the ragged edge, and he knew it. These rocket planes lost stability at high speed; engineers at Bell Aircraft had warned that the X-1A could not be trusted beyond Mach 2.3. This was close to the limit of what it could do, and Ridley had calculated a flight plan that would reach this speed. But it represented a single sudden leap of several hundred miles per hour beyond anything that Yeager or even Crossfield had achieved, and there was plenty of room for unpleasant surprises.

Accelerating under full thrust, he climbed steeply and reached the top of his arc. "Eighty thousand feet," he recalls. "A nighttime sky with flickering stars at ten in the morning. Up there, with only a wisp of an atmosphere, steering an airplane was like driving on slick ice." He dropped his nose and continued to accelerate, with six thousand pounds of thrust pushing an airplane that now was nearly empty of propellant.

His machmeter was showing 2.4 when his nose yawed left. He moved his rudder; it had no effect. He began to roll and tried to halt this motion by applying full aileron; again nothing happened. He realized he was too high and too fast. Then, very suddenly, the plane lost all semblance of stability and tumbled violently like a kicked football whipping end over end. Pummeled by forces as great as eleven g's, he

Preparation for flight: hydraulic lifts lower a B-50 mother plane onto an X-1.
(NASA)

slammed against his restraints. His body shot upward so strongly that his helmet cracked his cockpit canopy.

He knew he was going to die. He also knew that he had no more than a minute before he would drill a hole in the ground. He later recalled the experience:

> You're taking a beating now and you're badly mauled. You can see stars. Your mind is half blank, your body suddenly useless as the X-1A begins to tumble through the sky. There is something terrible about the helplessness with which you fall. There's nothing to hold to and you have no strength. There is only your weight knocked one way and the other as the plane drops tumbling through the air. The whole inner lining of its pressurized cockpit is shattered as you're knocked around, and its skin where you touch it is still scorching hot. Then as the airplane rolls, yaws, and pitches through a ten-mile fall, you suddenly lose consciousness. You don't know what hit you or where.[4]

Yeager regained consciousness as the plane fell into denser air. His mind still was foggy, but he remembered that he had set his movable stabilizer with its leading edge downward. He knew where to find its switch, and made an adjustment. His faceplate had misted over; he cleared it by switching on an electric heater.

As his vision returned, he saw that he was falling into rugged terrain. He set the plane's controls to follow its motion—and felt it go into a spin. This was what he wanted! He knew how to get out of that; he had even recovered from a spin in the X-1. He regained full control below thirty thousand feet, and put the X-1A into a normal glide.

Still breathless and under heavy stress, he radioed to Ridley, "Down to 25,000 feet over the Tehachapis," the mountains south of Edwards. "I don't know whether or not I can get back." Ridley replied, "That's twenty-five, Chuck?" Yeager continued, "I can't say much more. I gotta save myself."

His head cleared and he saw the lakebed ahead; he felt he might make it after all. He said, "I think I can get back to the base okay, Jack. Boy, I'm not gonna do that again. Those guys were so right," warning of instability that lay beyond Mach 2.3. "You won't have to run a structural demonstration on this damned thing," meaning that it had the strength to withstand heavy aerodynamic loads. He came down safely, later declaring that "no landing in my life was as sweet as that one."

He had indeed set a speed record, beating Crossfield and redeeming the good name of the Air Force. He had reached Mach 2.44, 1,650 miles per hour, but he also had broken the sound barrier while heading downward, falling 51,000 feet in 51 seconds. Nevertheless, he was back on the ground in one piece, as was his X-1A, and plenty of people were ready to see to it that he would be the man of the hour.

He flew to Washington in an F-80 and found that the press was waiting. He made the rounds of television shows, including the popular *Camel Caravan*. Then, as he was about to fly back to California, a Bell Aircraft executive approached him with a large box. A gift for Yeager himself would have been illegal, but this one was for Glennis. It came from Larry Bell, founder and president of the company: a beautiful jacket of Persian lamb, black and gray in color. Yeager had finally gotten the fur coat that he wanted for her, but it had nearly cost his life.

No one ever again tried to set a speed record in the X-1A. Indeed, it lasted less than two years before being destroyed due to another Ulmer leather explosion, with this one bringing the accident investigation that finally pinned down the problem. Yeager also made no further attempts at records. The Air Force sent him to Okinawa to test a captured MiG-15, a Soviet fighter that had seen much use in the Korean War. Then, having been a fighter pilot himself during his younger years, he received command of a squadron of F-86s in Germany. When he returned to Edwards, he was in charge of the Air Force school for astronauts.

The problem of high-speed instability remained unsolved for a time. An Air Force test pilot, Milburn Apt, learned what he could about it through test flights in the supersonic F-100. In September 1956, he flew the new X-2 and took it to Mach 3.2, becoming the first man to exceed two thousand miles per hour. Then he made his mistake, for he turned too quickly as he prepared to set up his return to the lakebed.

His plane went out of control, tumbled violently, and knocked him unconscious. He began to regain his senses as he entered denser air. The nose of the X-2 was detachable and could fall away, as a prelude to having its pilot bail out, and Apt pulled a handle to initiate this. The separation shocked him anew and knocked him again into unconsciousness. His capsule struck the ground, killing him instantly.

Ironically, the solution to the problem already was known by then. A NACA aerodynamicist, Charles McLellan, had proposed that the key was to break with the conventional practice of designing tail surfaces as small thin wings. Instead they were to be built as wedges with the sharp edges pointing forward. He tested this idea using a small model in a hypersonic wind tunnel, which reached speeds of Mach 7—and it worked. This discovery meant that tail surfaces of modest size could assure stability even at extreme speeds. The X-2 did not introduce such surfaces, but wedge-shaped vertical fins went onto the next research aircraft, the X-15. One could call it "the last airplane before the space shuttle," for the X-15 set speed and altitude records—Mach 6.70 and 67 miles—that remained unbroken until the shuttle *Columbia* flew to orbit in 1981.

As early as 1959, it became clear that the frontiers of aviation had leaped in barely five years from flight in the atmosphere at Mach 2 to flight into space at Mach 25. In April of that year, the astronauts of Project Mercury first met the press. Yeager might have been one of them, for he still was a test pilot in good standing, and he was only thirty-six years old. But he never had received a college degree, which was a prerequisite. He didn't mind; he was well aware that a new generation was coming to the forefront. Indeed, his school at Edwards went on to train a number of this generation's members.

His colleagues went forward within their careers, and sometimes to their fates. Crossfield became a test pilot at North American Aviation, builder of the X-15, and made a number of its early test flights. He retired from the air in good health, and went to Washington as a technical consultant to the House Committee on Science and Technology.

Jack Ridley died in 1957, riding in a C-47 that collided with Japan's Mount Fuji. People remembered him, and in 1980 they named the Edwards flight control center in his honor. Bill Bridgeman survived his missions as a test pilot, only to die on a personal flight to Catalina Island. No one named anything for him at Edwards, neither a street nor a building. He had been a Navy man, which put him beyond the pale.

The Yeagers continued to live happily together, celebrating their fortieth wedding anniversary in 1985. They did not see their fiftieth, for Glennis died of cancer five years later, at age sixty-six. Chuck served out his career in the Air Force, rising to brigadier general before he retired, and remains active and vigorous. As he noted in the conclusion of his autobiography, "I've had a ball."

The Quiet Rocket Man 19

THE ROSE BOWL in Pasadena stands within a desiccated riverbed called the Arroyo Seco. In 1936 this football stadium lay far in the future; the arroyo was merely a hot and dusty place that was well away from downtown. That made it very useful for a band of students from nearby California Institute of Technology, who were experimenting with rockets. They made their first test firing as they crouched behind a pile of sandbags. The rocket amounted to little more than a pipe stuck in the hard ground, and even that pipe had come from a company waste bin.

The rocket thus was as crude as could be, but the people who were there in the arroyo, or were following the work back at Caltech, included a good share of the eventual founders of the world's missile and rocket programs. The group's mentor was Theodore von Kármán, the nation's leading aerodynamicist, who went on to lead the postwar Air Force toward these new horizons. Also present was Hsue-shen Tsien, who eventually returned to China and built up that country's missile efforts. Three other members of the group, along with von Kármán, founded the firm of Aerojet General, one of the nation's first rocket companies.

Still another man was behind the sandbags, a tall, slim fellow in his mid twenties. He was William Bollay, and in time he established the main line of U.S. rocket engine development. He did this by pursuing a vision, not of flight to the moon, but of a long-range missile that would serve the needs of the Air Force. Navaho was its name; it established a focus for rocket efforts in the United States throughout the whole of the postwar years. Because of Navaho, the most advanced wartime rocket builders—the Germans, led by Wernher von Braun—joined in a partnership with American industry, a partnership that gave a solid base for the field's dramatic advances.

Bollay himself had been born in Germany, in 1911. The name is Huguenot in origin; his ancestors had fled religious persecution in

303

the France of Louis XIV, and his father was an officer in the German army. Then in 1924, amid the ravages of the postwar inflation, his family left their home in Stuttgart and emigrated to Evanston, Illinois, where the senior Bollay soon found work running a coalyard. The younger Bollay, staying in his hometown, went to Northwestern University. Then in 1933, as his wife Jeanne recalls, "he came bounding across the campus one day, his eyes sparkling. He'd gotten a $300 scholarship to Caltech."

They still were a year away from getting married, but she followed him to the West Coast, enrolling for her senior year at UCLA while he entered graduate school. "I'd go over to Caltech every weekend, in the big red streetcar," she remembers. "At Caltech, there wasn't much time for courting. Mostly, I sat by while he studied." His work won the attention of von Kármán, who picked him as an assistant. They did calculations for the dome of the Mount Palomar observatory; they tried to understand the hydrodynamics of oil wells. "Von Kármán would start thinking about 10:00 P.M., and they'd work till three in the morning," Jeanne continues. "Then Bill would come in bleary-eyed, and he'd have an 8:00 A.M. class the next day."

Bollay also fell in with another of von Kármán's grad students, Frank Malina, who had initiated the experiments with rockets. Malina had not been able to fire them at Caltech itself, which was as cloistered as a monastery, but he found the open space he needed at the Arroyo Seco. It was customary for graduate students to give seminars, and Bollay, spurred by Malina, gave one on building a rocket plane that would reach 1,200 miles per hour. The X-1 approached this speed little more than a decade later, but at the time, such performance lay at the far frontier of speculation.

Despite this interest in rockets, Bollay was not about to hitch his career to anything so uncertain. His Ph.D. dissertation was a solidly von Kármánesque piece of research on the theory of wings, which dealt with nothing more futuristic than practical aerodynamics. He stayed for a while at Caltech, as a young instructor, then went to Harvard as a junior faculty member. There he built a wind tunnel, in the basement of the engineering building, using surplus electric motors from the Boston subway.

Harvard was an ivory tower, but Bollay could hardly escape the looming prospect of war. The Nazis had an organization of U.S. supporters, the German-American Bund, and one of their members approached him, hoping that his German descent would make him recruitable. Jeanne recalls his response: "Bill was so outraged by the idea, that they thought he might help them, he went out and followed his brother Eugene, who had earlier joined the naval reserves." Eugene was a meteorologist; naval service offered a path to a career in this field. For Bollay, the Navy opened the door to a career in rocketry.

He went in for a physical in June 1941; the naval doctors turned him down, saying he was too skinny. Then in September they ordered him to active duty. He arrived in Washington—and found he was to deal with metal fasteners such as nuts and bolts. This didn't appeal to him, and he quickly found a way to pull strings. Some of his Caltech colleagues now were high-ranking naval officers, and he asked them to help. Within days, he found himself transferred to the Experimental Engines Branch of the Bureau of Aeronautics.

During the ensuing war years, this branch grew swiftly to become one of the nation's leading centers for work in advanced propulsion. Bollay won the key position, managing the development of jet engines. Close at hand were colleagues who held similar responsibilities for rocket engines and for ramjets. Their offices and labs were in Annapolis, Maryland, and Bollay had the opportunity to follow closely the activities that involved all three types of engine.

For the Navy's rocketeers, the task was to develop small boosters that could push a heavily loaded airplane into the air. Working in the group was Robert H. Goddard, who even then had almost legendary status as a prophet of space flight and an inventor of liquid-fueled engines. "He could have had us sitting around his knee," says Robert Truax, his boss, who had initiated the Navy's work with rockets soon after receiving his commission at the U.S. Naval Academy. "But he would never talk rockets. I think he was afraid someone would steal his stuff. His stuff wasn't that good. He was a physicist; his ability to do engineering was very limited. He had the vision, certainly. And there was almost nothing that was later developed successfully that he didn't try, at least once. But he was very much a loner. He had no one who knew how to weld, for instance. He had failure after failure. I'm amazed he even got a rocket out of the launch tower."

Goddard had the task of developing a liquid-fueled rocket unit for boosting aircraft at takeoff. "The result was a small disaster," Truax recalls. He did not make proper arrangements to cool the engine, leaving it prone to overheat. Then a senior manager insisted that they test the unit in a large patrol bomber, with this manager himself at the controls. "It burned out and spewed flame all over," says Truax. "It set the tail on fire." That was the end of Goddard's rocket project for the Navy.

The ramjet effort proved to be much more successful. The ramjet, or "flying stovepipe," was the simplest engine imaginable. It was no more than a length of tube equipped with fuel injectors. At high speed, air rammed into the front, to burn the injected fuel and heat up. This hot airflow then blasted out the back, to give thrust. For the tube, a group of researchers at the Navy's Applied Physics Lab, in nearby Baltimore, used nothing more complex than the exhaust pipe from a P-47 fighter. A cluster of small solid-fuel rockets provided the initial boost, which accelerated the ramjet to a speed where the air-ramming effect came into play. In June 1945 this makeshift arrangement reached a speed of fourteen hundred miles per hour, over twice as fast as the hottest aircraft of the day.

Bollay's own work focused on the design and production of turbojets. The British inventor Frank Whittle had built the first of them that the Navy knew about, and Bollay was anxious to get them into production. "The Navy took a while to get interested in turbojets," Truax recalls. "Their first jet airplane still had a propeller in front. It was a lot of fun. A pilot would cut the main engine, shut down the propeller—and then pull alongside someone else." Few aviators then had seen a jet plane, and the jet pilots hoped to mystify them as to how they kept up with and even passed them, without a propeller. By the war's end, though, the Navy was pursuing jet aircraft seriously. North American Aviation, in Los Angeles, was working on the FJ-1 Fury, which was to be carrier-based.

This fighter project brought initial contacts between Bollay and North American. Lee Atwood, the company's president after 1948, recalls that the end of the war had brought a drastic falloff in his firm's fortunes. "We had ninety thousand employees at the peak," he declares. Indeed, North American had been a mainstay in the nation's wartime aircraft production. But by the fall of 1945, amid sweeping production cancellations, the firm was down to only sixty-five hundred. What little work remained was largely in the new area of jet-powered bombers and fighters. To Atwood and his boss, James "Dutch" Kindelberger, they represented the way to the future. In Atwood's words, "It was quite apparent that the country would be needing new military aircraft, and we would participate."

A host of new technologies had come out of the war, brimming with potential: jet planes, rockets, radar, electronics, automatic control, atomic energy. Kindelberger decided that the way to proceed was to bring in the best scientist they could find and have him build up a new company research lab, staffed with experts in these fields. An executive recruiter in the Washington area recommended Bollay. He and Jeanne, along with their infant daughter Melodie, were in Los Angeles by Thanksgiving of 1945. They bought a big and rambling house on the bluffs of Pacific Palisades, across the street from the beach. Bollay set up shop in a red-brick building near the airport. It had been known as the tooling building, but soon won the name of Aerophysics Laboratory.

As he settled in, his old mentor Theodore von Kármán was pointing a path for the Air Force's future. At the request of its commanding general, Henry "Hap" Arnold, von Kármán wrote a report titled "Toward New Horizons." He predicted that the future would see supersonic jet fighters, long-range rockets tipped with atomic bombs, satellites in orbit. General Arnold was thoroughly pleased with the report, and told von Kármán that it would be used "for some time to come as a guide to the Commanding General in discharging his responsibility for research and development." There was little money for such efforts, but with Arnold's support, Bollay was in a position to go forward.

The Army Air Forces was preparing just then to enter the new realm of missiles. The initial step featured a simple desire to have people develop a broad range of ideas by means of study contracts. In November, officials at seventeen aircraft companies received invitations to submit proposals for design studies of specific weapons. These designs were to cover a number of categories, having different ranges. Working with the company's chief engineer, Raymond Rice, Bollay decided to respond with a concept for a missile with range of five hundred miles.

This was to improve substantially on the performance of the best missile flown to that date, which was Germany's wartime V-2. Wernher von Braun had led the effort that built it. It was a ballistic missile with a range of 190 miles. Over three thousand of them had been fired in anger during the war, mostly against London and Antwerp, Belgium. The new concept of Bollay and Rice called for more than twice this range, but these men saw that they could use the V-2 as a point of departure. Its builders had crafted a winged version, the A-9, that sought to stretch its range with a supersonic glide. In a test flight, a wing broke off and the rocket disintegrated high in the air. Nevertheless, the North American proposal offered to "essentially add wings to a V-2 and design a missile fundamentally the same as the A-9."

Bollay's rocket research began in a company parking lot, with parked cars only a few yards away. A boxlike steel frame held a rocket motor; a wooden shack housed instruments. The steel blade of a bulldozer's scraper shielded test engineers in case an engine blew up. A surplus liquid-fueled engine from Aerojet General, with a thousand pounds of thrust, served as the first test motor. The rocket researchers went on to build and test home-brewed engines as well, initially of fifty to three hundred pounds of thrust. Some of them were so small that they seemed to whistle rather than roar. In Atwood's words, "We had rockets whistling night and day for a couple of years."

Bollay had built a wind tunnel at Harvard; he now proceeded to build a small supersonic wind tunnel within his new laboratory. He also began to bring in specialists in gyros, electronics, and rocket motors. "We were feeling our way," says Atwood. "We had no coordinated plan; but what we were picking up was all aimed toward propulsion, aerodynamics, or control. Those were the pillars or legs on which things would be developed."

Bollay's small rocket engines were giving his people a basic introduction to the field, but Bollay wanted to work with the V-2 itself. It was the first truly large ballistic missile, forty-six feet tall with fifty-six thousand pounds of thrust. The U.S. Army had seized dozens of them; in addition, von Braun and a number of his fellow specialists had come to the United States and now were cooling their heels at Fort Bliss, Texas. Bollay launched an extensive program of consultation with these people. In addition, von Braun's assistant, Dieter Huzel, had collected a priceless trove of rocket documents. He went on to join the Aerophysics Laboratory as a full-time employee.

Bollay wanted to test-fire V-2 engines, but their thrust was far too great for the company's parking-lot test center. He needed a major set of test facilities, and Atwood was ready to help. "We scoured the country," Atwood recalls. "It wasn't so densely settled then—and we located this land." It was in the Santa Susana Mountains, at the western end of the San Fernando Valley. The land was stark and sere, full of rounded reddish boulders, offering spectacular views. It belonged to a family named Dundas, who allowed Hollywood film crews to use it for scenes of the Wild West. In March 1947, North American leased the land and went on to build a rocket test center, at an initial cost of $713,000 in company money, matched by $1.5 million from the Army Air Forces.

When the V-2 engine fired, recalls Jim Broadston, who was one of Bollay's leading rocket men, "I was amazed at the vibration. Your body shook from the noise." Certainly, though, it had plenty of room for improvement. Lieutenant Colonel Edward Hall, who was funding the work from Wright Field, declares that "it wasn't really a very good engine. It didn't have a proper injector, and that wasn't all. The heat transfer was wrong; they'd blow up on takeoff. It was ineffective, unsafe, unreliable. When we took it apart, we decided that was no way to go."

The Germans had developed this engine under the press of wartime urgency, and Bollay wanted to fix its deficiencies. He expected to carry through the design and test of a new rocket engine, which would improve on that of the V-2. In addition, work in supersonic wind tunnels refined the shape of his missile of five-hundred-mile range. During the early months of 1948, a workable preliminary design emerged. In this fashion, although Bollay had started with the V-2 and its engine as points of departure, he went forward to devise original concepts.

By then the U.S. Air Force had won its independence from the Army and had received authority over programs aiming at missiles with range of a thousand miles and more. Shorter-range missiles remained as the exclusive concern of the Army. Accordingly, at a conference in February 1948, Air Force officials instructed the North American management to stretch the range of their missile to a thousand miles.

The five-hundred-mile missile had featured a boost-glide trajectory, using rocket power to fly ballistically and then extending its range with a supersonic glide. This approach was not well suited for a doubled range. But at Wright Field, Colonel M. S. Roth proposed to increase the range anew by adding ramjets to the missile. A Navy effort, Project Bumblebee, had been under way in this area since the war; Bollay's Aerophysics Laboratory had carried out pertinent aerodynamic studies. In addition, at Wright Field the Power Plant Laboratory included a Nonrotating Engine Branch, which was funding development of ramjets as well as rocket motors. Its director, Weldon Worth, dealt specifically with ramjets; Lieutenant Colonel Hall, who dealt with rockets, served as his deputy.

Though designed for boost-glide flight, the new missile readily accommodated ramjets and their fuel tanks, for supersonic cruise. The revamped configuration called for two large vertical fins that each would mount a ramjet engine at the tip, Buck Rogers–style. These ramjets and their fuel added weight, which brought an increase in the power of the new rocket motor. It had been planned to match the thrust of the V-2—fifty-six thousand pounds—but in March 1948 this design thrust went up to seventy-five thousand pounds. The missile also received the name Navaho, reflecting a penchant at North American for names beginning with *NA*.

Bollay did not try to build the ramjets; the Air Force left that part of the problem to the engine-building firm of Wright Aeronautical. The rockets, however, would be all his own, and Colonel Hall expected them to find broader uses. "Navaho was the main line of things," he notes. "Although it was a cruise missile, we could put into it a large enough rocket motor to allow us to turn out engines that would be near the size we would need for a ballistic missile."

He already had his eye on such a weapon. At Convair in San Diego, the Belgian-born engineer Karel Bossart was working with design concepts for a ballistic missile named Atlas, after the Atlas Corporation that then owned his company. The necessary rocket engines and other technologies did not exist, but Hall expected that they would grow out of the Navaho effort. From the start, then, it was clear that Navaho was to lay the groundwork for this rival missile.

By mid 1949 it was clear that work on the new Navaho engine was not going well. "Engineers have a tendency to redesign and redesign, over and over," recalls Jim Broadston, who went on to direct engine testing at Santa Susana. Bollay thus needed a manager who would make decisions and push the project. He found his man in Sam Hoffman, a salty aircraft engine leader who had been chief engineer at the firm of Lycoming and then had become a professor at Penn State. Hoffman had dealt with Bollay during the war; both men had a similar combination of industrial and academic experience.

"I came out to get a rocket engine for them," Hoffman recalls. "Bill had a group of brilliant young fellows with no practical experience—which probably helped them with the new things that were coming along. Bill wanted me because I knew how to build engines, had built them, and brought practical experience to this group of young engineers. They all were a generation after me. I had had a career before, but these guys hadn't, except for being in the Army and Navy."

By Thanksgiving of 1949, the first version of this engine was ready for testing at the new Santa Susana facility. It lacked turbopumps; propellants were fed by pressure from heavy-walled tanks. The rocket crew proceeded cautiously, beginning with an engine-start test, at 10 percent of maximum propellant flow for eleven seconds. It was successful, and led to additional and somewhat longer starting tests during December. Then as the engineers grew bolder, they ratcheted up the thrust. In March 1950 the engine first topped its rated level of seventy-five thousand pounds—for four and a half seconds. Full-thrust runs during May and June exceeded a minute in duration and achieved good success.

Meanwhile, a separate effort was developing the turbopumps. The first complete engine, turbopumps included, was assembled at the end of March. Initial tests used water in place of propellants. Then, in August, this engine fired successfully for a full minute—at 12 percent of rated flow. The first full-thrust firing, late in October, reached seventy thousand pounds for less than five seconds. Bollay's crew ran off seven subsequent tests during 1950, but only one, in mid November, topped the rated thrust level.

The reason lay in problems of rough combustion during ramp-up to full thrust. Rough combustion was new; it ran beyond the German experience, for they had not encountered it in the V-2. "It was all relatively new," notes Paul Castenholz, a test engineer who worked at Santa Susana. "We hadn't any real experience" with important elements of their engine's design. "You had to go by logic and ease your way into it without doing too much damage to the hardware. You approached every test with your fingers crossed. Essentially, you'd hold your ears, close your eyes, and hope it would work okay."

Following the successful full-thrust test of November 1950, it took three and a half months to achieve the next fully successful test. It took until March 1951 before problems of rough combustion came under control. These problems stemmed from combustion instability within the engine, and their solution brought a milestone: for the first time, the Americans had encountered and solved an important problem that the Germans had not experienced. Combustion instabilities recurred repeatedly during subsequent engine programs, but this work of 1950 and 1951 introduced North American to methods of solution.

By then the design and the mission of Navaho had changed dramatically. The detonation of a Soviet atomic bomb in 1949, the fall of China to communism, and the outbreak of the Korean War in mid 1950 combined to put the nation once again on a war footing. But designers at the Aerophysics Laboratory, working with their Air Force counterparts, showed that they could anticipate vast increases in the range of Navaho, to as much as fifty-five hundred miles.

Conferences among Air Force officials, held at the Pentagon in August 1950, redefined the program and set this intercontinental range as a long-term goal. An interim version, Navaho II, with range of three thousand miles, appeared feasible as a near-term project, with a full-range Navaho III representing a long-term effort that would go forward in parallel. A letter from Major General Donald Putt, a director of research and development, became the directive instructing North American to pursue these goals.

The thousand-mile Navaho of 1948, with its seventy-five-thousand-pound engine, had taken approaches based on the V-2 to their limits. Navaho II, the initial focus of work, took shape as a two-stage missile with a rocket-powered booster. A ramjet-powered second stage was to ride this booster during initial ascent, much as the space shuttle rides its propellant tank today. Then, high in the stratosphere and at supersonic speed, Navaho's ramjets would kick in and the missile would separate from its booster to fly onward.

Its mockup reached completion in July 1952. Even today, half a century later, it continues to look like something out of *Star Wars*. It featured delta wings, side-mounted inlets, small forward-mounted wings known as canards, and a double vertical tail. Its fuselage was long, slim, and pointed. Two of the largest ramjets then conceivable, each four feet in diameter, were to provide the thrust. It was to cruise at 90,000 feet and 1,800 miles per hour, with a guidance system that could pick out

The X-10, a Navaho prototype, flew with turbojet engines. (U.S. Air Force)

selected stars even in the daytime, for use in navigation. It might feint or zigzag along its way. With its fuel burned off, it was to come in over the target at 95,000 feet. Using infrared sensors, it would feel for the warmth of a darkened city.

Such a missile needed more thrust for its boost than the 75,000-pound rocket motor could provide. Bollay and his colleagues thus undertook to design an engine with 120,000 pounds of thrust, featuring new and lightweight arrangements for its cooling. Two such engines, mounted at the base of the booster, would propel Navaho during launch.

In 1951 the Aerophysics Laboratory was a significant corporate division, with over sixteen hundred employees. Yet Bollay maintained and even strengthened his links to the academic world, taking a part-time professorship at UCLA. "He was a quiet, direct person," recalls Paul Castenholz, a student whom Bollay hired in 1949. "He was not flamboyant; he was to the point. Bill was tall, slender, looked active. You looked at him and you felt he was a dynamic person, ready to go somewhere." Jim Broadston remembers him as "a charming person. He looked well-groomed, as an engineer should." Jeanne Bollay uses the same adjective as Castenholz: "He was quiet; he thought a long time. Very amiable; the only problem I ever had with him was that he'd be off in some other world. He had a wicked sense of humor, in an understated, English way."

In his heart, he remained an academic man. As was true of von Kármán, his delight was to bring in highly intelligent people with new ideas, nurture them, and watch them grow. "Bill brought into North American an unusual bunch of highly gifted people," remembers Eugene, his brother. "And they were all like Bill. They all were pushing like mad to be the top in their particular field." Chauncey Starr, who rose to national leadership in atomic energy, was one of them. John R. Moore won similar leadership in guidance systems. Sam Hoffman built the rocket engines for the Apollo moon-landing program. Paul Castenholz designed the main engine for the space shuttle. Dale Myers, who was already at North American, became NASA's director for manned space flight.

In 1951 Bollay was technical director of the Aerophysics Laboratory. His boss, Lawrence Waite, was an assistant to the president, reporting to Lee Atwood. However, Bollay was increasingly at odds with Waite. "Bollay was oriented to university-type approaches," says Tom Dixon, who had managed the rocket work in the parking lot days. "He wasn't interested in 'management systems.' Larry Waite was an adamant fellow; he disagreed with the way Bill wanted to run things, and Bill just couldn't get along with him." Atwood has similar recollections: "Larry was from MIT and was technically able, but he shouldn't have held that job. Eventually we moved him over to Contracts and Pricing."

During that year, a reorganization of the Aerophysics Lab brought a reshuffle of management that led to Bollay's departure. Waite was promoted to corporate vice president. The Navaho effort received a new project manager, Dale Myers, who at the time was a young aerodynamicist. Hoffman continued to direct the rocket engine program. Bollay left North American entirely. He set up a new company of his own, became deeply involved in building battlefield missiles for the Army, and ceased to remain active in the development of rocket motors.

By then, however, the Navaho effort was sufficiently robust to proceed under its own momentum. The Korean War was on, and there was an upsurge of interest in missiles of all types. With the 120,000-pound engine in prospect, the Air Force now lost interest in the 75,000. By contrast, Army officials saw that it could power Redstone, a proposed missile of two-hundred-mile range. Colonel Hall remembers when a robust man with a thick German accent came into his office at Wright-Patterson Air Force Base. The following exchange ensued:

WERNHER VON BRAUN: I understand you are abandoning this engine. Could we have it?

HALL: What organization are you with?

VON BRAUN: The U.S. Army.

HALL: Well, then, just fill out an MIPR.

The MIPR (Military Interdepartmental Purchase Request) represented paperwork that helped to transfer this engine from Air Force to Army control. This seventy-five-thousand-pound engine indeed became the basis for Redstone, which was von Braun's first large rocket project since coming to the United States. It went on to launch America's first satellite, and carried the nation's first astronauts on short hops to the edge of space.

Also in 1951, the Atlas ballistic-missile project, which had been limping along on Convair company funds, sprang to life amid an upsurge in Air Force interest. The new design studies called for a behemoth of a missile, 160 feet tall, with seven of the 120,000-pound engines providing thrust. It was thoroughly unwieldy; this concept represented a basis for further studies, rather than an approach to a practical strategic weapon. Still, it marked a milestone. For the first time, the Air Force had a design for a rocket with range exceeding five thousand miles that could be pursued using rocket engines that were already in development.

Atlas itself had not been approved for development, which meant its engines had to be funded through a backdoor arrangement known as bootlegging. Bootlegging has been aptly described as taking money that had been aimed in one direction, and pointing it in a different direction. "We had a hell of a time funding Atlas," Hall recalls. "Navaho became a line item in the budget very early; we could fund it. The developmental work on the rockets for Atlas, as well as for those of Navaho that would be used in Atlas, were all done under the Navaho program."

Hall appreciated that engines for Atlas would have to differ from those of Navaho. The Navaho engines burned alcohol, which had served for the V-2. But to fly all the way to Moscow while remaining reasonable in size, Atlas would need a more energetic fuel: kerosene. Kerosene was likely to break down chemically within a rocket motor, releasing explosive gases or clogging thin tubes used for cooling, and triggering the engine's destruction. But during 1952, studies showed that the 120,000-pound engine indeed could be modified to burn kerosene.

Hall found his opportunity in plans for the fifty-five-hundred-mile Navaho III, which was to be larger than Navaho II, demanding a booster rocket of greater performance. The use of kerosene would reduce the booster's size, making Navaho III easier to transport and to deploy. "I called up Sam Hoffman," says Hall. "There were several of us on the phone. We said, 'Sam, we want you to lay out an engine for hydrocarbon use, we want to throw the alcohol.' Sam was shocked. And his reasons were good—a hydrocarbon is a mixed bag of cats; you don't really know what's gonna happen. Sam was unhappy, and he let us know he was unhappy. We said, 'No, you have to do it, and we want one hundred twenty thousand pounds out of it.'

"There were several weeks when it was in the balance, and we told Sam that we much appreciated what North American had done on the seventy-five-thousand-pound engine. But if his company would not take on the one-hundred-twenty-thousand-pound hydrocarbon engine—we'd have to give it elsewhere. And Sam then collapsed and said, 'Okay.'" In January 1953, Hoffman initiated an effort called REAP (Rocket Engine Advancement Program). Its purpose was to solve the problems of switching the Navaho engine from alcohol to kerosene. The engine that came from this work gave the Air Force more thrust than Hall had demanded: 135,000 pounds. It was initially slated for Navaho III, with three of them in the booster. At Convair, new design concepts also called for its use in Atlas.

For Atlas to proceed as a major program, however, the Air Force needed information on the size, weight, and explosive power of the nuclear weapons that were likely to become available within the next few years. The Atomic Energy Commission refused to let the Air Force in on these secrets. Theodore von Kármán, who was chairing that service's Scientific Advisory Board, responded by setting up a panel to explore this question. He recruited the mathematician John von Neumann to head it up, along with a number of the most noteworthy bomb builders: Edward Teller, George Kistiakowsky, Hans Bethe, and Norris Bradbury, who was director of the Los Alamos weapons laboratory.

Their report was ready by the fall of 1953. Within a few years, they concluded, it would be possible to build small hydrogen bombs of high yield, which could be carried aboard long-range rockets of reasonable size.

This was a breakthrough. It changed all the prospects for rockets and missiles. Trevor Gardner, a special assistant to the Air Force secretary, quickly put together his own committee, also headed by von Neumann, to look closely at both Navaho and Atlas. The thermonuclear breakthrough now meant that Atlas could be much smaller than had been projected; the final design called for only three rocket engines rather than seven. Early in 1954, this panel recommended that the Air Force should proceed with Atlas, and that this project should have the highest possible priority. Very quickly, the Air Force chief of staff and the secretary of defense endorsed this proposal, as did President Eisenhower's National Security Council. The age of big missiles had arrived.

During 1955, three new programs got under way. The Air Force's Thor and the Army's Jupiter, both of fifteen-hundred-mile range, featured an improved version of the Atlas engine. Titan, a second Air Force ICBM, used a closely similar rocket engine built by Aerojet General. There now were six missile programs—Navaho, Atlas, Titan, Thor, Jupiter, Redstone—that relied on Bollay's rocket motors or on variants. "We often talked about this basic rocket as a strong workhorse, a rugged engine," says Castenholz. "I think a lot of these programs evolved because we had these engines. We anticipated how people would use them; we weren't surprised when it happened. We'd hear a name like Atlas with increasing frequency, but when it became real, the main result was that we had to build more engines and test them more stringently."

Still, this plethora of missiles was more than the nation needed. Navaho and Atlas both went forward, for Navaho's early start had brought it well along in development. It appeared unwise to abandon this effort peremptorily, for it offered a valuable backup if ballistic missiles were to encounter major delays. But by mid 1957, Atlas and Thor were both in flight test, having made good Navaho's initial lead. In July the Air Force canceled Navaho.

"It came just as all cancellations come—out of the blue," Atwood recalls. Still, even he had to agree that ballistic missiles showed greater promise: "Navaho would approach the target at Mach 3; a good antiaircraft missile might shoot it down. But Atlas would come in at Mach 20. There was no way that anyone would shoot *it* down."

Atlas, Titan, Thor, Jupiter, and Redstone all achieved operational deployment. They all were liquid-fueled; by the mid 1960s, they gave way to solid-fueled rockets that were much less complex and could be launched instantaneously. The Army's Pershing replaced Redstone, while the Air Force's Minuteman and the Navy's Polaris, the latter being carried aboard submarines, took over the strategic role. But Thor and Atlas lived on and saw continuing use, as launch vehicles in the space program.

Thor led the way, serving as the nation's first rocket to the moon. During 1958, Air Force specialists fitted it with upper stages and a small lunar probe, then carried out three launches. The most successful of them reached over seventy thousand miles into space, and the project manager declared, "What we gained this weekend was a few seconds on infinity." That was only the beginning, for both NASA and the Air Force soon used Thors to launch a host of satellites.

These spacecraft supported serious efforts in military reconnaissance, observations of the world's weather, and probes of interplanetary space. The first communications satellites also rode atop Thor. In time, NASA added an improved upper stage and a better guidance system, christening the resulting rocket as the Delta. It remains in service to this day, having launched satellites by the hundreds. Its main engine, greatly improved through the decades, produces 205,000 pounds of thrust. Nevertheless, it traces its ancestry directly to Bollay's original rocket motor of 120,000 pounds.

Much the same is true of Atlas, which continues in use under that name. Larger and more powerful than Thor or Delta, it has flown with upper stages that have flung instrumented spacecraft as far as the planet Saturn. The Mercury astronauts, beginning with John Glenn, rode to orbit on the thrust of its engines. It too has been a mainstay of the space program, launching heavy satellites for both NASA and the Air Force.

Manned space flight has also relied largely on Bollay's legacy. As early as 1957, Wernher von Braun began planning to use a cluster of eight Atlas engines for a rocket called Saturn, which was to launch astronauts with over a million pounds of thrust. By then, Bollay's rocket group had organized as a new company division, Rocketdyne, with Sam Hoffman as its president. In addition, studies conducted within Rocketdyne convinced Hoffman that the basic Atlas engine could be scaled up very considerably, to yield a single engine—not a cluster—with over a million pounds of thrust.

The eventual Apollo moon rocket, which carried the astronauts, relied on both approaches. It featured a cluster of five engines in the first stage. Each engine, standing nineteen feet tall, produced 1.5 million pounds of thrust. In turn, its design amounted largely to relying on the basic layout of Bollay's original 120,000-pound engine, with its specific components being enlarged to heroic size.

The upper stages of this moon rocket, as well as the later space shuttle, relied on the high energy of liquid hydrogen for their performance. Here the link to Bollay involves nothing so specific as a basic engine plan that could be scaled up. The link rather is one of people, for the men who designed and built these hydrogen-fueled engines were the ones that Bollay had hired and promoted. They were the people of Rocketdyne, including Sam Hoffman and Paul Castenholz. Their engine proposals were the ones that won out, amid stiff competition from those of other rocket companies.

Bollay himself lived to see this legacy unfold, from the first launch of Redstone in 1953 to the first flight of the space shuttle in 1981. Following his work with battlefield missiles for the Army, during the 1950s, he spent several years as a consultant. In 1962 he returned to the academic world, spending a year at MIT and then moving to Stanford in

1963, where he spent the rest of his career. In 1977 he retired, at age sixty-six. But two years later he learned he had Alzheimer's. The disease developed rapidly, and he died in 1982.

His professional colleagues well understood what he had done, though his name remained little known outside that compact coterie. Yet his legacy ran deeper than rocket motors, deeper even than the generation of technical leaders to which he was a mentor. His real achievement can best be appreciated against the backdrop of that worrisome cry of the late 1950s and 1960s: "The Russians are ahead of us!"

Few issues in public life, during those years, were more potent. Beginning in 1957, the Soviets pulled off a stunning succession of accomplishments in missilery and space flight, to which President Eisenhower seemed unable to respond. Lyndon Johnson, then the Senate majority leader, lashed the Republicans vigorously over this state of affairs, and put them on the defensive. John F. Kennedy, urging the nation to meet its challenges with greater vigor, used the missile-gap issue with telling effectiveness in the 1960 election.

Yet the Soviet lead was never more than about a year. That was the margin of their advantage in launching the first large ballistic missile over an intercontinental distance. It also was the measure of their lead in launching the first heavy satellites, as distinct from small experimental models that Premier Khrushchev derided as "grapefruit." In the field of manned space flight, only ten months separated the orbital mission of Yuri Gagarin, the first cosmonaut, from that of John Glenn. That lead of a year or so nevertheless was enough to give the Soviets an image of overwhelming technical strength.

Without Bollay's early Navaho work, their lead would have been much larger. As Colonel Hall puts it, "I think it's correct that without Navaho, there'd have been no significant push in liquid rockets" until the thermonuclear breakthrough of the mid-1950s. The Air Force would have proceeded with the seventy-five-thousand-pound engine, out of a desire to go beyond the German V-2. Thereafter, though, "we would have gone beyond the seventy-five thousand, but very slowly. Without Navaho, we would have lost at least two years."

The Soviet lead then would have been three years or more, rather than one; their challenge in missiles and space would have been far more prolonged and galling. The view that communism stood for the future, and could readily outstrip the fumbling efforts of American democracy, would have been far more credible. These things did not happen; the Soviet technical challenge proved to be manageable. That may well be the most significant legacy of William Bollay, the quiet rocket man.

Clarence "Kelly" Johnson

20

W<small>HEN YOU JOIN</small> a company fresh out of college, with senior managers staking their hopes on a newly designed airplane, it's not a good idea to start by telling your boss that this plane won't fly. Kelly Johnson did just that in 1933, when he joined Lockheed—and he showed that he was right. It was the beginning of a close involvement with this firm that spanned Johnson's entire career, a career that brought him to the forefront as the nation's leading aircraft designer.

As a student at the University of Michigan, where he received bachelor's and master's degrees in aeronautical engineering, he had become quite proficient in the use of a wind tunnel. Although he still was taking courses, he worked on the side as a consultant as he used this tunnel to solve problems in industry. He improved the streamlining of cars built by Studebaker; he worked with racing cars from that firm that qualified for the Indy 500, and boosted their gas mileage substantially. He also ran tests on models of Lockheed's new airplane, the Electra.

It marked a substantial step forward. Lockheed's earlier aircraft had used single engines and had been built of plywood, but this one mounted two engines and featured all-aluminum construction. This meant that it could carry more passengers and reach higher speeds. Two knowledgeable specialists, a professor of aeronautics and a leading aircraft designer, had signed a report stating that the Electra would show acceptable stability in flight, based on the wind-tunnel results. Johnson disagreed, declaring that these experts were wrong.

The company's chief engineer, Hall Hibbard, responded by sending him back to the Michigan wind tunnel, with a model of the Electra in the back of his car. He found that the solution lay in replacing the conventional single vertical fin with a double tail, with a fin at each end of the horizontal stabilizer. Hibbard responded with a letter: "There was a big celebration around these parts when we got your wires telling about the new find and how simple the solution really was. It is apparently a rather important discovery and I think it is a fine thing that you should be the one to find out the secret."

Johnson now found a home at Lockheed. There were only six engineers, including Hibbard, and he was one of them. They worked together within a single large room, each with his own drafting table. He even married one of his coworkers, Althea Young. She was Lockheed's assistant treasurer, who came around on paydays to distribute the checks. Initially she was making twice as much as he did, for he had been hired with a starting salary of $83 per month. But by the time they got married, in 1937, he had redressed this imbalance.

The Electra flourished as his fortunes rose. Amelia Earhart bought one; he advised her on how to stretch its gas mileage when she tried to fly it around the world. She died at sea in the attempt, but in 1938, Howard Hughes flew his own Electra and circled the globe successfully. A variant, the XC-35, won the Collier Trophy for introducing a pressurized cabin that permitted flight at high altitudes. Another Electra carried Prime Minister Neville Chamberlain to his notorious meeting with Hitler at Munich, where he handed Czechoslovakia to the Nazis. Other versions won wide acceptance as airliners.

With war looming, officials at Britain's Air Ministry needed bombers for use in fighting submarines. They wanted Electras, but with substantial changes to accommodate gun turrets and other equipment. Johnson was the only engineer within Lockheed's group of visitors. He responded by purchasing a drawing board, T squares, triangles, and other drafting equipment, then setting to work on a redesign. He worked straight through for three days and nights, with brief catnaps in lieu of actual sleep. Then, with the new designs in hand, the Lockheed group returned to the Air Ministry.

Detailed discussions followed, but it was clear that everything rested on the quality of the work by Johnson, who was only twenty-eight years old. The chief of the Air Staff raised this point with Courtlandt Gross, a company manager whose brother was chairman of the board: "We're very unused in this country to dealing—particularly on transactions of such magnitude—on the technical say-so of a man as young as Mr. Johnson." Gross replied that he and his brother both had full confidence in their young engineer. The bomber that resulted, called the Hudson, led to large orders for Lockheed and entered service very early in the war. Johnson's redesign also led his company into the field of antisubmarine warfare, a field in which Lockheed continued to show leadership through the postwar decades.

In this fashion, Johnson contributed significantly to the success of the Electra and its military variant. Even so, the basic layout of the Electra had not been his; he had merely worked to modify an existing set of designs. But during 1939, he and Hibbard started with a clean sheet of paper as they crafted the design of an aircraft that was entirely their own. It was Howard Hughes's airliner, the Constellation, often called the Connie.

To this day, the Connie stands out for its unusually distinctive and even beautiful design. Francis Bacon wrote in the seventeenth century, "There is no excellent beauty that hath not some strangeness in the proportion." For the Connie, this included the fuselage and the triple tail.

The fuselage was subtle in shape, having the form of a long, slender shark. Its curvature cambered downward at the front to shorten the leg on the nose gear, sweeping upward at the rear to blend into the tail. Johnson claimed that this design added three miles per hour to the speed. Nevertheless, such fuselages appeared only on this airplane, for this tapering form created the "Connie seat problem." The Constellation lacked room to fit in the extra seats that could make the difference between profit and loss for an airline. By contrast, the rival DC-4 had a simple fuselage in the shape of a straight tube and accommodated all the seats that a plane of its size could hold.

The Connie's triple tail was another distinctive feature. It drew on experience with the Electra's double tail, offering good stability in flight. It made the plane easier to steer and to control, particularly with an engine out. It also lowered the tail, to fit the plane more easily into existing hangars. Yet this tail also merited description as strange, even though similar designs were appearing on contemporary aircraft from Boeing and Douglas. These firms, along with Lockheed, soon adopted single-tail designs, making them standard. As the Connie flew on through the postwar years, its triple tail stood out as a memento of designers' tastes from an earlier day.

This airliner gained brilliant success in the commercial world, while also flying in military versions. It featured a pressurized cabin, a legacy of Lockheed's XC-35, which suited it for a market whose customers demanded the high speed and freedom from airsickness of high-altitude flight. Although the basic design dated to 1940, Lockheed kept improved versions in production until 1959. These remained in service through the 1960s. In this fashion, the active life of the Constellation spanned some thirty years.

As the Connie prepared to spread its wings, designers were turning their attention to the jet. The first engines came from General Electric

Kelly Johnson's airliner, the Constellation. (Trans World Airlines)

and followed designs by England's Frank Whittle. Each unit delivered only 1,250 pounds of thrust, which wasn't much. Hence the experimental fighter that flew with this engine, the XP-59A, used two of them. It first flew at Muroc Air Base in October 1942, but even with jet power it failed to top four hundred miles per hour. Better engines subsequently enabled it to top this mark, but still it could not beat the latest versions of the piston-powered P-47 and P-38. Once again, then, there was the need to start with a clean sheet of paper.

As preparation for the jet age, Johnson and his colleagues had already carried through some highly pertinent work. Lockheed's P-38 was one of the first fighters that encountered compressibility. Its designers dealt with it by installing an auxiliary flap that would cause this plane to pull out of a high-speed dive. These engineers did not defeat compressibility, but they learned to recognize it and became familiar with some of its effects. In turn, this dive flap allowed the P-38 to achieve its high performance without killing its pilots.

Another Lockheed man, Nathan Price, set out to invent a turbojet engine. The successful wartime engines had poor fuel consumption but nevertheless were valuable because they combined high thrust with light weight. Price did not appreciate this; he thought that a jet engine would also have to excel in fuel economy. He proceeded to design an engine that was well beyond the state of the art.

That didn't bother Johnson; he took Price's engine design and used it as the basis for a fighter concept that was to reach Mach 0.94, or 625 miles per hour. This was probably the first time in the United States that a plane and an engine were designed as an integral whole, with this exercise giving Johnson a renewed appreciation of the interplay of engine and airframe that assures a successful design. With this plus his work on the P-38, Johnson probably knew as much about jet aircraft as anyone in the industry, short of having actually built one.

During 1943, as intelligence sources became aware of Germany's Me-262, General Arnold of the Army Air Forces decided that he needed something better than the XP-59A. He wanted it in a hurry, and he was not pleased with the Whittle-type jet engines of General Electric. Turning to the sources, he set his eyes on a British engine from the firm of De Havilland, the Goblin, which was to achieve three thousand pounds of thrust. That same British firm was also building a fighter, the DH-100 Vampire, that was to fly with this engine. Arnold was quite pleased at the thought that the Goblin would drive the Vampire, but he wanted this engine to power an American fighter of original design.

He turned to his development center at Wright Field. In May of that year, one of its officials invited Lockheed to prepare a proposal. The firm's technical staff drew it up within a matter of weeks, with Hibbard, the company's chief engineer and a corporate vice president, naming Johnson as the project manager. In mid June, Johnson took the proposal to Dayton, where he insisted that he could build the new plane from scratch in only 180 days. On June 17, Wright Field issued a letter contract instructing him to do just that, and to build a single prototype at a cost of $495,210. The new fighter received the name of XP-80.

Such a project ordinarily would require eighteen months rather than six. Johnson knew that to meet this schedule, he would have to introduce high-speed management to go with his high-speed plane. He already had been thinking about arrangements that would cut across lines of command and layers of management, allowing designers, machinists, and shop workers to collaborate closely. As he subsequently described it, he hoped to avoid "the delays and complications of intermediate departments to handle administration, purchasing, and all of the other support functions. I wanted a direct relationship between design engineer and mechanic and manufacturing."

He pulled together a picked group of two dozen engineers, supporting them with a staff of over a hundred mechanics. His directions called for each engineer to serve as "designer, shop contact, parts chaser and mechanic as the occasion demands." Secrecy was very tight, and the project needed a secure area where the work would be safe from prying eyes. Johnson found room near the wind tunnel, blocking it off with empty wooden boxes that had held engines for Hudson bombers. A rented circus tent served as the roof.

Across the street was a plastics works that was very smelly. A staff engineer, Irvin Culver, was a fan of the Li'l Abner comic strip, in which Hairless Joe brewed his Kickapoo Joy Juice in a still called the Skunk Works. Culver took to answering his phone by saying, "Skunk Works," and the name stuck. It came to mean a new way of doing business, featuring secrecy, small staffs, and freedom from outside interference, along with minimal red tape.

A meeting with Wright Field officials, on June 26, started the 180-day clock. A large red sign went up on the back wall: OUR DAYS ARE NUM-BERED. The wooden mockup was ready on July 15 and received approval five days later. In mid August the prototype itself was well along in assembly, with all fuselage bulkheads in place, attachment of aluminum skin in progress, and wing construction started. Soon only one important item was missing: the engine. Frantic telephone calls and overseas cables brought its arrival on November 2. A week later it was in place within the XP-80. This plane's wing and fuselage were soon under canvas and on a flatbed truck, bound for Muroc Air Base for flight test.

It took two months to get into the air. It had two side-mounted inlets, and during an engine run-up on November 16, suction from the Goblin engine caused both of them to collapse. Debris flew into the compressor and cracked its impeller, rendering the entire engine useless. There was nothing to do except to send to De Havilland for a replacement—which had to be removed from a Vampire prototype, thereby delaying that prototype's own flight for two and a half months. Finally, early in January 1944, the XP-80 took to the air.

If it had been capable of supersonic speed, it would have outraced the roar of its engine. It did not do this, but it came close. Wally Bison, one of the project engineers, recalls that first flight: "We were standing on this hill at dawn. All of a sudden somebody says, 'Here he comes!' and the plane passed by a couple of hundred feet off the deck in dead silence. Then the jet blast came, a sound we'd never heard before. I was goose pimples from the top of my head to the bottom of my feet."[1]

Though it was a true jet fighter, considerably faster than the XP-59A, it still was no world-beater. It barely topped 500 miles per hour in level flight, making it slower than the Me-262. Its hobgoblin was the Goblin; though this engine was rated at 3,000 pounds of thrust, it gave a maximum of only 2,460 pounds due to restrictions on its turbine speed. It

The F-80 fighter. (Lockheed Martin)

needed a better engine, and General Electric came to the rescue with its I-40, rated at 4,000 pounds.

A modified version of this plane, fitted with this new engine, became the XP-80A. The test pilot Tony LeVier took it up for the first time on June 10, four days after the Normandy invasion. The extra thrust increased its speed by as much as sixty miles per hour, and the Army Air Forces abandoned plans for continued use of the Goblin.

Amid the rapid advances of postwar jet propulsion, versions of the P-80—later redesignated F-80—remained in production only until 1949. Nevertheless, these planes saw plenty of action in Korea. The first all-jet dogfight pitted an F-80 against a Soviet-built MiG-15, and the F-80 shot down this enemy. Lockheed built over six thousand of these jet fighters, both for the United States and for its allies.

The F-80 also gave rise to two useful follow-on aircraft after Lockheed introduced a two-seat version. This became the T-33, a jet trainer. Fitted with an afterburner and with onboard radar, it also became the F-94 night fighter. In 1949 an F-94A shot down a target drone without the pilot ever seeing it. The radar operator, sitting in the backseat, gave steering instructions to the pilot until he could take aim using his own radar image. This plane remained in production until 1954, with the most advanced version, the F-94C, flying with a thrust of 8,750 pounds. This was nearly four times the thrust of the Goblin of 1944, showing that Johnson's original XP-80 had been built with plenty of opportunity for growth.

These early jet fighters grew out of World War II. For Johnson, the next step came from the Korean War. He visited Korea during that conflict and talked with pilots of existing fighters. They had plenty of complaints: that enemy fighters had the advantage in altitude, that Soviet or Chinese commanders could direct their own fighters by flying out of reach at fifty thousand feet, that American airmen had to throw out a lot of equipment to get better performance. Johnson returned to California with a determination to build a next-generation fighter that could top any rival, both in speed and altitude.

Two current developments spurred his hopes. At General Electric, the engine specialist Gerhard Neumann was building a lightweight turbojet suitable for flight at Mach 2. This was close to the limit of what Chuck Yeager and Scott Crossfield had not yet accomplished in their rocket-propelled X-1A and Douglas Skyrocket. But with this jet engine, Neumann expected that fighter aircraft would take off from the ground and cruise at such speeds, on afterburner.

In addition, Douglas Aircraft had built its X-3, which was intended to demonstrate such performance. People called it the Stiletto, for it had an extreme shape that indeed made it look like a dagger. Its nose was long and sharply pointed; its length of sixty-seven feet was three times greater than its wingspan. *Time* magazine described its wings as "thin, knife-edge trapezoids no bigger than dining-room tables" that "do not look as if they could lift it into the air." They did, but the takeoff speed of 260 miles per hour was faster than the top speed of aircraft built only twenty years earlier.

In flight test, the X-3 proved highly disappointing. It had been built to use a pair of powerful engines from Westinghouse, each with thrust of sixty-six hundred pounds. These engines never arrived, for Westinghouse lacked the facilities to carry through their development, and the keepers of the X-3 had to make do with turbojets of considerably less power. Thus, although this plane had been built to cruise at Mach 2, it had to go into a dive to top Mach 1, despite its sharply pointed shape. The test pilot Bill Bridgeman did what he could with it, but while Douglas Aircraft had hoped to use it to set records, it was Kelly Johnson who actually achieved them. He did this with his new superfighter, the F-104, which first flew in 1954.

It became known as "the missile with a man in it." When the test pilot Tony LeVier first saw it, he said, "Where are the wings?" It lacked the extreme proportions of the X-3, being twelve feet shorter and with slightly more wing area, but the family relationship was plain. Its lead-

F-104 fighters in close formation. (Lockheed Martin)

ing edges were so sharp that the ground crew covered them with wood. In *The Right Stuff,* Tom Wolfe wrote of the Air Force's "marvelous bricks with fins on them," of planes "which were like chimneys with little razor-blade wings on them." The F-104 was the archetype. Each wing spanned only seven and a half feet, from root to tip.

As a production jet fighter, it outflew some of the hottest rocket planes. It set a speed record of 1,404 miles per hour in 1958; a year later it climbed to 103,396 feet. For the Air Force, however, this was too much of a good thing. Successful fighters do not merely punch holes in the sky; they must effectively perform a variety of missions, such as striking ground targets. The F-104 proved less useful in operational service than some of its rivals. The Air Force purchased a number of these Lockheed fighters, but soon passed them on to other nations—or converted them to fast unmanned drones that served as targets to be shot down.

It was back to the drawing board for Johnson and his staff, to craft a modified design. This version included a ton of electronics and could carry out low-level missions, delivering bombs and other munitions in ground attack. The changes boosted its loaded weight by up to nine thousand pounds, which meant it no longer was effective in dogfights. But it was very good at penetrating enemy air defenses, and it could deliver nuclear weapons. West Germany selected it as a fighter-bomber for its revived Luftwaffe, which now was part of the North Atlantic Treaty Organization (NATO). Six nations proceeded to build it under license, with Italy's firm of Aeritalia adding further improvements as late as 1968.

With his F-80, F-94, and F-104, Johnson addressed Air Force requirements for advanced fighters. He also worked extensively for the Central Intelligence Agency, crafting the U-2 and SR-71 spy planes. The need for photoreconnaissance became evident after 1950, for the bombers of the Strategic Air Command had to prepare to launch a nuclear attack. Their crews needed photos of targets as well as information on air defenses.

Reconnaissance overflights counted in international law as acts of war, which meant that a certain amount of discretion was advisable. General Curtis LeMay, commander of SAC, began by sending B-45 bombers to England; the Royal Air Force flew them over the Soviet Union and shared their findings with the Yankees. LeMay soon expanded this activity by using his own B-47s, which had longer range. However, President Eisenhower did not approve of this Air Force freelancing. He elected to strengthen the nation's capabilities by initiating new programs within the Central Intelligence Agency.

The CIA needed a long-range aircraft that could cruise at very high altitudes, close to the limit where a jet engine would flame out. An initial competition led to the selection of the X-16, a twin-engine design from Bell Aircraft. A prototype was under construction when the Air Force's Trevor Gardner invited Johnson to submit his own competing proposal. This airplane, the U-2, was to use only one engine, making it simpler and more compact than the X-16, and Johnson declared that he could have it in flight test eight months after signing a contract. Johnson and Gardner won support from Defense Secretary Charles Wilson, from Secretary of State John Foster Dulles, and from the director of the CIA, Allen Dulles. These men met with Ike and persuaded him to accept Johnson's proposal, leaving the X-16 out in the cold.

Secrecy was extraordinary. The CIA's project manager, Richard Bissell, put together a staff that worked out of offices separate from those of the rest of the agency. They wrote their own contracts, kept their own financial records, and handled their own administration and security. Indeed, nearly one staff member in seven was a security officer. Bissell kept his cable traffic private; even Allen Dulles couldn't read it. Funding for the program came from an account that Dulles controlled. This allowed the U-2 to go forward without Congress appropriating funds for it—or even being aware that it existed.

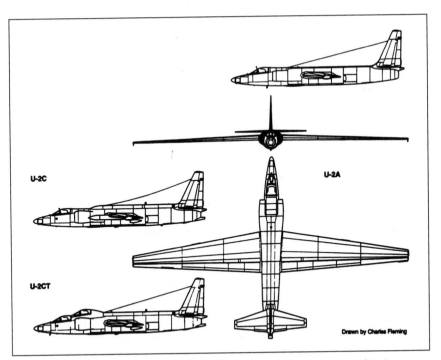

The U-2, in one- and two-seat versions. (Art by Charles Fleming, courtesy American Heritage)

New and classified aircraft had been flying out of Edwards Air Force Base for some time, but while it was good enough for the Air Force, it wasn't secret enough for the CIA. Bissell and Johnson flew over Nevada and found a new site, Groom Lake, Nevada, a dry lake that was ringed by mountains. It lay a hundred miles north of Las Vegas and adjoined the Yucca Flats area that served for tests of nuclear weapons. Bissell convinced Ike to annex Groom Lake to that site, with this CIA air base thus receiving the protection of the Atomic Energy Commission.

Wilson and the two Dulleses had made their pitch to Ike in November 1954. In July 1955, as promised, the first U-2 reached Groom Lake. It did not simply fly there from the Lockheed plant; it arrived in pieces and in crates, within a C-124 cargo plane. Reassembled at the test site, it displayed the broad wingspan of a sailplane, which would enable it to cruise above seventy thousand feet. That same wingspan allowed it to take off at speeds as low as sixty-five miles per hour. It entered operational service a year later, flying out of Incirlik, Turkey.

During its first month, which was July 1956, it conducted six overflights of the Soviet Union. But despite its high altitude, Soviet radar picked it up right at the outset. Following the second overflight, the Foreign Ministry in Moscow lodged a protest. The protests escalated, and by the end of that month, Ike ordered a stand-down. Subsequent missions required his personal approval; during the next four years, only eighteen took place.

Nevertheless, the U-2 showed its usefulness. There was much concern at the time over a "bomber gap," for Soviet officials had succeeded in fooling the Yankees as to their capacity for production and deployment. U-2s photographed known military air bases—and disclosed that the Soviets were building their bomber forces at a far slower rate than had been feared. In addition, pilots could deviate from planned courses to look at targets of opportunity. In this fashion, a U-2 discovered the Tyuratam launch site, which was Moscow's principal missile and space flight center. The CIA had not even suspected its existence.

This spy plane remained under cover, at least to the general public, until May 1960. Then a Soviet surface-to-air missile downed one near the city of Sverdlovsk. The Kremlin had relied extensively on espionage in developing nuclear weapons, and at that moment its officials were readying reconnaissance satellites as counterparts of the U-2. Khrushchev nevertheless declared that he was shocked, *shocked* to see the Yankees spying on him. He then walked out on a planned summit meeting with Eisenhower in Paris.

The U-2 never again overflew the Soviet Union, for it was vulnerable to that country's air defenses. It nonetheless continued to work in other regions, where the danger was less severe or the risk of loss more acceptable. Its finest hour probably came in October 1962, when overflights of Cuba revealed that the Soviets were installing long-range ballistic missiles. Photos of their sites led immediately to the Cuban missile crisis. This gave the U-2 a most unusual distinction: twice, in 1960 and again in 1962, it triggered Cold War imbroglios of a very serious nature.

Bissell had anticipated that one day it would be shot down over the Soviet heartland; he had regarded it as an interim craft, and did not plan on a long life in service against Moscow. Thus, almost as soon as the first of them went into action at Incirlik, he and Johnson began planning the next spy plane, which was to fly even higher while cruising at supersonic speed.

Initial plans centered on a program called Suntan, which again was classified at the most stringent level of secrecy. It called for flight at Mach 2.5 and one hundred thousand feet, using liquid hydrogen as the fuel. This highly volatile liquefied gas had seen use in the first hydrogen bomb, but like everything else having to do with nuclear weapons, this technology was closely guarded and Johnson had to start largely from scratch. Suntan made important advances in producing, storing, and transporting large quantities of this fluid, while burning it in jet engines of conventional design. The engine-building firm of Pratt & Whitney collaborated closely, learning lessons along the way that led to the successful use of liquid hydrogen in high-performance rocket engines. But the planned aircraft promised inadequate range, which could not be stretched. When this became clear, Suntan faded. Johnson then turned his attention to concepts that relied on hydrocarbon fuels.

During 1958 and 1959, he sent Bissell a succession of design studies that carried Skunk Works designations of A-1 through A-12. The last of these was the one that counted, leading in January 1960 to an initial contract for twelve of them. The program that followed was called Oxcart, which suggests slow speed and clumsiness, but the A-12 was more like a supersonic chariot. In its final form, as the SR-71, it cruised at Mach 3.2 and at eighty-five thousand feet.

This performance was comparable to that of Navaho, designed a decade earlier, but the differences in layout were striking. Navaho predated a time when turbojets could drive it at similar speeds; it needed ramjets. Then, because ramjets needed a boost to Mach 3 before they would light, North American put much effort into a large rocket booster, even though it merely offered an initial push. The SR-71 used neither rocket engines nor ramjets; a pair of afterburning turbojets provided all the power it needed, both for takeoff and cruise.

Navaho had been built with titanium and stainless steel. North American's XB-70, a jet-powered contemporary of the SR-71 that was also meant to cruise at Mach 3, used stainless steel quite extensively. For the SR-71, Johnson wanted to use a heat-resistant titanium alloy that had the strength of stainless but only half the density. However, this metal proved to be particularly demanding.

Early samples of the alloy were so brittle that they sometimes broke when they fell off a desk. They also were extremely hard and difficult to machine. Lockheed's machinists had drill bits that could cut through aluminum with ease, but their bits at first could drill only seventeen holes in this titanium before they wore out. Even when better tools became available, titanium remained extraordinarily sensitive to contaminants. A line drawn on a sheet of this metal with a Pentel pen would eat a hole in it within twelve hours. Bolt heads broke off when heated. Spot-welded panels held together when assembled in winter, but the same panels tended to fall apart when produced in summer.

The problem of the bolts proved to result from cadmium, which formed a thin rustproofing layer on workers' torque wrenches. The cadmium came off in tiny particles and reacted with the titanium bolt heads, sapping their strength. The spot-welded panels were weak because they had been washed with municipal tap water, which was heavily chlorinated during the summer months. Johnson's managers raided the workers' toolboxes for cadmium-plated wrenches and switched to chlorine-free distilled water for cleaning the panels. The problems disappeared.

Similar difficulties came to the forefront at Pratt & Whitney, which developed the engine. In the words of William H. Brown, a senior manager,

> We had to learn how to form sheet metal from materials which previously had been used only for forging turbine blades. Once we had achieved this, we had to learn how to weld it successfully. Disks, shafts, and other components also had to be fabricated from high-strength, temperature-resistant turbine-blade-like materials to withstand temperatures and stresses encountered. I do not know of a single part, down to the last cotter key, that could be made from the same materials as used on previous engines. Even the lubrication pump was a major development.[2]

Conventional rubber O-rings could not withstand high temperatures; the builders introduced steel rings. Penn State University came forward with a special lubricating oil; the SR-71 needed five gallons, with an oil change after every flight. If you took your '71 into the shop for such a job, it cost $650. Ordinary jet fuel would have boiled in flight. Johnson took this problem to the aviator Jimmy Doolittle, who now was a vice president at Shell Oil. Shell responded by developing a suitable fuel that also served as hydraulic fluid. It circulated in a single pass through the hydraulic system before being burned in the engines.

The test pilot Jim Eastham, one of the first to fly this plane, recalls seeing it for the first time in 1962: "I was in a state of shock. Who could imagine such a machine! Kelly reached down into his desk, pulled out a photo—and I just stared at it. I couldn't believe what I was seeing. The shape, the size." It was over a hundred feet long and far more slender than most aircraft. Each wing mounted an immense engine pod, wider than the fuselage itself. Nor did Lockheed merely build one or two prototypes; it put this plane into production. In 1963, with its very existence still tightly classified, ten of them were lined up in a row at Groom Lake.

At its cruising altitude of eighty-five thousand feet, the horizon lay some 350 miles away, and the curvature of the earth was plainly visible. The view from the cockpit rivaled that from orbit. In the words of one of its Air Force pilots, Steve Grzebiniak, "As we're going by Salt Lake

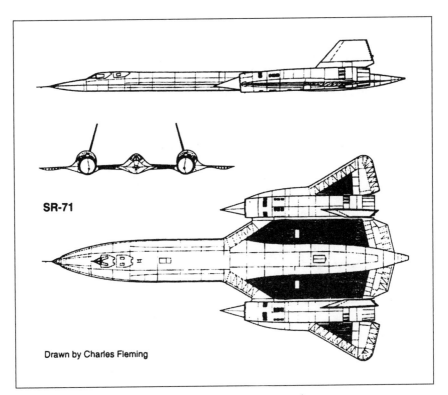

SR-71

Drawn by Charles Fleming

The SR-71. (Art by Charles Fleming, courtesy American Heritage)

City, which is well to our north, we can look back on a really clear day, see Pike's Peak behind us and start to see the coast looming up ahead of us." Farther on, "the coast is obscured by the mountain range. But you can see the mountains, and the ocean beyond. We could probably see the Los Angeles area, then maybe the Oregon border."

Eastham remembers more: "The sky doesn't get black but is a deep dark blue." The setting sun "is really quite spectacular because there's very little twilight. And it's rather eerie, because you see the sun—then you look down and it's pitch-black. The sun is a big glowing globe in the blackness. It approaches the hard vacuum of the moon, where everything is either sunlit or deep in darkness. Cities are sparkling jewels in the black. You could see the whole Los Angeles basin at one glance, and you could see the freeways if you looked for them. You could see Baja, though not to the tip. Really, it's the only way to travel."[3]

Air Force officials agreed. Working with their Lockheed counterparts, they actively promoted a plan to build an interceptor version, to be known as the YF-12A in prototype and the F-12B in production.

General Herbert Thatcher, head of the Air Defense Command, expected that a fleet of ninety-three such fighter aircraft could protect the entire United States against Soviet bombers. As an initial step, Lockheed built three YF-12As and proceeded with flight tests, beginning in 1963.

The results were spectacular. In 1965 this aircraft reached an altitude of 80,257 feet and a speed of 2,070 miles per hour, with the latter representing a world record. Further flights showed that the YF-12A could do useful work at such heights and speeds. In these tests, pilots used onboard radar to fire missiles at drone bombers in flight. The most demanding such mission involved a sortie from Eglin Air Force Base in Florida. With the plane cruising at Mach 3.2 and above 80,000 feet, the pilot detected an unmanned B-47 approaching head-on while flying 1,500 feet above the sea. He launched his air-to-air missile—and brought down the drone from a range of 120 miles.

Defense Secretary Robert McNamara was far less impressed. He had established the powerful Office of Systems Analysis within the Pentagon, to conduct studies of the nation's defense requirements and to assess the merits of proposed weapons in their light. Based on such recommendations, he judged that the Soviet threat would not be so severe as to require the F-12B. He took the position that other interceptors, offering less performance but also less cost, could better serve America's needs.

This led to a three-year conflict between McNamara and Congress, which backed the F-12B and repeatedly appropriated funds to support its production. McNamara simply impounded the money, refusing to spend it. In the mid 1960s there was no law akin to the Nixon-era Impoundment Control Act, requiring White House appointees to spend appropriated funds. The impasse thus persisted.

Late in 1966, with this conflict still unresolved, McNamara took an unheard-of step. He proposed that tooling for the SR-71 be broken up and sold for scrap. Ben Rich, one of Johnson's key lieutenants, was shocked: "When an aircraft still has value—when there's nothing like it—you want to hold on to the tooling." Johnson, backed by supporters in Congress, fought against this vigorously. He was well aware that if the tooling was destroyed, this would end all prospect not only for the F-12B, but for further production of the SR-71.

"We fought it for three years, trying to hide the tools," Rich recalls. "But we were not successful." The tooling was government-owned and had been paid for under Pentagon contracts, which meant that McNamara was within his rights to order its destruction. Finally the order came down anew, directly from the project office: destroy the tooling. There was no escape. By early 1970, Johnson was reporting to his Air Force superiors that "the large jigs have now been cut up and we are finishing the cleanup." The scrap metal that resulted was sold for seven and a half cents per pound.

This denouement was reminiscent of the destruction of Jack Northrop's flying-wing bombers. Indeed, the SR-71 was the last of Johnson's major projects. Still, its operational versions continued to fly, and everyone was aware that more than Northrop, Johnson had pushed the frontiers in a broad range of directions. He was, without question, the outstanding aircraft designer of his era.

One understands this by looking at his rivals. A number of them gained distinction but did not win public renown, for the profession of aircraft design was not one that lent itself to fame. Chuck Yeager broke the sound barrier in the Bell X-1, but few people noted the name of its chief engineer: Robert J. Woods. At Douglas Aircraft, Arthur Raymond gave wings to America by shaping a succession of airliners, from the DC-1 to the jet-powered DC-8. He won a full share of aeronautical awards, but he tended to step aside and allow Donald Douglas to take the credit.

Some companies divided their projects among several top designers. Boeing's bombers helped to win the war and preserve the peace; its jet airliners, from the 707 to the 747, picked up where Douglas Aircraft left off. Any single engineer who could have claimed all these airplanes would certainly have been a second Kelly Johnson. However, Boeing had several such men, including Edward Wells, Maynard Pennell, Joseph Sutter, and the aerodynamicist George Schairer.

North American Aviation turned out a succession of airplanes that were as varied and as excellent as those of the Skunk Works. These included the wartime P-51; the B-45, America's first production jet bomber; the F-86 that burned up the skies of Korea; and the F-100, the first jet fighter to go supersonic in level flight. Other such craft included Navaho, the XB-70, and the X-15. Again, though, this firm relied on several cooks to stir the broth. These included Raymond Rice, Edgar Schmued, Harrison "Stormy" Storms, and Charles Feltz.

There were outstanding individuals whose reach exceeded their grasp. Jack Northrop was a classic example; another was Alexander Kartveli of Republic Aviation. He had a penchant for speed, crafting the wartime P-47. He also built the F-84, the Air Force's second jet fighter, which improved upon the P-80 by introducing a jet engine of simple and particularly effective design. His F-105, which first flew in 1955, remained in service through the mid 1970s. It made its reputation as one of the best fighter-bombers in use, and flew extensively in Vietnam.

However, there were two important projects on which Kartveli promised more than he could deliver. The first, the XF-91, placed a set of rocket engines within an airframe that resembled the standard F-84. It seemed like a good way to win extra speed and altitude, but it meant two different engine installations along with three types of propellant: kerosene for the jet engine, alcohol and liquid oxygen for the rocket. The Air Force didn't like this complexity, and canceled the program after purchasing only two prototypes.

The second such project, the XF-103, sought Mach 3.7 and seventy-five thousand feet. The basic design dated to 1950; if it had gone forward at a good pace, it might have amounted to an SR-71 a decade before its time. Like Navaho, it used a ramjet, along with a turbojet for flight at lesser speeds. The program got as far as building a complete engine unit that operated in ground test using air from a wind tunnel. It worked successfully both as a ramjet and as an afterburning turbojet.

But the engine contractor, Wright Aeronautical, was also reaching too far. The ground tests, conducted in 1956, confirmed that this dual-mode installation had serious problems that would resist solution. By then the program had been under way for several years, and while Kartveli was building a prototype of the airframe, the effort was overrunning its budget and schedule. In 1957 the Air Force decided that the XF-103 had worn out its welcome, and canceled it.

Kelly Johnson had miscues of his own. He built an experimental fighter for the Navy that was supposed to take off and land vertically, like Flash Gordon's rocket ship. It proved unsafe, and the Navy abandoned it. Johnson lost no sleep over this; he set it aside and turned his attention to his next project.

Through his career, any plane from the Skunk Works carried his personal stamp. He did not manage using committees and review boards; he ran the Skunk Works himself, and he kept it small. This meant it could act quickly. He did not repeat the 143 days of the XP-80, from paper design to flight-ready prototype, but he never needed anything like the seven years of Kartveli's XF-103.

He held a keen eye, keener than those of many of his rivals, both for what was technically feasible and for what his customers wanted. In this fashion, he avoided falling prey to a Northrop-like personal vision, or to a Kartveli-like concept that couldn't be built. His Skunk Works remained elite, a group of picked specialists who repeatedly showed talent that set the pace in aviation. Other companies built their own high-performance aircraft, but they generally found that Johnson had been there first.

The industry has changed greatly since his heyday. His era was one of numerous new projects that brought abundant opportunities to learn, and to apply lessons from a recent design to a new one. During his career, he personally participated in the design and development of some forty aircraft. By contrast, the present day counts only a handful of programs, which often drag out for decades. The B-1B bomber took over twenty years from initial studies until it finally entered production, in 1982. NASA's space station grew out of studies dating to 1980; its first major element did not reach orbit until 1998.

Such practices may suit an industry that today often operates as a jobs program, which puts its emphasis on maintaining full employment. They did not suit Johnson, and we will not see his like again.

PART 5

Maturity

Launching the
Commercial Jet Age

21

THE JET AIRLINER entered American life late in the 1950s, when tail-finned automobiles were at their height of glory. Yet the jetliner was no mere exercise in style; it brought vast changes to the way we fly. Passengers appreciated not only their speed but their freedom from harsh vibration and their ability to fly above the weather. The new aircraft were large in size as well as speedy, and airline executives liked them because they were highly productive; they could do a great deal of work. The jets thus made flight more economical. This brought cuts in ticket prices, which encouraged more people to fly, which led the airlines to purchase still more of these planes. In only a few years, the old piston-engine airliners were swept from the skies.

But the jetliner did not emerge from anything so straightforward as a request from these executives for new equipment that could tap this engine's vast promise. It was fifteen years in the making. During much of that time the Air Force was laying the groundwork, while the airlines' interest remained focused on the latest piston-driven craft. Then, when they did begin buying the new jetliners, the competition for sales sparked a corporate battle in which pools of capital were as much a weapon as technical designs. The combatants were Boeing and Douglas Aircraft.

The backdrop to the jetliner lay in the struggles of the aviation industry to regroup in the wake of World War II. That industry had built over ninety-six thousand aircraft during 1944, the last full year of the war. In 1947 the planebuilders sold only fifteen hundred combat aircraft, along with a modest number of airliners. The changes were wrenching. Builders of fighter aircraft—Lockheed, Republic, North American—saw major federal contracts vanish virtually overnight. The same was true for the builders of bombers, Boeing and Convair. Indeed, at Boeing the payroll had been running at half a million dollars per day. When word of a contract cancellation came in at three-thirty in the afternoon, the president rushed to close the plant before the 4:00 P.M. shift change.

But two fields of activity offered hope: airliners and jets. Boeing, Lockheed, and Douglas had all been leaders in building military transports, as Uncle Sam paid for the production facilities and the development of their designs. These now went forward as a new generation of piston-engine airliners: the Lockheed Constellation, the Douglas DC-6, and the Boeing Stratocruiser. In addition, both the Air Force and the Navy were highly interested in jet propulsion. They were already purchasing jet fighters from Lockheed at war's end. Similar projects were under way at Republic, Northrop, North American, and McDonnell.

Jet airliners grew out of jet bombers, and the first steps dated to 1943. Five manufacturers—Boeing, Northrop, Martin, North American, and Convair—received contracts to design and build the nation's first experimental jet-powered bombers. These companies' managers were free to use their imaginations, for there was very little data to use in preparing their concepts. The conventional wisdom, such as it was, held that a jet bomber would have long, straight wings like those of a B-29, with these wings being thin for less drag and greater speed. In turn, the jet engines were to mount directly to these wings' undersides. In most design offices this approach held sway, and the aircraft that emerged were built accordingly.

Boeing, by contrast, had the opportunity to seek a different approach. This company had what its competitors lacked: a large wind tunnel capable of testing designs at airspeeds close to the speed of sound. It entered service in 1944, and Boeing's engineers expected to use it to carry out systematic studies of a host of aerodynamic alternatives. They were ready to challenge the conventional wisdom, seeking the best possible shape for a large jet plane.

Right at the outset there was a serious problem. The jet engines of the day were extraordinarily fuel-hungry, gulping over twice as much as piston engines of equivalent power. The Air Force wanted its bombers to have good range, which put a premium on fuel economy. Fortunately, the efficiency of these turbojets went up as their speed increased, while greater speed also brought greater range in its own right. To satisfy the customer, then, Boeing had to use its wind tunnel to wring out every possible advantage of speed.

The first important advance along this path came from Germany. The Germans had lost the war in the air but had nevertheless remained masters of the air, for that nation counted many of the world's foremost aerodynamicists. These people had cherished friendships and close professional ties with their American and British counterparts, prior to the war. One of them, Adolf Busemann, had proposed a particularly important invention: the swept wing. In May 1945 Boeing's chief of aerodynamics, George Schairer, visited Germany along with a party of scientists who were there to learn that country's secrets. Busemann told Schairer and the others of his work, and had the satisfaction of sparking a great deal of interest.

Why was the swept wing important? The reason was that the speed of jet aircraft stood to be limited not by a shortage of power, but by a sharp and marked rise in drag as an aircraft approached the speed of sound. Swept wings promised to put off this rise to higher speeds, and to keep it from occurring until a plane was flying considerably closer to sonic speed. Then, when it did occur, this drag rise would be less than with a conventional straight wing. Wing sweep thus offered a simple path toward a bomber that could fly faster and get the most out of its engines.

This concept, swept wings, quickly became a major topic of Boeing's research. Among the issues they raised was the question of where to put the turbojets. To place them in the conventional position, against the wings' undersides, seemed madness. Too many of Boeing's wartime bombers had gone down in flames as fires in their piston engines had spread to the adjacent wings, which were full of fuel. George Martin, the chief designer, wanted to hang the engines at the ends of struts, separate from the wings. The question then was what sort of strut would work best, and again Schairer found the answer. His wind-tunnel work showed that the proper engine position was below and in front of the wing. It is followed to this day.

The new bomber, called the XB-47, reached its basic design by April 1946. To look at it today, across half a century, is to see it indeed as the shape of things to come. It had wings that swept dramatically, engines on struts, and swept tail surfaces. One may compare it with a current design such as the Boeing 747. The latter has a particularly wide fuselage and mounts its wings low on the body. Except for such details, however, the two aircraft appear as very close cousins.

Pilots adored it, for it had the speed and maneuverability of a fighter. But it drew considerably less enthusiasm among generals such as Curtis LeMay of the Strategic Air Command, who had the job of preparing to attack the Soviet Union from bases in the United States. The B-47 lacked range, and therefore counted as no more than a medium bomber. Boeing did all it could—installing a fuel tank in the fuselage, hanging droppable tanks beneath the wings—but it wasn't enough. The B-47, though valuable, still counted as something of a sideline. By contrast, LeMay saw the Air Force's future as lying in the heavy bomber, able to carry the atomic bomb across intercontinental distances. Such aircraft represented an entirely different game.

In this realm of the heavies, the Air Force held considerable hope for the B-50. It was an advanced version of the B-29 that had dropped the atomic bombs on Japan. By 1946, its replacement was already in view in the B-36, a six-engine behemoth. Its performance was described as "10,000 pounds for 10,000 miles," enough to carry such a bomb to Moscow and then return, all in a single, unrefueled round-trip. It was not yet in production, but was entering flight test, and at the Pentagon it was the focus of high hope.

Yet even the B-36 was piston-powered, and with the jet engine in full flower, some advanced thinkers were starting to assert that it was already time to think of using similar engines in the next heavy bomber, after the B-36. Again there was a conventional wisdom: that its engines would be turboprops, in which a jet's internal flow of hot gas was to spin turbines, driving a propeller with great power. That contrasted with the situation in a turbojet, a standard jet engine, in which the hot gas blasted out the back to produce thrust in the manner of a rocket. Turboprops tantalized designers, for they offered greater speed and power than piston engines, along with excellent fuel economy. They would not match the speed of turbojets, but they pointed a clear direction beyond the pistons of the B-36.

Boeing's president, William Allen, was determined that his firm would take the lead in pursuing this approach. He had risen to prominence by advancing both with his company and with Seattle, its city. Allen had grown up in a small town within Montana's Bitterroot Range, but had found his way to Harvard, winning a law degree. He then returned to the Pacific Northwest and joined a law firm in Seattle, which then was a boomtown whose main business was timber. Allen started by handling the legal business of Boeing, which at the time paid him no more than $50 a month. But his career rose as the company grew. At age thirty, in 1930, he joined the board of directors. During the next fifteen years, he became intimately knowledgeable about the firm's finances.

Then in 1945, with the war nearly over, the company needed a new president. Allen held his colleagues' high esteem and stood as a consensus choice. Still he resisted, believing himself to be unqualified. When he finally succumbed and took the job, as he later remarked, "I was incompetent. I told them so and they knew it was true. I told each of them that they were going to have to put out a little bit more for that reason, and they did." He needed all the help he could get, for as he was taking office, the government was canceling Boeing's wartime contracts. Undaunted, he soon decided to stake much of what was left by building the Stratocruiser, a new airliner with four piston engines. Boeing lost money on this venture, but it helped keep the company's key people together during the lean postwar years.

Like a judge taking testimony, Allen knew how to lead by listening. In Schairer's words, "Anytime there was a big decision to be made, he'd call all the interested parties in and he'd go around the table asking for opinions. He'd just sit there writing in a notebook he always carried into a meeting. As each spoke, Allen wouldn't say anything himself except to ask a question now and then. He refused to make any decision, or provide any leadership, until he had gone completely around the table listening to everyone have his say."[1] Many of the discussions were technical, for a byword within the firm was, "We hire engineers and other people." Still, though he lacked such a background, Allen proved to be the man who showed the way. He did it by going after more business from his main customer: the Air Force.

In June 1946, Boeing won a contract to conduct studies on a post–B-36 heavy bomber with turboprops. Two years later it had a well-considered design, featuring four such engines. By then, though, the turboprop engines themselves were in trouble. They would subject their propellers to unprecedented stresses, as a consequence of their high power. At one meeting with Air Force officials, representatives of three propeller companies and two engine manufacturers were present. They all said that they did not know how to build a shaft that would hold a propeller to its turboprop motor, amid the stresses and vibrations it would have to withstand.

In 1948, however, a new prospect was causing heads to turn: refueling in the air. With this technique the restricted range of jet-powered bombers could be increased at will, and the drive for refueling came from the top. In March of that year, with not even basic experiments having been conducted, Air Force Secretary Stuart Symington told the Senate Armed Services Committee that new bombers, using "the most modern development of refueling technique," could "bomb any part of Russia and return to American bases."

That weekend, with rhetoric running ahead of reality, a group of airmen borrowed a hose from a local fire station and conducted "Operation Drip," transferring water between two B-29s in flight. More realistic tests quickly followed, and that summer the Air Force confirmed its commitment to this procedure. The B-47 was to use aerial refueling to stretch its range, and General Kenneth Wolfe ordered it into production.

At the same time, managers at the engine-building firm of Pratt & Whitney were offering the prospect of considerable improvement in the basic jet engine itself. Their approach was to offer two turbojets in one, an inner jet engine placed within an outer unit. The combination was designed to produce particularly high pressures within the engine's core. Pratt's managers had all come up in the world of piston motors, where it was a matter of common experience that high internal pressures led to more power and better fuel economy. In the new realm of the turbojet, this principle held as well.

The new engine became known as the J-57. In 1948 it existed only on paper, and not even as a well-considered design; its prototype lay well in the future. It nevertheless drew strong interest at the Air Force development center of Wright Field, where a jet-engine expert named Woldemar Voigt was at work. He had led the design of the wartime Me-262 jet fighter, and had come to the United States to join the winning side. Now he was advising Colonel Peter Warden, who worked with General Wolfe and who was a strong supporter of jets. Warden also was the man with whom Boeing's managers usually dealt in day-to-day activities. Voigt thought it would be a good idea to see what those managers could do if they could look ahead to flying with the J-57. Warden responded by inviting Boeing's people to carry out a quickie study of a new heavy bomber, over a weekend in October.

It is part of aviation lore that the concept of what became the B-52 emerged during that weekend, at the Van Cleve Hotel in Dayton, Ohio. Edward Wells, the program manager, directed the work. Colonel Warden received the resulting thirty-three-page report the following Monday, sent it up through channels, and saw the B-52 emerge as an eight-engine jet bomber that indeed won the role of replacing the B-36. This represented another milestone along the road to the jetliner, for it showed that the turbojet could power aircraft that were both very large and vital to the national interest. No longer would these engines raise doubts, at least within the Air Force. They had won in competition over not only the piston engine but the turboprop.

The next year, 1949, saw another milestone as the world's first commercial jet airliner entered flight test. This was the Comet, the product of Britain's firm of De Havilland as well as of a government policy that gave strong support to civil aviation. In the late 1940s the standard aircraft in service was still the DC-3, with a cruising speed of 180 miles per hour. The Comet promised to raise this to 480. Certainly there was a strong flavor of subsidy from the Crown in the affair, for British Overseas Airways Corporation (BOAC), the government-owned airline, had ordered Comets as early as 1947. But De Havilland was risking £12 million of its own money as well, some $34 million. Sir Geoffrey de Havilland, the chairman, was pioneering in his own right.

At Boeing, a small design group had been studying concepts for similar aircraft since 1947. The aerodynamicist Jack Steiner stood close to this group, and he recalls that among the airlines, "there was no faith in jets whatever. None." The reason was that air carriers, as commercial enterprises, in no way could accept their costs and performance limitations. The jet engines of the postwar years still were fuel guzzlers; aircraft that they powered would be limited in range. Aerial refueling might be fine for the Air Force, but to a CEO it looked like sending two aircraft to do the work of one. And the jet engines of the day demanded much maintenance, which would drive operating costs even higher.

Airline executives certainly were highly interested in new aircraft, but these were not Comets. Instead they were lining up to buy late-model piston planes such as the Douglas DC-7. It promised nonstop service coast to coast while raising speeds to 330 miles per hour. C. R. Smith, president of American Airlines, soon declared that "we can't go backward to the jet," adding that "a DC-7 will cost $1.5 million compared to at least $4 million for a U.S. jet." Ralph Damon, president of TWA, had a similar view: "The only thing wrong with the jet planes of today is that they won't make money."

As William Allen continued to look for new ways to expand his product line, he moved in a different direction, toward jet-powered tankers. Tanker aircraft were drawing attention, amid the Air Force's burgeoning purchases of new bombers. Operational squadrons had been using another Boeing product, the piston-driven KC-97, but it had problems. The peak of its speed barely matched the lowest suitable value of the jet bombers' speed, making refueling inconvenient. When it did take place, it typically occurred at altitudes of only about fifteen thousand feet, amid choppy air that brought further complications. But a jet tanker could avoid all this.

The J-57 engine also offered new hope to advocates of a post-Comet jetliner. With its improved fuel economy and good thrust, it encouraged thoughts of an aircraft that would be large, fast, economical, and reliable, offering a package that would strongly tempt the buyers. Yet Allen could not simply order up a design and bring it through to production, for to do that would amount to betting the company on a gamble. Such a project would cost money, which could only come from Boeing's own coffers as an up-front expense. Nor could Allen expect to recover these expenses quickly, even if the plane were to sell well. Airline executives, their eyes on the bottom line, would demand the lowest possible sticker price. Boeing then could expect to turn a profit only through profit, by selling hundreds of them, and that might take as long as a decade.

But Allen was ready to pursue a different strategy. He hoped to craft a design that could serve both military and civil needs, and sell it first to the Air Force as a tanker. The Pentagon then would pay the cost of development while purchasing the tooling and production equipment—and much of this would carry over to the jetliner. That would reduce its front-end costs as well as the financial risk. In particular, Allen would use company funds to build a prototype, then offer it to both the civil and military markets. The cost would be $16 million, a huge sum for a single airplane. But Boeing could afford it, flush as it was with Korean War profits.

This plan nevertheless drew objection from among Allen's own top executives. The problem was that Boeing had never built a financially successful airliner. Its few efforts in this area had been spotty and intermittent; the firm had long since become an outfit that sold most of its production to one customer, the Air Force. And in entering the commercial market it would be going head to head against the world leader in commercial aviation: Douglas Aircraft.

Douglas had pioneered the successful airliner by introducing the DC-3 during the mid 1930s. The firm then had introduced the first four-engine airliner, the DC-4, and had followed with a host of popular successors: the DC-6 that flew above the weather for passenger comfort, the economical DC-6B, the top-of-the-line DC-7. Boeing also faced potential competition from Lockheed, whose triple-tailed Constellation aircraft were virtually poems in flight. Boeing, of course, had the advantage of its vast experience in building large jets. But this advantage could quickly vanish once Douglas entered the field.

Even so, in April 1952 Allen made the decision to build the prototype. He insisted, however, that the emphasis was to fall on selling it to the Air Force as a tanker. In earnest of this, he christened the prototype as Model 367-80. Model 367 had been the company's designation for the KC-97. This was his way of inviting people to knock off the skylarking about jet airliners and settle down to the serious business of a new military project.

Ten days after this decision, the Comet entered service and astonished the world. It quickly demonstrated enormous appeal, acquiring the cachet that the Concorde would win two decades later. Passengers, praising its vibration-free and relatively quiet flight, bought up available tickets for weeks ahead. More remarkably yet, BOAC found itself making money with its new jets—a feat that soon brought other airline executives over for a look. Within a year BOAC had jet routes running to the Far East, while three other airlines, including Air France, were putting their own Comets into service. *Fortune* magazine, declaring that "1953 is the year of the Coronation and the Comet," noted that fifty-six had been sold and another fifty were in "serious negotiation."

It was almost too good to last, and it didn't. Early in 1954 a Comet with the designation Yoke Peter, flying out of Rome, exploded at an altitude of some thirty thousand feet. The planes were grounded and carefully checked; nothing turned up, and they were back in service in March. Two weeks later another of them, Yoke Yoke, blew apart in an entirely similar fashion. The Comets now were grounded anew as Prime Minister Winston Churchill called for a formal court of inquiry to determine the cause of these accidents.

Ironically, it proved to lie neither in the jet engines nor the high speed of flight. The cause lay in the aircraft structure. It had weakened under repeated strains and finally broke, much as you would break a wire by bending it back and forth. These findings represented a body blow to the Comet; four years passed before a redesigned version qualified for service. In the meantime, the Americans had the field to themselves.

Boeing rolled out its prototype of the 367-80, which everyone called the Dash-80, in May 1954. The rollout of a new airplane is somewhat like the entrance of a queen, and to heighten the drama the plane was painted in yellow and coppery brown. The guest of honor at the ceremony was William Boeing, the company's founder. He had washed his hands of the firm some twenty years earlier, selling his stock in bitterness after a new federal law forced the breakup of a corporate group that had included Boeing Aircraft. Now he was back, at age seventy-two, watching with emotion as his wife, Bertha, swung a bottle of champagne as if she was launching a ship.

The new prototype proved to be timely. In June Air Force Secretary Harold Talbott announced a competition of designs for that focus of Allen's hope, a jet tanker. Lockheed and Douglas entered as well. But the Dash-80, making its first flight in July, was Allen's ace in the hole. Company officials argued that regardless of the decision in the competition, the Air Force should do itself a favor by buying Boeing tankers as interim models. They would cost less because they would be based on the already-existing Dash-80, and would be available sooner.

Less than a month after that first flight, Talbott gave Boeing an order for twenty-nine such tankers, with an understanding that the final order would total as many as a hundred. Lockheed won the competition the following March, but its victory proved hollow. The Air Force elected not to pursue its design but to stick with Boeing's. In Steiner's words, "We got our nose in the tent and they never got it out."

The new tanker, designated KC-135, was to be built in government-owned facilities using government-furnished tooling. Could Boeing rent these assets from the Air Force for use in building jetliners? Allen won Talbott's assent in August 1955, after pointing out that such rental payments would "obviously be of substantial benefit to the Air Force and to the country." This meant that the new airliner could emerge from its

Rollout of the Dash-80, prototype of the Boeing 707: May 15, 1954. (Boeing)

larval form as a tanker, once Allen received one more thing: orders from the airlines.

Meanwhile, at Douglas Aircraft, similar jet-powered thoughts were on the mind of Donald Douglas. Unlike Allen, who had risen to his corporate presidency by winning his colleagues' esteem, Douglas held his post of company chairman by virtue of having founded the firm. He was a full-blooded Scotsman, able to play the bagpipes and to quote Robert Burns, and he ran the corporation as an extension of his own personality. He had a big dog named Wunderbar, "the best-informed dog in aviation," who shared his office and attended conferences. He had been grooming his son for the presidency and gave him the title in 1957, but refused to grant him any real authority. The lad was forty years old and had spent his life in aviation, but his dad felt that he still needed more seasoning. Yet while Douglas ran his firm like a feudal lord of the manor, his strong personal integrity gave him a high level of respect among airline executives. People dealt with him by telephone, relying on his word and his handshake, and letting the paperwork catch up in its own good time.

He had a project group that had been studying jetliners for several years, but he was in no hurry to enter this new field. He had built jet fighters and twin-engine bombers, but never anything as large as a B-47 or B-52, which meant he lacked experience with big jet aircraft. He also would have to carry through the development of a jetliner entirely on his own, with no cost-sharing with the Air Force. Meanwhile, his company was riding merrily along on its pistons, and had a solid command of the market. Its latest model was the DC-7C, the "Seven Seas," with enough range to fly nonstop from New York to Paris.

But a major customer was about to force his hand: Juan Trippe, chairman of Pan American World Airways. That airline was the largest in the United States and Europe, which put Trippe in a class by himself when it came to ordering equipment. Airline presidents were accustomed to having planebuilders craft designs tailored to their wishes. Trippe had the clout to drag them into building what he sought whether they liked it or not, for he could play corporate leaders against one another until he got his way.

His interest in jetliners dated to the late 1940s. As early as 1949 he had begun talking with planebuilders, though three years later he found that only De Havilland was willing to quote prices and delivery dates. In 1952 he had placed an order for three Comets, and everyone in the industry knew that if he liked them, he would order many more. Now it was 1955, and he was cherishing a clear view of what he wanted. It would have to be a true transatlantic jetliner, able to cross the Atlantic without a refueling stop. William Allen was pitching his new offering, called the Boeing 707. But Trippe wasn't biting, for it lacked the range.

To make the range, he knew an airliner would need an engine even more advanced than the J-57. Fortunately, Pratt & Whitney was working on just such a turbojet, the J-75. With it, an airliner could be larger in size and could carry more fuel. Unfortunately, the J-75 was not available. It was an Air Force project, still in an early stage of development. Fred Rentschler, Pratt's chairman, was in no position to offer the performance guarantees that an airline would demand.

Trippe responded by letting people know that he might turn to the British firm of Rolls-Royce, whose Conway engine was drawing excellent notices. That would hit Rentschler where he lived; he wanted badly to supply engines for America's upcoming jetliners, and he would do a lot to keep the British from taking his business. In the J-75, the crux of the problem lay in its use of high-temperature metals, which would improve its performance. Rentschler decided he could offer a preliminary version that would use standard metals and that would amount to a more powerful J-57. Such an engine carried less technical risk, and Rentschler recommended it as an alternative. Trippe responded by ordering 120 of them, for $40 million. He now had engines on the way, and he was ready to use them as levers to get planes to go with them.

To Douglas, Trippe's move offered a new and encouraging prospect. Douglas now could hope to play the tortoise to Boeing's hare. Boeing, stuck with a shorter-range design, was likely to find itself locked in and unable to respond to Trippe's initiative, for the 707 was to use the J-57. Douglas, unfettered by such a commitment, could proceed from the start to build a longer-range craft that would use the J-75. Further, Trippe's initial order might crack open a huge market. Other airline executives might distrust the jet, but they would have to match Trippe's purchases or lose business to him on their lucrative Atlantic routes. The Comet had shown that jet flight indeed would be popular, and Trippe would stand ready to repeat its success, forcing other carriers to fall in line. They might well buy their planes from Douglas.

In June 1955 Donald Douglas gave formal approval for development and construction of his own jetliner, the DC-8. Very quickly Boeing's people began to see, in the words of one of them, that the Dash-80 "was a millstone around our necks." Douglas, with no prototype, "had a rubber airplane and could promise anything." Then on October 13, Trippe dropped the other shoe. He announced that he had decided to purchase twenty 707s and twenty-five DC-8s.

At Boeing this decision brought more consternation than joy. Frank Gledhill, the Pan Am executive who brought the news, emphasized that Trippe really preferred the DC-8 because of its range. Pan Am still wanted the 707, but only because it would be available sooner than the DC-8. When these Douglas jets entered service, Trippe intended to sell his 707s and to go over completely to DC-8s.

For Boeing, this raised the strong likelihood that the 707 would repeat the experience of the Stratocruiser. That airliner had taken shape as a commercial counterpart of the successful C-97, an Air Force transport. But that military ancestry had doomed it to failure in the market. Pentagon requirements had made it heavy and therefore costly, both to purchase and to operate. In turn, that weight had led Boeing to use Wasp Major piston engines, which had plenty of power but proved to be low in reliability. No way existed to turn this ugly duckling into a graceful swan; the company built only fifty-six of them, while Douglas continued to rule the skies.

Now, in 1955, the 707 was again emerging as a warmed-over version of an Air Force project, the KC-135 tanker. The two aircraft were to have a great deal of commonality in their engines, fuselage, and wings, greatly reducing the cost of the equipment necessary to build these jetliners. Even so, Boeing faced substantial outlays for start-up of production. If the firm failed to sell them in large numbers, it would take a bath.

The alternative would be to break commonality and to go over to a redesigned and enlarged 707, capable of using the J-75 and of crossing the Atlantic nonstop. The new engines would demand a new and larger wing, and this would be costly. Such a wing would need its own jigs, frameworks built to high accuracy for use in final assembly. The redesigned 707 would demand lengthy flight tests, to convince the Civil Aeronautics Administration that the new wing was safe. Lack of commonality with the KC-135 would also drive up the overall cost of production. In all this, Boeing again would take a bath.

Nevertheless, the two alternatives were far from equivalent. To maintain commonality would amount to standing pat, refusing to respond to the demands of the market. That way lay certain failure. To break commonality would respond to those needs, and while this alone could not guarantee success, at least it would help Boeing to regain a level field as it pursued this competition.

The upshot, for several Boeing managers, was a weekend that strongly resembled the one in Dayton's Van Cleve Hotel in 1948. Then the goal had been to launch the B-52; now it was to save the 707. Ed Wells again was in charge, as these officials laid out concepts for the larger wing. The new design was the 707 Intercontinental. With it, Allen hoped to win orders not only from Pan Am but from European carriers.

Meanwhile, Trippe's decision was bringing consternation to other airlines, as well as to Boeing. They now would have no choice but to place their own jet orders, or face a Pan Am monopoly over the Atlantic. Three other carriers proceeded to announce their own purchases during the month that followed October 13, setting their industry irrevocably onto this new course.

United Airlines was next to decide. It had built a mockup with a 707 cabin interior at one end and that of a DC-8, three inches wider, at the other. Visitors had preferred the roomier DC-8 cabin, and on October 25 William Patterson, president of United, announced that he was buying thirty DC-8s. For Boeing, this was a serious blow. Early in November, National Airlines also ordered DC-8s. American Airlines, the largest domestic carrier, would be the next to commit, and if it went for the DC-8, the trend might become overwhelming. And American had been studying jets jointly with United. Further, in the words of its vice-president of operations, "our preference for doing business, our history, was all with Douglas."

But American's president, C. R. Smith, was impressed by Boeing's promise of earlier deliveries. He was willing to go for the 707, if it could be made roomier than the DC-8. "So we widened it," said Wellwood Beall, a senior vice president. "By four inches." This broke commonality with the fuselage of the KC-135 as well as with the wings, driving costs still higher. But Smith's business was a potent persuader. With this change, Boeing literally won by an inch. On November 9, Smith announced that he would buy thirty 707s.

This experience showed clearly how a willingness to make changes, even major ones, could represent a vital tactic in winning sales. During subsequent months, Boeing went on to use this tactic repeatedly. Pan Am's Trippe decided that he liked the Intercontinental, and switched some of his earlier 707 orders to the new model. For Braniff, serving high-altitude airports in South America, Boeing offered its standard 707 with more powerful engines. Qantas purchased thirteen short-body 707s built for that airline alone. To win the business of United, Boeing crafted still another short-body variant called the 720.

With this, Allen turned the tables on Douglas. Douglas had expected that the Dash-80 would set the design of the 707, as a one-size-fits-all configuration that would try to serve both military and civil uses. His DC-8, designed from the start as an airliner, then might do much better. But with its extensive custom offerings, Boeing turned the DC-8 into the one-size-fits-all airplane, for Douglas lacked the financial resources to develop his airliner in multiple versions. He offered a choice of engines, with the J-57 being available prior to the J-75, but in no way would he match Boeing's eagerness to please.

Even so, these early rounds of sales did not establish Boeing as the winner. As 1955 ended, Boeing had 72 orders to Douglas's 100, and the most anyone could say was that the Seattleites had established a significant commercial presence. But during 1956, as Boeing's strategy took hold, the 707 outsold the DC-8 by a margin of three to one. At the end of that year the 707 held the overall lead, 141 to 123. In effect Allen and Douglas had been conducting a duel, with tanks of capital as weapons. Allen's deeper pockets put him in position to sell more airliners and hence to leverage his outlays into more sales.

Then, beginning in 1957, sales of the DC-8 virtually dried up. During the next four years, Douglas sold fewer than fifty of them. Part of the problem stemmed from sheer haste in the DC-8's development, for unlike Boeing, Douglas moved quickly toward production without first building a prototype. That too had been a tough decision; a prototype offered advantage in finding bugs within the design during flight test. However, it would delay the program. In turn, a program delay would have given buyers even more reason to head for Seattle, where early deliveries of aircraft were a key selling point.

The first DC-8 rolled out in April 1958 and made its initial flight in May. That was only five months after the first flight of a production 707.

This DC-8 was itself a production model, intended for delivery to United, and it carried out much of the flight testing. It indeed proved to have problems, and with DC-8s already in production, they had to be fixed on the assembly line. This was far more costly than changing a prototype's blueprints. Major retooling became necessary, while airplanes nearing completion had to go back for rework and modification.

As recently as 1955, Boeing had not even been a serious player in the realm of commercial aviation. The Dash-80 represented its bid for success in this field, but its prospects had carried no guarantee. Its new strength stemmed from Allen's decision of October in that year: to break commonality between the 707 and KC-135, and to accept the added costs of building custom versions to meet market demand. And since Boeing's subsequent fortunes turned upon that decision, it is worth a second look at just what it involved.

It has been commonplace to describe such choices, and similar ones made by other aviation leaders, using words appropriate to Las Vegas. *Time* magazine, writing of the Dash-80 venture, pronounced it a "gamble in the sky." John Newhouse of *The New Yorker* later wrote that to launch a new airliner project amounted to "betting the company." Yet Allen was not gambling; he was accepting risk, which was something very different.

It is true that his choices involved alternate ways of spending large sums of money, amid uncertain prospects. But he was not offering a product on a take-it-or-leave-it basis, leaving its fate in the hands of airline executives and of competing planebuilders who were ready to work vigorously to offer better selections. Instead, Allen used his dollars to mobilize the strengths of his designers and his marketing staffs, who were prepared to show their own vigor.

He did not trust passively to fate or luck; he did all he could to influence the outcome. In this fashion, he set his company on a course toward dominance within the industry. This dominance emerged during the 1960s, as Boeing and Douglas competed through two further rounds of jetliner development.

22 Room at the Bottom

THERE WAS so much power in the new jet engines, in packages so compact, as to change quite dramatically people's views as to what constituted a big airplane. The wartime B-29 had appeared immense in its day, with initial versions offering loaded weights as great as 120,000 pounds. At the dawn of the commercial jet era, the French built a twin-engine airliner called the Caravelle that weighed in at 110,000 pounds, with full load. Yet it counted as no more than a small jetliner that served short-range routes. At the other end of the scale, the various models of 707 and DC-8 spanned a range from two to three times heavier. The biggest of them, the 707 Intercontinental, approached the loaded weight of that postwar behemoth, the B-36.

Between the Caravelle and the big jets lay a market opportunity. A shrewd planebuilder might come in with a jetliner of intermediate size and range, carrying somewhat more than a hundred passengers on distances that were shorter than New York to Los Angeles. Along such routes the propeller still ruled, late in the 1950s, with airlines providing this service by using their DC-6s and other such aircraft. A substantial body of opinion held that the jet would have a hard time offering competitive economics, and that within this realm, the turboprop would have its day. Lockheed accepted this viewpoint, bypassing jet designs and offering its turboprop Electra for such intermediate markets. But at Boeing and Douglas, people had other plans.

Both firms faced the question of whether they could offer new jetliners that would prove suitable. The answers came from preliminary designs, airplanes studied on paper. This contest was under way as early as 1958, even before the first 707s and DC-8s entered service. Both companies offered to build downsized versions of their respective jetliners, as two- or four-engine models, depending on customer preference. Within each company, the board of directors decreed that two major airlines would have to place orders before the new project could go ahead.

Four carriers stood as potential first customers: Eastern, United, American, and TWA. These were the largest domestic airlines, but not all of them were in a position to make early purchases. TWA was having financial problems, and was not likely to buy anyone's medium-range airliner. American had recently purchased a substantial number of Lockheed Electras, and was also likely to hold back. By contrast, United was potentially an eager customer, but with a caveat. It operated a major hub in Denver, a center for its routes, and its executives knew that the city's mile-high altitude would demand an extra engine. This would assure safe takeoff if one of them were to fail during the roll down the runway. Douglas therefore put its two-engine version on the shelf, agreed with United to proceed with its four-engine design, and tried to line up the additional customer that would permit the firm to go ahead.

This move put considerable pressure on Boeing, which had been emphasizing its twinjet design. That concept was drawing interest at Eastern, which was ready to order new jets if their economics were suitable. Charles Froesch, Eastern's vice president of engineering, took the view that this would demand a two-engine airliner. Eastern and United thus indeed represented two potential customers, but each wanted its own number of engines. Douglas looked unstoppable, because of the strong response it had received from United, and hope faded for the new Boeing project.

But these hopes revived during 1959 as Froesch began to talk of needing a larger model that could require three engines. He wasn't the only one; TWA's chief of engineering, Robert Rummel, was also suggesting that Boeing should pursue a trijet. If Eastern would come up from two engines to three then United might go from four to three, for a trijet would still address that carrier's Denver requirements. This approach drew encouragement from Boeing's in-house studies.

"We had to find a middle ground between United's desire for four engines and Eastern's desire for two," said Jack Steiner, who was managing those design studies. "The middle ground proved to be a three-engine airplane, and it was this, more than any other one factor, that led to the three engines." The new project was the Boeing 727, and it had a specific mission: to fly out of La Guardia Airport on instrument runway 4-22, which had a usable length of 4,860 feet, and proceed to Miami nonstop. That put a premium on being able to take off and land in short distances, and this called for a new type of flap.

Flaps, dangling behind a wing's trailing edge, had long been used to add lift during takeoff and landing. For the 727 the design chief, Bill Cook, introduced what amounted to three flaps in one. As one airline pilot later remarked, "On this bird you don't lower the flaps. You disassemble the whole damn wing." This indeed provided short-runway capability, while allowing the 727 to climb and descend unusually rapidly. This was important; it meant that even on flights of a few hundred miles, the plane could spend most of its time at high speeds and altitudes, which saved fuel.

During 1959 and 1960, as these design efforts proceeded, the financial prospects of Boeing and Douglas offered background that was strongly influencing these firms' willingness to pursue their programs. Of the two companies, Boeing was by far the healthier. It had two major Air Force projects, the B-52 and the KC-135 tanker, as well as the 707. Its backlog of unfilled orders stood at $2 billion in 1959, while its sales of $1.6 billion were the largest in the industry. It ran in the black during that year, with both sales and profits continuing to rise during 1960. It had written off $165 million as the cost of developing the 707, and was in good shape for the 727 venture.

By contrast, Douglas was swamped in the backwash of the DC-8. As noted earlier, the firm had launched this project not only with no prototype akin to Boeing's Dash-80, but with no experience in building large jet aircraft, and with no cost-sharing involving the Air Force, such as Boeing had with the KC-135 (which amounted to a variant of the 707). In essence, then, Donald Douglas had sought to proceed by advancing directly from the drafting board to the production line.

Like Boeing, Douglas was to receive revenue both from down payments when it booked new orders and from lucrative final payments when it delivered finished airplanes to its customers. During the late 1950s, Douglas did poorly in both areas. New orders fell off; from 1957 through 1961, Douglas sold only forty-seven DC-8s. The design proved to have bugs that had to be fixed on the assembly line, delaying delivery; in 1959 the firm completed only twenty-one of these jetliners.

Even so, Douglas found itself depending increasingly upon the fragile prospects of these new airliners. It was building fighter aircraft for the Navy but was failing to bring in any large amount of new military business. Its 1960 backlog of $1.4 billion—down by one-third in only four years—was more than half commercial aircraft. Sales slumped as well, falling from $1.2 billion in 1958 to under $900 million in 1959, little more than half of Boeing's. The company ran at a loss during both 1959 and 1960, with much of the reason lying in continuing heavy write-offs for DC-8 development.

The firm was prepared to live with these costs and to hold onto the DC-8, hoping that someday it might become a moneymaker. But it could not accept the risk of having two such turkeys on its hands. In competing with the Boeing 727, Douglas did not go over to a trijet design; the company stayed with its four-engine layout and continued to seek the additional customer, in addition to United, that would allow the project to proceed. The stakes were high, for Douglas's financial situation gave it much less leeway than Boeing. Nothing less than a large and solid block of orders would justify such a commitment. These orders did not arrive, and Donald Douglas made the wrenching decision to abandon the effort.

In Great Britain, a similar project also went nowhere. The firm of De Havilland offered its own three-engine jetliner, the Trident—and proceeded to shoot it down before it ever flew. The Trident was potentially a good airplane that might offer strong competition to Boeing, but it was designed for one airline and one man: Lord Sholto Douglas of Kirtleside, chairman of British European Airways. To fit the needs of this carrier, he insisted that the Trident should offer eighty-passenger capacity and one-thousand-mile range. This meant that it amounted to a Caravelle with an extra engine, having negligible appeal to other airlines.

Lord Douglas's decision flew in the face of the attitude of people such as those of Boeing, who knew that when a customer said "jump," the appropriate response was "how high." But BEA had its subsidies, as did De Havilland, which meant that Lord Douglas could feel quite comfortable about the whole affair. As he put it, "They don't change one hair of that airplane without my permission."

Meanwhile, United Airlines indeed was signing on as Boeing's second customer, accepting that the trijet 727 would serve its needs. In November 1960, Boeing's William Allen signed contracts with Eastern and United for delivery of up to eighty of these aircraft. The total value of the two orders was $420 million, the largest to date in the industry.

Moreover, for the second time in a decade, a twist of fate was wiping out competition and boosting Boeing's potential market. The British had been first with a jetliner; their De Havilland Comet was carrying passengers as early as 1952, when the 707 existed only on paper. It might have been a strong alternative, but then came its withdrawal from service in 1954, after two of them exploded in midair due to defects in the design of its pressurized fuselage. Lockheed's Electra might have competed vigorously with the 727, but met a similar end.

In two accidents, during 1959 and 1960, this plane lost wings during flight. In the second of these, over Indiana, both wings came off; the plane darted into the ground like an arrow, mangling the passengers so severely that only seven could be identified. The technical cause proved to be subtle. The normal maneuvers of flight can cause an engine to wobble on its mounting with considerable force. But the stiffness of the mounts, and of the nacelle, or engine housing, dampens these oscillations and keeps them from intensifying. Within the Electra, minor damage from a hard landing or similar mishap could reduce this stiffness, even though there was little loss of strength. Then when the engine wobbled, it might do so with growing power, setting up destructive motions that could break a wing's main structural spar.

Once this became known, it proved fixable—at the cost of fourteen hundred pounds of extra stiffeners in each aircraft. But there is something peculiarly terrifying about an airplane that can't keep its wings on, and the Electra became thoroughly unpopular. Lockheed had made a good move in aiming it at the medium-range market, where it could outspeed its piston-powered competitors. But that firm's commitment to the project dated to 1955, when few people anticipated that the early jets would prove so successful, and the Boeing 727 took away its market quite thoroughly.

Boeing went on to build 1,832 of these planes during the next quarter century, with no Douglas-built alternative ever being offered. The 727 thus gave Boeing a monopoly on such aircraft—and a solid leg up on Douglas in their ongoing rivalry. Indeed, its significance proved to be deeper still. Douglas's failure to challenge the 727 represented its first withdrawal from the role of offering aircraft in all the categories of size and range that a major airline would demand.

In turn, the popularity of jetliners turned them into moneymakers for the airlines. In flight, they showed reliability. Gone now was the too-common experience of shutting down an engine while in the air, leaving passengers to wonder why the propeller wasn't turning. With their speed and reliability the new jets could make several flights a day, each plane doing the work of several of the piston models. This offset their higher purchase prices.

At the dawn of the jet era, worried airline executives noted that a single 707 or DC-8, flying on a frequent schedule, would carry as many passengers across the Atlantic in a year as a major ocean liner such as the Queen Mary. Where, they wondered, would the ticket-buyers come from, to fill all those empty seats? The answers soon proved evident, as people responded in droves to the jets' appeal.

After 1960, as the jets took over the airways, the airlines' operating costs fell sharply. These carriers passed the savings on to their customers, and ticket prices fell. That brought more people to the airline offices. The annual number of passengers leaped between 1960 and 1965, rising from 60 million to 100 million. In this fashion the success of the jets boosted demand—and created a need for the airlines to purchase still more jets.

These burgeoning new markets meant that planebuilders could find opportunities galore during the 1960s, in all sizes and ranges of aircraft. The big four-engine models, such as the 707, drew the headlines and the glamour as they winged nonstop to London. But the average domestic trip was running at around 550 miles. This was not even far enough to get from New York to Chicago, let alone Miami. Indeed, some three-fourths of all domestic routes were shorter than 250 miles.

These flights were at the bottom when it came to glamour. But there was plenty of room at the bottom, because there was so much demand. These connections represented the last stronghold of the piston engine, being served by a motley array of DC-6s, twin-engine Convairs, and even leftover DC-3s. The only aircraft newly entered in this field were the turboprops and the Caravelle, neither of which were taking the world by storm. Anyone who could offer a low-cost jet would be sitting on a gold mine, for the main competition would consist of piston-powered retreads that had nowhere else to fly.

However, experience with the Caravelle had shown that to win this gold mine would call for a good deal of digging. The problem was that during takeoff and at low speeds, a propeller could still outperform the jets. Jets were unsurpassed when flying high, fast, and far. But a short-range flight consisted largely of takeoff and low-speed operation, and here the propeller still could win out. The Caravelle, for instance, had shown high operating costs; its routes generally were too short for its jet engines to show what they could do.

Nevertheless, the British once again took the lead, trying for success in this market. Their instrument was British Aircraft's BAC 111, which carried more passengers than the Caravelle but had only three-fifths the weight when loaded. This cut its purchase price, and greatly reduced its operating costs by allowing it to use less fuel. Braniff Airways was an early buyer, ordering its first half-dozen late in 1961. Its president used them on the 240-mile route between Dallas and Houston, estimating that he would save over half a million dollars per year. Mohawk Airlines, the largest in a class of regional carriers, also bought these planes. Then in 1963, BAC sold the first of thirty aircraft to American Airlines, which was one of the biggest.

As these developments unfolded, a number of people at Douglas Aircraft were watching closely. Having lost out to the Boeing 727, that firm had salved its wounds by arranging to serve as the U.S. agent for sales of Caravelles. Little came of this; United Airlines purchased twenty of them, but this purchase was the only one of its kind. Still, Donald Douglas was not yet ready to end his days as an exhibit in the Smithsonian. Working with his son, he again showed the old spirit as he brought in new blood—and new business.

Together they put through a major corporate shakeup, as ten vice presidents resigned or were fired between 1959 and 1962. They reorganized the company into two groups, one dealing with missiles and space, the second carrying forward the traditional focus on aircraft. They strengthened the latter group by bringing in Boeing's Wellwood Beall as vice president of operations. This was a significant coup, for Beall had stood at William Allen's right hand. Allen had him resign because he was having problems with alcohol, but Boeing's loss proved to be its rival's gain.

Within the Aircraft Group, centered in Long Beach, California, the immediate question during 1961 was what to do about the DC-8. It looked like a lost cause; since its inception in 1955, the firm had received only 154 orders. Moreover, Douglas Aircraft just then was at its nadir. Its backlog was continuing to erode, while its losses in 1959 and 1960 had totaled $53 million. Donald Jr. took the view that the DC-8 would catch on, and he called for new emphasis in selling it. He soon had his reward, for by then the plane had its bugs worked out and the upsurge in passenger growth was in full swing. The company earned a profit in 1961, and sales of DC-8s began again to pour in.

The head of the Aircraft Group was Jackson McGowen. He had been chief project engineer for the DC-6 and DC-7, and had held major responsibilities on the DC-8. In 1963, with the firm's prospects continuing to improve, he persuaded Donald Douglas to challenge the BAC 111 and to enter the short-haul market. He particularly asserted that Douglas Aircraft should go forward with a brand-new twinjet, the DC-9, and moreover should do so even without orders from customers. The market, in his view, was just that tempting. And Preliminary Design had an attractive layout.

The DC-9 followed the basic appearance of the Caravelle and BAC 111: uncluttered wings, engines mounted at the fuselage rear. It was about fifty miles per hour faster than its British rival in cruising speed, and put particular emphasis on cost-saving features. Ease of maintenance was a strong point; mechanics could change an engine in twenty-eight minutes, compared with four hours for a DC-8. Douglas ordered the plane into development in April, and he was not flying blind; he had been talking with C. E. Woolman, president of Delta Airlines. In May Woolman ordered his first batch of DC-9s. With this, the program was well and truly launched.

Meanwhile, what was Boeing doing? That firm had completed its production of B-52s, but was rolling merrily along with the 707, 727, and KC-135. For the short-haul market, though, the view was that two was company but three would be a crowd. The company's managers had no wish to compete with both the BAC 111 and the DC-9. Nor did it escape their attention that sales of the DC-9 were proceeding slowly, with fewer than sixty of them being ordered during 1963 and 1964. But during 1964, Boeing's people devised a unique design that promised significant advantages and might win customers from the other twinjets.

This called for a long, narrow nacelle for each engine, mounted beneath the wing. Such an arrangement promised to set up an airflow that would produce less drag from the wings. Then, with reduced drag in those quarters, higher drag from the fuselage would be acceptable. It could grow wider. Indeed, it could be a short version of Boeing's standard fuselage, used on both the 707 and 727: 148-inch diameter, with six-abreast seating. Passengers were accustomed to it; airline executives liked it because they could cram in more seats. In turn, Boeing would draw on long experience and build it inexpensively.

The new airliner was the Boeing 737. But it came along some two years after the DC-9, and Douglas fought to keep the advantage. During part of 1964 the focus was on Eastern Airlines, with both planebuilders in the role of suitors. Douglas weighed in with a proposal to stretch the basic DC-9, increasing the number of seats. To everyone's vast satisfaction, the new model promised operating costs only slightly higher than the standard version, which meant that the extra passengers would be pure profit. That was good enough for Eastern, which placed its order in February 1965.

However, Boeing did not go away empty-handed. Lufthansa, with many short routes in Europe, had been cheering from the sidelines, and placed an order for 737s during that same month. This represented an initial purchase in what quickly became a flood of orders, as domestic and overseas carriers bought nearly three thousand 737s during the next quarter century. Boeing also helped its cause by stretching the standard 737, following the lead of Douglas. That won a nice order from United Airlines.

More significantly, these stretching exercises substantially increased the appeal of both the DC-9 and the 737, enabling their sales to really take off. The DC-9 began to demonstrate this appeal during 1965, as Douglas's orders began to zoom. Late in 1966, *Fortune* magazine noted that "the figure stands at a spectacular 400, plus 101 options, with a total value of $1.8 billion. The plane looks increasingly like the hottest Douglas product since the DC-3."

With this, the victory of the jetliners was complete. They had trumped the competition over all the important classes of aircraft size and route length. It is true that a few of the golden oldies continued to fly. Commuter aircraft continued to sport propellers; even after 1980, one could still see a row of DC-3s lined up at Boston's Logan Airport, ready to fly to destinations such as Provincetown. But as orders rolled in for the DC-9, Douglas Aircraft soon found itself choking on its own success.

"Sell the planes and we'll find a way to build them," Jackson McGowen had told his salesmen. They were responding most handsomely, but McGowen soon found himself beset by problems in assembling the DC-9. The buildup for its production coincided with the Vietnam escalation, and both the workforce and the base of suppliers came under increasing strain. In the course of a year and a half, during 1965 and 1966, the company hired some thirty-five thousand people. Many of them proved marginal in quality, and although Douglas set up a costly training program, over a third of them were fired or quit. McGowen had planned on constructing a DC-9 with forty-eight thousand work-hours. Instead, it needed eighty thousand.

This threw a large monkey wrench into his plans, for he had counted on reducing his production costs by taking advantage of the "learning curve." This summed up industry experience dating to World War II: as a production run continues, workers gain skill while each of them learns to do more. Each successive doubling of cumulative production—from twenty to forty total aircraft assembled, for instance, or from forty to eighty—will reduce labor costs by some 20 percent. The resulting cost savings can be immense; McGowen's experience showed that the learning curve would cut the labor costs by as much as 85 percent during production of the first forty to fifty planes. But faced with both low-quality labor and rapid turnover, production costs of the DC-9 stayed stubbornly high.

Another problem lay in an accounting practice called "managed earnings." For decades, Douglas Aircraft had followed the conservative practice of writing off development costs of new aircraft as they were incurred, accounting for them as expenses charged against current receipts. But in 1963, amid the company's reforms, it acquired a new financial officer, A. V. Leslie. He took the view that this standard practice produced big cuts in profits during development phases, along with artificially inflated jumps once cash from sales began to roll in. Managed earnings, by contrast, would delay reporting these expenses. It would treat them instead as part of the production costs, charging them pro rata against each DC-9 to come off the line.

The downside was that if the company reported a loss, the true loss might be considerably worse. Soon Leslie's new practice, combined with stubbornly high labor costs, brought bad news. McGowen had planned for an average loss of $1.15 million on each of the first twenty aircraft. This was normal; he expected that the first planes would be quite costly to build but that manufacturing costs would drop as the program advanced down the learning curve. After twenty airplanes, the loss would drop to $400,000 on each plane, and prosperity would be just around the corner.

It didn't happen. Losses on the first twenty produced $10 million more in total red ink than McGowen had anticipated. And even after delivering more than fifty planes, each new one was bringing a further loss of $600,000. This meant that profitability lay somewhere off in the distant future. It would be very difficult to bring down costs, through the learning curve, to where the company could recoup its losses by means of sales volume.

There also were problems aplenty in securing the parts and equipment needed to build each DC-9. As company president Donald Jr. soon declared, by early 1966 "our lead time on all materials was expanding almost on a week-by-week basis. If you could get a forging in eight weeks it would go to ten weeks and pretty soon twenty weeks and thirty weeks. They would find they were running out of engines and tires and brakes and everything." The reason lay, again in his words, in "the tremendous impact that the rapidly accelerating Vietnam war was having."[1]

Aircraft galleys offered a case in point. Most of them came from one source, the Nordskog Company in Van Nuys, California, and that firm was up to six months late in filling some orders. It couldn't get the stainless steel and sheet aluminum it needed, while copper was also proving harder to find. For the DC-9 this caused real problems, for the galley was an integral part of the plane's structure. More significantly, military pressures on Pratt & Whitney brought delays of up to three months in delivering jet engines.

Other problems were of Douglas's own making. For a time it built both the DC-8 and DC-9 on the same production line, even though the two planes had different production speeds. The firm didn't split the line until early 1966, and even then it took months to smooth the operations of supply and support. In addition, Douglas proved too enthusiastic in taking to heart the idea of customizing the aircraft. Such custom designs could boost sales in normal times, but now they were hostage to problems of supply. For the DC-9, customers ordered a hundred different configurations of the galley alone. The plane featured one, two, or three fuel tanks, plus supplemental tanks in two different sizes. The engines had four different power ratings. The interiors had eight hundred items offering choices as to color or finish. "We have 32 shades of white paint," said McGowen. As Donald Jr. put it, "That's three versions of the DC-9 and three versions of the stretched DC-8 and cargo versions of all six."

All this meant production delays. The 1965 annual report had promised ninety-three DC-9 deliveries during the coming year. This number fell to sixty-three. The company couldn't receive revenue from its sales until it delivered the product. And it had another problem with its money as well, which also stood as a legacy of the estimable A. V. Leslie.

He had come in when Douglas was flush with cash, and had initiated the practice of loaning it to airlines to help them buy new planes. That was fine as long as inflation and interest rates stayed low. But when they rose, Douglas found that it was lending money at lower rates than it was paying for its own borrowed funds. The amounts weren't small, either; they were running into the hundreds of millions.

To top it off, the company lacked a modern system for controlling its costs. Its senior management relied on quarterly reports, which offered considerable depth but took a month to compile. The consequences proved to be highly inconvenient. In 1965 the firm showed a profit, and during the following spring, its management went ahead with plans for an offering of debentures. On April 20, at the annual meeting, Donald Jr. told stockholders that the company was "in one of the most satisfactory phases of its history." But only six weeks later, at the end of May, he declared that "earnings this year, if any, will be nominal."

The debenture sale went ahead anyway, in July—and then the roof fell in. As recently as April, the company had been forecasting a profit of $20 million or more. It actually sustained a loss of $27.6 million, and its bankers learned the bad news late in September. Earlier disclosures of loss had already sent the firm's securities into a nosedive, the stock losing nearly three-fourths of its value, the debentures trading as low as 73 cents on the dollar.

The sudden appearance of this loss was distressing. More so was the fact that the management didn't really know how to identify or correct the causes. Worst of all, from the bankers' view, was that the Douglases, *père* and *fils,* both believed that nothing was really wrong. All they needed was another $200 million in new credit. The company had been drawing on an existing line of credit, but on October 10, Morgan Guaranty and Chemical Bank cut it off. These financiers put the firm on the shortest of leashes, doling out funds only week by week, to meet payroll and other bills.

There was little prospect for the $200 million, for the company's equity, unmortgaged by existing long-term debt, was as low as $45 million. A new issue of stock was a possibility, for although the company was insolvent it was far from broke, and it held a healthy backlog. But Wall Street by then had lost confidence in the firm's financial statements, to say nothing of the two Douglases. Merrill Lynch, which had underwritten the recent debentures, took the view that the Securities and Exchange Commission would not allow another public issue of any kind. This meant that Douglas Aircraft was unbankable.

One more move remained on the chessboard: merger. Some other outfit might take over the company; the depressed value of its stock meant that this need not be costly. At $350 million, its total debt was not excessive, when measured against its backlog and its 1966 gross sales of over a billion dollars. Antitrust concerns, however, would be highly significant. To avoid trouble with the Justice Department, such a union could not seriously diminish competition within the planebuilding industry.

Merrill Lynch was the obvious choice to act as a marriage broker, but there was a problem. After the bad news about profits broke in September, some people who had bought debentures in July sued both Merrill Lynch and Douglas, claiming that the prospectus had been misleading. It would be awkward to have Douglas represented by a co-defendant, so the firm turned to another brokerage, Lazard Frères. A partner in this house was Stanley Osborne, who had been a White House adviser in 1963. He took the lead in talking to the serious bidders. He had the legal obligation to consider alternatives to merger, and he found that Douglas indeed faced a liquidity crisis; it would need over $400 million to finance its operations over the next eighteen months. Concluding that a buyout indeed was unavoidable, he promptly lined up six candidates.

The successful bidder would have to pump in upward of $100 million while bringing in a great deal of new management. It also would have to show a strong record in exercising tight financial controls. Bidders included General Dynamics, North American Aviation, and the aerospace firm of McDonnell, with the latter being in a strong position. Its chairman, James McDonnell, had made a play to take over Douglas as early as 1963, while his three hundred thousand shares of stock made him by far the largest single shareholder.

The issue of Douglas's future came down to a board meeting in January 1967, on Friday the thirteenth, as a five-man committee reviewed the bids. Lee Atwood, the chairman of North American, was probably the bankers' favorite, for his company was sound and conservative. It had over $2 billion in annual sales and more than half a billion in assets. McDonnell was also a plausible choice, for as the magazine *Fortune* would note, "his company seemed to have several years of good earnings and an expanding capital base ahead of it. It had a history of good cost controls and an aggressive group of young middle-management men. There were also those 300,000 shares. Old Mac never mentioned the possibility of a proxy fight if the committee chose another entry; he didn't have to."[2]

Sweetening a previous offer, he agreed to pay $68.7 million for 1.5 million shares of Douglas common, a controlling interest. He also agreed to buy this stock without any guarantee that the Justice Department would approve the merger, and in this he accepted a considerable risk. If the merger failed on antitrust grounds, he would be left holding the bag, or rather the shares, which then would have little value. At this point Atwood's conservatism worked against him, for he would not take this risk; he would purchase shares only after the Justice Department gave its approval. That meant that he was folding, and that McDonnell would win. The full board of directors accepted the latter's proposal, and Donald Jr. phoned James McDonnell with the news. Still, this was a day that the old patriarch, Donald Douglas, had only lately anticipated. In the words of a friend, "He walked out of the room like a dead man when it was over."

The new firm of McDonnell Douglas stood as the fourth largest American planebuilder, after Boeing, North American, and Lockheed. The activities of the two merging firms complemented each other well. McDonnell was a preeminent builder of fighter aircraft, but had no presence in commercial aviation. Douglas, by contrast, had little military work but was strong both in airliners and in spacecraft. Before the merger could go into force, though, Stanley Osborne of Lazard Frères had one more errand: to meet with Ramsey Clark, President Johnson's attorney general. Clark was uneasy about the merger but agreed at last to go along with it. With that, the last roadblock was clear.

James McDonnell proceeded to take over his new holdings like William the Conqueror. Donald Douglas received the new title of honorary chairman, which amounted to a kick upstairs into insignificance. Donald Jr. took a $50,000 pay cut and moved to St. Louis, McDonnell's center of operations, to work under the old man himself. A key McDonnell man, David Lewis, went out to California to take over, finding that both workers and executives were sitting disconsolately within a plant that they feared would soon shut down. He did not rally them with a pep talk; instead he ordered that the plant should receive new paint. That looked like a good omen, for an unneeded factory would not receive such attentions, and people took heart.

McDonnell had plenty of cash, along with access to credit, and the flows of money soon washed away the problems. During 1967 and 1968, Douglas delivered nearly five hundred airplanes. Costs went sliding down the learning curve; by mid 1968 the company once again was running at a profit. Better yet, by the end of that year Douglas went on to repay $460 million in debt.

This amounted to clearing the decks for action. James McDonnell very much wanted to get into the airliner business, and to launch a new aircraft. The point of departure for his thoughts was the Boeing 747, which in 1967 existed only on paper but nevertheless was ready to

Assembly of Boeing 747 airliners. (Boeing)

reshape the airline industry. The 747 was to draw its power from a new generation of engines known as fanjets, mounting a large whirling fan in the front and delivering unprecedented levels of thrust. Like the 707, the 747 drew on the joint leadership of Boeing's William Allen and Pan Am's Juan Trippe. Tailored specifically to the needs of Pan Am, this behemoth amounted to a legacy for these two men, one that would continue to fly down the long decades that lay ahead.

At American Airlines, Frank Kolk was vice president of engineering. He took the view that while the 747 might be fine for Trippe, it was far too large for the domestic market. He was impressed by the 747's principal features: fanjet engines, wide-body cabin with plenty of room for passengers. However, he wanted to see these features replicated in an entirely new airliner, intermediate in size. At Douglas Aircraft, the preliminary design group had been exploring ideas for such a plane, the DC-10. As the firm's prospects brightened in the wake of the merger, it became increasingly clear that the time for it was at hand.

Yet in aviation as in true love, there was no way to guarantee that the path would run smooth. The DC-9 offered a cautionary tale in which a new airliner had brought its builder to the brink of insolvency, not because it sold poorly but because it proved to be too popular for its own good. The DC-10 brought consequences that were considerably more far-reaching. The pursuit of Kolk's concept led to nothing less than a reshaping of the entire commercial airplane industry.

If Douglas had been left alone to build its DC-10, it would have commanded a substantial market and strengthened its position as Boeing's leading rival. But Lockheed was also in the picture, as a third major builder of commercial airliners. This firm had missed its chance quite badly with its Electra, but Kolk's concept offered a chance to recoup. Lockheed lost little time in offering its own version, the L-1011, which competed directly with the DC-10.

Here was a bad case of wasteful duplication, as both firms went on to proceed with development, flight test, and production of two closely similar airplanes. Each company had to incur the full costs of their projects, and by splitting the market, Douglas and Lockheed both emerged with heavy losses and permanent weakness. Lockheed built 252 L-1011s and then retired from the commercial realm, offering no further airliners and earning its living entirely with the military. Douglas did somewhat better, selling 446 DC-10s, but this too was not enough. It continued to build new versions of the DC-9 and DC-10, but never again launched an entirely new project.

The DC-10 and L-1011 were well suited to a growing market, and might have filled a continuing demand. However, both of them mounted three engines. A decade later, at the end of the 1970s, it became clear that the future lay with wide-body twinjets, similar in size, range, and capacity, but with one less engine. This meant that after incurring debilitating weaknesses by building what was essentially the same airplane, Douglas and Lockheed both saw their products superseded by new and simpler designs. Boeing's 767, announced in 1978, became America's wide-body twin. There also was strong activity in Europe.

The success of Boeing, matched against the weakness of its domestic competitors, threatened to give the Seattleites a near-monopoly in several important classes of airliner. Demand remained strong for small aircraft; the 737 and DC-9 continued to compete vigorously. But Boeing was in the driver's seat with everything that was larger. This did not suit the world's airline executives, who liked to play one planebuilder against another so as to get the lowest prices and the best terms. These executives therefore watched with approval as the French firm of Sud Aviation took the lead in putting together a Europe-wide aviation consortium, Airbus Industrie.

Airbus proceeded to fill the gap left by the weakness of Lockheed and Douglas. It started during the 1970s by offering its own wide-body twinjets, the A-300 and A-310. During the 1980s it expanded its prod-

Last of a proud line: the MD-80 series of Douglas Aircraft. (*McDonnell Douglas*)

uct line, offering a range of aircraft that competed directly with Boeing in all classes other than the top-of-the-line 747. Boeing continued to hold its position as the world's premier builder of commercial aircraft, but Airbus took a strong second place, settling in with some 30 percent of the global market.

The years continued to roll along. In 1977 Douglas announced plans for a new and improved version of the DC-9, called the Series 80. But the designation DC meant Douglas Commercial, and Douglas now was part of McDonnell Douglas. A few years later the company changed the plane's name to MD-80. It proceeded to spawn its own variants—the MD-81, -82, -83, -87, and -88, corresponding approximately to the year of introduction—and this series of airliners became a mainstay for the firm.

After 1990, with the Cold War over and won, the aerospace industry came under considerable strain because there were too many companies for the available military orders. The solution lay in a controlled downsizing paced by mergers, as most of the airframe builders combined into three large groups: Northrop Grumman, Lockheed Martin, and Boeing. Boeing was by far the biggest, absorbing the whole of McDonnell Douglas along with what had formerly been North American

Aviation. With this, Douglas Aircraft ceased to operate as a rival to Boeing and came under the same management.

Decades earlier, Boeing had gained advantage amid the misfortunes of two rival airliners, the Comet and the Electra. Now its board of directors was ready to help their cause more directly. Douglas had continued to cherish hope for the MD-11, a variant of the old DC-10. But these hopes proved stronger than the plane's sales, and Boeing stopped taking new orders. Within the MD-80 and the newer MD-90 series, several models competed directly with the 737 product line; they too went overboard. As with the MD-11, Boeing stood by its legal commitment to build the planes that had already been purchased. But it also looked ahead to a shutdown of their assembly lines.

Nevertheless, there still was room at the bottom, for Boeing elected to keep one last Douglas jet in production. This was the MD-95, a short-range plane with seats for a hundred passengers. It was too small to compete with any current version of the 737, but it filled a significant market niche and offered a counter to similar small jets built by Airbus. As Boeing took it over, it received a new designation: the Boeing 717. This had initially referred to the KC-135, but that designation had never caught on, and the jet tanker had been out of production since 1965. Hence its number was available for reuse.

A half-century ago, Douglas airliners ruled the sky as Boeing struggled to play catch-up. Today, the remnants of this once-proud commercial empire continue to operate in Long Beach. But their prospects are in other hands, and like a wife who takes her husband's name after marriage, the name they bear is not their own.

King Lear

23

THE WINDS OF WINTER were cold near Reno, Nevada. They swept down from the nearby Sierras and crossed the stark concrete of a runway, with a hangar of corrugated steel echoing hollowly amid the gusts. Peeling paint on the hangar's side revealed the name LEARFAN, along with a faded corporate logo in colors that once were a bright red, green, purple, and blue. Yet this place was not completely abandoned, for there was a light in a corner window. It came from the office of Moya Lear, in what was virtually a candle to the memory of her late husband Bill. Eager and active, she continued to come to the office every day, hoping for a phone call. It was to come from a savior, an investor who could put the Learfan effort back together, vindicating the vision that led him to design his last airplane.

William Lear was a great stout paradox of a man, brilliantly creative yet restless and insecure, lighting up skies with his inventions while at times facing bankruptcy, founding major corporations but proving unable to run them. In a world of technologists with advanced degrees, he succeeded repeatedly with self-taught technical insight. A high school dropout, he won a full share of honorary degrees. He was a salesman of the first order, but at his death he left a company that wound up half a billion dollars in debt. All doors opened for him, but in the privacy of his home he sometimes threatened suicide.

He cherished and depended upon the love of Moya, his wife of over thirty years, yet lived the life of an international playboy. He spent his career seeking inventions that could secure his fame. Yet when his name indeed became a household word, it was for an exercise in style and pizzazz: the Learjet.

William Lear was born in 1902 in Hannibal, Missouri, and grew up there during his first eleven years. The young boy had a particular problem in his mother. She spent his earliest years repeatedly walking out on her husband and living with a series of men, taking little Willy along. Then in 1908, she met the man she wanted and stayed with him. Even so, the young boy found little stability. Repeatedly, during subsequent years, his mother abused him severely. She raged at him, lashed him with vicious insults, and beat him until her man pleaded with her to stop. Until he turned eighteen, she sat on the bathtub rim and watched him as he used the toilet.

The family, such as it was, moved to Chicago in 1913. There the lad found escape in the world of technology and books. Here was no capriciousness, no unpredictability or abuse; if you learned what you needed to know and did things properly, your equipment would work as you wished. At age twelve he built his first radio receiver, with earphones, and assembled a telegraph. He had few friends, but one of them had a father who worked with electricity. He spent long afternoons in the friend's basement, tinkering with coils and batteries.

He also discovered the local library. Here he read everything he could on electricity, along with the adventure stories of Tom Swift and the rags-to-riches tales of Horatio Alger. Later, at age seventeen, he began hanging around the local airport. He did chores for the mechanics; he admired the pilots and once in a while wangled a flight. Already he had all the formal education he would ever receive, for he had dropped out of high school in his freshman year.

This was the boy that became father to the man. Lacking warmth and affection in his youth, he went on to surround himself with the sycophants and admirers who readily flock to a man with money. Denied the ordinary reassurances of a normal upbringing, he lived a life of compulsiveness, demanding to have it all. Abused as a child, he abused the women who loved him with infidelities. He had a continuing passion for mistresses, with some of these relationships being quite serious.

He dressed nattily, spent money freely, went out of his way to win people's attention—and through it all he nourished an unslakable insecurity, a driving fear of being inadequate. Fame, fortune, professional success would never be merely the results of applying his ingenuity to difficult tasks. He looked to them instead as sources of reassurance, candles in the night that might hold at bay the dark memories of his youth.

Because he expected to depend on other people to attain his wishes, he quickly learned the value of a well-dressed appearance and a confident, self-assured manner. These, along with his self-taught background in electronics, launched him into the world of radio in the 1920s. He tried a succession of jobs—salesman, disc jockey, circuit designer—and grew bored. None of them promised a quick path to success. In 1925 he was living in Tulsa, with a wife named Ethel and two babies. He was building an airplane in his backyard, from a kit; he also had fallen in with Elmer Wavering, who went on to become president of Motorola. None of this satisfied him.

He took to drinking chocolate sodas at the local drugstore, and soon became smitten with a waitress named Madeline. He pursued her avidly, taking her off to Dallas for a weekend in a hotel. That was no innocent escapade, not in 1925. It violated the Mann Act, and Lear found himself facing jail for the crime of transporting a woman across state lines for immoral purposes. He beat the rap by divorcing Ethel and marrying Madeline. Then, a few years later, he began cheating on Madeline before he divorced *her,* keeping steady company with a secretary. He kept that woman as one of his principal mistresses.

Meanwhile, he set out to make his name as an inventor. He returned to Chicago, where there was plenty of radio business, and in 1928 he made his first invention: a miniaturized coil, wound with fine wire. Seeking to sell these coils to established firms, he approached a radio company headed by one Paul Galvin, who hired Lear as chief engineer. The following year, auto radios suddenly emerged as the latest thing, and Lear was ready to make a move.

The car-radio problem was technically demanding, for spark plugs were potent sources of static. Lear thought he knew how to muffle the static, and with help from Wavering, whom he brought in to assist him, he succeeded. The new radio needed a catchy name, and Galvin came up with "Motorola." Lear went on to introduce important simplifications that further improved this product, making the 1932 Motorola the first truly practical car radio on the market.

With this, Lear quickly lost all interest in auto radios. He abandoned this field, in which he was ready to prosper, as precipitously as he had abandoned his wives, Ethel and Madeline. And the reason was the same: he had found a new love. He had purchased an airplane; he now plunged deeply into aviation, flying frequently and often bringing his mistress as a passenger. Victory, to Lear, quickly grew stale; he would leave to others the fortunes of Motorola. Both at the workbench and in bed, what mattered was the pursuit and the conquest.

Drawing on his experience with car radios, he built and sold the Radioaire, an airplane receiver for use in navigation. Hoping to boost his sales, he moved his operation to New York City, where he could meet many more pilots. High living and business expenses soon drove him into debt. He saw an opportunity in another inventor's patented radio tuner, made some improvements, sold the new instrument to RCA in exchange for a fat consulting arrangement, and went back to aviation radio. He continued to use his Radioaire receiver as a point of departure, as he introduced a succession of improvements in his navigational system. His hand-tooled prototypes were good enough for Amelia Earhart, who used Lear's equipment on several of her flights. This helped him to make sales overseas, which grew into his mainstay.

He used rotating loop antennas that relied on an electric motor to turn the loop with precision, aiming at a distant radio transmitter while avoiding an overshoot or an undershoot. With the technology of the day, this was difficult to achieve. Lear thus became highly interested in the work of the inventor Arling Rydberg, who had built a clutch that could disengage a motor from a shaft with particularly high accuracy. Lear called this the "fastop clutch" and made it a feature of his instruments.

By then World War II was breaking out and President Roosevelt was calling for fifty thousand planes a year. Every one of them might use Lear's instruments. But the Army Air Corps wouldn't touch his stuff, for he had a bad reputation in mass production. He did very well at hand-crafting his items in small numbers, for use by the world's Amelia Earharts. But when it came to building instruments on an assembly line, Lear was very bad at quality control. His free-spending habits often left him short of cash, leaving him to cut corners by using low-quality coils or capacitors. He rarely kept production workers long enough to let them learn their jobs adequately, and to perform them with skill.

Even so, the fastop clutch saw him and his company, Lear Avia, through the war. He adapted it to a host of uses on a wide variety of aircraft. This clutch became a key element in a line of electrical actuators, lightweight controls that could move aircraft parts with great precision. Such actuators replaced the clumsy and heavy hydraulic systems that had been in common use. They represented Lear's niche in aviation, his contribution to the war effort.

Lear Avia thus was a vendor, a supplier of aircraft subsystems. It was on a par with similar companies that were supplying fuel pumps, cockpit instruments, alternators and generators. Lear had hoped to ride his inventions to glory, but the Army did not even award him contracts to build navigational instruments such as he had developed. Those plums went to Bendix, RCA, and General Electric. He was far from unhappy, however. He had money aplenty—more than he could spend, for once—and he had a new wife, Moya Olsen. In contrast to the models and chorus girls who were his frequent companions, she looked like Popeye's Olive Oyl. But she understood him particularly deeply. Her own father had been a womanizer; she knew that a man could be unfaithful and still be a good husband in other respects. She gave him acceptance and nurturing warmth that had been rare in his driven life. He responded by calling her Mommie. They were together from 1942 until his death, thirty-six years later.

Although few new planes were on order after the war, there were some, and they all needed Lear's proprietary electrical actuators. Such orders kept him in business, but offered little challenge or opportunity for growth. Again, then, he faced the need to find something new. He found it in aircraft autopilots.

Early versions had interested him for years. He was fond of taking a woman for a flight in his personal plane, putting it on autopilot, then repairing with her to a bed he had installed in the back while the plane automatically stayed straight and level. However, those autopilots were heavy and slow in reaction, suitable only for bombers and transports. Lear wanted a lightweight version that would give fast response, making it suitable for fighters.

He faced competition from big firms such as Bendix and RCA, which had grown fat and sassy on wartime contracts. Being big, however, made them sluggish and bureaucratic, while Lear was vigorously entrepreneurial. He needed such an edge, for the technical problems were formidable. The autopilot had to fit within a forty-pound package. It needed advanced gyroscopes of reduced size and exquisite precision. Its electronic control circuits were so intricate that they needed advanced math for their design, along with a simulator to test them as their designs evolved.

It took Lear two years, from 1945 to 1947, to piece together the necessary technology. Then he learned that his instrument, which he had designed for the piston-driven fighters of the war, wouldn't work with jets. He had always flight-tested his own instruments; he got the Air Force to teach him to fly the F-80, thereby becoming one of the few civilians to qualify for these hot new planes. Within months, he had the instrument his sponsors wanted. They responded by giving his firm an order that was worth nearly a billion dollars over the next twelve years.

This autopilot steered planes on a straight and level course, even in clouds. He modified it to respond to radio beacons at an airport that indicated direction and glide path, turning his instrument into a blind-landing system. These achievements won him the Collier Trophy. It was one of aviation's most prestigious prizes, and brought him and Moya to the White House, to receive this award from President Truman. It was another major success for Lear, and he reacted characteristically: he went into a funk. Once again, he needed something new to do.

He found it, not in autopilots or instruments, but in one of the planes he had used for their testing. Some time earlier, the Air Force had given him a Lockheed Lodestar, a twin-engine plane dating to the 1930s, as a test bed for his autopilots. Lear called it the Greenie Weenie. After winning the Collier Trophy, he began customizing it. He remodeled its interior, putting in carpet and adding paneled walls along with a bar. Then one of his friends fell in love with the new plane, so Lear sold it to him. It was a turning point; from now on, airplanes rather than instruments became his principal focus.

This marked his entry into business aviation. It represented a specialized branch, intermediate between private ownership of Cessnas or Beechcrafts and airline ownership of commuter aircraft. Business airplanes allowed corporations to set their travel plans without regard to airline schedules, allowing key people to travel when and where they pleased. To own such aircraft was a sign of prosperity; these planes were frequently used to entertain clients and customers. Moreover, the business-aircraft field was ripe for innovation. It offered Lear an irresistible combination of technical challenge, salesmanship, and style.

With great delight, he decided that there was a large market for his reconditioned Lodestar, which he called the Learstar. Some two hundred of these planes still existed; he could buy them cheaply. He met little success, selling only about sixty of these rebuilt aircraft. But an advanced business airplane was precisely what he built next.

In the mid 1950s, amid growing European prosperity, he moved to Switzerland to set up a subsidiary. Here he lived a life of wealth and luxury, while keeping a sharp eye for useful ideas. He found what he wanted in a Swiss-built jet fighter-bomber. Here, he decided, was the basis for his new business plane. It emerged a few years later as the Learjet.

It became a legend, turning Lear from a company president into a cult figure. Hence it is worth appreciating why it was significant. Technically, it offered little that was new; it drew on what already existed in the late 1940s. It amounted to a reconditioned version of that Swiss military jet, just as the Learstar had been a reconditioned Lodestar. But its military background gave it particularly high performance. Light in weight, it could reach seven hundred miles per hour, and was highly maneuverable.

To the public, the Learjet came close to being the ultimate status symbol. Everyone appreciated that a rich man might own a limousine, a yacht, a penthouse in Manhattan, a mansion in the country. But now a wealthy man might also own, not merely a private plane, but a jet—and an agile, beautiful craft that seemed ready to break the sound barrier even when sitting on the runway. Less than half of the general public had ever flown at all; the phrase "jet set" described those glamorous people who could fly to Europe in *commercial* aircraft. To go further, to actually own a personal jet, was as exciting a thought as to be close to the Kennedys.

The Learjet was derived from a Swiss-built fighter plane. (Learjet, Inc.)

As the famous and glamorous beat a path to Lear's door, this driven and insecure man finally won the adulation he had craved for so long. Arthur Godfrey and Danny Kaye became personal friends. He secured celebrity endorsements from the Smothers Brothers, performers Steve Lawrence and Eydie Gorme, singer Roger Miller, television newsmen Peter Jennings and Howard K. Smith. Next to the astronauts, few people in aviation held greater public renown.

He now was more than an inventor or corporate leader; he was a superstar. He had an adoring league of Learjet owners who would gladly invest in any venture he proposed. He had achieved the status of being believed without having to prove what he asserted; people were ready to trust him on faith. But he and his close associates soon would learn what lay beyond the end of the rainbow. There indeed was a land of Oz waiting at the end of the yellow brick road. Within this land lay overextension, failure, bankruptcy, and financial collapse. Like a Napoleon whose ambition knew no bounds, Lear entered this realm as he proceeded recklessly to work in areas of which he knew almost nothing.

At the outset, beginning in 1968, he decided to address the problem of air pollution. He decided he could lick this problem by inventing a steam engine to power the cars and buses of the future. This engine was to use a miracle fluid called Learium, which he wanted to invent. (In the end, it was ordinary water.) With characteristic ambition, he announced that he would build a steam-powered car that would win the Indianapolis 500.

He built a steam-powered Monte Carlo; it crossed the Sierras, then broke down. His steam bus was a city bus of ordinary appearance, with STEAM IS BEAUTIFUL lettered across the top of the front. It carried passengers around San Francisco during August 1972, and indeed emitted less pollution than a conventional diesel. But its fuel mileage was three to five times worse. No further support came forth, and Lear wrote off a $15 million loss with nothing to show for it.

He invaded the business-jet field a second time in the mid-1970s, with a design called the Learstar 600. It called for an advanced wing and for new fuel-saving engines. Lacking facilities to build such a plane himself, he sold the design in 1976 to Canadair. This Canadian firm bought it for the Lear name and as a spur to their own engineers. He didn't realize that. They modified his design extensively, while playing him off against their own engineers by encouraging him to put forth additional ideas. After stringing him along in this fashion, they dropped his work for that of the home team. Moya recalls that when he learned this at a meeting with Canadair executives, "he was *white*. It was a *bad* time for him. I just put my arms around him and said, 'Honey, it's a great airplane, and someday we'll take it someplace.'"

In Reno, within his company, two of his managers decided that he needed a new airplane to work on. These engineers, Richard Tracy and Rod Schapel, saw that he was aging and declining in health. In Tracy's words, "Bill's gonna die if he doesn't get one more last shot." Schapel set out to work on a concept for a small business turboprop, based on an idea that Lear had kicked around as early as 1954. This was that two turbine engines should join together to drive a single rear-mounted pusher propeller, for safety following engine failure.

Lear took the view that when twin-engine aircraft crashed, it was usually due to pilot error amid the strain of coping with the unbalanced thrust from that surviving motor. As he put it, "The second engine always has enough power to get you to the crash site." But if both engines drove a single prop, it could have "centerline thrust," to prevent violent yawing when an engine shut down. The pilot would simply push both throttles forward, then learn at leisure which engine had the problem.

Lear returned to Reno and soon found that he would have to lay off some people. He didn't like that. He had paid little heed to the proposal of Schapel, but now he grabbed at it greedily, hoping it would make him again the daring entrepreneur of his youth. Very quickly he added several touches of his own. The most important was that the plane was to be built entirely of carbon-fiber composites. In the mid-1970s, these new materials tantalized the engineering mind. They offered lighter weight than aluminum, and considerably greater strength. In the course of Lear's work on the Learstar 600, he had prepared designs that made use of carbon composites. Now he wanted something considerably more far-reaching: an entire aircraft built of them.

When it came to technology, he was like a kid in a candy store. He grabbed at anything in sight, without worrying about technical problems. At Boeing, for instance, composites were also entering use—but slowly, with more of them appearing on successive generations of jetliners as they proved themselves in service. By contrast, Lear wanted to ride with an all-composite design on his first try.

His proposed power plant also raised questions, for it fit no existing category for aircraft engines. Should it count as a twin-motor design? Or would its single propeller, driveshaft, and gearbox relegate it to the single-engine world? Lear wouldn't accept that; twin-engine craft were what the market demanded. Then how would his propulsion win certification; how would the FAA qualify it for use, since they had no rules to go by? Answering such questions demanded what the Boeings of the world call "research," and leave to NASA. Lear had different ideas. "How are you going to maintain the engines?" his son asked. He replied, "We don't need any maintenance."

He christened this design Learfan. Under his strong hand, it took shape during 1977 and early 1978. Then, quite suddenly, Lear learned that he had leukemia. It progressed rapidly, and at age seventy-five, he knew he did not have long to live. He met this news characteristically. Two days before he died, he refused to go to the hospital. "I want to go to the plant," he told Moya. When he died, his nurse was at his side stroking his hand. He thought she was Moya. "Finish it, Mommie," he gasped. "Finish it!"

The plane existed only on paper. But Lear had a successor, a long-time associate named Sam Auld, who now was company president. Auld had spent much of his career in Lear's shadow, and he needed a good man to run the program. In a major coup, he succeeded in hiring Bill Surbey, an experienced project manager from Cessna. Surbey smoked a pipe and dressed casually. His whole manner was one of calm, unflappable confidence. He had been managing the Cessna Citation program, a top-of-the-line business jet with a budget of half a billion dollars. And he had dreams of his own; he wanted to become a company president. But Cessna was too big, and was likely to keep him in project management. He'd have to go elsewhere for his chance, and in this fashion he fell in with the dreamers who were nurturing the Learfan.

Auld had never developed or built a new aircraft, and didn't really expect to do this even now. He hoped to construct a prototype, fly it as a demonstration, then sell the design to some other firm such as Canadair. All this would cost only $20 million, and the money looked to be available. But this gave Surbey a soggy feeling. He argued that this plan wouldn't work, that the aircraft industry was not set up to build other people's designs. Beech, Cessna, even Canadair were not job shops. They had large engineering staffs to prepare original designs, and they weren't likely to buy Lear's. If the Learfan was to go ahead, Auld and Surbey would have to build a factory and do it themselves. In turn, that would cost $100 million.

Auld responded by beating the bushes for support. He was solidly plugged in to the network of Lear's fans, and knew a variety of investment bankers. He made his way to Oppenheimer and Company, a New York outfit that specialized in attracting research-and-development money from private individuals. The owners of Learjets, who knew little about designing new aircraft but who cherished the name of Bill Lear, thus received the opportunity to put up $30 million for their boy's newest hot rod.

The Oppenheimer people wanted guarantees that the Learfan would actually go into production. Another of Lear's old friends, the plane-builder Robert Adickes, proved helpful. He suggested that Auld talk to the British government, because Prime Minister Margaret Thatcher was looking for opportunities to build factories in economically depressed Northern Ireland. Auld flew to London, but it didn't come easily: "There are all sorts of tire-kickers who like to talk about such projects. But to nail the money down, to make it happen—that's something else."

On a dark and rainy evening in February 1980, it came together. A group of Mrs. Thatcher's ministers met in a room of Parliament and decided to put in $50 million. The Oppenheimer group then chipped in with their $30 million, while another $20 million was already available from other sources. The Learfan would proceed.

The project was jerry-built, to say the least. Its technology existed as a wing and a prayer. The engineering group and most of the management lacked experience in planebuilding. The factory was to be in Belfast, nine time zones distant from Reno. The financing was a mix of speculation together with Maggie Thatcher's pork barrel. Within this brew, the Oppenheimer group soon added a new ingredient: management instability.

They wanted to stir up a sense of excitement, to build confidence among the investors. The way to do that was to name a new company president, a well-known executive from one of Learfan's competitors.

This would show that Learfan could attract a leader in the industry. As a result, Sam Auld was kicked upstairs, which left him quite bitter: "I'd been working night and day, seven days a week, to raise the $100 million. And then three weeks later I was no longer in charge."

His replacement was Linden Blue, executive vice president at Gates Learjet. This firm, headed by Charles Gates, had purchased rights to the Learjet, and was building and selling them commercially. One of Lear's longtime associates, who asks not to be identified, remembers Blue well: "He spent money like a drunken sailor. Linden was about to get the boot from Charlie Gates because of his prolific spending, when we were so fortunate as to pick him up. The guy was uncanny at spending money. He spent eighty thousand dollars fixing up his office, adding a bathroom and a kitchen. After the whole airplane was pretty thoroughly designed, he bought a CAD-CAM computer for seven hundred fifty thousand dollars. He put in a data telemetry system for the aircraft that was second only to NASA's. We all got new cars, too. And this attitude soon pervaded its way down to the janitors: 'Wow, we've got all this money, let's buy a lot of things.'"

Blue did more. His background was in marketing; he decided that to sell more airplanes, the design had to change. For what the customer would be paying, the cabin was to be lengthened by a foot. ("That change alone cost about a million dollars an inch," says Robert Jacobsen, the chief engineer.) The cabin door was in the wrong place, too. By unpleasant coincidence, Blue's objections fitted in with some manufacturing problems that were troubling the technical managers. Their inexperience in working with composites had led them to a design that would be difficult to build. They thought they could make it simpler and more manufacturable, while at the same time accommodating Blue's design changes.

This tended to drive up costs without limit. The engineers were eager to learn the latest in composites and to improve their designs. But such changes ramified through the system, delaying the program. There now was a large and costly factory near Belfast—and amid these delays, its people would be working to no good purpose, all the while drawing their salaries. Hence there was a need for a strong hand in engineering management, to winnow and judge these changes. Bill Surbey had the needed experience. But he found himself spending most of his time on other things.

Someone had to show the flag in Ireland, and Surbey was volunteered for this. It meant commuting between Nevada and the Emerald Isle, with a flight every two weeks. During his half-month in Belfast, he could not keep up with what the engineers were doing back home.

The Learfan in test flight. (*San Diego Aerospace Museum*)

During the alternating two weeks, in the States, he had to spend a lot of time meeting with bankers and investors. He was the last man who might have kept the costs under control, and he couldn't.

Nevertheless, the Learfan effort was building an airplane. By agreement with the British, the first flight of the prototype was to take place by the end of 1980. On the afternoon of December 31, a crew was conducting high-speed taxi tests prior to takeoff. Suddenly a brake overheated and a tire caught fire. The plane was still on the runway, enveloped in smoke. Technicians rushed out to it, as people's hopes sank with the sun. These mechanics quickly changed the brake and tire, as if in the pits at the Indy 500, and the plane once again was ready. Then during checkout the copilot hit the wrong switch; a fire extinguisher sprayed its carbon dioxide into the engines. It took past sundown to replace the extinguisher, delaying the flight to the next day.

But on January 1 it flew successfully. "Torch" Lewis, the vice president for sales, remembers the moment: "To see it go off, and it was going to be a success. We had the money, we had the airplane, we had sold one hundred eighty of them. The world was our oyster." It looked like a vindication of Bill Lear's genius. He had conceived this revolutionary airplane with its new power plant, combining the reliability of twin engines with the safety of centerline thrust. His designers had leaped far ahead of the competition, pioneering a lightweight, all-composite layout that promised exceptional speed and fuel economy. He had dreamed boldly, planned with audacity—and there it was, a real airplane in flight. To the British and the other investors, everything looked to be in excellent shape.

It wasn't. To build a single new aircraft was the easy part, the sort of thing Lear had always excelled at. Indeed, other entrepreneurs—Burt Rutan, Bob Adickes, Leo Windecker—were building their own airplanes as well, without $100 million in backing. The hard parts would come later: certification, developmental testing, the solution of a myriad of technical issues that meant the difference between a prototype and a useful, reliable airplane. These were things that the world's Cessnas and Canadairs could do well. They also were tasks that had rarely interested Lear, and which the Learfan effort was ill-prepared to face.

By early 1982 the financial handwriting was on the wall: they needed a lot of new money, and soon. But the company was carrying a great deal of debt, which made it unattractive to investors. Linden Blue left in April and took over as president of Beech, where he planned to buy out Learfan at distress prices. The British became antsy. Their laws would not allow a company to operate if it had no prospect of success. In the United States a firm might use bankruptcy law to stave off its creditors in an effort to survive. But British law demanded that such a company was to sell its assets and go out of business.

What saved Learfan was an Arab prince, Sultan bin Salman bin Abdul Aziz al Saud. As a student in California he had wanted to buy a Mercedes, but his papa wouldn't send him the money. He soon found help from a Denver banker and oil wildcatter, Robert Burch, who became the prince's financial adviser. Prince Sultan was an aviation buff. He was an early buyer of Learfan orders, and flew aboard the space shuttle *Discovery* in 1985, when it launched the Arabsat communications satellite. Now Burch convinced him to buy out Learfan and make him its new president. Burch had no aviation experience.

He knew this, and brought along a friend, Allen Price. Price had been an aircraft salesman, and had carried out an evaluation of the Learfan for Burch. He had never worked as an engineering manager or directed a development program, but he looked quite aeronautical to Burch. The Denver wildcatter proceeded to fire Sam Auld and Bill Surbey, along with a number of other experienced people. Moya Lear remembers more: "He took Bill's portrait down! From its place at the top of the stairs, and it had been there forever. He fired my secretary, who'd been with us sixteen years. This company had a spirit, but when Mr. Burch walked in, it was over."

What was not over were the engineering problems. They had not yet even begun.

The first bad one showed up in December 1982, when a wing was being stressed under load. Suddenly there was a loud crack as its interior structure gave way. It had been designed using techniques that were standard for aluminum, but carbon-fiber composites demanded a different approach. It took a year to make the fix. All through that year the Belfast factory hung on like an albatross around everyone's neck, eating into their capital. Nor was the wing problem the only one of its kind. In a 1984 test, a fuselage was put under pressure and bent. It blew up with a loud bang. After that problem was fixed, another fuselage was pressurized and bent in the opposite direction. It exploded as well, bursting under the pressure.

The power plant proved to be even more intractable, though this had not been obvious at the outset. The arrangement, with two turbine engines driving a single propeller through a gearbox, was quite new for fixed-wing aircraft. But it was a standard design for helicopters. Pratt & Whitney had a "Twin-Pak" engine set, in which a pair of such engines drove a single rotor through a common gearbox. The Learfan's design was less complex, and its managers anticipated that they would certify it using the rules for the Twin-Pak.

The FAA was skeptical. The Learfan was to fly over the ocean, but helicopters rarely did this, and had a margin of safety because their whirling rotors could generate lift simply by being allowed to freewheel. A helicopter in distress thus could descend slowly to an emergency landing rather than crash. Even so, the FAA was willing to proceed with helicopter-like rules, at least at first. One of their rules covered the possibility that the Learfan's gearbox might lose its oil during a long flight at sea. The FAA wanted that gearbox to "run dry" for thirty minutes, without lubrication. This was the rule that the Twin-Pak and similar helicopter installations had to meet.

In an early test the gearbox cracked and produced an oil leak. Learfan engineers traced this to a flaw in the casting, and introduced stringent inspection procedures to prevent a recurrence. The FAA was not mollified, and upped the requirement to ninety minutes. This meant that the power plant engineers now had to design and certify an entire new system, to spray a fine mist of oil onto the gears in case of need. This was one more system that might go wrong.

In another test, engineers undertook to run the power plant for two hundred hours on the ground. The propeller spun within an enclosure that lacked circulating air, which subjected it to unusually severe vibration. This was part of the test, and the power plant flunked. It showed fretting, a type of wear from friction, at the junction between the main gear and the propeller shaft. The gearbox went back for a redesign, followed by another two-hundred-hour test. The fretting was reduced, but it still was there. This meant that the gearbox needed still another re-design and yet another two-hundred-hour test.

These problems were annoying, but they were no more than what any design group might face in trying to push the state of the art. But the Learfan managers could not accommodate the resulting delays, as they found themselves in a very bad situation. If they had operated on a shoestring, they would have carried the overhead of only a modest engineering staff and a hangar. Then, at reasonable cost, they might have solved these problems and worked toward a manufacturable airplane. If they had been set up as an established firm like Cessna, their factory would have stayed busy producing existing designs while the engineers pushed ahead. As it was, the Belfast plant was producing nothing salable for Learfan; yet it had to be fed.

The company's money was dwindling. It had $210 million in all, including funds from the prince and down payments from purchasers, but that wasn't enough. After each major problem arose the management stretched out the schedule, laid off some people, and tried to carry on. After they had done this several times they were left with only a few million dollars, along with very little in the way of a staff that could solve the problems. As 1984 turned into 1985, Bob Burch said that it would take $50 to $80 million more to finish the project. That money was nowhere in sight.

While this financial noose tightened, other aircraft firms began to offer attractive alternatives. The promise of the Learfan all along had been that of a pathbreaker, combining composite materials, twin-engine operation, and centerline thrust. But by 1985, buyers could look ahead to the Beech Starship, initiated by Linden Blue, which offered the first two of these three. Robert Adickes was pursuing the Avtek 600, with these same features. Amid the delays and the problems, the Learfan increasingly looked like a pioneering effort whose time had come—and passed.

So it was that in May 1985 the company filed for bankruptcy. Its directors listed $475 million in debts, and only $7 million in assets. But before its collapse became final, one more act played out. A man approached Moya Lear, describing himself as Dominic Ferretti, an Italian financier. He claimed he had access to $257 million in new money with which to save Learfan, and he would be glad to help her if she would start by advancing him $65,000. She and her executives proceeded to celebrate with a party in a Reno hotel. Then sheriff's deputies crashed the party and arrested the "financier." He was a parole violator from California named George Upton, with a record of pulling off scams, and had been convicted earlier of grand theft. With that, the Learfan story indeed was finished.

Was it merely a story of mismanagement, of entrepreneurs who misjudged the difficulties and ran out of funds? It was much more. The tale of Learfan shows what lies beyond success, beyond achievement, past the end of the rainbow.

In his heart and by his nature, William Lear had been neither an engineer nor an entrepreneur, but an artist. He had dropped out of high school; his technical knowledge was largely a matter of feel and intuition. He lived his life in the conviction that technical progress was a matter of will, of daring to break through conventional thinking to seize the moment. This attitude appealed enormously to other engineers, trapped in stodgy organizations. That is why Bill Surbey, among others, left solid jobs at places like Cessna to join him. That is why serious, experienced managers at the top of their form were willing to follow him.

If that had been all, then Lear might have gained a strong reputation within the field of aeronautics, while remaining little known in the world at large. But he did more; so much more, in fact, as to dazzle those whom his work touched. His Learjet became an icon of its era. Lear himself became one of the people who set the pace during the 1960s, along with Stanley Kubrick, Bob Dylan, and Robert Kennedy. That made him dangerous. It meant that people would believe him without requiring him to prove what he proposed.

Was his Learfan, then, foredoomed from the start? At best, it would have ridden the margins of what was feasible, both technically and financially. Even if it had succeeded, the program would not have turned the skies white with these new aircraft. By the mid 1980s there were simply too many business jets and turboprops on the market, along with a sizable number of used aircraft for resale. Even a successful Learfan in no way would have repeated the triumph of the Learjet, which was credited with introducing a generation of business executives to jet-powered corporate aircraft. At most, the Learfan might have scored a modest success and capped his career with one final achievement.

Years after the project went bankrupt, his widow continued to tend the dying embers of this, his last vision. In her mind the effort had suffered setbacks but remained feasible and viable, waiting only for the magic kiss of money. (It did not come from a prince.) Well past age seventy, she continued to cling to the faith that she could finish it and vindicate her husband's last wish. That was why she drove to that hangar every day, with the runway looming in emptiness and winds blowing cold from the Sierras in winter. She greeted her secretary, answered her mail, and sat at her desk. And she waited for the phone to ring.

Voyager

24

"OKAY, YOU ARE CLEARED, Edwards to Edwards, flight-plan route, maintain 8,000 feet."

These words, transmitted from the control tower at Edwards Air Force Base, sent the *Voyager* aircraft on a flight that circled the world. Nine days later, without a single stop for fuel, it soared out of the morning mist. It flew over the crowd that had come to greet its pilots, Richard Rutan and Jeana Yeager, then touched down for a landing. The craft had flown 26,178 miles on a single load of gas.

It was more than a pathbreaking achievement; it stood as a testament to human courage. In an age of mass organizations, it stemmed from the work of a small number of brilliant individuals. This contrasted sharply with such accomplishments as the Apollo flights to the moon, wherein the astronauts had been backed by three hundred thousand people working on the ground. The *Voyager* flight thus could rank with such similar triumphs as the first four-minute mile, the ascent of Mount Everest, the descent to the oceans' ultimate depths.

Moreover, this achievement held a surprising and unexpected character. Everest, the moon, the oceanic abyss—all in turn had been predicted decades in advance, by Jules Verne and other writers, and had been pursued over long periods of time. By contrast, nonstop flight around the world lay almost outside the realm of the imaginable. No Verne or similar writer had foreseen it; there was only a satiric 1931 short story by James Thurber, "The Greatest Man in the World," to hint of the possibility. In turn, this possibility became a serious prospect only when the *Voyager* crew was actively preparing for their flight.

Voyager stemmed from the work of Burt Rutan, who may well be the world's most original aeronautical designer. His interest in this field began about 1953, when he was ten years old. It was a family affair; his dad was working toward a pilot's license, while his brother was building flying models. His father recalls that when young Burt set out to build a model, "he didn't ask for a kit; he asked for a sheet of paper." He designed and constructed a display model of the Boeing 707, which then was quite new. This was his first plane; it also was the last nonflying aircraft he ever built.

He started working seriously with flying models while in junior high school, eventually winning some thirty trophies at competitions sponsored by the National Air Modellers. Many of these were at the local level, but he also won at the national level. He took first prize while still in high school by building a model of a turboprop commuter plane that flew at the end of a control line. He had designed it from three-view drawings ordered from the company.

He also worked with radio-controlled models, which allowed him to experiment with unusual designs. He built a radio-controlled plane that featured canards, small control surfaces set well forward that amounted to an extra set of wings. This introduced him to canards, which in time became his hallmark as a designer.

He spent his college years at California State Polytechnic, graduating with a B.S. in aeronautical engineering in 1965. Along the way, he invented a method for using his station wagon as a wind tunnel. He mounted an aircraft model on a long pole or boom, holding it away from the disturbed air flowing near the car. Then, driving full tilt down a road, he took data on the model's performance by using instruments inside the car that were linked to the boom.

He also used a radio-controlled model for flight test. He measured the aileron response to control commands, and applied aerodynamic theory to predict how this response would cause his model to yaw. Then he built miniaturized instruments to fly aboard the model itself, measuring the yaw directly. There was close agreement between theory and test. For this work, he won first prize in a nationwide undergraduate competition.

He received his degree with honors and joined the technical staff at Edwards Air Force Base. He started at a junior level, helping to write test manuals. Soon, though, his unusual ability won him management of a flight-test program of his own. This was LAPES, the Low Altitude Payload Ejection System. It called for a transport aircraft to fly ten feet off the ground while parachutes pulled a sled with a twenty-five-ton load from the cargo hold. The sled was to hit the ground and skid to a stop. LAPES proved unsatisfactory in practice, but it gave Rutan his first taste of project management.

He liked the work at Edwards, but by the early 1970s his interests were broadening. He preferred to work by himself and take full responsibility for a task. That wasn't easy in the Air Force, where colonels and other officers kept making him wait. He also was taking steps toward involvement in homebuilt aircraft. His interest in novel designs now focused on a Swedish fighter, the Viggen. It mounted a canard, which was unusual for a combat aircraft. He sought to learn how the Viggen flew, making a number of tests using his cartop wind tunnel. These experiments encouraged him to attempt a homebuilt plane of similar design, which he called the Vari Viggen.

By 1972 his independent spirit was leading him strongly toward entrepreneurship, but he still wasn't ready for this move, and he still was with the Air Force. Then he received an offer from Jim Bede, president of Bede Aircraft. His firm was working on a high-performance design for the private-pilot market, the BD-5, and he wanted Rutan to take principal responsibility for its aerodynamics. Rutan soon realized that he could take a long-term leave from the Air Force, holding that as a fallback position, while serving what would amount to an entrepreneur's apprenticeship at Bede. He soon moved to join it at its location in Kansas, with his experimental Viggen in tow.

At Bede he redesigned the BD-5 to use a jet engine. The plane that resulted went on to appear in the James Bond movie *Octopussy*. Rutan was in charge of both engineering and flight testing. But the BD-5 in its original version, with a piston motor, encountered serious problems with this engine during development. He decided, correctly, that the company was heading for bankruptcy, and he did not propose to go down with the ship. In 1974 he left Bede, returning to California to launch his Rutan Aircraft Factory.

His experimental Vari Viggen was to be his product. It had already cost him his first marriage, for as he later noted, "I was spending all my time building the Vari Viggen in my garage. At one point my wife said, 'It's either me or that airplane.' God, that was an easy decision." His second wife proved more amenable, for she became one of RAF's three employees.

He had been taking this airplane to air shows and hobbyists' gatherings, and had received a warm response. Its canard drew particular attention, for it amounted to a road not taken in the design of horizontal stabilizers. Such a stabilizer was necessary to achieve good stability, and conventional design placed it at the rear, as part of the tail. This was particularly important for airliners, for such a tail reduced the landing speed and cut the length of the runway.

Rutan's canard was a stabilizer mounted at the front. This was not new; the Wright brothers had used this. A canard raised the landing speed, but helped prevent dangerous stalls that could kill a neophyte, and it also reduced an airplane's weight. Other designers had worked with canards, but had found that their aircraft were unstable, tending to flip onto the back when pitching up. Rutan treated the canard as a second wing, crafting what amounted to a biplane with the wings fore and aft. This proved to be the key to a stable design.

He did not offer finished aircraft for sale, knowing only too well that this would trap him in a morass of requirements for FAA certification. Indeed, a decade later it was the inability of the Learfan to win certification that brought its costly demise. But the FAA was far more lenient toward homebuilt designs intended for the personal use of a hobbyist. Rutan therefore began to sell books of plans and directions for construction. The Vari Viggen was not a commercial success, but he kept experimenting.

He wanted to power a plane with an air-cooled Volkswagen engine, and built an experimental version of what he called the Vari-Eze (pronounced "very easy"). Seeking a quick and simple construction method, he turned to a technique called fiberglass-on-foam. He had used it with radio-controlled models; others were applying it in building sailplanes. No one had tried it for a piloted plane with an engine, and Rutan initially viewed it simply as a stopgap. He had used conventional wood construction in his Vari Viggen, and expected to do so again. But as his tests continued, he realized that fiberglass-on-foam possessed adequate strength. It also proved simple to implement.

Its basic materials were styrofoam or urethane foam along with fiberglass and epoxy. The foam formed a stiff core for the fuselage and wings. The builder cut it with an electrically heated wire, almost as if one were trimming balsa wood for a model. Templates, fixed to each end of a long foam block, defined airfoil shapes; hobbyists shaped the wing to its proper form by running a stretched hot wire along these templates' curves. Then they covered both wings and fuselage with layers of epoxy-impregnated fiberglass. Near the wing root, up to an inch of fiberglass was often needed.

This technique eliminated the need for wing spars and other structural members. The fiberglass shell itself took all the loads, with the filling of foam adding stiffness. Homebuilders embraced this construction technique with enthusiasm, for it enabled them to construct complete flying aircraft for as little as a few thousand dollars. In this fashion, Rutan introduced a highly significant construction method to complement his innovative designs.

Rutan switched to a different aircraft engine, which was more reliable than the Volkswagen motor, and saw his Vari-Eze win quick success in the world of hobbyists. Most of them were flying biplanes, with top speeds of around 90 miles per hour. The Vari-Eze cruised at 175, with a top speed of 200, which put it in a class with factory-built craft that were fully certificated. Rutan sold some six thousand instruction sets for his airplane, at $100 each.

However, the Vari-Eze proved not to be the very easiest. It called for a hand-cranked propeller; homebuilders who installed an alternator and starter found their aircraft becoming tail-heavy, requiring more weight in front to trim the plane. It also developed a reputation for being too sensitive for the controls. Rutan addressed these problems by developing a new airplane, the Long Eze. He designed it to use a slightly larger aircraft engine, permitting the use of an alternator and a starter while providing more luggage space. He also smoothed out the handling qualities. This instruction set cost $200, and he sold even more of them than he had of plans for the Vari-Eze.

During the late 1970s, his fiberglass-on-foam technique drew the attention of NASA. Decades earlier, its aerodynamicist Robert T. Jones had independently invented the swept wing for high-speed jets. Recent military aircraft—the Navy's F-14, the Air Force's F-111—used a swing wing with adjustable sweep, spreading widely for takeoff and landing while folding sharply for flight through the sound barrier. Jones had lately introduced a further innovation: the oblique wing. It looked like a surfboard mounted atop a fuselage, and was to pivot in sweep, like a scissor. It amounted to a new type of swing wing, accommodating flight at a range of speeds. It also promised lower drag, greater range, reduced weight, and a much simpler structure for wing pivoting and support.

Oblique wings had been studied in wind tunnels, but NASA needed a flight test. A proposal to convert an existing naval jet stood to cost up to $7 million. Rutan stepped in with a fiberglass-on-foam design, the AD-1. It eventually flew as a single-pilot aircraft powered by two small jet engines, at speeds approaching two hundred miles per hour. Its cost, with engines, came to $239,000.

Rutan designed the AD-1 but did not build it; he left its construction to the firm of Ames Industrial Corporation, a U.S. subsidiary of a French firm, Microturbo, that supplied this plane's jet engines. He continued this partnership by garnering two additional projects: a subscale prototype of a jet trainer, and an experimental jet-powered shallow-draft boat for the Navy. Together with the AD-1, these efforts demonstrated that Rutan's fiberglass-on-foam technique could produce inexpensive subscale aircraft for flight test.

Then in 1981, Microturbo, which owned Ames, decided to get out of the aircraft-fabrication business and to concentrate entirely on its small turbojets. With this, Rutan realized that he would have to fabricate as well as design his subscale demonstrators. Joining with a longtime associate, Herb Iversen, he attracted $750,000 in venture capital and launched the firm of Scaled Composites.

They soon landed a key customer: Beechcraft, which contracted with Rutan to design the Starship business aircraft, and to build a demonstrator at 85 percent scale. He now was running two companies, Scaled Composites and his own Rutan Aircraft Factory. The former soon was taking much of his time, for it gave him full opportunity to pursue his love of innovative design.

His design methods remained informal, with personal computers from Apple, along with IBM PCs, playing a large role. "We use a lot of TLAR—That Looks About Right—and then use the computers mainly to check our seat-of-the-pants feeling," noted John Roncz, one of Rutan's chief engineers. "Aerodynamics is like an equation where the first three terms give 99 percent of the answer. If you understand the physics you've got that. Most people spend too much time modeling the last one percent to death. We leave that to flight testing." The emphasis was on intuition and aerodynamic insight, with changes made to an aircraft as needed. "We can get out there and whack the model around," he added.[1]

Rutan's brother Richard, five years older, joined his activities. He had been a fighter jock in Vietnam, flying 325 missions. After 1980 he worked increasingly closely with a fellow pilot, Jeana Yeager (no relation to Chuck). They soon became sweethearts, and she moved in with him. "She brought along some furniture that filled my tiny apartment," he wrote. "It was cramped and simple, but I have never been happier in my life. I would be working in the cramped kitchen, and she would scamper up onto the counter like a little cat, cross her legs, and sit there just watching everything I did and looking into my eyes. We were very much in love. Life felt like one long honeymoon, and the skies were big and blue when we would go flying together."[2]

One day in 1981, Burt joined them at lunch and made a radical suggestion: that it now was possible to build an aircraft that could circle the globe with a single load of fuel. The existing distance record dated to 1962, when a B-52 flew unrefueled from Okinawa across the United States to Spain, covering 12,532 miles. That airplane carried 68 percent of its takeoff weight as fuel, and Burt was well aware that he would have to design an airplane that could hold even more.

He proceeded to sketch such a plane on a napkin. That first design concept was not *Voyager*, however; there were many more drawings before its eventual configuration emerged. Despite his ingenuity, a suitable design did not come easily, for here he truly was breaking new ground. He was not attempting merely to craft another sporty airplane for his hobbyists and homebuilders. He was proposing to build a craft with a range of over twice the world's distance record, three and a half times the longest scheduled commercial nonstop routes.

Everything revolved around the fuel supply. Each additional gallon demanded tankage, an enlarged wing to carry the load, then still more fuel to carry the resulting additional weight. It took more to carry more, around and around in a spiral. In the end, each extra pound of weight at takeoff demanded four additional pounds of fuel to go the distance.

Burt's design studies showed that such a craft needed long, heavy auxiliary tanks riding on the wings. Such tanks would be hard to accommodate within a lightweight design. However, he turned this difficulty into an advantage. He did this by making the tanks longer still, stretching them until they became twin fuselages, each carrying landing gear. A canard was essential; it was his professional trademark, but its real significance lay in making the plane lighter, in a situation where every ounce counted. The canard and the main wing served as structural beams, joining the twin fuselages in a crossbraced structure that would be strong as well as light. In turn, the central fuselage shrank to become a cockpit and cabin for the pilots, along with arrangements for mounting the engines.

These engines raised their own issues. In any other airplane, a designer could take for granted that the motors would run continuously, from start to finish. But this conflicted with the fact that *Voyager* was to be five times heavier at takeoff than at landing. For the flight to succeed, the plane needed both low drag and high efficiency. To reduce the drag, the plane was to cruise at low speed, 110 miles per hour on average. To keep this speed from increasing as the plane burned fuel and became lighter, it would be necessary to reduce the engine power. However, aircraft engines are not efficient over a wide range of throttle settings, and at low power the efficiency would fall off markedly. How, then, could Burt have both good efficiency and low speed?

The answer lay in an unusual engine-installation arrangement that Burt himself had used earlier, in an aircraft called the Defiant. It called for two engines mounted respectively at the front and back of the craft, one pushing and one pulling. At takeoff, both motors were to run at maximum power. As the flight progressed, this power was to be cut back, but only to a degree. When the plane grew sufficiently light, one engine was to be shut off, with *Voyager* proceeding entirely on the power of the second.

This approach promised not only to preserve the engines' efficiency, but to add a measure of safety. The turned-off engine would be available for use in an emergency. In addition, both engines were to have center-line thrust, with the direction of their thrust passing through the plane's

Burt Rutan's Defiant. This plane showed the canard and the characteristic wing-form of Rutan's designs. The fore-and-aft mounting of its engines foreshadowed the design of his Voyager. *(Rutan Aircraft Factory)*

center of gravity. This represented a considerable improvement over conventional twin-engine designs, wherein the shutdown of one engine tended to make the plane veer to the side.

The motors themselves demanded considerable care in their selection. They came from the firm of Continental Teledyne in Alabama. The front motor was a standard air-cooled design of 130 horsepower, which had been in production from 1962 to 1980. Hence it was reliable and well understood, with all its bugs long since worked out. It served as the auxiliary engine during takeoff, climb, and the first part of the cruising flight, while furnishing additional power for climbing over storms.

For the main engine in the rear, the Rutans and Yeager chose a liquid-cooled model that offered high efficiency. Liquid-cooled designs are heavy and hence are rarely used in aviation, but for *Voyager*, such a motor promised a tempting gain in fuel economy. Indeed, it made up for this extra weight in fuel saved during just the first half-day. This resulted from its ability to maintain closely the tolerances, or gaps between moving parts, specified by the designer.

For best performance, for instance, an engineer might determine that there must be 0.0005 inches of clearance between the piston rings and the cylinder walls, no more and no less. If the gap is 0.0006 inches, then these parts may allow high-pressure gases to leak past, reducing performance and producing excessive wear. If the clearance is 0.0004 inches, then there may inadequate lubrication, again leading to increased wear. In turn, such tolerances depend on the engine maintaining a specified temperature. Metal parts expand and contract as their temperature changes, leading to variations in the clearances or tolerances. Liquid-cooled engines can maintain a design temperature far more effectively than an air-cooled motor, which depends on the somewhat variable cooling provided by the airstream as it rushes past.

For *Voyager,* the more accurate fit of the engine parts meant that the liquid-cooled motor could achieve a higher compression ratio. Indeed, when the pistons were at maximum compression they approached within 0.04 inches of the cylinder head. Within this confined space, the injected fuel-air mixture swirled in turbulent eddies, thoroughly mixing the fuel and ensuring better combustion. This brought a welcome gain in fuel economy, with the engine's overall efficiency coming to 36 percent, compared with 25 percent or less for auto engines. Each carefully husbanded gallon of fuel thus delivered more power to the propeller and lost less as waste heat.

In addition to seeking every possible advantage from the engines, Burt also left few stones unturned in improving *Voyager's* aerodynamics. His existing aviation experience was invaluable, but a round-the-world flight would press a design to its limits. Hence it was essential to be able to predict its performance with high accuracy. Major aircraft firms were accustomed to relying on wind-tunnel tests for the needed data, but the Rutans had no access to a wind tunnel. Such manufacturers in recent years had succeeded in predicting performance through lengthy calculations using supercomputers, but the Rutans had no such advanced mainframes.

However, they did have their ordinary desktop models. Burt appreciated that at the low speeds that interested them, these computers could give useful results by using highly simplified mathematical representations of the airflow. These methods were far too simple for the high speeds of commercial jets, but they suited *Voyager* well.

The choice of materials was critical. Conventional aluminum was out of the question; it was far too heavy. Yet the fiberglass-on-foam technique was also unsuitable, for it filled most of a plane's interior with polymer foam, leaving little room for fuel. *Voyager* relied instead on carbon composite, which also served as the basic structural material for the Learfan. Aircraft designers have long relied on materials with high strength and low density; carbon composites possess these characteristics to an unusual degree.

How good are they? Standard aircraft aluminum approaches the strength of some structural steels, with barely one-third the density.

Some fibrous materials do far better. Glass fibers are as light as aluminum, and ten times as strong. Carbon fibers give nearly the same strength but are only two-thirds as dense. However, these fibers do not stand alone as structural materials. They form composites, being embedded in a resilient surrounding substance that holds them together. In fiberglass, for instance, the glass fibers lie within a matrix of plastic. Composite materials do not achieve the full strength of their fibers, for the matrix materials are considerably weaker than the glass or carbon. But composites often are substantially lighter and stronger than aluminum.

Carbon composites begin with a specialized carbon-rich compound. When heated in the absence of oxygen it gives off gases and turns to carbon fiber, much as wood turns to charcoal when heated under similar conditions. Workers gather the fiber into bundles and weave them into a thick, flexible fabric resembling a place mat. The manufacturer then impregnates the fabric with epoxy adhesive. This is not the common household form, which hardens when mixed with a catalyst from a tube. The epoxy is an industrial-grade type and hardens when heated in an oven, which is commonly called an autoclave.

The resulting carbon composite is sold in wide rolls, like fabric in a department store. It is shiny and black, dry rather than sticky to the touch. In building *Voyager,* it served as a lamination on panels of Nomex honeycomb. The Nomex resembled strong paper; the honeycomb formed from it closely resembled that of a beehive. This material, a quarter-inch thick, had no useful strength of its own. Instead, it served as the filler for a "sandwich," with carbon-epoxy being laminated on each side. After being cured or hardened in an autoclave, this sandwich formed strong, stiff panels weighing only four ounces per square foot. The carbon-epoxy provided the strength; the honeycomb filler gave stiffness, for the carbon fabrics would have been excessively flexible if bonded together directly.

Voyager's builders fashioned the wings around a spar, or long beam, made entirely of carbon-epoxy, cured in an autoclave. To form the wings to the proper shape, they prepared templates, or molds, and laid panels of the carbon-honeycomb sandwich within them, using air pressure to force these panels against the forms for a true fit. These also went into the autoclave; when the wing panels emerged, the builders fitted them to the spar, top and bottom, and secured them with industrial adhesives. Body panels, used for constructing the fuselages, were fashioned with the aid of templates in the same manner.

A few bulkheads, or walls, went into the fuselages for extra strength, but mostly the plane relied on the inherent stiffness of the carbon-honeycomb sandwich. Near the wing roots, where the wings and fuse-lages joined, the builders used sandwiches of fiberglass and Kevlar, a commercial fiber from Du Pont with strength and light weight similar to carbon. These sandwiches gave greater toughness than carbon, while allowing the structure to stretch slightly as needed.

The final craft used no structural metal, but relied entirely on these composites. If you were to x-ray the airplane looking for metal, you would have seen only a few rivetlike fasteners. Its wingspan was 111 feet, longer than that of a Boeing 727; you could walk along its length and come close to wondering where it would end. Yet the wing was only 3 feet across, to reduce its drag. You could take hold of a wingtip and flex it up and down, perhaps hearing the sound of gasoline sloshing within.

Without engines, fuel, or other supplies, the basic *Voyager* aircraft weighed only 939 pounds. Its engines doubled this, to 1,858 pounds. At takeoff, the eventual fuel load came to 7,011 pounds. *Voyager* was virtu-ally a flying gas tank, with its weight in fuel coming to over seven times the weight of the composite structure that contained it. In turn, the complete airplane was quite spindly in appearance, for its wings, canard, and fuselages all were long and considerably narrower than customary.

As preparations proceeded, flight instruments also received unusual care. These came from the firm of King Radio, whose chairman ap-proached the Rutans and offered to "open the catalogue" for them, sup-plying whatever was needed. The autopilot was particularly important. It was viewed as "mission critical" because it was to take over much of the routine and wearisome task of maintaining speed, course, and alti-tude. Without an autopilot, *Voyager*'s crew would have to put far more physical and mental effort into flying this airplane, particularly in stormy weather.

Conventional small-aircraft autopilots control the plane by automat-ically moving the ailerons on the wings. This works well for most such planes, which are maneuverable and responsive. By contrast, *Voyager* was sluggish in responding to its controls, hard to maneuver, and prone to bend or oscillate in highly uncomfortable ways. To deal with this, King Radio engineers modified the autopilot to control *Voyager* by mov-ing its right rudder rather than its ailerons. They also incorporated a circuit to vary the speed of the autopilot's response, to compensate for the aircraft's large change in weight as its fuel burned off.

Other instruments served for navigation and communication. To set their course, the pilots steered by using an existing global array of seventeen ground stations, each broadcasting navigational signals by radio. The onboard equipment received these signals and calculated the

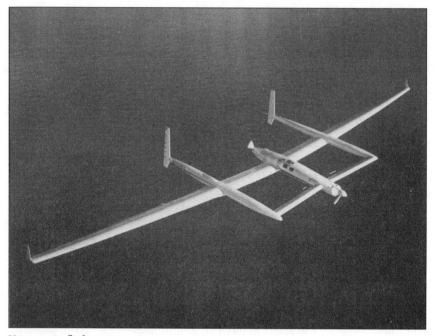

Voyager *in flight.* (*Rutan Aircraft Factory*)

shortest route between any two points in the flight plan. Cockpit instruments displayed the plane's course and position, direction and distance to navigational checkpoints, true speed over the ground, and the speed and direction of winds aloft. For communication, Voyager relied on a high-frequency radio whose signals would bounce off the ionosphere and reflect back to earth, to be received by distant stations. A separate system provided communications by satellite.

Voyager carried a compass, gyrostabilized to keep it from bouncing around wildly in turbulent air. It also was linked electronically to the autopilot, to provide information on the plane's course. The pilots had an onboard radar as well. Using a four-color video monitor, it could show thunderstorms up to two hundred miles ahead, while displaying coastlines and the shapes of islands.

Finances grew tight as the project went forward; Dick Rutan and Jeana Yeager, who were to pilot Voyager, had to get along without receiving salaries. They moved from their apartment into his parents' home, where his mom kept the refrigerator full. Their materials and equipment were gifts from various firms, and they relied to the full on volunteer labor. They ran a small tourist business on the side, selling T-shirts and other mementos, along with club memberships at $100 each. In addition, donations were always welcome. Even so, many expenses were unavoidable; the hangar alone cost $110 per day. As the time for flight approached, they were hundreds of thousands of dollars in debt.

"It's not going to be anything like fun," declared Dick. "Just being inside this flailing carbon structure, a long way from home, listening to engines and hoping they keep running." The fight plan called for up to twelve continuous days in the air, along with a good deal of hard work. For instance, oil had to be pumped into the motors with a hand crank. "I had to lie on my back and reach over my right shoulder to turn the crank," Jeana later wrote. "It took four hundred cranks per quart to get the oil into the system."

Air scoops for engine cooling needed adjustments to minimize drag. This meant crawling to the back, opening a door, and pulling on a lever. Fuel required frequent transfers, to keep the plane balanced. Onboard systems demanded continuing close checks. There were logs to keep, a navigational computer to program with updates, a ground crew to talk to by radio—and a workload that would increase markedly whenever they flew into stormy weather. There wasn't much time for sleep.

The two pilots were to take turns at the controls. The cabin, where the off-duty pilot could try to sleep, was two feet wide. The cockpit had a width of twenty-two inches, with headroom of only forty inches. The central fuselage, where they were to live, has been aptly described as resembling a pair of joined-together megaphones with an engine at each end. The pilots had earphones to filter out the noise, but these proved to be of only limited help.

They consulted with astronauts who had flown two-week missions in highly cramped quarters, and applied this experience in preparing for the flight. Food came in prepackaged pouches, with the flight plan calling for one full meal a day along with snacks the rest of the time. Wastes were to be collected and disposed of in plastic bags, as on space missions.

As a trial run, these pilots took *Voyager* on a mission of four and a half days in July 1986, covering nearly twelve thousand miles as they looped back and forth over California. Dick, a macho fighter pilot, wondered if he could trust fragile Jeana with the responsibility of flying the craft. He watched her closely during the first two days, losing considerable sleep. In time he decided she could do it and he relaxed; then he overslept. All this put great stress on her. She failed to eat or drink enough, losing six pounds from her normal weight of ninety-seven pounds. She became dehydrated, and fainted frequently during the week that followed the flight.

This experience showed them what they had to do to achieve success in the round-the-world effort. An important point was to monitor their food and water intake, drinking water according to a schedule so as to prevent dehydration. The July flight also showed the need for soundproofing within the cabin. With this, and with several fixes to mechanical problems, they were ready to try to girdle the globe. They were well aware that they might not succeed, that it might take more than one try before they could make it.

In attempting to circle the world, *Voyager* offered an astonishingly lengthy list of ways to crash. Most of them stemmed from its eggshell-like fragility. There were seventeen fuel tanks in the wings and fuselages, for instance, and if anyone had tried to load them up by pumping in gasoline as you fill up your car, the resulting weight would have broken the aircraft. It took six hours to fill the tanks, in a meticulous procedure that added a few gallons at a time to each of them, in a calculated sequence.

Prior to its round-the-world flight, the plane had never been completely fueled and tested at full weight, not even to check its ability to taxi on the runway. Such a fully loaded condition was so dangerous that no one wanted to attempt it on more than the one occasion when it truly would be necessary: the flight itself. Fully fueled, the wings dragged on the runway during the takeoff roll; the resulting abrasion damaged both wingtips. The tires were under considerable stress; if one of them had blown during takeoff, the consequent strain would have broken the landing gear, pitching *Voyager* into a fiery crash. The tires held, but the plane accelerated so slowly that it used up all but seven hundred feet of its fifteen-thousand-foot runway before reaching flying speed.

Takeoff occurred on December 14, 1986, just after 8:00 A.M. At that hour, the winds were close to dead calm. This was important, for *Voyager* faced danger from anything stronger than a mild breeze. It did not climb quickly, but gained altitude at only fifty feet per minute. This left it vulnerable to a downdraft. As it flew over California's coastal mountains, there was further danger from turbulence. Had the aircraft been buffeted or tossed about with force, its wings would have broken. And once under way, there was no opportunity to turn back. The crew had no means to dump fuel in an emergency, and their plane was far too heavy to land safely.

Dick was the more experienced of the two; he spent fifty-five of the first sixty hours at the controls. Near the end of the second day, they encountered a typhoon over the western Pacific. He maneuvered close to its northern edge to pick up its powerful tailwinds—and then had to double back briefly to avoid additional bad weather. A day later, crossing the South China Sea, he had to steer between thunderheads to the south and the unfriendly coast of Vietnam to the north. The State Department had asked the Vietnam government to permit emergency overflight, but they had refused.

The passage over Africa, on the fifth day, was harrowing. A line of thunderstorms lay athwart the path, and *Voyager* climbed to twenty thousand feet to surmount them. Even so, the plane was tossed about quite badly. Both pilots began breathing oxygen, but they suffered hypoxia by not using enough. Jeana, badly fatigued, went to sleep with her oxygen bottle. Dick soon noticed that she was cool to his touch, and was far too quiet for his comfort. Fearing for her life, he succeeded in waking her up, then turned up the valve on her oxygen flow.

She came away with a severe headache and with nausea that made her vomit. But she remained lucid, which helped when Dick experienced his own hypoxia. He began to hallucinate, believing that the instrument panel was swelling and bulging in his face. He pointed this out to Jeana, who now was fully alert and who reassured him: "Don't worry about it. I'll take care of it."

They cleared the African coast—and Jeana, now at the controls, saw a red warning light. Loss of oil! The main engine began overheating because the weary pilots, hypoxic and preoccupied with the bad weather, had neglected to replenish the supply. Fortunately, they solved the problem by putting in fresh oil, and the temporary lack proved not to have caused damage. As they headed out over the Atlantic, Dick radioed, "I'm tired. I want to go to bed in California."

But there was no rest for them. They ran into another bad storm over the ocean, which flipped their craft into a ninety-degree bank. It had never flown at so extreme an attitude, but Dick drew on his skill as a pilot and slowly leveled the wings. Then, off South America, his skills suddenly left him as he hit a wall. "One minute I was fine," he wrote, "and the next minute I couldn't remember how to do anything. I was in a haze, and I could simply not make my mind work." He drifted into a blissful reverie, and he didn't care: "None of it mattered anymore." But though overcome by fatigue, he retained the presence of mind to call to Jeana for help. She took over from him, allowing him to get some much-needed sleep.

They hugged the north coast of South America as they entered the Caribbean. Eight days into the flight, they crossed Costa Rica and once again were over the Pacific. This was their last full day in the air, and they cruised northwestward off the Mexican coast.

Then, with only a few hours to go, the craft barely avoided complete disaster. It was pitch-dark, in the early hours of the last morning, and the engine was drawing fuel from one of the tanks. Dick thought it still held plenty of gasoline, but it didn't. He learned of this only when the engine sputtered and quit. They had been running with that single motor, holding the front engine in reserve. Now they had to start it, knowing that if they didn't, they would have to ditch at sea amid the blackness of night.

"We were a glider for five minutes," Dick later remarked. It took several attempts, but they indeed succeeded in starting that engine— after losing more than half their altitude. As they resumed their flight, fuel flowed backward through a tube and fed the failed rear engine, allowing it to restart as well. To avoid any further possibility of trouble, they elected to complete the flight with both motors running.

In the cool of early morning, nine days almost to the minute from takeoff, Dick brought the plane in to the Edwards runway and gently eased it down. Jeana, still game, climbed atop the cabin and waved to a large crowd that had come to hail their arrival. Dick joined her, as a friend handed him a black cowboy hat. With that hat on his head, he threw his arms outward in a gesture of victory. They had done it, and with gas to spare. Eighteen gallons remained, enough to take them hundreds of miles farther.

Six days later, Jeana and both Rutans drove into Los Angeles. At the Century Hotel, President Reagan hailed their achievement and presented all three with the Presidential Citizens Medal. *Voyager* went to Washington, for display in the National Air and Space Museum. Dick and Jeana laid travel plans of their own, for the project still was deep in debt. By giving talks in both Europe and the United States, they received lecture fees that covered what they still owed.

Since then, Burt Rutan has also continued to flourish. His company, Scaled Composites, retains the flavor of the early Skunk Works, with little more than a hundred employees. He designed a sail for the boat that won the 1988 America's Cup, and he continues to build proprietary designs for his clients. "Burt sometimes seems to think that if it's radical, it's better," says his longtime colleague John Roncz. "He knows how to create the kind of shapes that get on the covers of magazines." Burt agrees: "My number one priority is having fun. If you're having fun, you're more likely to be productive."

He nevertheless is not the Kelly Johnson of our time, not by a long shot. Johnson's Constellation set the pace in airliner design until the coming of the jets. His fighters—the P-80, the F-94, the F-104, and the YF-12—defined the mainstream of advanced work in the military realm. By contrast, Burt has never certificated an airplane. He has continued to work within the FAA's loophole, which dispenses with certification for aircraft that qualify as experimental. Yet within this niche, he has continued to show that there still is plenty of room for ingenuity, both with piston engines and with jets.

Keepers of the Flame 25

I'T'S NOT EASY to be ahead of the times. For a number of years, that stood to be the fate of a small community of propulsion experts. They had invented and nurtured the scramjet, an engine that they knew would offer a path to the ultimate airplane—one with no practical limit on speed or altitude. Such aircraft, indeed, could someday fly from a runway to orbit.

The concept held daunting technical difficulties, but for a few years the Air Force and NASA took their ideas seriously, and these people flourished. Then, amid budget cutbacks, their projects were canceled and their efforts faded into obscurity. Still these specialists kept their hopes alive, as if they were keeping a flame that never quite died out. Then, during the mid 1980s, their hopes blazed anew, as President Reagan himself endorsed their work.

The leader of this community was Antonio Ferri. During World War II he was director of one of Europe's most advanced wind tunnels, a supersonic facility near Rome. In 1943 the Nazis took over Italy. Ferri had received military training, and left his post to lead a force of guerrillas that fought with considerable effectiveness. The Allied advance drove back the Germans; the Office of Strategic Services, predecessor to the CIA, sent an agent to find him and brought him to the United States in September 1944. Here he quickly established himself as a leader in the infant field of supersonic research.

He lectured on this subject to other engineers, then collected his lecture notes and wrote the first textbook in this field. He had already been on the faculty at the University of Rome, and he returned to the academic world. In 1951 he joined Brooklyn Polytechnic Institute, where he proceeded to build up an aerodynamics research lab. Soon he was consulting for major companies, drawing in so many contracts that his graduate students couldn't handle the work. Ferri responded by setting up a company, General Applied Science Labs.

With financial backing from the Rockefellers, GASL grew into a leading center for research in high-speed flight.

He was a formidable man. As one former student recalls, "You had to really want to be in that course, to learn from him. He was very fast. His mind was constantly moving, redefining the problem, and you had to be fast to keep up with him." Another ex-student—John Erdos, now the president of GASL—adds that "if you had been a student of his and later worked for him, you could never separate the professor-student relationship from your normal working relationship." He always was Dr. Ferri to his old students, never Tony, even when they rose to become company officials.

During the 1950s, Ferri's work as a consultant brought him into a close friendship with Alexander Kartveli, chief engineer at Republic Aviation. As noted earlier, he was a rival of Kelly Johnson, challenging Johnson for boldness in aircraft design. When he began working with Ferri, his focus of attention was the proposed XF-103 interceptor. It was designed to use a ramjet for propulsion and to reach speeds of twenty-five hundred miles per hour, altitudes of seventy-five thousand feet.

Ferri and Kartveli were both Europeans and learned men; they liked opera and history. They complemented each other professionally, Kartveli studying designs for new airplanes, Ferri emphasizing the details of difficult problems in aerodynamics and propulsion. As they worked together on the XF-103 they fed off each other, each stimulating the other to think bolder thoughts. Among the boldest was a belief that Ferri first put forth and that Kartveli then supported with more detailed studies: that there was no natural limit to aircraft speeds or performance.

This meant Air Force jets could fly with unrestricted speed and altitude, to outrun or outclimb any foe. Better yet, it would bring the advent of true spaceplanes, flying from a runway to orbit and offering vast improvements over the use of rockets. Rockets carried liquid oxygen in a tank, which added weight. Yet all the while there was oxygen in the atmosphere, free for the taking. If it could be tapped and used in advanced jet engines, then space flight might be accomplished with vehicles resembling a supersonic airliner.

The key was to be a new type of engine, an advanced type of ramjet. Ramjets were the simplest engines in use, amounting to carefully shaped ducts with fuel injectors. They rammed into the air at high speed, compressing it; the air heated up from the burning fuel and expanded out the back to give thrust. This is what gave plausibility to the fantastic speed of the proposed XF-103. Advanced ramjets were already in flight, powering the experimental X-7, an unmanned missile. It reached 2,881 miles per hour, or Mach 4.31, setting a speed record for jet planes that stands to this day.

But to Ferri and Kartveli, even the ramjet wasn't fast enough. The airflow had to slow down within its interior, dropping below the speed of sound, to burn its fuel. As the air slowed down it heated up—and there was only so much heating the system could take. Above four thousand miles per hour, this internal heating would prove so severe as to set a speed limit for such ramjets. By contrast, it took eighteen thousand miles per hour to get to orbit.

There was a way around this. Just as a slower internal airflow was hotter, within the ramjet, so a faster flow would be cooler. Such a flow would be supersonic; by burning fuel within it, a ramjet might reach far higher speeds. Ferri thus proposed to fly to orbit by burning fuel in a supersonic internal airflow within a ramjet.

This approach raised a host of difficult technical issues, which Ferri did not solve. But he asserted that it was possible to address them, giving specific examples of approaches that looked promising. He pointed out the powerful advantages that such engines would offer, attending international conferences and bringing these ideas to a wider technical audience. His strong professional reputation ensured that he would be taken seriously. He went on to conduct experiments at GASL, seeking to prove his claims. His efforts helped to turn such engines from an idea to an invention, which might be developed and made practical. In turn, his studies gave strong encouragement to other propulsion specialists.

Near Los Angeles, the firm of Marquardt was strongly involved in ramjets, building test versions that were flying on the X-7. In 1957 the Soviet Union launched Sputnik as the world's first satellite, sowing panic in Washington and bringing urgent appeals to build rocket-powered launch vehicles to match their achievement. But at Marquardt, some people already were looking beyond rockets as they made calculations concerning ramjet-powered boosters. These too were to rely on supersonic internal airflow, and were to fly to orbit with considerable savings in cost.

Within a Navy research center, the Applied Physics Lab of Johns Hopkins University, a small group led by William Avery was also making calculations. They raised eyebrows, and interest, by asserting that a ramjet-powered craft of a type they specified could produce useful thrust even beyond orbital velocity. One of Avery's analysts, Fred Billig, spent weeks at his desk with a Friden adding machine, as he struggled with his equations in that precomputer era.

Billig soon gave the new engine a name. "We need a snappy name," said Avery, his boss. Billig sat down with a set of lettered tiles and came up with SCRAM: Supersonic Combustion Ramjet, a designation that reflected its reliance on burning fuel in a supersonic airflow. At Marquardt, other people picked up this name and modified it into "scramjet."

Still another man was stirring the pot: Weldon Worth, technical director at the Aero Propulsion Lab at Wright-Patterson Air Force Base. As early as 1957 he was launching the beginnings of Air Force work in hypersonic propulsion. Hypersonic flight represented the next step beyond the supersonic; it called for flight beyond Mach 5, in a realm where problems due to aerodynamic heating would stand in the forefront. In 1959 he organized the first conference on hypersonic propulsion, held in Boston.

Beginning around 1960, he built up a program of basic research called Aerospaceplane. It did not aim at anything so specific as a real airplane that could fly to orbit. Rather, it conducted design studies and supported basic research in advanced propulsion, seeking to build a base for the development of such aircraft in the distant future. Marquardt and GASL were heavily involved, as were General Dynamics, Republic, North American, and Douglas Aircraft.

Aerospaceplane was classified, but it proved too hot to keep under wraps. A steady stream of leaks brought continuing coverage in the trade magazine *Aviation Week*. At the *Los Angeles Times,* the aerospace editor Marvin Miles developed his own connections, which led to banner headlines: "Lockheed Working on Plane Able to Go into Orbit Alone"; "Huge Booster Not Needed by Air Force Space Plane."

At Republic, Kartveli's group presented an Aerospaceplane concept that was virtually all scramjet. The engine wrapped around the entire vehicle, with auxiliary turbojets to provide an initial boost. Robert Sanator, one of Kartveli's colleagues, recalls the excitement of the work: "This one had everything. There wasn't a single thing in it that was off-the-shelf. Whatever problem there was in aerospace—propulsion, materials, cooling, aerodynamics—Aerospaceplane had it. It was a lifetime work and it had it all. I naturally jumped right in."

At Marquardt, a manager named Art Thomas directed the work. This company collaborated closely with GASL, merging for a time into a single company with Ferri as a vice president. As Thomas recalls, "Ferri would swing by and would give me and my staff about four times more work than we could accomplish. I complained about this to one of Ferri's colleagues, who replied, 'He knows that; he only expects you to accomplish one-fourth of what he gives you. Your problem is to figure out which one-fourth does he want.'"

Amid the hype about flight to orbit, there also was a modest effort aimed at building a small scramjet that could fly at much lower speeds. GASL, led by Ferri, undertook to develop it. Marquardt was to add equipment for fuel supply and control. Lockheed set out to build a small hypersonic aircraft that would carry four such engines. It was to ride

Aerospaceplane concept of Republic Aviation Corporation in the mid 1960s.
(Courtesy Robert Sanator)

atop a solid-fueled rocket, which would boost the craft to five thousand feet per second. Then the scramjets were to kick in and add an extra thousand.

The Air Force's Scientific Advisory Board kept watch with a skeptical eye. By 1963, with real achievement lagging, it had had enough. In October, it declared that

> today's state-of-the-art is inadequate to support any real hardware development, and the cost of any such undertaking will be extremely large. The so-called Aerospaceplane program has had such an erratic history, has involved so many clearly infeasible factors, and has been subjected to so much ridicule that from now on this name should be dropped. It is also recommended that the Air Force increase the vigilance that no new program achieves such a difficult position.[1]

Lockheed by then was preparing to test-fly its aircraft—but it didn't have the scramjets. They were still on the lab bench at GASL, where the builders were shooting for a thrust of 644 pounds. They got 517, or 80 percent of what they wanted, but they didn't deliver a completed engine to Marquardt in the time before the funds ran out. Years later, Art Thomas still was miffed at GASL for this.

Meanwhile, what was NASA doing? Langley Research Center, where Ferri had worked after the war, had a rich tradition in high-speed flight. This work was culminating in its X-15 research airplane, which was to carry out flights up to Mach 8 while carrying a small experimental engine. Kennedy Rubert, a Langley manager, arranged to have this engine designed as a scramjet, which was called the Hypersonic Research Engine (HRE). GASL and Marquardt were testing scramjets in wind tunnels, but the HRE effort sought to test them in piloted flight.

The HRE designer was Tony Du Pont, a member of the famous Du Pont family in the chemical industry. He was a casual and easygoing man who had already shown an uncanny eye for the technologies of the future. As a student, as early as 1954, he had applied for a patent on a wing made of composite materials—thirty years before *Voyager* flew with such structures. Du Pont had flown as a copilot with Pan American; he had managed studies of Aerospaceplane at Douglas Aircraft. Then Cliff Garrett of the firm of Garrett AiResearch, who was strongly interested in scramjets, recruited Du Pont to direct his own company's efforts. Neither Du Pont nor AiResearch had ever built such an engine, and they were competing with three major propulsion firms: Marquardt, General Electric, and Pratt & Whitney. But Du Pont pulled it off, winning the contract to design the HRE.

He did it in part by avoiding some of his competitors' mistakes. Marquardt lost points by proposing to use some of Ferri's technical concepts, which were unfamiliar to NASA and which in any case looked like a rehash of what that company already had been doing for the Air Force. General Electric lost in part because it submitted a budget and schedule that in effect warned of overruns ahead—a candor for which GE was judged "nonresponsive." But Du Pont also won by being fast on his feet.

At that time, the premier hypersonic ground-test facility was the Navy's Ordnance Aerophysics Laboratory in Daingerfield, Texas. It stood next door to the Lone Star Steel Company, which had a large air-separation plant to provide oxygen for its steelmaking. Often its air compressors were not needed for this purpose, and the Navy took advantage by using those compressors to run this wind tunnel with a continuous hypersonic flow. By contrast, most other high-speed wind tunnels used compressed air from a tank, for run times of less than a minute. But the Daingerfield facility could run for hours if necessary. It accommodated test engines up to two feet across, with these engines burning fuel at speeds up to Mach 5.

NASA's managers offered an opportunity to the HRE competitors. They could spend a month in Daingerfield testing hardware—if they could build scramjet components on short notice. Du Pont responded by constructing a scale model of an HRE combustor, in sixty days. His colleagues took it to Texas, where they obtained over five hours of test data. This was unprecedented; a subsequent NASA effort, using tank-fed wind tunnels, worked for nearly a decade and accumulated only about three hours of total run time. NASA's contract group was impressed both by Du Pont's initiative and by his massive quantity of test data, and made their decision accordingly.

This contract award came in mid 1966. By then, though, the scramjet was in serious trouble. The Vietnam War was escalating, squeezing research funds. There was no clear need for an airplane that could fly to orbit; rockets would do the job for as far into the future as anyone could see. Eugene Fubini, the Pentagon's director of research, had already canceled Aerospaceplane. Now Robert McNamara, the secretary of defense, decided that the Air Force would not continue to support research with the X-15.

That left the X-15 entirely in NASA's hands. This agency, with budget problems of its own, responded by sharply cutting back its planned schedule of flights. With this, the HRE effort had to change direction as well. Rather than focus on a flying test engine, this engine now would undergo testing only in wind tunnels.

Still, there was the opportunity do one more thing: to build a dummy HRE engine, with the proper size and shape but with no fuel-burning, and to mount it to the X-15 during a few of its fastest flights. Major William Knight was the pilot on the mission that set the speed record, as he took this rocket plane to 4,520 miles per hour, or Mach 6.7. "It was a very exhilarating flight," he recalls. "I didn't have much time to look out the window; the maximum altitude was one hundred thousand feet. The view from the altitude flights—two hundred and fifty thousand, three hundred thousand feet—was much more impressive. But this was the culmination of a test pilot's profession, in terms of 'this is the ultimate and I am one who has been selected to do this.'"

Knight was flying full tilt into unexplored realms, and he encountered an unusual form of aerodynamic heating. Superhot air burned through the lower fin that was supporting the dummy scramjet. "We burned the engine off," he continues. "I was on my way back to Edwards Air Force Base; my concern was to get the airplane back in one piece. I didn't know I had lost the engine at all."

It was symbolic of the rapidly diminishing fortunes of the leaders who had pursued the scramjet in its days of promise: Ferri, Billig, Thomas, Du Pont. They had hoped to be pioneers, inventors who could open up a new road into space. They all had dedicated their professional lives to this. But with the demise of Aerospaceplane and the redirection of the HRE into ground test, these visionaries now faced a kind of professional limbo. They had to find other things to do, even as they worked to keep alive their vision of flight without limits.

Antonio Ferri was the first to face this. Aerospaceplane had been GASL's mainstay; when that was lost, he left the firm. New York University recruited him, offering him an endowed professorship. In the spring of 1967 he took this new appointment. He proceeded to build a new supersonic-research lab, this one in the Bronx. Yet as one of his colleagues recalls, "He felt he was only half a researcher. His love was to do experiments." But his facilities in the Bronx were far less extensive than those he had used at GASL, and his opportunities were correspondingly reduced.

For Marquardt's Art Thomas it was worse. "I was chief engineer and assistant general manager," he recalls. "I got laid off. We laid off two-thirds of our people in one day." No one else had a scramjet group that he might join, but he hoped for the next-best thing: conventional ramjets, powering high-speed missiles. "I went all over the country. Everything in ramjet missiles had collapsed." Solid-fuel rockets had taken their place. He had to settle for a job working with turbojets, at McDonnell Douglas in St. Louis.

Fred Billig was able to go forward, but he had less to start with. His research group had never been a major participant in either Aerospaceplane or HRE. The Navy kept him going; his sponsors thought that someday they might want scramjet-powered missiles, so they kept him around, just in case. At times he had only enough money to support a handful of people in his group, but he kept plugging ahead.

Tony Du Pont also did not give up. He proceeded to invent a new type of scramjet, one that could take off from the ground under its own power. Takeoff was a real problem; the scramjet needed a boost to around Mach 3 before it could begin to give thrust. This demanded auxiliary propulsion. For Aerospaceplane this had taken the form of turbojets, but these were heavy and represented dead weight when not in use. Du Pont proposed to provide this initial boost using a clever arrangement of rockets, heat exchangers, and fuel injectors. He patented his concept and set up his own consulting firm, Du Pont Aerospace, hoping to win NASA or Air Force support.

He went forward with what came to hand. "We did whatever we could," he recalls. "Some years I could bring in consulting income." At every turn, he promoted his scramjet that could take off from the ground. As one of NASA's managers recalls, "He aggressively peddled this proposal throughout NASA, to the congressional staffs, to the Nixon

White House staff, and elsewhere. He was a skillful and brilliant sales-man and manipulator of arguments."

He didn't get very far. By the late 1970s he was reduced to building a small model of his boost-at-takeoff apparatus, using wood and plexi-glas. He tested it in a friend's backyard, using an air compressor that he bought at Sears. By then he was becoming well known at the Pentagon's Defense Advanced Research Projects Agency (DARPA), where he hoped to win funding. He wanted to build a larger version of this backyard en-gine to test at GASL, but even this seemed out of reach.

Did these people ever doubt the value of their work? "Never," says Billig. One of Ferri's longtime colleagues gives the same answer: "Never. He always had faith." These people had full confidence in the scramjet, but they had to overcome the doubts of others and find backers who would give them new funding. From time to time a small opportunity appeared. Then, as Billig recalls, "we were highly competitive. Who was going to get the last bits of money? As money got tighter, competition got stronger. I hope it was a friendly competition, but each of us thought he could do the job best."

Amid this dark night of hypersonic research, one small candle still flickered. This was the Hypersonic Propulsion Branch at NASA-Langley, which continued to conduct wind-tunnel experiments with the HRE. In the early 1970s even this work faded, but the Langley group did not give up the scramjet. Instead they launched a new research effort, albeit with very low funding. They arranged to carry out wind-tunnel tests of new experimental scramjets, at speeds up to Mach 7. The engines were small, but they were the real thing.

This new effort brought Ferri back into the scramjet world. A cor-porate reshuffle brought the return of GASL to its original owners, in-cluding Ferri, who came back in 1972 as its president. GASL had stayed alive doing whatever came to hand: pollution studies, coal-combustion studies, high-speed trains, low-drag wings. But Ferri wanted to lead the firm back into scramjets. He succeeded in winning the NASA contract to design and fabricate the small new scramjets for Langley. It wasn't much, not after the high hopes of Aerospaceplane. But at least Ferri and his closest associates were once again doing the work they loved. Ferri nevertheless did not enjoy it for long. He died late in 1975, struck by a heart attack at age sixty-three.

Billig, Thomas, Du Pont, and Ferri had been keepers of the flame, nurturing and holding to the idea of the scramjet across a number of lean years. But after 1980, circumstances changed dramatically. Their flame blazed anew and became a powerful fire, as scramjets came again to the forefront.

An important reason lay in Air Force dissatisfaction with the space shuttle. It made its first flight in April 1981, but it was a NASA launch vehicle, which meant the Air Force didn't control it. A senior technical director, General Lawrence Skantze, responded with a study of rocket-powered craft that might prove suitable as replacements—and was highly dissatisfied with the results. Later, when presented with the concept of the scramjet, he embraced it with open arms.

The director of DARPA, Robert Cooper, also was interested in new ideas. He wanted to build new experimental aircraft. One such effort was already under way: the X-29, with a highly innovative array of wing designs, control systems, and advanced materials. Cooper was open to suggestions regarding other such projects.

In addition, the early 1980s were years of President Reagan's defense buildup. The Pentagon had plenty of money, and was receptive to new proposals. Reagan himself became a strong booster of space projects. He showed this by taking the lead in launching the space-based Strategic Defense Initiative, for defense against Soviet missiles. He also supported NASA's plan for a space station.

The technical scene offered new opportunities as well. Scramjets had faced a serious obstacle, for there was no way to build wind tunnels that were speedy enough to test them during their development. But the rise of supercomputers, with advanced computer programs in aerody-namics, offered a way out. Existing high-speed wind tunnels might test and validate the correctness of these "flow codes"—and these codes, running on the supercomputers, in turn could calculate solutions that would assess the merits of a scramjet design. In addition, the NASA-Langley researchers had gained success. They had demonstrated by ex-periment that their small scramjets from GASL could operate properly even under highly demanding conditions.

General Skantze's studies proved critical, as he sought a next-generation shuttle. He was particularly interested in an air-breathing launch vehicle, but no suitable engines existed, even on paper. Du Pont thought that his engine might help, and learned that Tony Tether was the DARPA man who was attending the pertinent meetings. Du Pont met several times with Tether, who finally decided to send him up to talk with the boss, Robert Cooper. Cooper listened to Du Pont and then asked one of DARPA's best aerodynamicists to check him out.

Cooper's man, Robert Williams, was a longtime Navy expert in heli-copters. He also had a wide range of interests, particularly in high-speed flight. He was interested in the Outer Air Battle missile, a proposed tac-tical weapon that might use a scramjet. This had brought him into discussions with Billig, who had educated him. As a result, Williams became known within DARPA as the man to talk to if anyone was interested in scramjets.

He had his own hopes for air-breathing flight to orbit, but no one he knew could tell him of an engine that could do it. William Escher, a Marquardt man who had nurtured ideas similar to Du Pont's, recalls a lengthy phone conversation in which he was unable to satisfy Williams's hopes—a phone call in which Williams had become so engrossed that he missed an airline connection. Williams now raised this issue with Du Pont.

He telephoned Du Pont and said, "I've got a very ambitious problem for you. If you think the airplane can do this, perhaps we can promote a program. Cooper has asked me to check you out." "He gave me three days," Du Pont recalls. "I stayed up all night; I was more and more intrigued with this. Finally, around 7:30 A.M., I called him back: 'Okay, Bob, it's not impossible. Now what?'"

Du Pont had spent that night making calculations; Williams responded by giving him $30,000 to prepare a report. Soon Williams was talking with Art Thomas: "How'd you like to work on hydrogen-powered scramjets?" "Hydrogen!" Thomas replied. "You've got to be out of your mind! There's no application!" "Well, I'm not so sure," said Williams. "I have a report. . . . " It was Du Pont's. This started a snowballing process, for Du Pont's conclusions were encouraging enough to permit Williams to go to his management and break loose more funding, to sponsor more research.

This new work fitted in with ongoing DARPA activity that was seeking temperature-resistant alloys that might see use in a spaceplane. Late in 1983, Cooper convened a classified meeting near San Diego, as a number of specialists spent several days discussing air-breathing flight to orbit. "I went into that meeting with a high degree of skepticism," Cooper recalls. However, the technical presentations brought him around: "For each major problem, there were three or four plausible ways to deal with it. That's extraordinary. Usually, it's—Well, we don't know exactly how we'll do it, but we'll do it. Or, We have *a* way to do it, which may work. It was really a surprise to me; I couldn't pick any obvious holes in what they had done. I could find no reason why they couldn't go forward."

This brought an expanded program of studies and analyses during 1984, a $5.5 million effort known as Copper Canyon. Its conclusions appeared promising, and Cooper elected to seek funding for a full-blown program. Williams spent much of 1985 giving briefings to senior federal officials, working to win their support. One of the most important of these meetings came in July 1985, when Cooper accompanied Williams as they gave a presentation to General Skantze himself.

They gave their talk within a darkened office, projecting viewgraphs on a wall. As Cooper recalls, "He took one look at our concept and said, Yeah, that's what I meant. I invented that idea." He certainly did not invent the scramjet, but he had come to understand that he wanted something like it—and here it was. "His enthusiasm came from the fact that this was all he had anticipated," Cooper continues. "He felt as if he owned it." His support was vital, for he headed the Air Force Systems Command, which dealt with advanced technology.

He wanted more than viewgraphs; he wanted to see Du Pont's engine on a test stand. Funds from Copper Canyon had allowed Du Pont to build a small version that was under test at GASL, and Skantze wanted to go there and watch. "I called in my motley crew of technologists," says Williams. "We had a countdown for our engine run. A young technician got a little too excited and forgot to throw the igniter switch. Hydrogen poured into the engine. Then, realizing his mistake a little too late, he threw the igniter switch—into a very hydrogen-rich mixture inside the engine. There was a very strong detonation. The thrust gauge went slamming off scale amid a tremendous roar from the engine. I jumped about two feet in the air. The general remarked, 'This engine sure does develop thrust, doesn't it!'"

With this, Williams adds, "the Air Force system began to move with the speed of a spaceplane. In literally a week and a half, the entire Air Force senior command was briefed." Later that year the secretary of defense, Caspar Weinberger, granted a briefing. Members of Weinberger's staff were there, along with senior people from NASA and the military services. Williams brought a blue-and-white model of a spaceplane, with a needle nose and wings that resembled fins on a dart.

Weinberger had just returned from a meeting in Brussels, and still was weary from jet lag. Williams recalls that as he started his briefing, "I was appalled to see that the secretary was very tired. I grabbed the spaceplane model and slid it across the table, almost impaling him and somewhat alarming his staff." Williams certainly had no thoughts of harming Weinberger: "I was determined that he get a good look at the model.

"We finished our briefing," Williams continues. "There was silence in the room. The secretary said, 'Interesting,' and turned to his staff. Of course, all the groundwork had been laid. All of the people there had been briefed, and we could go for a yes-or-no decision. We had essentially total unanimity around the table, and he decided that the program would proceed as a major Defense Department initiative. With this, we moved immediately to issue requests for proposals to industry."

Weinberger had the clout to make this commitment, for there was support at the White House as well. Williams had met with Reagan's science adviser, George Keyworth, who had responded with enthusiasm. When Reagan prepared his State of the Union message, which he delivered early in 1986, Keyworth was among the presidential appointees who contributed to it. Reagan then declared that he personally supported this new initiative, called the National Aerospace Plane (NASP).

It would be pleasant to state that with this broad base of endorsement, this NASP program went ahead with strong budgets and solid success. It did no such thing, for from Day One, it had rested on optimism. Du Pont was the chief optimist, winning strong support from Williams. Indeed, the main point of the Copper Canyon studies had been to come up with concepts and results that would vindicate Du Pont's conclusions. Williams was quite firm on that point; he committed himself totally to Du Pont's ideas, and established them as the baseline. When other contractors responded with doubts, Williams replied that if people worked hard enough, they could achieve Du Pont's goals.

Billig disagreed. He knew a great deal about inlets, which were to play an essential role. A scramjet inlet was to capture the onrushing hypersonic airflow, compress it while slowing it somewhat, and channel it to the combustor that burned the fuel. Billig had been studying such inlets since his days with the Friden calculator, back in the 1950s, and he insisted that Du Pont's claims for inlet efficiency were out of reach. For this and for similar sins, Williams froze him out of the program, even though Billig was among the nation's most knowledgeable scramjet specialists.

Some of the nation's best designers avoided NASP entirely. Ben Rich of Lockheed, who had succeeded Kelly Johnson as head of the Skunk Works, attended the 1983 conference near San Diego. Even so, six years later he still was saying, "I've never seen a scramjet producing net thrust." Scott Crossfield, who had ridden to glory with the Douglas Skyrocket and who later flew the X-15, met with Johnson and told him that he was working on NASP. The following discussion ensued:

JOHNSON: Separate yourself from that damn thing.

CROSSFIELD: Kelly, you told me that about the X-15.

JOHNSON: Yes, seemed like I did. That turned out pretty well,
             didn't it?

CROSSFIELD: I remember when you said, all it would do is prove the bravery of the pilot.

JOHNSON: Yes, I did say that, didn't I? I remember that meeting.

Yet while Johnson did not press his criticism with Crossfield, who was an old friend, he remained unconvinced.

Other experienced people—Marquardt's Artur Mager, Princeton University's Seymour Bogdanoff—insisted that Du Pont was wrong when he dreamed of a lightweight vehicle that would fly to orbit using relatively little fuel. They insisted that the overall performance would fall short of Du Pont's hopes, and that this vehicle would need far more fuel, making it considerably heavier and more costly.

This point was critical, for NASP had won support on the basis of Du Pont's estimates. Its promise did not lie in the hope of winning success someday, after everyone had retired. Instead, Cooper had drawn on the work of Copper Canyon and had touted the idea of a spaceplane that could be ready in as little as three years. As time passed and as further work tended to support the skeptics, NASP lost favor and its budget came under attack.

Late in 1987, Williams became convinced that he needed someone with clout to stave off cuts in his funding. He worked his way up the chain of command, but found no one who would help him. There was a reason: the Air Force secretary, Edward Aldridge, endorsed the cuts and anticipated further budget reductions as well. In desperation, Williams wrote a letter to White House Chief of Staff Howard Baker, asking him to have Reagan help.

The letter never reached Reagan; instead, Baker sent it onward to the new head of DARPA, Robert Duncan. Duncan knew insubordination when he saw it, and quickly decided that Williams had to be fired. This suited the Air Force; it was paying most of the cost of NASP, but this program was in the hands of DARPA. Williams's replacement was indeed an Air Force man, Robert Barthelemy, who had been a senior technical director at Wright-Patterson Air Force Base. He did not love Du Pont, whose influence swiftly faded.

The coming of the Bush administration, early in 1989, launched a round of cutbacks in the defense budget. The leading champions of hypersonics—Cooper, Skantze, Williams—now were gone from government or were greatly reduced in influence. Their successors and other senior people, particularly within the Air Force, had much less interest in this field. Soon after taking office, Defense Secretary Richard Cheney presented a plan to terminate Air Force involvement in NASP, turning over whatever might be left of it to NASA.

Anthony Du Pont's initial National Aerospace Plane concept, circa 1985, showed a slender shape. (NASA)

At this point, a paper from the Rand Corporation titled "Assessment of NASP: Future Options" proved to have significant influence. The Rand Corporation was a think tank that for decades had helped to shape Pentagon policy. The authors of this paper, Bruno Augenstein and Elwyn Harris, argued that NASP should not be pursued with an eye toward development of operational hypersonic craft in the relatively near future. They pointed instead to a number of important NASP technologies: advanced propulsion, new materials and structures, new ways to use computers in design and analysis. They declared that these would be pertinent to both future military and civilian aircraft.

This represented a call for a program aimed at developing new and broadly useful technology, rather than one that focused on a near-term spaceplane. It appears to have swayed Air Force Secretary Donald Rice, a longtime president of Rand. It also drew interest within the National Space Council, headed by Vice President Dan Quayle. During the summer of 1989, the Space Council made recommendations that the Air Force accepted. The redefined program thus won a few more years of life.

Still, NASP all along had emphasized the development of a new experimental airplane, the X-30, which was to fly to orbit. During the mid 1980s, with Du Pont riding high, Cooper had envisioned it at around

50,000 pounds, the weight of a fighter plane. When Williams met with Weinberger and slid his model down the table, that model had a slender shape, reflecting the expectation that it would need only a modest fuel supply. But as estimates of its performance fell off, designers responded by making it fat with fuel. The configuration of 1990 resembled a pregnant whale and called for a weight of as much as 300,000 pounds. Soon, this too appeared optimistic. Program officials considered that to reach orbit, the X-30 would need a loaded weight of at least 550,000 pounds.

The program cost and schedule expanded accordingly. Estimates of 1986 had declared that the X-30 would cost $3.1 billion, with flight tests beginning in 1993. When that year arrived, the cost estimate was five times greater, at $15 billion or more, and Air Force officials were hoping for first flight in 2004. This represented a slip of eleven years from the 1986 plan, put forth only seven years earlier.

The X-30 never got off the drawing board; its designers built nothing larger than a fuel tank. NASP itself went no further than to test experimental scramjets in wind tunnels. Nor did it last long. It withered away amid further budget cuts, with participants delivering last rites early in 1995.

Nevertheless, hope springs eternal, and the scramjet still may see its day. It is a remarkable fact that despite decades of research, no scramjet has actually flown under NASA or Pentagon auspices. But that is about to change. A new NASA program called Hyper-X is about to achieve the first test flight of a working engine in an experimental aircraft, the X-43.

The flight-test program is quite limited, calling for two flights at Mach 7 and one at Mach 10. The vehicle is only twelve feet long and will ride a Pegasus rocket to the test speed. The scramjet engine will then burn for only around seven seconds. Yet there is a reason why these tests are to be both brief and few: the scramjet community already holds high confidence that such engines can be built to work as planned.

This confidence stands as a legacy of NASP. It stems from close agreement between data taken from wind tunnels and computational simulations. The breakthrough that underpins this confidence is the advent of good mathematical models that capture the details of hypersonic flow. The power of these computer programs, which calculate those details, enables NASA to learn much from only a few flights of the X-43. Those flights are to supply experimental data that will be compared with the computed results, and NASA's researchers anticipate good agreement.

A successful X-43 program will show that radically new flight vehicles, as well as their engines, can be successfully designed by relying on computers. As the power of these computers continues to grow, designers will introduce improvements aimed at boosting the performance of

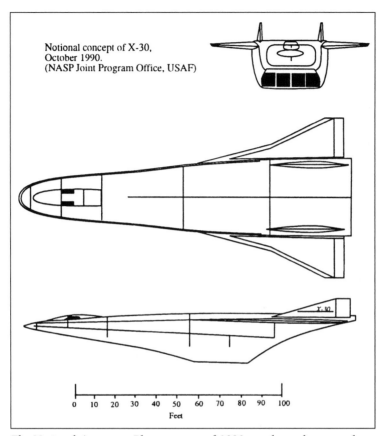

Notional concept of X-30,
October 1990.
(NASP Joint Program Office, USAF)

The National Aerospace Plane concept of 1990 was large, heavy, and fat. (U.S. Air Force)

scramjets—and will see if they can succeed. Meanwhile, other researchers will continue to push the development of the advanced materials that will go into actual aircraft.

The scramjet, and its prospect of air-breathing flight to orbit, stands today as an unsolved issue for the new century. Despite decades of research, no one today can demonstrate credibly that this ultimate airplane can be built in an attractive form, inexpensive and modest in size. Yet the experience of NASP seems to show that even if such a design is not yet in view, it lies just over the technical horizon. The keepers of the flame are older now; soon they will be gone. But the concept of the scramjet remains alive, ready to entice a new generation.

A Look Ahead

About fifteen years ago, I had the pleasure of writing a speculative book chapter on the subject of World War III, setting it in the year 2018. I did not envision that by then the Soviet Union and its Eastern European empire would have long since ceased to exist; my imagination was not that vivid. I therefore presented this war as an armed conflict between the superpowers, centering on a Soviet tank invasion of West Germany. However, this war did not escalate to a nuclear exchange. Instead of being fought with weapons of mass destruction, the combatants relied on weapons of discrete and precise destruction. As in 1943, Hamburg received heavy blows:

> The city had also been crippled by the air strikes of July 2018. But at war's end, one could fly over Hamburg and scarcely see any damage. At first glance, the port appeared untouched—until you noticed the twisted masses of steel beams that had been the cranes for container ships, essential for the port's operation. Tugboats lay blasted and sunk. The port captain's office was flattened. Railroad bridges and highway overpasses lay crumpled; the airport's runways and control tower looked like the cratered surface of an asteroid. But that was it. The residential and office districts had been completely untouched.
>
> Much the same was true in other cities. In Cologne, the Rhine bridges lay in the river as piles of steel junk, but there was no other damage. Near Wyhl, further up the Rhine, was a nuclear power plant. Its transformer yard had been blown to pieces, its administration building was a wreck—but the reactor domes had merely been nicked by shrapnel. In Munich there had been a central telecommunications building, which now lay destroyed as by a wrecker's ball. In the adjacent buildings, windows had been broken by the concussions; and that was all.[1]

This form of warfare first came to public notice late in the Vietnam War, when the Air Force used precision-guided bombs that homed in on an illuminated spot made by a laser. These weapons destroyed bridges in Hanoi that were strongly defended and had withstood attacks using standard munitions. Such "smart bombs" were useful, but they required a plane and its pilot to fly in harm's way. They also called for skill in marking the target with the laser while avoiding antiaircraft fire.

Standoff weapons, capable of being fired from a distance, addressed these issues. They took shape as cruise missiles such as the Navy's Tomahawk. They navigated by computer, using a radar altimeter and a map of the terrain stored in memory. Cruisers and other warships could carry them in substantial numbers, while aircraft could launch them as well.

Such weapons remained few in number during the war with Iraq in 1991. The bomb tonnage still was mainly unguided types that might have been left over from World War II. Yet these precision munitions had an impact vastly disproportionate to their numbers. They took out specific targets in downtown Baghdad; they destroyed antiaircraft sites and command centers. They contributed markedly to the U.S. victory.

In turn, this victory made a powerful impression on other countries in the region. They had watched Iraq and Iran battle to a standstill during a war that spanned most of the 1980s. Both nations were well armed with modern weapons; yet they had achieved nothing more than stalemate. Then the United States sent its expeditionary force, building it from scratch in no more than a few months. It crushed the Iraqis outright, winning complete victory with very little loss of American life.

In Kosovo during 1999, Yankee power won even stronger success. Whereas the Gulf War had featured a major invasion of Iraq by ground forces, this intervention in the Balkans relied entirely upon air strikes. President Clinton took the view that the American people had no stomach for combat casualties; pilots therefore were ordered to stay out of danger, although this compromised their effectiveness. But this air war, relying heavily upon smart weapons, forced the invading Serbs to retreat—without the loss of a single American.

The aircraft that deliver such ordnance will bear comparison to those of World War II. During that war, the B-17 counted as a heavy bomber. It was a large airplane with four engines and a crew of ten, and weighed up to fifty thousand pounds when fully loaded with fuel and munitions. Today's F-16 fighter is a single-engine plane flown by a single pilot, with a maximum loaded weight of forty-two thousand pounds. This approaches the weight of that B-17; yet the F-16 counts as a light-weight fighter. Standard-size fighters—the F-14, the F-15 and the F/A-18—range up to eighty-one thousand pounds. They carry substantial weapons loads, and can fly two or three missions in a day where the B-17 often flew two or three in a week.

These fighters all carry precision-guided weapons, launching them from standoff distances of some fifty miles. The accuracy of these munitions raises the effectiveness of their air strikes enormously. The bombers of World War II were quite good at burning cities to the ground, but when it came to hitting specific targets, they often did far more poorly.

For instance, as noted earlier, the Germans had a plant in Norway that was supporting their atomic-bomb research. One hundred forty B-17s dropped seven hundred bombs, which did some damage but missed the main building entirely. The British also conducted a night raid on Peenemünde, the German center for rocket and missile development. They missed the main facilities and killed plenty of workers, but only one top rocket scientist. The Americans hammered Schweinfurt with its ball-bearing factories, but failed to disrupt this industry—while sustaining unacceptable combat losses.

Precision weapons would have made short work of any of these targets. To continue to deliver them, the Pentagon is proceeding with two new aircraft: the Lockheed Martin F-22 and the Joint Strike Fighter. Critics have questioned the need for such programs, noting that today's planes are effective enough. But the Navy's F-14, a mainstay of the carrier fleet, is thirty years old, while the F-15 and F-16 are only slightly younger. The Russians have lost the Cold War but nevertheless remain active. Their new Sukhoi-27 fighter can outfly these aircraft, and Moscow is in a position to sell this warplane to America's adversaries.

The F-22, an air superiority fighter, will soon go into production, entering service in November 2005. Plans call for building 348 of them. Its supporters declare that it will require only twenty minutes for turnaround between missions. It also is to win advantage through stealth, maneuverability, and "supercruise."

Supercruise means supersonic cruise without use of an afterburner. Afterburners use a great deal of fuel; fighters have been flying with them for decades, but their thirst for fuel has limited these warplanes to only brief bursts of supersonic flight. The F-22 is to fly at these speeds routinely. It will do this by relying on new engines that combine high thrust with light weight.

Stealth is to be another strong point, allowing the F-22 to avoid detection by radar. Stealthy designs have tantalized the Air Force since the 1970s. The Lockheed F-117A, a product of the Skunk Works, pushed stealth to the limit; its designers started with a highly irregular shape that had good radar-evading properties and crafted it into an airplane. The F-22 does not go so far, for it looks like other modern fighters. But it achieves its own stealthiness, in part through extensive use of composites in its structure—which also save weight.

The Joint Strike Fighter is even newer. Lockheed Martin and Boeing are competing for the contract award, with both firms having built flying prototypes; because Lockheed already has the F-22, Boeing is likely to win the JSF. It will be tomorrow's lightweight fighter, serving the Air Force, the Navy, and the Marines, while replacing the F-16 and all but the newest versions of the F/A-18. Maneuverability is to be its strong suit; by swiveling the thrust of its engines, it will gain exceptional ability in the air and will be able to land vertically. Plans call for it to enter service in 2008, with up to three thousand of these fighters being built during subsequent decades.

While existing aircraft such as the F/A-18 continue to receive significant upgrades, the F-22 and JSF show that technology continues to advance in ways that justify entirely new designs. Nevertheless, today's situation contrasts markedly with that of the postwar decades. Jet propulsion brought a rapid succession of new fighters that pushed the frontiers of flight beyond Mach 2. Planebuilders of the 1960s and 1970s crafted the large versions that fly today; the 1980s brought the F-117A and its stealth. But while the F-22 and JSF will receive their own upgrades in time, it may be half a century before there is enough new technology to support another new fighter, crafted from scratch.

For bombers, this maturation has already occurred. After 1945, it took less than a decade before the Air Force received the first B-52s, eight-engine jet bombers with intercontinental range. Later versions approached half a million pounds in maximum loaded weight. After that, the situation remained essentially frozen for some thirty years. The 1980s brought the Rockwell B-1B and Northrop's B-2, both of which are now out of production. It will be a long time before the next truly new bomber takes to the skies.

The B-52 was a large but rather plain design, fast for its day but lacking supersonic speed along with any semblance of stealth. Boeing built 744 of them between 1952 and 1962. Many of them have long since been recycled into beer cans; the aluminum-can industry uses ten times more of this metal per year than the aircraft industry. But a few dozen B-52s remain in service. They carry cruise missiles with a range of seven hundred miles. They also are useful in carpet bombing, laying down swaths of nonnuclear destruction that recall those of World War II.

The B-2, the stealth bomber, echoes the F-117A in placing stealth above all else. It is a flying wing, a shape that gives a very poor radar return. It is crafted from composites, which are far stealthier than aluminum, and it uses a radar-absorbing coating. This coating demands continuing maintenance, but the analyst John Pike declares that "when properly maintained, the stealth bomber is profoundly difficult for radars to track." The Air Force calls this bomber the Spirit: It's there, but you can't see it.

The B-1B Lancer—another splendid name—is more conventional in appearance. It flies supersonically and looks like a fighter plane, but its top weight of 477,500 pounds matches that of a large wide-body airliner. It lacks the exotic shape and materials of the B-2, but it also is stealthy. Its radar signature is only one percent of that of a B-52, which has wings and tail surfaces that stand out like a barn.

During 1945, the Allies struck at Berlin with over a thousand heavy bombers during individual raids. By contrast, today's bomber force is noted for being few in number. In addition to the small remaining force of active B-52s, there are fewer than a hundred B-1Bs, along with only twenty-one B-2s. (Each B-2 is named for a state of the Union, like a battleship.) However, the use of smart weapons again means that each of these bombers is extraordinarily capable.

These limited numbers are associated with high cost. The B-2 program set records in this respect, as it came to $45 billion, over $2 billion for each warplane. This paid for the extensive staffs of people who generated the paperwork necessary to cope with its unfamiliar technology and novel manufacturing methods; at its peak, the B-2 program was churning out a million sheets of paper per day. The F-22 program is doing better, with a current estimate of $64 billion for its 348 airplanes. Still, this tops $180 million per aircraft.

A single word justifies such costs: survivability, the ability to avoid being shot down in today's combat environment. Philip Klass, a longtime military specialist at *Aviation Week,* notes that today's warplanes all can carry nuclear weapons as well as smart bombs, making it far more desirable to knock them down. At the same time, antiaircraft missiles make it far easier to destroy them, rendering survivability more difficult. Klass notes that the United States couldn't field a force of a hundred thousand F-80s from the Korean War; they wouldn't be survivable.

Advanced electronics represent a large share of the cost of new military aircraft, and their importance continues to increase. Some people say that the warplane of the future will be fully automatic, and will have a pilot in the cockpit—along with a dog. The pilot will be there to feed the dog; the dog will bite the pilot if he should try to touch the controls. However, military electronics are expensive. You can buy a fine home computer at Radio Shack that is quite affordable, but this low cost results from spreading the costs of development and of production facilities over millions of units. Military electronics are far more demanding.

Yet when specialized packages must serve as few as twenty-one B-2s, or a hundred B-1Bs, there is no way to spread this over a large and ongoing production run.

Modern warplanes can take decades to germinate. The B-1B existed as a well-considered prototype design as early as 1970, but amid the vacillations of political leaders, it did not reach production until the early 1980s. In service, this bomber and other warplanes must operate for additional decades. Meanwhile, potential enemies continue to advance in their own capabilities, which leads to major design changes that drive up program costs. That is why there are overruns.

Klass notes that "if you are a colonel in charge of developing the next fighter, you go to the CIA and you say, 'What kind of Russian fighters will we face in twenty years?' You design to meet that threat. Then the CIA says, 'No, the threat will be like this. We've seen this new fighter at Ramenskoye'—Moscow's flight-test center—'and it's twice as fast as we'd believed.' What do you do? Do you stick with your original design, which now is no longer survivable? Or do you go to a larger, more powerful engine and greater capability? Of course, you do the latter—and then it gets entered as a cost overrun."[2]

The world of commercial airliners brings its own issues. As recently as thirty years ago, the United States had three strong builders of jetliners: Lockheed, McDonnell Douglas, and Boeing. Today only Boeing remains, with Lockheed having abandoned the civilian world and with the remnants of the commercial programs of Douglas having gone over to Boeing. Yet these Seattle planebuilders now face stronger competition than before, from Airbus Industrie. This European consortium, centered on France's firm of Aerospatiale, draws strength from subsidies received from its member governments. In recent years, it has given Boeing quite a run for its money.

In the commercial realm, the strength of a planebuilder lies in its ability to offer aircraft covering all important combinations of range and passenger capacity. Boeing today indeed covers the field, from its small short-range 717 and 737 twinjets to the 747-400, which carries 421 passengers across the Pacific nonstop. Airbus still cannot truly match the 747-400, but it comes close. Its A-340 offers long range along with up to 380 seats. In all other categories of design, the two firms compete directly.

Both firms continue to sell substantial numbers of their small twinjets. However, their most significant competition involves wide-body airliners only slightly smaller than the 747-400. Boeing has introduced its 777, a big twin-engine wide-body with 305 to 328 seats, depending on the layout. Airbus has responded with its A-330/340, which amount to two jetliners in one. The A-330 again has two engines and carries up to 295 passengers, making it only slightly smaller than the 777. The A-340 is a 330 with two additional engines; it resembles earlier versions of the 747.

These companies expect to maintain their competition for decades, as they struggle to win market share. Boeing's 747-400 gives it an advantage, for this airliner is highly prized, and the Seattleites have considerable freedom to name their price: up to $177 million. Profits at Boeing from the 747-400 then permit price cuts when wooing customers for the 777 and other aircraft. Airbus lacks such an ace in the hole, but its subsidies enable it to win customers by offering its own price cuts. For decades to come, these aircraft will be familiar sights at our airports. Advanced versions of the 777 may remain in production until 2050, with some of these planes catching the rays of the sun on the first morning of the twenty-second century.

What of future designs? Since 1960, two prospects have drawn continuing attention: the supersonic transport (SST) and the very large four-engine wide-body. The Concorde remains in service to this day, built in very limited numbers but continuing to cross the Atlantic at Mach 2. But prospects for a next-generation SST are far more problematical, for people remember the last American attempt. It foundered on the shoals of a surging environmental movement, and no one cares to repeat this experience.

Boeing tried to build this SST, which was to fly at Mach 3. It drew on technology from recent military projects—the Navaho missile, the XB-70 bomber, the SR-71—all of which approached or exceeded this speed. No one at the time had ever heard of an environmental impact statement, for no law required them. Even so, Boeing demanded and received federal funding for 90 percent of its development cost. When Congress canceled the program by refusing to vote additional funds, this SST effort vanished like the morning dew.

Environmentalists opposed it because its supersonic flight promised to produce sonic booms, sudden loud blasts of sound that people found unacceptable. Moreover, there was great concern that exhaust from its engines would damage the ozone layer in the upper atmosphere, which absorbs cancer-causing ultraviolet rays from the sun. A third source of opposition came from the noise of those engines, which critics declared would be fifty times louder than that of a 747.

A modern SST might serve the lucrative transpacific market, which hardly existed during the 1960s. The 747-400 can take more than fourteen hours to cross the Pacific, while an SST could greatly shorten this time. And because the plane is flying over water, its sonic boom would not be heard. In addition, today there is reason to believe that new SST engines would not harm the ozone.

Nevertheless, the issue of noise remains. In commercial aviation, quiet engines are heavy, and design studies have shown that an SST could not carry this weight. To meet regulations that mandate low noise, such an airplane would either fall short in range, or would be unattractively heavy and costly. Hence, with the SST concept faltering even when merely studied on paper, no one nowadays is pushing to revive it. In this sense, the world was closer to an SST in 1960 than it is today, for no such program is now in prospect.

The four-engine behemoth has had considerably better prospects; it has existed since 1970, as the Boeing 747 family. Successful airplane designs tend to grow in the course of their lives, and the 747 indeed has done this. The well-known bump on its upper fuselage, which initially held little more than a cocktail lounge, has since grown into a true upper deck, carrying some sixty-nine passengers. Boeing retains the opportunity to stretch it further, into a full-length upper cabin. The 747 then would become a genuine twin-deck airliner, powered by new engines and fitted with a new wing.

At Airbus, executives are highly interested in challenging Boeing within this field. They know that Airbus would gain a powerful advantage by offering the world's largest airliner, particularly if it was a completely new design while Boeing had merely a new version of its old 747. Competition from such an aircraft would strike at Boeing's bottom line by forcing it to cut the price of its 747s, thus diminishing its freedom to offer sweet deals on its other airliners.

Airbus holds a detailed design for this jetliner, which it calls the A-3XX. It too would have two full-length decks, and would carry up to 656 passengers. The 1999–2000 edition of *Jane's All the World's Aircraft*, a standard reference, reports plans for development that would place the first of them in commercial service during 2005. Even so, there is excellent reason to expect that it will not amount to much.

Such a behemoth would make sense if airline traffic, domestic and international, tended to funnel between a modest number of gateways such as New York and London. High volume along their connecting routes then would dictate the construction of jetliners that would be large indeed. But the globe-spanning range of today's aircraft allows passengers to choose direct routings, such as nonstop flights from Los Angeles to Rome. Increasing demand for seats has led to increases in the size of the airplanes that serve such connections, but existing craft such as the A-340 and the 747-400 remain quite suitable.

The A-3XX would cost up to $12 billion to develop, and Airbus continues to wait in hope that the market, as it continues to grow, may one day support such an investment. The alternative is a program that would fail in this market, by selling too few airliners. Meanwhile, executives at Boeing have watched bemusedly as Airbus has slipped the start of development of its A-3XX from one year to the next.

With no SST in prospect, and with no behemoth immediately in sight, the airliners of today are likely to remain in production for quite some time to come. This suggests that what exists today is what will serve the future, and that there is no new thing under the sun. It also means that the commercial realm, like its military counterpart, is on the threshold of maturity. Like the railroad industry, which has seen little technical change since the advent of diesel locomotives, aviation as we see it today may persist with only modest technical advance during the coming half-century.

Notes

1 Beautiful Balloons

1. Gillispie, *Montgolfier*, p. 42.
2. Ibid., p. 62.
3. Kirschner, *Balloons*, p. 11.

2 Airplanes of the Mind

1. Cayley's paper is reprinted in Pritchard, *Cayley*, Appendix III.
2. Ibid., p. 206.

3 The Problem of Control

1. Vaeth, *Langley*, p. 45.
2. Moolman, *Kitty Hawk*, p. 94.
3. Jakab, *Visions*, p. 196.
4. Moolman, *Kitty Hawk*, p. 151.

4 Zeppelins

1. Robinson, *Giants*, p. 40.
2. Lehmann, *Zeppelin*, pp. 154–155.
3. Ibid., p. 164.

5 The Red Baron

1. Kilduff, *Richthofen*, p. 36.
2. Bowen, *Knights*, p. 25.
3. Kilduff, *Richthofen*, p. 49.
4. Ibid., pp. 55–56.
5. McKee, *Friendless*, p. 149.
6. Norman, *Air War*, p. 158.
7. Titler, *Red Baron*, frontispiece.

6 Visions of Air Power

1. Hezlet, *Aircraft*, p. 63.
2. Mansfield, *Vision*, p. 82.

7 Lindbergh

1. Lindbergh, *Spirit*, p. 463.
2. Berg, *Lindbergh*, p. 427.

8 Ships in the Sky

1. Edward R. Murrow, "I Can Hear It Now." Vol. I, 1933–1945. New York: Columbia Records, n.d.
2. Toland, *Ships*, p. 329.
3. *Aeronautical Journal*, October 1975, p. 445.

9 Night and Fog

1. McGregor, "Beam"; Smith, *Seat*, pp. 139–140.
2. Davenport, *Gyro!*, p. 112.
3. *Aeronautical Journal*, August 1976, p. 329
4. Langewiesche, *Blind*, pp. 73–74.
5. "MLS 21" (product literature), Allied-Signal, Bendix Avionics Division, Fort Lauderdale, Florida, November 1986.
6. Komons, *Bonfires*, p. 341.

10 Donald Douglas and His Airliners

1. *American Heritage of Invention and Technology*, Fall 1988, p. 6.

11 The Battle of Britain

1. *Los Angeles Times*, November 28, 1982, pt. v, p. 5.
2. Churchill, *Finest*, pp. 22, 193; Copeland, *Speeches*, pp. 460, 474.
3. Shirer, *Third Reich*, p. 990.
4. *Oxford Dictionary*, p. 150.

12 Yamamoto Fights at Sea

1. Prange, *Dawn*, p. 406.
2. Hall, *Lightning*, pp. 41, 199–200.

13 *"The War Is Over"*

1. Churchill, *Finest*, pp. 548–549.
2. Middlebrook, *Hamburg*, p. 95.
3. Ibid., p. 244; Rhodes, *Atomic*, p. 473.
4. Rhodes, *Atomic*, p. 474; Middlebrook, *Hamburg*, pp. 264–267, 269, 274, 276, 374.

14 *General Curtis LeMay*

1. LeMay and Kantor, *Mission*, p. 373.
2. Manchester, *Glory*, p. 373.
3. *American Heritage*, June 1995, p. 70.
4. Rhodes, *Atomic*, p. 732.
5. Allen and Polmar, *Downfall*, p. 286; Rhodes, *Atomic*, pp. 745–746.
6. Aeschylus, *Prometheus Bound*, Episode 4.

15 *Germans Invent the Jet*

1. Heinkel, *Stormy*, pp. 212, 213.
2. Ibid., p. 224.
3. Boyne and Lopez, *Jet Age*, p. 74.

16 *Howard Hughes*

1. Rummel, *Howard*, p. 5.

17 *Jack Northrop*

1. Coleman, *Northrop*, pp. 140–141.
2. Von Kármán and Edson, *Wind*, p. 175.

18 *Chuck Yeager*

1. Yeager and Janos, *Yeager*, p. 130.
2. Ibid., p. 180–181.
3. Crossfield and Blair, *Always*, p. 177.
4. Ibid., p. 183.

19 *The Quiet Rocket Man*

This chapter draws extensively on personal interviews with:

J. Leland Atwood	Colonel Edward
Eugene Bollay	Hall
Mrs. Jeanne Bollay	Sam Hoffman
Jim Broadston	Dale Myers
Paul Castenholz	Robert Truax
Tom Dixon	

20 *Clarence "Kelly" Johnson*

1. *Audacity*, Fall 1994, p. 23.
2. *Lockheed Horizons*, Winter 1981–1982, p. 9.
3. Personal interviews, Jim Eastham and Steve Grzebiniak.

21 *Launching the Commercial Jet Age*

1. Serling, *Legend*, pp. 70–71.

22 *Room at the Bottom*

1. Eddy, Porter, and Page, *Destination*, p. 54.
2. *Fortune*, March 1967, p. 224.

23 *King Lear*

This chapter draws extensively on personal interviews with:

Sam Auld	"Torch" Lewis
Linden Blue	Dave McClenahan
Roger Bratland	Bill Surbey
Robert Jacobsen	Richard Tracy
Moya Lear	Leo Windecker

24 Voyager

1. *Aerospace America*, June 1985, p. 72.
2. Yeager, Rutan, and Patton, *Voyager*, p. 37.

25 *Keepers of the Flame*

1. Hallion, *Hypersonic*, p. 951.
This chapter draws extensively on personal interviews with:

H. Lee Beach	William Knight
Fred Billig	Ernest Mackley
Robert Cooper	Louis Nucci
Scott Crossfield	Ben Rich
Tony Du Pont	Robert Sanator
John Erdos	Art Thomas
William Escher	Robert Williams

Afterword: *A Look Ahead*

1. Clarke, *2019*, p. 271.
2. Personal interview, Philip Klass.

Bibliography

Books and Reports

Allen, Frederick Lewis. *Only Yesterday*. New York: Harper and Row, 1931.

———. *Since Yesterday*. New York: Harper and Row, 1939.

Allen, Oliver. *The Airline Builders*. Alexandria, Va.: Time-Life Books, 1981.

Allen, Thomas B., and Norman Polmar. *Code-Name Downfall: The Secret Plan to Invade Japan and Why Truman Dropped the Bomb*. New York: Simon and Schuster, 1995.

Barker, Ralph. *The RAF at War*. Alexandria, Va.: Time-Life Books, 1981.

Bartlett, Donald L., and James B. Steele. *Empire: The Life, Legend and Madness of Howard Hughes*. New York: W. W. Norton, 1979.

Becker, Beril. *Dreams and Recollections of the Conquest of the Skies*. New York: Atheneum, 1967.

Becker, Carl. *Modern History*. Morristown, N.J.: Silver Burdett, 1958.

Belote, James H., and William M. Belote. *Titans of the Seas*. New York: Harper and Row, 1975.

Bender, Marylin, and Selig Altschul. *The Chosen Instrument*. New York: Simon and Schuster, 1982.

Berg, A. Scott. *Lindbergh*. New York: Putnam, 1998.

Biddle, Wayne. *Barons of the Sky*. New York: Simon and Schuster, 1991.

Botting, Douglas. *The Giant Airships*. Alexandria, Va.: Time-Life Books, 1981.

Bowen, Ezra. *Knights of the Air*. Alexandria, Va.: Time-Life Books, 1980.

Boyne, Walter. *The Aircraft Treasures of Silver Hill*. New York: Rawson Associates, 1982.

———. *Clash of Wings: Air Power in World War II*. New York: Simon and Schuster, 1994.

———. *Messerschmitt 262: Arrow to the Future*. Washington, D.C.: Smithsonian Institution Press, 1980.

Boyne, Walter, and Donald Lopez, eds. *The Jet Age*. Washington, D.C.: Smithsonian Institution Press, 1979.

Brickhill, Paul. *The Dam Busters*. New York: Ballantine, 1965.

Brooks, Peter W. *The Modern Airliner*. Manhattan, Kans.: Sunflower University Press, 1982.

———. *Zeppelin: Rigid Airships, 1893–1940*. Washington, D.C.: Smithsonian Institution Press, 1992.

Caidin, Martin. *Black Thursday*. New York: Ballantine, 1968.

Churchill, Winston. *Their Finest Hour*. New York: Bantam, 1962.

Clarke, Arthur C., ed. *Arthur C. Clarke's July 20, 2019: Life in the 21st Century.* New York: Macmillan, 1986.

Coffey, Thomas. *Iron Eagle: The Turbulent Life of General Curtis LeMay.* New York: Crown, 1986.

Coleman, Ted. *Jack Northrop and the Flying Wing.* New York: Paragon, 1988.

Constant, Edward. *The Origins of the Turbojet Revolution.* Baltimore: Johns Hopkins University Press, 1980.

Copeland, Lewis, ed. *The World's Great Speeches.* Garden City, N.Y.: Garden City Publishing, 1949.

Crickmore, Paul F. *Lockheed SR-71 Blackbird.* London: Osprey Publishing, 1986.

Crossfield, A. Scott, with Clay Blair Jr. *Always Another Dawn: The Story of a Rocket Test Pilot.* New York: World Publishing, 1960.

Crouch, Tom D. *The Bishop's Boys: A Life of Wilbur and Orville Wright.* New York: W. W. Norton, 1989.

———. *The Eagle Aloft: Two Centuries of the Balloon in America.* Washington, D.C.: Smithsonian Institution Press, 1983.

Daley, Robert. *An American Saga: Juan Trippe and His Pan Am Empire.* New York: Random House, 1980.

Davenport, William Wyatt. *Gyro! The Life and Times of Lawrence Sperry.* New York: Scribner, 1978.

Davies, R. E. G. *A History of the World's Airlines.* London: Oxford University Press, 1964.

———. *Airlines of the United States since 1914.* London: Putnam, 1972.

Dempster, Derek D. *The Tale of the Comet.* New York: David McKay, 1958.

Dependable Engines . . . since 1925. East Hartford, Conn.: Pratt & Whitney, 1990.

"Development of a Strategic Missile and Associated Projects." Report AL-1347, Los Angeles: Aerophysics Laboratory, North American Aviation, 1951.

Dwiggins, Don. *The Complete Book of Airships—Dirigibles, Blimps and Hot Air Balloons.* Blue Ridge Summit, Pa.: Tab Books, 1980.

Eddy, Paul, Elaine Porter, and Bruce Page. *Destination Disaster.* New York: Quadrangle/New York Times, 1976.

Ege, Lennard. *Balloons and Airships.* New York: Macmillan, 1974.

Fairlie, Gerard, and Elizabeth Cayley. *The Life of a Genius.* London: Hodder and Stoughton, 1965.

Galland, Adolf. *The First and the Last.* New York: Henry Holt, 1954.

Galloway, Jonathan F. *The Politics and Technology of Satellite Communications.* Lexington, Mass.: Lexington Books, 1972.

Gauvreau, Emile, and Lester Cohen. *Billy Mitchell.* New York: Dutton, 1942.

Gerber, Albert B. *Bashful Billionaire.* New York: Lyle Stuart, 1967.

Gibbs-Smith, Charles H. *Aviation: An Historical Survey from Its Origins to the End of World War II.* London: Her Majesty's Stationery Office, 1970.

———. *Ballooning.* London: Penguin Books, 1948.

———. *The Invention of the Aeroplane (1799–1909).* New York: Taplinger, 1965.

Gibson, James N. *The Navaho Missile Project.* Atglen, Pa.: Schiffer, 1996.

Gillispie, Charles C. *The Montgolfier Brothers and the Invention of Aviation.* Princeton, N.J.: Princeton University Press, 1983.

Godson, John. *The Rise and Fall of the DC-10.* New York: David McKay, 1975.

Graham, Margaret B. W., and Bettye H. Pruitt. *R and D for Industry: A Century of Technical Innovation at Alcoa.* New York: Cambridge University Press, 1990.

Green, Murray. "Stuart Symington and the B-36." Ph.D. diss., American University, Washington, D.C., 1960.

Gunston, Bill. *Fighters of the Fifties.* Osceola, Wis.: Specialty Press, 1981.

Hall, R. Cargill. *Lightning Over Bougainville.* Washington, D.C.: Smithsonian Institution Press, 1991.

Hallion, Richard, ed. *The Hypersonic Revolution: Case Studies in the History of Hypersonic Technology.* 3 vols. Bolling Air Force Base, Washington, D.C.: Air Force History and Museum Program, 1998.

———. *Legacy of Flight: The Guggenheim Contribution to American Aviation.* Seattle: University of Washington Press, 1977.

———. *On the Frontier: Flight Research at Dryden, 1946–1981.* NASA SP-4222. Washington, D.C.: U.S. Government Printing Office, 1984.

———. *The Wright Brothers: Heirs of Prometheus.* Washington, D.C.: National Air and Space Museum, 1978.

Hammond, Paul Y. *Super Carriers and B-36 Bombers: Appropriations, Strategy, and Politics.* New York: Bobbs-Merrill, 1963.

Hardy, M. J. *The Lockheed Constellation.* New York: Arco, 1973.

Heinkel, Ernst. *Stormy Life.* New York: Dutton, 1956.

Heppenheimer, T. A. *Hypersonic Technologies.* Arlington, Va.: Pasha, 1993.

———. *Hypersonic Technologies and the National Aerospace Plane.* Arlington, Va.: Pasha, 1990.

———. "Voyager: The Plane Flown 'Round the World." In *1989 Yearbook of Science and the Future,* ed. David Calhoun, pp. 142–159. Chicago: Encyclopaedia Britannica, 1988.

Hezlet, Vice Admiral Sir Arthur. *Aircraft and Sea Power.* New York: Stein and Day, 1970.

Howard, Fred. *Wilbur and Orville: A Biography of the Wright Brothers.* New York: Knopf, 1987.

Howarth, David. *The Dreadnoughts.* Alexandria, Va.: Time-Life Books, 1979.

Hudson, Heather E. *Communication Satellites.* New York: Free Press, 1990.

Hughes, Thomas Parke. *Elmer Sperry: Inventor and Engineer.* Baltimore: Johns Hopkins Press, 1971.

Hunley, J. D., ed. "Toward Mach 2: The Douglas D-558 Program." NASA SP-4222. Washington, D.C.: U.S. Government Printing Office, 1999.

Jackson, Robert. *Airships.* Garden City, N.Y.: Doubleday, 1973.

Jakab, Peter L. *Visions of a Flying Machine: The Wright Brothers and the Process of Invention.* Washington, D.C.: Smithsonian Institution Press, 1990.

Jane's All the World's Aircraft. 1999–2000 and earlier editions. Alexandria, Va.: Jane's Information Group, 1999 and earlier.

Jenkins, Dennis. *Messerschmitt 262 Sturmvogel.* North Branch, Minn.: Specialty Press, 1996.

Johnson, Clarence "Kelly," and Maggie Smith. *Kelly: More Than My Share of It All.* Washington, D.C.: Smithsonian Institution Press, 1989.

Keats, John. *Howard Hughes.* New York: Random House, 1966.

Keegan, John. *The Price of Admiralty.* New York: Viking, 1988.

Kelly, Fred G. *The Wright Brothers: A Biography.* New York: Dover, 1989.

Kennett, Lee. *A History of Strategic Bombing.* New York: Scribner, 1982.

Kilduff, Peter. *Richthofen: Beyond the Legend of the Red Baron.* New York: John Wiley and Sons, 1993.

Kirschner, Edwin J. *Aerospace Balloons from Montgolfière to Space.* Fallbrook, Calif.: Aero Publishers, 1985.

Komons, Nick. *Bonfires to Beacons: Federal Civil Aviation Policy Under the Air Commerce Act, 1926–1938.* Washington, D.C.: U.S. Government Printing Office, 1978.

Langewiesche, Wolfgang. "Flying Blind." In *Great Flying Stories,* ed. Frank W. Anderson Jr., pp. 61–75. New York: Dell, 1958.

Lehmann, Ernst. *Zeppelin.* New York: Longmans, Green, 1937.

LeMay, General Curtis E., and MacKinlay Kantor. *Mission with LeMay.* Garden City, N.Y.: Doubleday, 1965.

Levine, Alan J. *The Strategic Bombing of Germany, 1940–1945.* Westport, Conn.: Praeger, 1992.

Levine, Isaac Don. *Mitchell: Pioneer of Air Power.* New York: Duell, Sloan and Pearce, 1958.

Lewis, Peter. *British Aircraft 1809–1914.* London: Putnam, 1962.

Ley, Willy. *Rockets, Missiles, and Space Travel.* New York: Viking, 1957.

Lindbergh, Charles. *The Spirit of St. Louis.* New York: Scribner, 1953.

Loftin, Laurence K. *Quest for Performance.* NASA SP-468. Washington, D.C.: U.S. Government Printing Office, 1985.

Lord, Walter, *Incredible Victory.* New York: Harper and Row, 1967.

McGregor, Ken. "Beam Dream." In *Saga of the Air Mail Service, 1918–1927,* ed. Dale Nielson. Washington, D.C.: Air Mail Pioneers, 1962.

McKee, Alexander. *The Friendless Sky: The Story of Air Combat in World War I.* New York: Morrow, 1964.

McRuer, Duane, Irving Ashkenas, and Dunstan Graham. *Aircraft Dynamics and Automatic Control.* Princeton, N.J.: Princeton University Press, 1973.

Manchester, William. *The Arms of Krupp.* New York: Bantam, 1970.

———. *The Glory and the Dream.* Boston: Little, Brown, 1974.

Mansfield, Harold. *Billion Dollar Battle.* New York: David McKay, 1965.

———. *Vision: A Saga of the Sky.* New York: Madison, 1986.

Maynard, Crosby. *Flight Plan for Tomorrow: The Douglas Story.* Santa Monica, Calif.: Douglas Aircraft, 1962.

Melhorn, Charles M. *Two-Block Fox.* Annapolis, Md.: Naval Institute Press, 1974.

Middlebrook, Martin. *The Battle of Hamburg.* London: Allen Lane, 1980.

———. *The Berlin Raids.* London: Viking, 1968.

Miller, Frank. *Censored Hollywood: Sex, Sin and Violence on Screen.* Atlanta: Turner Publishing, 1994.

Miller, Jay. *The X-Planes, X-1 to X-29.* Marine on St. Croix, Minn.: Specialty Press, 1983.

Miller, Ronald, and David Sawers. *The Technical Development of Modern Aviation.* New York: Praeger, 1970.

Moolman, Valerie. *The Road to Kitty Hawk.* Alexandria, Va.: Time-Life Books, 1980.

Morison, Samuel Eliot. *The Two-Ocean War.* New York: Ballantine, 1972.

Musgrove, Gordon. *Operation Gomorrah: The Hamburg Firestorm Raids.* New York: Jane's, 1981.

Neufeld, Jacob. *The Development of Ballistic Missiles in the United States Air Force 1945–1960.* Washington, D.C.: U.S. Government Printing Office, 1990.

Neufeld, Michael. *The Rocket and the Reich.* Cambridge, Mass.: Harvard University Press, 1995.

Nevin, David. *Architects of Air Power.* Alexandria, Va.: Time-Life Books, 1981.

Newhouse, John. *The Sporty Game.* New York: Knopf, 1982.

Nolan, Michael. *Fundamentals of Air Traffic Control.* Belmont, Calif.: Wadsworth, 1990.

Norman, Aaron. *The Great Air War.* New York: Macmillan, 1968.

Our Twentieth Century World. Milestones of History. New York: Newsweek, 1973.

The Oxford Dictionary of Quotations. New York: Oxford University Press, 1980.

Pedigree of Champions: Boeing since 1916. Seattle: Boeing, 1985.

Prange, Gordon W. *At Dawn We Slept: The Untold Story of Pearl Harbor.* New York: McGraw-Hill, 1981.

Preston, Antony. *Aircraft Carriers.* New York: Grosset and Dunlap, 1979.

Pritchard, J. Laurence. *Sir George Cayley.* London: Max Parrish, 1961.

Rae, John B. *Climb to Greatness.* Cambridge, Mass.: MIT Press, 1968.

Ramo, Simon. *The Business of Science.* New York: Hill and Wang, 1988.

Rashke, Richard. *Stormy Genius: The Life of Aviation's Maverick, Bill Lear.* Boston: Houghton Mifflin, 1985.

Reynolds, Clark. *The Carrier War.* Alexandria, Va.: Time-Life Books, 1982.

Reynolds, Quentin. *They Fought for the Sky.* New York: Rinehart, 1957.

Rhodes, Richard. *The Making of the Atomic Bomb.* New York: Simon and Schuster, 1988.

Richelson, Jeffrey T. *American Espionage and the Soviet Target.* New York: Morrow, 1987.

Robinson, Douglas, and Charles Keller. *Up Ship!* Annapolis, Md.: Naval Institute Press, 1982.

Robinson, Douglas H. *Giants in the Sky.* Seattle: University of Washington Press, 1973.

Roskill, Stephen. *Naval Policy between the Wars.* Vol. 1, *1919–1929.* New York: Walker, 1968.

Rummel, Robert W. *Howard Hughes and TWA.* Washington, D.C.: Smithsonian Institution Press, 1991.

Ryan, Cornelius. *The Last Battle.* New York: Simon and Schuster, 1966.

Schairer, George. "The Engineering Revolution Leading to the Boeing 707." Paper presented at the AIAA Seventh Annual Applied Aerodynamics Conference, Seattle, July 31–August 2, 1989.

———. "The Role of Competition in Aeronautics." Paper presented at a meeting of the Royal Aeronautical Society, London, December 5, 1968.

Schlaifer, Robert, and S. D. Heron. *Development of Aircraft Engines and Fuels.* Boston: Harvard University, 1950.

Serling, Robert J. *The Electra Story.* Garden City, N.Y.: Doubleday, 1963.

———. *Howard Hughes' Airline: An Informal History of TWA.* New York: St. Martin's/ Marek, 1983.

———. *The Jet Age.* Alexandria, Va.: Time-Life Books, 1982.

———. *Legend and Legacy: The Story of Boeing and Its People.* New York: St. Martin's, 1992.

Shirer, William. *The Rise and Fall of the Third Reich.* New York: Crest, 1962.

Sloop, John L. *Liquid Hydrogen as a Propulsion Fuel, 1945–1959.* NASA SP-4404. Washington, D.C.: U.S. Government Printing Office, 1978.

Smith, Dean. *By the Seat of My Pants.* Boston: Atlantic-Little, Brown, 1961.

Solberg, Carl. *Conquest of the Skies.* Boston: Little, Brown, 1979.

Steel, Ronald. *Walter Lippmann and the American Century.* Boston: Atlantic-Little, Brown, 1980.

Steiner, John E. *Jet Aviation Development: One Company's Perspective*. Seattle: Boeing, 1989.

Steipflug, Steve. *McDonnell Douglas, Douglas Aircraft Company, 1st Seventy-Five Years*. Long Beach, Calif.: South Coast, 1995.

Thomas, Lowell, and Edward Jablonski. *Doolittle: A Biography*. Garden City, N.Y.: Doubleday, 1976.

Titler, M. *The Day the Red Baron Died*. New York: Bonanza Books, 1970.

Toland, John. *Ships in the Sky: The Story of the Great Dirigibles*. Seattle: University of Washington Press, 1973.

Tuchman, Barbara. *The Guns of August*. New York: Macmillan, 1962.

Vaeth, J. Gordon. *Langley: Man of Science and Flight*. New York: Ronald Press, 1966.

Van Ishoven, Armand. *Messerschmitt Aircraft Designer*. Garden City, N.Y.: Doubleday, 1975.

von Kármán, Theodore, with Lee Edson. *The Wind and Beyond: Theodore von Kármán*. Boston: Little, Brown, 1967.

Wescott, Lynanne, and Paula Degen. *Wind and Sand: The Story of the Wright Brothers at Kitty Hawk*. New York: Harry N. Abrams, 1983.

Wilson, John R. M. *Turbulence Aloft: The Civil Aeronautics Administration amid Wars and Rumors of Wars, 1938–1953*. Washington, D.C.: U.S. Government Printing Office, 1979.

Wolfe, Tom. *The Right Stuff*. New York: Farrar, Straus and Giroux, 1979.

Wooldridge, E. T. *The P-80 Shooting Star*. Washington, D.C.: Smithsonian Institution Press, 1979.

———. *Winged Wonders: The Story of the Flying Wings*. Washington, D.C.: Smithsonian Institution Press, 1983.

Yeager, General Chuck, and Leo Janos. *Yeager: An Autobiography*. New York: Bantam, 1985.

Yeager, Jeana, Dick Rutan, and Phil Patton. *Voyager*. New York: Knopf, 1987.

Periodicals

Aeronautical Journal
   Dirigibles: October 1975, p. 439.
   Flight instruments: August 1976, p. 343.

Aerospace America
   Learfan: October 1985, p. 52.
   Voyager: June 1985, p. 70.

Aerospace Engineering
   Doolittle, James: October 1961, p. 14.

Air and Space
   Boeing 247: March 1997, p. 74.

Air Power History
   Navaho: Summer 1997, p. 4.

American Heritage
   Atomic bombs: June 1995, p. 70.

American Heritage of Invention and Technology
   Berlin airlift: Fall 1998, p. 42.
   DC-3: Fall 1988, p. 6.

Astronautics and Aeronautics
  X-15: February 1964, p. 52.

Atlantic Monthly
  World War II in the Pacific: March 1999, p. 51.

Audacity
  Skunk Works: Fall 1994, p. 18.

Aviation Engineering
  Automatic pilots: January 1932, p. 16.

Aviation Week and Space Technology
  Voyager: July 21, 1986, p. 26; August 11, 1986, p. 72; December 22, 1986, p. 18;
    January 5, 1987, p. 22.

Bee-Hive (Pratt & Whitney)
  Jet engines: January 1954, p. 3; Summer 1968, p. 2.
  Wasp Major engine: January 1946, p. 8; Spring 1947, p. 10; January 1949, p. 7.

Business Week
  Aircraft market: March 23, 1963, p. 52.
  Boeing: February 11, 1961, p. 64.
  Douglas Aircraft: October 22, 1966, p. 175; December 3, 1966, p. 42.

Fortune
  Aircraft market: January 1948, p. 77; June 1960, p. 134; July 1960, p. 111.
  Airliners: April 1953, p. 125; May 1953, p. 128.
  Boeing 707: October 1957, p. 129.
  Douglas Aircraft: December 1966, p. 166; March 1967, p. 155.
  Hughes, Howard: February 1954, p. 116; January 1962, p. 64; February 1962,
    p. 120.

High Technology
  Voyager: December 1986, p. 29.

Journal of the Royal Aeronautical Society
  Dirigibles: January 1966, pp. 44, 114.

Lockheed Horizons
  SR-71: Special Issue, Winter 1981–1982.

Los Angeles Times
  Northrop, Jack: December 8, 1980, p. 1.

Los Angeles Times Magazine
  Rutan, Burt: November 21, 1999, p. 14.

Naval Institute Proceedings
  German navy: May 1991, p. 20.
  Postwar carriers: January 1990, p. 44.

Newsweek
  Douglas Aircraft: April 7, 1958, p. 85; January 18, 1965, p. 64; January 23, 1967,
    p. 77.
  Voyager: September 22, 1986, p. 86; December 29, 1986, p. 34.

Scientific American
  Wright brothers: July 1979, p. 86.

Time

Boeing: July 19, 1954, p. 68.

High-speed flight: April 18, 1949, p. 64; April 27, 1953, p. 68.

McDonnell Aircraft: January 20, 1967, p. 73; March 31, 1967, p. 79.

Missiles: January 30, 1956, p. 52.

Voyager: June 28, 1986, p. 53; December 29, 1986, p. 10; January 5, 1987, p. 28.